SECRET AGENT 666

SECRET AGENT 666

ALEISTER CROWLEY, BRITISH INTELLIGENCE, AND THE OCCULT

BY
RICHARD B. SPENCE

Feral House

ISBN: 978-1-932595-33-8

Feral House
1240 W. Sims Way #124
Port Townsend, WA
98368

www.FeralHouse.com www.FeralHouse.com

10 9 8 7 6 5 4 3 2 1

Design by Dana Collins

TO THE MEMORY OF

"MACK THE RICE"

A.K.A.

FAN CHA-LI

ACKNOWLEDGEMENTS

I owe a very special thanks to three persons: Steve Jackson, Phil Tomaselli, and my wife, Ingrid, for their help, insights, encouragement, and many valuable suggestions.

My sincere thanks also goes out to William Breeze, Ben Brower, Brady Brower, Douglas Burbury, Kelly Chapman, Nancy Dafoe, Shane Davis, Bill Heidrick, Nicholas Hiley, Peter Koenig, Jason Louv, Claudio Mauri, Paul Newman, Marco Pasi, Julian Putkowski, Geoffrey Pocock, Vance Pollock, Charles Rice, Lawrence Sutin, Martin P. Starr, Elena Tsvetkova, Chris Volpe, John White, and Pingchao Zhu.

To any I neglected to mention, my apologies.

SECRET AGENT 666

TABLE OF CONTENTS

intRODVCtion
~
SIX DEGREES of ALEISTER CROWLEY
~

IN 2002, THE BBC POLLED its viewers and listeners to compile a list of the Top 100 Britons of all time. Political figures (such as #1, Winston Churchill), literati, and assorted celebrities dominated the list that emerged, to no surprise.[1] Coming in at #73, just behind King Henry V and just ahead of Scotland's Robert the Bruce, was Aleister Crowley. Best known in his day as the "Wickedest Man in the World" or, as he liked to call himself, "The Great Beast 666," Crowley seems an odd entry for such a list. During his time on Earth, his infamy grew far greater than his fame. Nevertheless, in the nearly sixty years since his death in relative obscurity, Crowley has become a countercultural icon. Even if this falls short of the god-like status he yearned for, it doubtless would gratify him.

Aleister Crowley is, few would argue, the father of modern occultism, neopaganism, and New Age spirituality. Today's Thelemites (avowed followers of Crowley and his spiritual doctrine of Thelema) far outnumber the small cadre he recruited in his lifetime. His motto "Do What Thou Wilt" has had a subtle and profound influence on modern culture. While some still fear and loathe him, Aleister Crowley inspires fascination, even admiration, in others.

Crowley's identification with the occult overshadows his achievements in other spheres. He was a record-setting mountaineer, an outstanding chess player, and a talented or at least popular poet and writer. He also collected an amazingly wide array of friendships and acquaintances, albeit mostly brief, and some regretted. Aleister Crowley had connections of but a few degrees to many of the prominent literary, artistic, and political figures of the early twentieth century. For example, his erstwhile friend and famed military theorist Col. J.F.C. Fuller was also a guest at Adolf Hitler's fiftieth birthday celebration. Another friend, the journalist Walter Duranty, became Stalin's favorite and apologist. Crowley had numerous links to Churchill, among them the writer Frank Harris, a guest at Churchill's nuptials.

A large number of Crowley's associates shared his interest in the occult, and a substantial minority were his partners in sex, drug-taking, magical rites, and other activities licit and illicit. Much less appreciated is that many of these same individuals also connected Crowley to the intelligence world. Throughout his adult life, Crowley associated with people who were, had been, or would be spies. When one of this ilk moved out of Crowley's life, another, as if by magic, appeared to take his or her place. These relationships and transitions were more than coincidence. Hidden behind his occultism and real or feigned depravity was Crowley's sporadic work as a secret agent for Her/His Majesty's Government. This book illuminates that deliberately obscured and much-disputed aspect of his life.

In 1999, I was deep into researching the complicated and perplexing career of the "Ace of Spies," Sidney Reilly. Intriguing synchronicities kept appearing between the movements of Reilly and Crowley. Most intriguing was the men's overlapping presence in World War I in New York City, where Reilly was working, in his own devious way, for Britain's "secret service." Crowley later claimed to have been doing the same, despite the blatant anti-British propaganda he had been writing for pro-German magazines during much of that time. Not surprisingly, Crowley's subsequent protestations of loyal secret service to England mostly were dismissed as face-saving fantasy.

Still, the question seemed interesting enough to merit a look at whatever American security agencies' records might hold on the subject. Eventually the files of the U.S. Army's old Military Intelligence Division yielded a thin dossier on Crowley's WWI activities. This handful of documents contained one critical piece of information: during the war, American investigators, while probing the activities of suspected German spies, discovered that "Aleister Crowley was an employee of the British Government . . . in this country on official business of which the British Consul, New York City has full cognizance."[2] Thus Crowley's claim to have been His Majesty's servant was true after all, at least to some degree. Of course, this leads to the harder questions: what he did and with whom, and *why*. My preliminary exploration of those and related issues, "Secret Agent 666: Aleister Crowley and British Intelligence in America, 1914–1918," appeared in the *International Journal of Intelligence and Counter-Intelligence* in fall 2000.[3] Still immersed in the Reilly book and with other research projects in the pipeline, I did not intend to dig any deeper into Crowley's intrigues.

Over the next few years, however, the article achieved a peculiar life of its own. Crowley fans, Crowley-haters, and others simply intrigued spread it across the Internet. Before long, I was receiving messages offering comments, information, and above all encouragement to look further into Crowley's involvement in espionage. Reluctantly at first, but with mounting enthusiasm as pieces of the puzzle came together, I went to work. The result is this book.

One of the first things to become apparent was that Crowley's secret activities during WWI were part of an involvement in clandestine affairs dating back to his student days at Cambridge University and continuing into the Second World War. The central problem, and my main reservation about the topic, was the dearth of documented, i.e. hard, evidence. The answers to most of the key questions presumably would be in the archives of the British intelligence and security services, MI6 and MI5. Unfortunately, those records were subject to a blanket exclusion from public access, an exemption that remains in effect even under the more recent freedom-of-information statute in the U.K.[4]

I knew from personal experience, however, that the same agencies made the rare exception to this rule when it suited their purposes to do so. As one of a handful of persons to receive access (dubbed a "briefing") to Sidney Reilly's MI6 dossier, I hoped that an appeal to the same authorities might result in like access to Crowley's. After due consideration, MI6 politely but firmly declined my request.[5] Per standard procedure, they even avoided admitting outright that any such file existed. They were thoughtful enough, however, to provide an interesting list of press references to Crowley that must have come from just such a file.

I had greater hope of success with MI5, the British internal security agency. Over the past several years "5" has declassified and released to the public numerous files on persons and events of "historical significance," particularly those connected to espionage. Someone as notorious as Aleister Crowley, a man of numerous and dubious associations and publicly accused of treason, degeneracy, satanism, and worse, could not have escaped their notice. MI5's initial reply in early 2003 was therefore a surprise. "I am afraid we are unable to help you in your quest for material on Crowley," it read, "as, contrary to your assumption, it would appear we never had a file on him."[6] The letter went on to explain that this was not necessarily as strange as it might seem, because "despite his bizarre antics the view may well have been taken that that Crowley did not represent a threat to security." Was this an indirect admission that Crowley had collaborated with MI5, or at least that the agency had some assurance that his "antics" presented no threat?

Not long after I received that letter, a 1930s MI5 document emerged from the Public Record Office (the main component of the British National Archives) that bore a cross-listing reference to another agency file, PP 2573, CROWLEY. Further evidence showed this was, indeed, Aleister Crowley. So I wrote again to MI5. After considerable delay, the ever-polite response began with an apology for "having misled you . . . when we said we thought we never held a record for Aleister Crowley."[7] In fact, the writer continued, my most recent letter "has helped us establish that we did indeed hold a record for him under that PP reference. . . . Sadly, it was destroyed (we think) in the 1950s when large numbers of records which seemed at that point to have outlived their usefulness were destroyed." Furthermore, there was no indication, the letter concluded, as to "why or when Crowley attracted our attention."

I was confused and dissatisfied to say the least. First MI5 asserted that there had never been a file; then, confronted with evidence of it, they admitted its existence and theorized that it had been destroyed. The matter took a further twist with the discovery of another document, a page from a 1916 British "Black List," which cited *two* Crowley MI5 files, and evidently much earlier ones. And so I wrote a third letter. One of the indicated files, PF ("Personal File") 2573, appeared to be an earlier version of the file noted above, but with a different prefix. That turned out to be so, but MI5 could offer no information about the change in prefix or even what "PP" meant. The eventual answer is intriguing, as we will see. The second file, PF 1943, somehow was overlooked not once but twice by MI5's archivists. Their only theory about it was that it had been "destroyed some years ago also."[8]

Was all this vacillation the result of untidy files, or part of a calculated secretiveness? Why would Crowley's files have been destroyed, when older dossiers on persons of no more "historical significance" were preserved? A reasonable person could suspect that the explanations were not altogether complete or forthright.

Of course, even if MI5 and MI6 had revealed the contents of their Crowley files, questions would have remained, and for every question answered, at least one other would be raised. Moreover, such files end up in the researcher's hands only after thorough "weeding." This can leave a meager or misleading residue of the unredacted version. Furthermore, as items may be excised from a dossier, so too may they be *added*.

Other archival materials in Britain still offered hope of information on Crowley. An appeal to the records of the Home Office, including the WWII Office of Home Security, produced a flat denial of having any files on Crowley. A like query to the Metropolitan Police (i.e. Scotland Yard) produced no response whatsoever beyond an automated acknowledgment of the request. As we will see, at least one person claims to have seen a Crowley MI5 file during WWII, and the Beast himself acknowledged that Scotland Yard kept an extensive record of his antics.

A search of the voluminous files of the British Foreign Office, however, had more promising results, or so it initially seemed. The Index to Foreign Office Correspondence, 1906–1919 yielded three file references, including two, FO 371/2541 and 371/4264, that related to Crowley's 1914–1919 activities. But it was the same old story. Many of these older files have not survived past purges, and all three were among the missing. An imaginative person might suspect a concerted effort to erase Aleister Crowley from the official record.

Such difficulties were not exclusively on the British end. Inquiries as recent as 2006 to the FBI under the U.S. Freedom of Information Act elicited the reply that the Bureau held "no records" relevant to Aleister, a.k.a. Edward Alexander, Crowley.[9] This reply somehow overlooked a small file on the Beast that the Bureau had released in response to another FOIA request in 1982.[10] Moreover, a *second* Crowley file surfaced amid the WWI-era records of the FBI's predecessor, the Bureau of Investigation.

I recount all this to sketch what I looked for, what I found, and the pitfalls and frustrations I encountered. The historian's saving grace in cases of such bureaucratic secrecy is the weeders' inability, no matter how hard they work, to expunge everything. As documents travel from one agency to another and are cross-referenced to other files, things fall between the gaps. From such gaps had the Crowley MI5 references appeared.

The practical result of this lack of documentary record is that I must rely more on circumstantial evidence and informed speculation than I would prefer. That almost led me to abandon the project, before I pieced together everything I had. That synoptic view, a reminder that the weight of circumstantial evidence can be compelling, and has sent more than one man to Death Row, encouraged me to go on.

Traces of the Beast's intelligence-related activities roughly divide into three evidentiary tiers. First are those persons and things with *known* connections to Crowley. Second come those that are *probable* in light of all the evidence. Finally there are mere *possibilities* generated by circumstances and relationships. Throughout the book, I will do my best to make these categories clear and distinct. The main focus of the book is on 1914–1919, both because Crowley's clandestine activities are better documented for that period, and because it was his most intense and prolonged involvement in espionage. Nevertheless this book will also demonstrate Crowley's long, if episodic, relationship with British and other intelligence bodies, involving many well-known historical events and persons.

One thing I want to make clear up front is that I neither follow Crowley's esoteric teachings nor have an ax to grind for or against him or them. Moreover, this book is not intended as a general biography of Crowley nor in any way a treatise on his writings or thought, and it takes no position on the reality of magic and the supernatural. However, I recognize that Crowley and many others did and do place great faith in such things. This book examines many of Crowley's better-known actions and associations in a new a light, taking some of them as indications of secret intelligence work. While such interpretations may seem to cast doubt on his mystical motives, this need not be so; the same magical retreat may be both essential to the health of the spirit and useful as a cover for spying.

Numerous Crowley biographies are available, offering a range of interpretations of the Magician. I found the recent works of Martin Booth, Richard Kaczynski, and Lawrence Sutin particularly useful, which is not to slight any others.[11] Even so, I have tried to avoid being too influenced or guided by any one work and always endeavored to stick to my own leads and intuitions. Inevitably, I developed my own opinion on Crowley, and it is fair to state that as best I can. Views of the man pretty much fall into three broad categories. Some see the self-proclaimed Great Beast 666 as little better than the Devil incarnate, a depraved, evil, and insidious spiritual influence on his generation and those since. While this view has declined in recent decades, Craig Heimbichner's *Blood on the Altar*, which portrays Crowley as the propagator of "the world's most dangerous secret society," demonstrates its enduring appeal.[12] Next are such works as Daniel P. Mannix's obscure and sensationalist *The Beast* and Roger

Hutchinson's more recent and mainstream *The Beast Demystified*.[13] These also take a dim view of Crowley, but as a sadistic, oversexed, egotistical monster whose mystical wisdom and "magickal" powers were so much delusion and fakery. Any talents he had, in this view, were insignificant beside his perverted and selfish behavior. The last view, arguably the most common, is that Crowley, despite many glaring flaws, was a man of genuine courage and brilliance, even genius. In many respects he was ahead of his time and misunderstood, and suffered accordingly. Generally, I agree with this last estimation. If not the monster some have described, Crowley certainly was capable of immense emotional and physical cruelty. Real flashes of insight illuminate his writings, but if he developed anything to an art, it was selfishness. Aleister Crowley would indeed have been fascinating to meet, but, as others have noted, I would be reluctant to leave my children or my money in his hands.

It might seem that someone so obsessively self-centered and disdainful of common decency as Aleister Crowley would make a poor spy. On the contrary, those very qualities helped to qualify him for the job. A strong, even ruthless, ego is essential for motivation and self-preservation; the only person the spy ultimately can rely on is himself. Espionage, street-level spying anyway, is at best morally suspect. One British intelligence veteran, Bickham Sweet-Escott, recalled being told at his recruitment, "All I can say is that if you join us, you mustn't be afraid of forgery, and you mustn't be afraid of murder."[14] A 1950s contract agent for the CIA, George Hunter White, revealed this mindset with brutal candor when he recollected, "I toiled wholeheartedly in the vineyard because it was fun, fun, fun. Where else could a red-blooded American boy lie, cheat, steal, rape and pillage with the sanction and blessing of the all-highest?"[15] Crowley, the proponent of "Do What Thou Wilt," would have found such an environment both convivial and rewarding on many levels.

Still, what would move a man with such evident contempt for the existing order to serve, indeed risk his life for, King and Country? In his *Confessions*, referring to 1914, Crowley explained his brand of patriotism:

> I still think the English pot as black as the German kettle, and I am still willing to die in defense of that pot. Mine is the loyalty of Bill Sykes' dog . . . the fact that he starves me and beats me doesn't alter the fact that I am his dog, and I love him.[16]

More simply put, perhaps, "my country, right or wrong."

Crowley was a pariah and spiritual rebel, but he also longed for the "regular life of an English Gentleman."[17] His role as a secret agent appealed not only to his ruthless, amoral side, but also to a profound sense of *Englishness* and an idiosyncratic but genuine sense of honor and duty.

1   www.bbc.co.uk.pressoffice/pressreleases/stories/2002/08-August/21/100_britons.shtml.

2   U.S. National Archives [USNA], Record Group 165, Military Intelligence
    Division [hereafter MID] file 10012-112, "General Summary", Intelligence
    Officer, West Point, New York, 23 Sept. 1918

3   *International Journal of Intelligence and CounterIntelligence*, Vol. 13, #3 (Fall
    2000), 359–371.

4   This Act went into effect in January 2005.

5   J. Grey, Historical and Records Section, Cabinet Office to author, 9 Dec. 2002.

6   MI5, T. Denham to author, 20 Jan. 2003.

7   *Ibid.*, 8 April 2005.

8   *Ibid.*, 18 Oct. 2005.

9   David M. Hardy, Section Chief, Record/Information Dissemination Section,
    Federal Bureau of Investigation to author, 8 May 2006.

10 Thanks to Martin P. Starr for bringing this to my attention.

11 Martin Booth, *A Magick Life: The Biography of Aleister Crowley* (London:
    Hodder & Stoughton, 2000), Richard Kaczynski, *Perdurabo: The Life
    of Aleister Crowley* (Tempe, AZ: New Falcon, 2002), Lawrence Sutin, *Do
    What Thou Wilt: A Life of Aleister Crowley* (New York: St. Martin's Griffin,
    2000). Certainly not to be ignored are John Symonds' early and critical
    The Great Beast: The Life and Magick of Aleister Crowley (London: Rider,
    1951) and its later editions and Martin Booth's *A Magick Life: The Biography of
    Aleister Crowley* (London: Hodder & Stoughton, 2000).

12 Craig Heimbichner, *Blood on the Altar: The Secret History of the World's Most
    Dangerous Secret Society* (Coeur d'Alene, ID: Independent History and
    Research, 2005).

13 Daniel P. Mannix, *The Beast* (New York: Ballantine, 1959), and Roger
    Hutchinson, *Aleister Crowley: The Beast Demystified* (Edinburgh and London:
    Mainstream, 1998).

14 Bruce Page, David Leitch and Philip Knightley, *Philby: The Spy Who Betrayed a
    Generation* (London: Sphere Books, 1969), 135, quoting Sweet-Escott, *Baker
    Street Irregular* (London: Methuen, 1965).

15 Martin Lee and Bruce Shlain, *Acid Dreams: The CIA, LSD and the Sixties
    Rebellion* (New York: Grove Press, 1986), 32–35.

16 Aleister Crowley, *The Confessions of Aleister Crowley: An Autohagiography*
    [hereafter, *CAC*], ed. by John Symonds and Kenneth Grant (New York: Hill &
    Wang, 1969), 761.

17 Sandy Robertson, *The Illustrated Beast: The Aleister Crowley Scrapbook*
    (Boston: Weiser Books, 1988), 39.

PROLOGUE

~

THE DOOMED SHIP

~

ON THE AFTERNOON OF 7 MAY 1915, THE RMS LUSITANIA, PRIDE OF THE BRITISH CUNARD LINE, STEAMED east along the southern coast of Ireland. Six days out of New York, the big liner was bound for her home port, Liverpool. So far it had been a routine voyage for the more than 1,200 passengers and 650 crew. Britain was at war, however, and the *Lusitania* was sailing through a declared war zone. Shortly before 1:30 p.m. the *Lusitania* was spotted by the German submarine *U-20*, and its commander, *Kapitan-Leutnant* Walther Schwieger, with two torpedoes left in his racks, moved in for the kill.

Almost three months earlier, the German Admiralty had proclaimed a policy of "unrestricted" submarine warfare in the waters around Britain. Under this controversial edict, any vessel carrying goods to Germany's enemies was subject to attack without warning. Berlin believed that the *Lusitania* was bearing a heavy cargo of war material, and probably also armament. At approximately 2:10 p.m., Schwieger fired a single torpedo that struck the liner just behind the bridge. A second, larger explosion soon followed. Almost at once, the big ship took on a list, and to Schwieger's surprise, and to that of many on board, she started to sink rapidly by the bow. In a mere eighteen minutes she was gone, taking with her almost 1,200 souls. Among the dead were 128 Americans.

At first glance, the *Lusitania*'s fate seems like simple bad luck; she was in the wrong place at the wrong time and took the torpedo in the wrong spot. From the immediate wake of the ship's sinking right up to the present day, however, recriminations, controversy, and conspiracy theories have swirled around the tragedy. Perhaps the most startling of these theories, to be examined in more detail later, is that the British Admiralty instigated the destruction of the "*Lucy*" with the aim of outraging Americans and bringing the U.S. into the war.

The charge is not as outlandish as it may first sound. Whether or not the *Lusitania* was specifically targeted as the sacrificial victim, elements in the Admiralty's intelligence section were endeavoring to provoke the Germans into inflammatory actions, and they had placed agents into the enemy camp for just that purpose. One such operative, who had successfully insinuated himself into the confidence of German agents and diplomats in the United States, was Aleister Crowley. He later claimed not only to have helped convince his German friends that the *Lusitania* was a man-of-war, but also to have encouraged them to disdain and provoke the Americans. When in 1917 the U.S. finally severed diplomatic relations with Berlin, the first step toward war, Crowley gave himself some credit for helping to bring that about.

Why would the Admiralty, or any other responsible agency of British officialdom, enlist for such sensitive duties a man publicly reviled as a reprobate, degenerate, and satanist? Why would a man with such apparent contempt for decent society and basic morality volunteer to serve his country in any capacity? Why would the Germans take this dubious Englishman into their confidence and even put him to work as a propagandist? Finally, how did Crowley subsequently avoid legal repercussions in Britain for this apparent treason? The answers to these questions and many others lie ahead.

CHAPTER ONE

~

God, Country, King, & Lodge

~

EDWARD ALEXANDER CROWLEY, SORCERER, PROPHET, SPY, AND "WICKEDEST MAN IN THE WORLD," first revealed himself on 12 October 1875 in Royal Leamington Spa, a pleasant mid-England town near Stratford-on-Avon. The new arrival, dubbed "Alick," was the first born and only surviving offspring of Edward and Emily Crowley. Though commoners, the Crowleys were well-off, in most respects solid members of the Victorian middle class. Edward Crowley originally owed his prosperity to a share in the family brewing and eatery enterprise, but he had diversified, investing shrewdly in water works and land reclamation.

Edward Crowley's secure finances permitted him to pursue his heart's true calling, preaching the gospel. Religion differentiated him and his family from most of their neighbors and relations. Most of the Crowley kin were Quakers, already nonconformists, but he and Emily adhered to a small, recently formed evangelical sect, the Plymouth Brethren. The Quakers thought the Brethren a bit fanatical. The apocalypse-minded Plymouth Brethren anticipated the imminent end of the world with smug satisfaction, if not outright glee. They rejected the official Church and most other forms of Christianity as misguided and hell-bound. The Exclusive Brethren, the sub-sect to which the Crowleys belonged, eschewed communion and most other contact with persons outside their narrow community. By today's standards, the sect bore certain characteristics of a "cult."

As noted in the Introduction, this book is not a comprehensive biography of the Great Beast, but some consideration of his family and formative years is in order. After his death a story circulated among the Crowley clan that attributed his beastly behavior to a bad streak inherited from his grandmother, Mary Sparrow.[1] Overall, Alick appears to have had a happy childhood within the narrow world of his parents and, save for chronic asthma, a healthy one. When he was eleven, however, his father died, leaving the boy to the mercies of his mother and her brother, Thomas Bishop, an official in HM Customs and a pious bully who bore no affection for his nephew (and vice versa). Whether the diminutive Emily Crowley was truly the "brainless bigot" that her son and others have portrayed is open to question; perhaps she simply was overwhelmed by her precocious and rebellious son.[2] It was she who, in a fit of frustration, first branded him the "Beast of the Apocalypse," and it says something about their relationship that he embraced that identity as his alter ego for the rest of his life. Certainly his maternal relationship had something to do with his tempestuous dealings with the opposite sex. Whether Crowley drove women crazy or simply was drawn to those already halfway there, his love life never ran smoothly.

Alick seemingly inherited none of his father's financial acumen. Although blessed with an inheritance that would have, with prudent management, supported him for the rest of his life, his basic approach to money was to spend until it was gone and then pray for more to drop into his lap. Oddly, this approach usually worked, although it kept him swinging from one extreme to the other and frequently fretting over impending destitution. As we will see, however, the future *Mega Therion* was never without means to keep himself fed, housed, and clothed, usually quite comfortably, and seldom was so stretched that he could not afford such indulgences (necessities, he might argue) as drugs and whores. He would credit this to the benevolence of the gods, but we must wonder whether sometimes it was another, more mundane, agency at work.

In one respect the Beast did follow in his father's footsteps. Edward Crowley sought to save the souls of poor sinners by converting them to his faith. His son, broadly speaking, spent most of his life trying to do the same. Just a step from the Plymouth Brethren's rejection of mainstream Christianity are Crowley's repudiation of Christianity altogether and his advocacy of a new religious order, Thelema.

Crowley had a deeply conflicted personality, with both manifest and shadow aspects. His repudiation of conventional morality and a somewhat sadistic compulsion to shock and humiliate mirrored an obscure longing for "the regular life of an English Gentleman." If he held the Established Order in contempt, he also secretly craved its admiration and acceptance. His observation about having an anarchistic mind and aristocratic heart speaks to a certain talent for duplicity. Perhaps his great unrealized career was not messiah, poet, or mountaineer, but actor. These aptitudes would serve him well as a secret agent.

In an interview with the BBC, espionage author John Le Carré talked about why people become and remain spies and the subtle rewards it offers. Le Carré (David Cornwell) had a long career in British intelligence, something long assumed by many of his readers but only recently acknowledged by the author. He likened his recruitment while a student at Oxford University to a religious awakening: "I really believed at last that I had found a cause I could serve. . . . It was if the whole of my life had prepared me for that moment," he continued, "It was like joining the priesthood."[3] It is easy to imagine Crowley saying much the same. Le Carré also added to the equation an inner, somewhat perverse, satisfaction in deception and "the dignity which great secrecy confers upon you." He noted the requirement of "flexible morality" or "a necessary sacrifice of morality" which, if disturbing, also had a "voluptuous quality" of near sexual gratification. Put another way, espionage work permitted, often demanded, that one do things normally considered wicked and not only get away with them, but be rewarded for them. Defying moral conventions while simultaneously serving some patriotic greater good would have been irresistible to the Beast.

The pursuit of the occult has more than a little in common with espionage. In his later novel *Moonchild*, Crowley's character "Lord Anthony Bowling" opines that "investigation of spiritualism makes a capital training-ground for secret service work, one soon gets up to all the tricks."[4] That Bowling was a thinly disguised portrait of Everard Feilding, one of the Beast's longest and most important contacts in British intelligence, illuminates this remark. Crowley offered that the goal of magic was to effect changes in the physical world "in accordance with will," i.e. to manipulate behavior and natural forces without observable action. Toward the end of his life, he further reflected on that when he compared the Secret Chiefs, the supposedly invisible and inaccessible masters of the "Great White Lodge," to "Captain A. and Admiral B. of the Naval Intelligence Service."[5] Both carefully concealed themselves and their actions from public scrutiny to the point that their very existence could be questioned. They worked in mysterious ways to achieve their ends, often without the full cognizance or understanding of those who served them.

There is an incident in Crowley's early years that says something about his peculiar relationship with England and his sense of duty. During his time at Malvern College (a boarding school) in 1891–1892, he joined the Cadet Corps of the 1st Worcestershire Royal Artillery Volunteers. This required him to take an oath of loyalty to the Crown. In a section later removed from his autobiographical *Confessions*, the Beast noted that whatever his personal issues with British government and Society, and those were many, he always felt himself bound by that oath. He added that "every time I perform an act in support of my original oath, I strengthen the link [to England]."[6] Therein may be the key to his future secret service.

While Crowley's adolescence was typically rocky, he did note some bright spots. One was an older Scottish cousin, Gregor Grant. Crowley credits Grant with exposing him to the works of Robert Burns and Walter Scott and turning him into a "romantic

Jacobite"—that is a partisan of the Stuart Dynasty that had lost the thrones of England and Scotland almost two centuries before.[7] As we will see, their reaccession remained a viable cause for some. The Celtic influence moved Alick to adopt the moniker "Aleister" in place of his given name, though he never effected a legal change. (Grant also encouraged Crowley's interest in climbing. In July 1894, for instance, they ascended the Devil's Chimney, a small but treacherous chalk pinnacle near Beachy Head.[8])

Another positive early influence was Aunt Annie, the second wife of his uncle, Jonathan Crowley. In some ways she was his mother-substitute.[9] Annie was well-educated and active in the Primrose League. Named for Disraeli's favorite flower, the League was a auxiliary of the then dominant Conservative Party, which Lord Randolph Churchill, father of Winston, helped found.

The Primrose League may have facilitated Crowley's introduction to clandestine work. Modeled on the Orange Order, the secretive fraternal hard core of Irish Protestantism, the Primrose League broke ground by admitting women (like Aunt Annie), and acted like the popular front of "Tory Democracy." It also constituted a kind of secret society within the Conservative Party, an early form of political action committee that, e.g., spied on perceived enemies of Toryism. Despite his associations with the extremes of Left and Right, Crowley maintained that he always was a Tory at heart, and that may have been as true a statement about his political persuasion as he ever made. The Primrose League could have used a young man of such versatility and conviction–e.g., by using young Crowley's interest in Celtic revivalism and dissident Jacobitism to monitor their adherents.

Through Aunt Annie's efforts, Crowley claimed, he gained the patronage of two Primrose League luminaries, Charles Thomson Ritchie (later 1st Baron Ritchie) and Robert Gascoyne Cecil, the Marquess of Salisbury. Cecil was not only Grand Master of the League, but also reigned as prime minister for most of 1885–1902. Ritchie was Salisbury's loyal cabinet member and a former Secretary of the Admiralty. In 1895, Ritchie became the new member of Parliament for Croydon, home to Annie and Jonathan Crowley and Crowley Ale's main brewery. As a well-heeled and active supporter of Ritchie's campaign, Annie Crowley could command his attention and, through him, solicit the help of Salisbury, who was always looking for young "men of ability."[10] This supports Aleister's claim that he entered Cambridge in the autumn of 1895 with the help of Lord Salisbury and earmarked by him for a career in the Diplomatic Service.

By the time he entered Cambridge's Trinity College, the former Alick had grown into a tall, strong young man, although still plagued by asthma. For the next three years he was, he said, a sporadically brilliant but generally unmotivated student. A better description might be "unchallenged." He delved into math and chemistry and read voraciously; he was searching for something unknown within the confines of

Trinity. Chess provided one outlet, poetry another. His abiding passion, though, was mountaineering, which drew him from Britain's high places to the forbidding Swiss Alps. Climbing strengthened his lungs, but more importantly it assuaged an appetite for physical danger and a desire to test and stretch his limits. So, of course, would spying.

Crowley at Cambridge kept his distance from most of his fellow students, just as he preferred solo climbing. He did, however, develop a mighty interest in sex, in many of its varieties. In addition to indulging in the favors of the willing "younger women" of the vicinity, he allegedly had a liaison with Herbert C. J. "Jerome" Pollitt, an older man who provided Crowley with an introduction to the Bohemian demi-monde where he sometimes entertained as a female impersonator.[11] While Crowley later confessed an intense friendship with Pollitt, he denied any "physical passion."[12] Be that as it may, Crowley preferred women, though bisexuality, innate or cultivated, became part of his persona. Perhaps this was another manifestation of his chameleon-like ability to assume attitudes and roles. Among the presumably platonic friends he made at Cambridge was a budding painter, Gerald Festus Kelly, later a noted portraitist and president of the Royal Academy of Art. Five years after meeting at school, Crowley and Kelly became brothers-in-law; later on both became wartime operatives in His Majesty's Secret Service.

It seems likely that Crowley, like Le Carré and many before him, had his first brush with the intelligence work while still in school. During the summer "long-vacation" of 1897, he broke with his habit of scaling to Alps to visit St. Petersburg, Russia. His purpose, ostensibly, was to improve his Russian, for he not only had determined on a career in the Diplomatic Service but was aiming at an appointment to "the most interesting and brilliant court in Europe"—that of Tsar Nicholas II.[13] He added that "the subtlety of intrigue has always fascinated me."[14] Intrigue, of course, is not the stock in trade of a diplomat, but the remark makes sense if Crowley was consciously or unconsciously indicating the true purpose of his Russian sojourn.

Russia at this time was a minefield for any representative of the British Crown. The Empire of the Tsar was Britain's most dangerous international rival and potential enemy. Each empire engaged in vigorous espionage against the other. Most of this activity was handled through embassies and consulates; just about any British diplomat in Russia could expect to do some sort of spying and to be spied upon. Of course, a young, affluent and cultivated Briton traveling on his own to sight-see and refine his Russian would seem an innocent commonplace. Therefore, he could be a useful observer of local conditions and sentiments and, if reliable, a courier of information. Crowley's St. Petersburg foray fits the pattern of a test-run for a prospective agent. (Amado Crowley's claim that the Beast used this 1897 sojourn to meet with the later-to-be-notorious Grigori Rasputin is pure fantasy.[15] Rasputin was then busy siring children in far-off Siberia.)

We need to pause and consider a few basic facts about espionage and briefly examine the organization of British intelligence at the close of the nineteenth century. First we must distinguish between an intelligence "officer" and an "agent." The terms often are used indiscriminately, and Crowley has been described as both, but there is a crucial difference. An officer of an intelligence service is a formal, often career, employee of the government—someone who merits a salary and maybe a pension. He may have an officer's commission in a military service or an intelligence service rank of equivalent stature. The functions of an intelligence officer are most often managerial; he might engage in hands-on spying, but generally the job consists of recruiting and managing *agents* to do the dirty work. A case-officer directs or "runs" one or more agents, who may also be referred to as *assets*.

Agents, therefore, are compensated discreetly, and are seldom regular employees of the service. The identity of agents is often a closely guarded secret, even decades after their service and death. Agents can be divided into sub-varieties ranging from simple informants to deep-cover operatives used to penetrate opposing organizations. A sub-variety is the *agent provocateur*, who works from the inside to compromise or disrupt the target organization. Aleister Crowley always was an agent, never an officer, and his most important roles, as we will see, were infiltrator and *agent provocateur*.

Perhaps the most important thing to understand about Crowley's relationship with British Intelligence is that the latter was a house of many rooms, undergoing continual remodeling. The origins of the British secret service go back at least as far as the reign of Elizabeth I, when the redoubtable Sir Francis Walsingham organized a network of agents to aid Queen Bess in her struggles against enemies foreign and domestic. Two of those agents were the scholar and magus Dr. John Dee and his equally occult-versed assistant, the disreputable Edward Kelley. Dee's secret signature is said to have inspired Ian Fleming to adopt "007" as the codename for his fictional secret agent, James Bond. [16]Crowley fancied himself the reincarnation of Kelley, a conceit that may have helped draw him into clandestine labors.

The British secret establishment as we know it today, dominated by the agencies MI5 and MI6, did not exist in the late nineteenth century. During the 1870s and '80s, first the War Office (WO), followed by the Admiralty, set up Intelligence Divisions mostly for the purposes of gathering foreign military information. These agencies served, among other masters, the Foreign Office (FO), which controlled a modest "Secret Service budget" for clandestine operations. Most intelligence-gathering was run out of embassies and consulates, with attachés and other diplomats handling the recruitment of agents and processing the raw information. Beyond this, the Indian Civil Service ran its own spy and counter-subversion network, and the Colonial Office dabbled in intelligence-gathering, as did the Board of Trade through its Commercial Intelligence Division.

At the close of the nineteenth century, Britain's *domestic* security lay in the hands of trusty Scotland Yard, above all its Special Branch (SB). The dominant figure of that body was Irish-born William Melville, a.k.a. "M" (the original one), a man who served as Conan Doyle's model for Sherlock Holmes's friendly rival, Inspector LeStrade.[17] Melville was not squeamish about his methods or choice of agents. He recruited, and even seems to have preferred, dubious and unsavory characters. One such recruit in the mid-'90s was a young Russian Jew with a revolutionary and criminal background, known as Sigmund Rosenblum. A few years later, with Melville's help, he restyled himself as Sidney George Reilly, British intelligence's so-called "Ace-of-Spies."[18] Melville was the nemesis of all "subversive elements," whether they be Irish Republicans (Fenians), anarchists, or foreign spies.

Melville provides another example of the blending of public and private intelligence gathering, to be encountered often in the coming chapters. In autumn 1903, the fifty-three-year-old Inspector retired from Scotland Yard, but barely a month later he was running the office of "W. Morgan, General Agent," a private detective agency. In reality, the outfit was a front for a War Office organ monitoring "all cases of suspicious Germans (and) Frenchmen and foreigners generally."[19] It was the precursor of MI5.

By the time Crowley left Cambridge in summer 1898, he had steered far away from a diplomatic career, the orderly life of an English gentleman, and most other conventional paths. He had become a seeker of spiritual enlightenment, and to that end a student of occult wisdom and practices. A critical early experience occurred at the end of 1896, a spiritual crisis or mysterious "calling" he experienced while visiting Stockholm. What he was doing in the Swedish capital is a mystery. British records show that Crowley received a passport on 28 December 1896, just in time for the boat to Stockholm. Curiously, British subjects did not require a passport to visit Sweden or much anywhere else. One place that did require the document was Russia, and Stockholm was a main transit point to Russian-ruled Finland and thence to St. Petersburg. Could Crowley's "crisis" have been a tyro spy's jitters over a pending mission?

What really seems to have started him down the twisting trail of occultism was the *Book of Black Magic and of Pacts* by a self-proclaimed expert, Arthur Edward Waite. So taken was Crowley by this work, with its suggestions of mystic brotherhoods and ancient traditions, that he wrote to Waite seeking further guidance. Waite responded by suggesting that he take a look at *The Cloud on the Sanctuary*, an obscure tome by an equally obscure eighteenth-century German mystic, Karl von Eckartshausen.[20] Eckartshausen had studied at the Jesuit University of Ingolstadt under Adam Weisshaupt (or Weishaupt), later the infamous founder of one of the most notorious secret societies, the Bavarian Illuminati. What, if anything, Crowley made of that connection is uncertain, but he did latch onto Eckarthausen's allegorical work as further evidence of a Secret Church and a "hidden community of Saints" guided by mysterious, illuminated adepts.

The young Beast plunged into, or deeper into, a study of alchemy, tarot, magic, demonology, and like arcana. Knowingly or not, he had found his true calling. As Crowley later told the tale, his lucky break came during a late summer climbing expedition to Switzerland. One evening in a lodge near Zermatt, he was pontificating to some fellow guests about alchemy, unaware that within earshot sat Julian Baker, an accomplished chemist and practicing alchemist, and much better versed in the latter than Crowley. He later took Crowley aside to instruct him, and over the next few days the eager Cambridge graduate became Baker's constant companion, pressing him for more information. Baker revealed himself as a member of an exclusive mystical society, the Hermetic Order of the Golden Dawn, and promised to introduce Crowley to other members when they returned to London.

Besides luck or divine providence, there is another way to read the above encounter. Arguably, Crowley knew who Baker was and that he was near. The Beast initiated talk of alchemy to get Baker's attention. Crowley's aim, it seems reasonable to suppose, was to win Baker's confidence and, through him, an introduction, and ultimately admittance to, the Golden Dawn.

Back in London, Baker introduced him to Frater Nolo Noscere (a.k.a. George Cecil Jones), who introduced Crowley to the Order's leading figures, including William Wynn Westcott, Florence Farr, and William Butler Yeats. It turned out that Waite himself was a member of the Golden Dawn. Perhaps Crowley knew that all along, too. It would take a little longer for Crowley to meet the patriarch of the Order, Samuel Liddell MacGregor Mathers.

The Golden Dawn was, in theory, highly selective in its membership . Beyond getting a recommendation from a current member or trusted associate, the candidate had to undergo a background check and an interview by members of the Inner Circle as well as an "'astral' or 'psychic' interview."[21] Somehow, Crowley passed all these tests, and on 18 November 1898 he joined the Golden Dawn's Isis-Urania Lodge.

The theory here is that Crowley sought this initiation not only out of curiosity, but also as part of an intelligence assignment, most likely from William Melville. But why would Melville or any British official have been interested in this small group of harmless, indeed respectable, eccentrics? Again one must look at the Golden Dawn and Crowley's occultism in the context of late Victorian society. The latter was part of what historian James Webb has dubbed "The Age of the Irrational." In late nineteenth-century Britain, a fascination with the occult was commonplace, especially among the educated classes. Secret societies abounded, and by far the largest and most influential of these was Freemasonry. Freemasons therefore figure in a variety of conspiracy theories, which portray them as everything from a corrupt fraternity to seditionists and Satanists.[22] To be fair, most mainstream Masons then and now reject any association with occultism and even reject the label "secret society," preferring "society with secrets."

While Freemasonry had become a worldwide organization by the 1890s, with various branches and jurisdictions, the United Grand Lodge of England and Wales (UGLE) remained the largest regular body, and Britain the most Masonic of countries. By 1900, the UGLE boasted almost 3,000 lodges with nearly 200,000 brethren.[23] That was still a tiny minority out of a general population of some 33 million, but Masonic affiliation had become a virtual union card for admission to the British establishment. Thus, the proportion of Masons in governmental service (including intelligence agencies) was much, much higher than in the population generally.

By becoming so mainstream, however, regular Freemasonry lost much of its air of exclusivity and mystery. Those seeking a more exclusive mystical experience gravitated to such "appendant" or "para-Masonic" bodies as the Scottish, Yorke, or more esoteric Egyptian and Martinist Rites, with their bevy of higher degrees and arcane orders. No doubt many doctrinaire Brethren would be relieved to know that Crowley was never a member of any UGLE-recognized lodge. Nevertheless he accumulated an impressive array of "irregular" initiations and degrees.

Masonry also provided the main recruiting ground for avowedly occult groups, among them the *Societas Rosicruciana in Anglia*, founded in 1865. Rosicrucianism had its roots in mystical works, probably spurious, that cropped up in the early seventeenth century. The nineteenth-century version was mostly an amalgam of ritual magic, alchemy, and Jewish Kabbalah (a magical system based on numerology). The same elements would constitute the core of Crowley's brand of magic.

Another pervasive influence in British occultism was Theosophy, Russian-born Helena Blavatsky's concoction of Hindu, Buddhist, and Western mysteries. Founded in 1875, the Theosophical Society was particularly important in promulgating (though it did not originate) the notion of a secret body of Ascended Masters or "Mahatmas" somewhere in the vastness of Central Asia (or the Astral Plane) who guided the spiritual progress of mankind.[24]

The 1880s also saw the founding of the Society for Psychical Research (SPR), which investigated all aspects of the "paranormal." Its members included the statesman Arthur James Balfour (nephew of Lord Salisbury) and *Times* publisher W.T. Stead.[25] Yet another luminary was the aforementioned Everard Feilding, later one of the Beast's most important contacts in the intelligence world.

Formed in 1888, the Hermetic Order of the Golden Dawn (HOGD) merged most of these currents. Almost all of its founding members were Rosicrucians, and most of those Freemasons of one sort or another. Like the Primrose League, the Golden Dawn broke with Masonic practice by welcoming women. Among the Golden Dawn faithful, Theosophy's Mahatmas were renamed the "Secret Chiefs." These powerful beings worked in mysterious ways, and whether they were human was debatable. As mentioned, Crowley compared the Secret Chiefs and their mysterious ways to the heads of an intelligence service, noting that both spy chiefs and Secret Chiefs "keep us in the dark for precisely the same reasons."[26] The HOGD claimed to be the British branch of a much older occult lodge in Germany, though whether this was puffery remains a matter of debate.[27]

Still, none of this would make the Golden Dawn a threat to the established order. Unconventional spirituality, however, often intersects with unconventional politics. Within the Order were political currents that would have aroused any watchful guardian of the State. Back at Cambridge Crowley had become enamored with Jacobitism, or (as most of its adherents preferred to call it) "Legitimism." The English Legitimists, though few, included popular writers, clergymen, and even members of the peerage.[28] A prominent example was Bertram Ashburnham, the fifth Earl of Ashburnham. His large estate in Wales included, among other amenities, its own military training ground. Ashburnham revived the moribund Jacobite cause in 1886 by forming, or re-forming, the Society of the Order of the White Rose (SOWR), which became the main public face of British Legitimism. Closely associated with SOWR were the Thames Valley Legitimist Club and the more exclusive Legitimist League, "a secret society which takes care to allow as little of its doings as possible to transpire to the public."[29] Ashburnham belonged to an array of other secret orders. He was, for instance, a Knight of Malta and Grand Master of the cultish and quasi-Masonic Order of St. Thomas of Acre.

There is no evidence that Ashburnham was a member of the Golden Dawn, but politics definitely linked him to a fellow ultra-Jacobite, Samuel MacGregor Mathers, who claimed spiritual authority over the HOGD as chosen mouthpiece of the Secret Chiefs. His authority, however, was increasingly questioned in London, in part because he secluded himself in Paris to better pursue his Legitimist intrigues.[30] He dabbled in plots against various governments, including Spain's, Portugal's, and probably Britain's. Crowley first met Mathers in Paris in May 1899.

For Ashburnham and Mathers, Jacobitism was a deadly serious business. Regime change, by armed rebellion if necessary, was their aim. They complained that Queen Victoria and her Saxe-Coburg-Gotha line were German usurpers, though their candidate was hardly any less foreign. That dubious honor fell to Maria Theresa Henrietta Dorothea de Austria-Este-Modena, daughter of the Duke of Modena and wife of Ludwig, Regent (later King Ludwig III) of Bavaria. By the late 1890s, however, British Legitimists had begun to shift their hopes to her son, Prince Rupprecht, or Robert as they imagined him on the thrones of England and Scotland. Coincidentally or not, Ashburnham, MacGregor Mathers, and friends were buying arms in Bavaria.[31] (Recall the Golden Dawn's claim to be a branch of a German secret society.)

Ashburnham and McGregor Mathers favored a radical scheme of devolution for the British Isles that would grant wide autonomy to Scotland, Wales, Ireland, and even Cornwall. This calculated appeal to Celtic separatist sentiments encouraged the presence of Yeats, (according to Melville, a professional paranoid), Maude Gonne, and other Irish nationalists in the Golden Dawn. The Legitimists were a tiny band, but so were the Irish Fenians, and in some ways that made both all the more elusive and dangerous. Their common opposition to the existing order made Jacobite-Fenian collusion likely.

The neo-Jacobite crowd also favored the "more extreme forms of Anglo-Catholicism," advocating the return of Britain to the Roman fold.[32] Ashburnham was a Catholic convert, and others of that ilk were disproportionately represented in the Legitimist movement. Cardinal Rampolla, no less than the Vatican's secretary of state, conferred "the choicest blessing of Heaven" on the Thames Valley organization for its staunch support of the Papacy.[33] Rampolla will return in a different role in the next chapter.

Crowley associated with two other outspoken proponents of Jacobitism and Celtic nationalism. The first, Louis C. R. Duncombe-Jewell, a.k.a. Ludovic Cameron, had also been born into the Plymouth Brethren but, following Ashburnham's example, jumped ship for Roman Catholicism. He was a sometime reporter for the *Daily Mail* who dreamed of raising a "Celtic Empire" that would embrace Scotland, Ireland, Wales, Cornwall, and Brittany. The Beast described him as a "passionate Jacobite" but claimed to find his political schemes "rather childish."[34] Even so, the two were chummy; Duncombe-Jewell later stayed with Crowley in Scotland and was a witness at his 1903 wedding. Duncombe-Jewell also was up to his neck in such Legitimist intrigues as "carrying out delicate and not always safe missions" in Germany and elsewhere.[35]

Much the same could be said for Henry Jenner, the so-called "Bard of Cornwall." Crowley's connection with him seems to have been indirect, through Duncombe-Jewell and probably Ashburnham.[36] Jenner served as "Chancellor" of Ashburnham's Order of the White Rose. He also was the Jacobite movement's chief "cryptographer" and the man handling secrets negotiations in Bavaria and elsewhere.[37] Crowley thus insinuated himself into a group of active international conspirators with seditious intentions.

Ashburnham and his fellow schemers saw themselves as part of a bigger Legitimist movement in Europe. They championed the claim of Don Miguel to the throne of Portugal and in France dreamed of restoring a Bourbon monarchy. The great hope of Legitimism, however, was another Bourbon, Don Carlos of Spain, the only claimant with a real chance of seizing power. The nineteenth-century uprisings of his partisans, the Carlists, plunged Spain into three episodes of bloody civil war. A fresh opportunity for Don Carlos II seemed to arrive in 1899. The weak government in Madrid was reeling from the recent, humiliating defeat by the United States. The northern provinces, the Carlist heartland, seethed with unrest. Carlos' supporters, domestic and foreign, pressed him to unfurl his banner and launch a new insurrection.

Ashburnham, MacGregor Mathers, Duncombe-Jewell, and Jenner were all embroiled in this Spanish adventure. So was Crowley. Ashburnham lent his estate for the training of British volunteers. Our man later recounted how in the service of Don Carlos he "obtained a commission to work a machine-gun, took pains to make myself a first class rifle shot, and studied drill, tactics and strategy."[38] The crucial moment came in summer 1899. In Madrid, the government moved to ratify the peace treaty with the United States. The disgruntled ex-commander of the Spanish forces in Cuba, General Valeriano Weyler y Nicolau, talked of a coup d'état while secretly negotiating with the Carlists.[39] At the same time, Ashburnham loaded his personal yacht, the *Firefly*, with Gras rifles purchased in Germany and dispatched it to Spain under the command of a White Rose stalwart, Royal Navy Lieutenant Vincent John English.[40] On 15 July, however, on the last leg of its third gun-running trip, the *Firefly* ran into trouble in the French port of Arcachon. An alerted Spanish consul demanded that French customs seize the vessel. As Crowley put it, the "conspiracy was disclosed."[41] Listed among the crew of the *Firefly* was a "C. Alexander," an early example of Crowley's many aliases.[42] The fiasco ended the uprising, although Carlist rumblings continued well into 1902.

Thirty years later, the Beast remained oddly reticent about his Spanish escapade, offering only that "there is a great deal more to this story; but I cannot tell it—yet."[43] The likely reason is that revealing his true role would reveal the hand of the British "Secret Service." Among those suspected of the betrayal is Crowley himself.

Ashburnham's and his cronies' aid to Don Carlos was not unselfish. They expected, realistically or not, that the newly installed Carlos VII would support their own ambitions. This may even connect to Crowley's earlier visit to Russia. In 1896, Don Carlos' son, the Young Pretender Don Jaime, accepted a commission in the Russian Imperial Army. He was favored by Tsar Nicholas, and there was reason to suspect that the Russians secretly supported his father's cause. That doubtless gave persons in London additional incentive to nip Carlos' hopes in the bud.

When he joined the Golden Dawn, and for a time thereafter, Crowley took on the identity of a Russian nobleman, Count Vladimir Svareff. The Beast later unconvincingly explained the impersonation as a half-baked sociological experiment and effort to hide his occult activities from his family. As we will see, he had that penchant for disguises and false identities that any decent spy would cultivate. He cannot have made a convincing Russian, certainly not to real ones, so whom was he trying to deceive? Could the impersonation have been a half-baked scheme to smoke out Russian agents in or around the Golden Dawn?

This brings us back to the theory that, like his encounter with Baker in Switzerland, Crowley's entry into the Golden Dawn, his cultivation of MacGregor Mathers, Ashburnham, *et al.*, and his enlistment in the Spanish plot were all part of a plan to spy on and thwart these men. Everything about his association with the HOGD smacks of an agent provocateur. Personality conflicts already rent the Order, and Crowley's behavior escalated them. He rose rapidly through the levels of the Order, too rapidly for some. His arrogance and all-too-avid interest in sexual matters also made waves.

The schism came in late 1899 when members of the senior Second Order, led by Farr and Yeats, refused to grant the upstart admission to the Adeptus Minor degree. An enraged Crowley rushed to Paris and convinced Mathers to initiate him, thus driving the wedge between Mathers and the London group. Later, Mathers dispatched his young acolyte back to London in a bizarre and brazen attempt to take physical control of the Order. In a black mask and highland garb, brandishing a ceremonial dagger, Crowley stormed about the lodge but failed to cow its denizens. He and Mathers ended up expelled from the Order, which triggered its irreversible disintegration.

So far as the Order is concerned, the Beast's probable aim was not to destroy the Golden Dawn, but to undermine the Jacobite Mathers' authority. In the aftermath, their superficial friendship quickly degenerated into mutual charges of fraud, blackmail, and attempted murder (by magical means). Crowley's allegations against Mathers included "Jacobite conspiracies to overthrow the throne of England."[44] That probably was the truth. Later still, in his novel *Moonchild*, Crowley thinly disguised Mathers as a German spy and the tool of an evil cabal of magicians called the Black Brotherhood. They were the enemies, naturally, of the benevolent Great White Brotherhood.

Crowley's joining the Golden Dawn with the ulterior motives of spy and provocateur is entirely consistent with a sincere interest in magic. He had the opportunity to milk the Order for the (possibly meager) knowledge it could provide. His determination that the HOGD's leadership was full of posers, swindlers, and traitors simply made its ruination that much easier.

1   Mary Crowley and Ian Glover, "The Crowley Family", www.manicai.net/
    genealogy/gam_aleister.html "Crowley Family," 17.
2   *Ibid.*, 19, and CAC, 36.
3   John Le Carré, "I Really Was a Spy," //archives.cnn.com/2000/books/
    news/12/26 john.lecarre, quoting from BBC documentary "The Secret Centre,"
    2000.
4   Aleister Crowley, *Moonchild* (London: Mandrake, 1929), 308. There are
    various later editions of the book and an online version at: www.hermetic.
    com/crowley/moonchild.html.
5   Crowley, *Magick Without Tears*, online version of 1st 1954 edition:
    www.hermetic. com/crowley/mwt/mwt_09.html.
6   William Breeze to author, 3 Feb. 2008, quoting deleted section.
7   *CAC*, 121.
8   In 2001, "Devil's Chimney" collapsed into the sea after a series of powerful storms.
9   *CAC*, 68.
10 Carroll Quigley , *The Anglo-American Establishment: From Rhodes to Cliveden*
    (San Pedro, CA: GSG & Assoc., 1981), 15.
11 J. Edward Cornelius (ed.), "The Friends and Acquaintances of Aleister Crowley
    [hereafter FAAC]: Herbert C. J. Pollitt," *Redflame: A Thelemic Research Journal*,
    www.redflame93/Pollitt.html, and Alex Owen, "Aleister Crowley in the Desert,"
    excerpt from *The Place of Enchantment: British Occultism and the Culture of
    the Modern* (Chicago: Univ. of Chicago Press, 2004), 186–202.
12 *CAC*, 142.
13 *CAC*, 115.
14 *Ibid.*
15 Amado Crowley, *The Secrets of Aleister Crowley* (Leatherhead: Diamond
    Books, 1991), 1. Amado Crowley, who claims to be the Beast's natural son,
    is a figure of considerable controversy in the Thelemic community, largely
    because he also claims to be his "father's" spiritual heir. My citation of Amado
    C's works here and elsewhere should not be taken as an endorsement of his
    dubious claim of paternity or anything else. On the other hand, I see no
    reason to ignore or dismiss something simply because he mentions it.
16 According to Richard Deacon [Donald McCormick], Dee's "007" symbol was
    meant to represent a pair of hand-held spectacles or all-seeing eyes: see *A
    History of the British Secret Service* [hereafter *BSS*] (NY: Taplinger, 1969),
    12–13, 27–30.
17 On Melville, see: Andrew Cook, *M: MI5's First Spymaster* (London: Tempus, 2004).
18 On Reilly's picaresque career see: Richard Spence, *Trust No One: The Secret
    World of Sidney Reilly* (Los Angeles: Feral House, 2002).
19 United Kingdom, National Archives, Kew [hereafter UKNA], "Melville
    Memoir," KV 1/8.

20 Eckartshausen lived 1752-1803; *The Cloud on the Sanctuary* appeared in 1802.

21 Sharron Lowena, "Noscitur A Sociis: Jenner, Duncombe-Jewell and Their Milieu," in Philip Payton (ed.), *Cornish Studies 12* (Exeter: Univ. of Exeter Press, 2004), 69.

22 On this, see Stephen Knight, *The Brotherhood: The Secret World of the Freemasons* (New York: Dorset Press, 1984) and A. Ralph Epperson, *The Unseen Hand: An Introduction to the Conspiratorial View of History* (Tucson, AZ: Publius Press, 1985).

23 Knight, 36.

24 The basic works of Theosophy are Blavatsky's *The Secret Doctrine: The Synthesis of Science, Religion and Philosophy* and *Isis Unveiled: Another Key to the Mysteries of Ancient and Modern Science and Theology.*

25 Quigley, 31–32.

26 *Magick Without Tears, ibid.*

27 The Golden Dawn Research Center, "The Truth about the Cipher Documents," www.golden-dawn.org/truth_ciph1.html.

28 James Webb, *The Flight from Reason: Vol. 1 of the Age of the Irrational* (London: MacDonald, 1971), 202–203.

29 Lowena, 66.

30 *Ibid.*, 70.

31 *Ibid.*, 68.

32 Webb, 204–205.

33 *Ibid.*, 205.

34 CAC, 361, 368.

35 Lowena, 68.

36 Paul Newman, *The Tregerthen Horror: Aleister Crowley, D. H. Lawrence & Peter Warlock in Cornwall* (Lulu/Abraxas, 2005), 12.

37 Lowena, 68.

38 *CAC*, 121.

39 *The New York Times* [hereafter *NYT*] (27 July 1899).

40 "The Carlists of Today," *Pall Mall Gazette* (10 Oct. 1901), 1–2 and (19 Oct.), 4; (23 Oct.), 11.

41 *CAC*, 121.

42 Lowena, 68, citing *Firefly* pay list, 26 Aug. 1899, in the Ashburnham Carlist Papers, Lewes.

43 *CAC*, 123, n.1.

44 Crowley (writing as "Leo Vincey"), "The 'Rosicrucian' Scandal" (1911) in Sandy Robertson (ed.), *The Illustrated Beast* (Boston: Weiser Books, 1988), 65.

~

CHAPTER TWO

THE MOVEABLE BEAST

~

SOON AFTER THE GOLDEN DAWN MELTDOWN, the Beast retreated to Boleskine, his newly acquired house near Loch Ness. There he played at being a local laird and performed "magickal" operations to perfect his command of the occult arts. Ever restless, however, in summer 1900 he left Britain, supposedly for New York, and for the next several years roamed the world, returning occasionally to his Scottish lair.

If he entered Gotham it was off the immigration record, nor does any American port or border crossing reveal his presence. He must have used an alias, but which and, above all, why, remain a mystery. In any case, Crowley's true destination was Mexico, where he surfaced in July. He seems to have spent most of the next few months mountaineering, but he also took time to befriend Don Jesus de Medina, a fellow occultist and a leading figure in Mexican Scottish Rite Freemasonry. Don Jesus awarded the visiting Englishman his Rite's coveted 33°, and the pair even formed their own secret society, the "Lamp of Invisible Light."[1]

In Mexico, Crowley also caught up with the Anglo-German alpinist Oscar Eckenstein. Their relationship appears to have been based on a common love of climbing, although German businesses were vigorous in Mexico and generally allied with British ones against the even more aggressive Yanquis. We will give more consideration to that below.

Another acquaintance Crowley either made or renewed in Mexico was with peyote (Anhalonium lewinii). The drug had made its way to Europe before 1900, and a German chemist had synthesized its main psychoactive component, mescaline, in 1898, so the Beast may have taken it before. Still, he was now in its native habitat and would not have missed such an opportunity. The peyote experience remained of interest to Crowley for years, for magical and other applications.

While in Mexico, Crowley also experimented with "making [him]self invisible," a lifelong obsession. His rituals to attain this goal had only limited success—a merely "flickering" state.[2] Not long after, however, when forced to protect himself against robbers and an angry mob, he stumbled upon the key, or so he believed. The

Beast attributed his escape, and his subsequent ability to slip in and out of others' perception (consciously and unconsciously), to a "peculiar type of self-absorption which makes it impossible for people to be aware of one."[3] This mental state, he added, "distracts people's attention from one automatically, as a conjurer does deliberately." Self-hypnosis, and perhaps hypnosis of the observer, probably was the root of this. Whether or not he ever mastered genuine invisibility, Crowley cultivated a knack for convenient inconspicuousness, a talent invaluable to a secret agent.

Aside from magic, drugs, and mountain climbing, Crowley's Mexican sojourn may have involved intelligence-gathering. His efforts among the Jacobites and the Carlists having proved his worth, the logical step was to send him further afield. An agent always needs a cover, a credible pretext to be somewhere or do something. Almost any British subject abroad was a potential asset, and it was a patriotic duty to keep one's eyes and ears open and report anything noteworthy to the proper authorities.

Britain's greatest concern in Mexico at this time was oil. The Admiralty had already begun to contemplate oil as replacement for coal in powering the world's greatest fleet. Throughout the vast Empire, however, the black stuff was scarce. During 1900–1901, the Admiralty's presiding "oil maniac," Second Sea Lord John "Jacky" Fisher, anxiously sought concessions in oil-rich places such as Mexico and Persia. In Mexico they faced stiff competition from American oil-men such as Edward Doheny, who just happened to be on the scene staking claims for his Pan-American Petroleum.[4]

In the end, though, a British entrepreneur, Weetman Pearson (later Lord Cowdry), took the lion's share of Mexico's oil. Pearson appeared just after Crowley left Mexico for San Francisco, which may be more than coincidence. The secret to Pearson's success was the personal backing of Mexico's dictator, Porfirio Diaz—Grand Master of the same Scottish Rite Masonry to which his acquaintance Don Jesus and more recently Aleister Crowley belonged. Freemasonry pervaded and subtly influenced Mexican politics, which probably facilitated Pearson's victory.[5] Did Crowley the British agent help also cultivate Brother Diaz through Don Jesus?

A similar question arises about Crowley's activities on the northern frontier of India in early 1902. His outward purpose, again, was climbing, in this case a daring ascent of one of the Himalayas' highest and most treacherous peaks, K-2 (a.k.a. Goodwin-Austen or Chogo-Ri). The mountain lay on the vague northern boundary between British-controlled Kashmir and Chinese Sinkiang. Close by lay the frontiers of Afghanistan, the Russian Empire, and Tibet, the last a source of anxiety for the British. Tibet's ruler, the Dalai Lama, was courting Russian support, and rumors abounded about the activities of the Tsar's agents in the Land of Eternal Snows. St. Petersburg's aim was to make Tibet a client state. In 1903, such concerns led to an outright British invasion of Tibet led by Francis Younghusband.[6] The only easy route by which Russian agents and aid could reach Tibet was through the passes and valleys close by K-2, making this region a rich source of information. The K-2 expedition's original leader, Crowley's friend Oscar Eckenstein, was arrested by British authorities on vague charges before they reached the mountain, putting the Beast in de facto control. Was that part of someone's larger plan? The climb itself ended in failure after two tries, when Crowley called off the ascent to save the life of a comrade stricken by pulmonary edema.

He displayed less heroism and compassion on his second expedition to the Himalayas in summer 1905. With a small team he attempted the formidable Mt. Kangchenjunga. Like K2 the peak lay near a strategic spot on the northern frontier where India's border met those of Tibet and Nepal. This climb ended in a mutiny said to have been sparked by Crowley's tyranny and the deaths of four men in an avalanche. Whatever his past accomplishments, Crowley's mountaineering reputation, and his reputation as a whole, never recovered from his seemingly callous and vindictive delay in helping the stricken men and recovering the bodies.

In the meantime, the Beast made his way back to Britain, where in August 1903 he married Rose Kelly, the older sister of his Cambridge chum Gerald Kelly. Their six-year marriage was almost as severe a disaster as the attempt on Kangchenjunga. Rose became the Beast's first Scarlet Woman, an embodiment of the powerful feminine spirit "Babalon" and all-around magical helpmate. Perhaps the role was too much for Rose, who soon fell into a downward spiral of alcoholism and insanity. In April 1904, in Cairo, she played her most important part in the career of the self-proclaimed Great Beast 666, To Mega Therion, by serving as medium for the spiritual entity Aiwass in the channeling of the Liber AL vel Legis, or Book of the Law. Crowley saw Aiwass as his "guardian angel," and himself as the prophet of a new age, the Aeon of Horus, and its new religion, Thelema ("Will").

A few months later, Rose gave birth to a girl, the grandly named Nuit Ma Ahathoor Hecate Sappho Jezebel Lilith. Out of either intense, albeit misguided, devotion or blind selfishness, Crowley dragged his wife and infant daughter with him back to India in 1905. After the failure on Kangchenjunga, they also followed him on a grueling trek through the wilds of southern China.

This commenced in autumn 1905, soon after the end of the Russo-Japanese War. The defeat of a European power by an Asiatic one sent shock waves throughout the East (and West), not least in China, which groaned under the weight of both Western and Japanese imperialism. Crowley's route took him from northern Burma through the Chinese province of Yunnan and on into neighboring French Indochina.

Yunnan was a major opium producer, but the trade's future was uncertain. In China itself, where an estimated quarter of all men were slaves of the poppy, a campaign was growing to curtail or ban the opium trade. Similar efforts were underway in Britain, which in 1906 stopped Indian opium exports to China. The next year saw an Anglo-Chinese pact to reduce export from, and cultivation in, China itself. Crowley was very much aware of this.[7] The Beast recounts that among his goals on the trip was to "get available information about the effects of smoking opium."[8] This in part served his personal interest in psychoactive drugs, on which he eventually collected "a vast quantity" of data, but it also allowed him to collect intelligence about quantity, quality, price, and distribution of the local product.[9]

The anti-opium pact hurt France's tax revenues in Indochina, where sale of opium was legal. Bordering Burma and Indochina, Yunnan had long been a sphere of Anglo-French competition, no less since the recent entente between London and Paris (1904). During Crowley's sojourn, tensions were peaking because of a French construction project, the Yunnan-Tonkin Railway, that looked like a path to annexation of Indochina. Crowley notes that the French had "flooded Yunnan-Fu [the provincial capital, today Kunming] with agents," something a British agent would notice where a simple tourist would not.

A further clue to his ulterior motives is Crowley's interest in a dubious Bengali doctor whom he suspected of writing anti-British propaganda, just the sort of intelligence that authorities back in India would have appreciated. Yet another clue is his passing mention of having "settled my little official affair with the Consul General" in Yunnan-Fu.[10] That suggests that he made a report and received his due reward.

With consuls and other eyes and ears scattered throughout south China, why would John Bull have needed the services of Aleister Crowley there? First, one can never have too many sources of information, and as Crowley mentions with perverse satisfaction, many of those eyes and ears were not up to the task. He was especially disparaging of the abilities of the Christian missionaries. The Beast, on the other hand, claimed special insight into the Oriental character. In matters such as opium, he brought other special skills to bear. Furthermore, an eccentric Englishman traveling with a wife and small child did not look much like a spy at first glance.

After reaching the Indochinese port of Haiphong at the beginning of April, the Mage sent Rose and Nuit back to India. He then set off alone across the Pacific and Canada, to New York and, ultimately, to England. His first stop, though, was bustling Shanghai, where he lingered for a couple of weeks. One attraction there was Elaine Simpson, a past sister from the Golden Dawn and a partner in both physical and astral sex. His eagerness to renew the affair helped motivate getting Rose out of the way.

Again, there is the suggestion of an intelligence agenda in Shanghai. In *Confessions*, Crowley tells of using Tarot cards to solve the mystery of a missing packet of 80,000 rubles.[11] The local "postmaster," a German friend of Simpson, was alarmed by the disappearance of the packet, which was addressed to a bank in Beijing. The mention of rubles indicates a Russian bank, and, of course, if there was anyone London was more suspicious of in the Far East than the French, it was the Russians. The affair sounds like a scheme to track the movement of Russian funds. One interested party would have been the venerable Inspector General of the Chinese Customs Service, Sir Robert Hart, a longtime servant of the British Crown. The Beast certainly knew who Hart was. Some years later, Crowley recalled, via his literary alter ego Simon Iff, that "When I last left China—for my sins—I traveled in the same steamer as Sir Robert Hart."[12]

Using the Tarot, Crowley determined that the culprit was a junior clerk in the office, but the crisis ended when the missing money miraculously appeared at its destination after all. The postmaster and clerks involved were all employees of the Imperial Chinese Maritime Customs Service, a strange entity based in Shanghai and largely run by the British, but employing many Germans and other nationals. In addition to its main job of collecting customs on foreign vessels, the Service ran its own postal service, policed ports and river traffic, and routinely collected intelligence about conditions in the Chinese interior. Having just come from Yunnan, the Beast could have given Hart's outfit valuable help.

Reaching London in June 1906, Crowley was heartbroken to learn that his tiny daughter had died of typhoid in Rangoon. He blamed Rose, fairly or not, and even the birth to them of Lola Zaza the next year could not mend the disintegrating relationship. In 1909, he and Rose finally divorced. Two years later she, now a hopeless alcoholic, entered an asylum. Another casualty of the marriage's failure was his friendship with Gerald Kelly.

Before their break, though, Gerald Kelly introduced the Beast to William Somerset Maugham. All three men would eventually find themselves in the service of British intelligence. Maugham's and Crowley's paths would cross on more than one occasion, and they developed a distinct dislike of each other. In 1908, Maugham published a novel, *The Magician*. The villain, Oliver Haddo, he based on Crowley, and the portrayal was ugly enough to make Crowley contemplate a libel action. He did not pursue the suit, but neither did he ever forget or forgive the insult.

In the interim, the Beast plunged into his own writing, both poetry and esoteric works, and always deeper into magic. In 1907 he founded his own occult order, the A∴A∴. This supposedly stood for Astrum Argentum or Argenteum Astrum ("Silver Star"), though others insist the true name was (and is) Adepts of Atlantis.[13] In any case, the group was less a secret society than Crowley's private club, to which he admitted whomever he wished, however he liked. The Order even had its own official organ, *The Equinox*. The A∴A∴ drew an interesting assortment of recruits, though determining who was a member can be tricky. Actual or purported members include artists and writers such as Austin Osman Spare, Frank Harris, the Franco-Russian George Raffalovitch, and Victor Neuberg. Also involved were George Cecil Jones and the British-born journalist and future apologist for Stalin, Walter Duranty, with whom Crowley shared drugs, a mistress (Jane Cheron), and the occasional act of ritual sodomy.

More pertinent to our inquiry, though, are the military members. One was a British Army officer, Capt. John Frederick Charles (J. F. C.) "Boney" Fuller. He had connection to military intelligence during the Boer War. Years later, Fuller would become one of the founders of the British Army's Tank Corps, a noted military theorist and great admirer of Hitler. In this period, though, Fuller was an admirer of Crowley and even wrote a book, *The Star in the West*, in praise of his teachings.[14]

Another important brother was a Royal Navy man, Commander Guy Montagu Marston. In his *Confessions*, Crowley describes Marston as "one of the highest officials of the Admiralty," a bit of an overstatement.[15] According to his naval service record, Marston was a navigation officer, and a good one.[16] Nothing obvious suggests an intelligence connection, or precludes one, but Marston's participation in actions against slave traders and rebellious chieftains in Africa during the 1890s shows an adventurous side. More intriguing was his request to visit Russia around 1902 on undisclosed business. The Commander was "especially interested in sex, anthropology and magic" which doubtless explains his attraction to Crowley.[17] In May 1910, his secluded Rempstone estate in Dorset was the scene of a magical "working" in which the Beast and his assistants invoked Bartzabel, the "spirit of Mars." Marston asked the spirit if nation would rise against nation and received a prophetic reply that war with Turkey or Germany would come within five years.[18] Besides his avid interest in the occult, Marston's other dirty little secret was a love affair with his cousin, Daisy Bevan. In an odd coincidence (or not), her husband, Edwyn Bevan, was the brother of two other persons who would encounter the Beast, or his reputation, a decade or so down the line.

Marston could have provided an indirect link between the Mage and the Admiralty's Naval Intelligence Division (NID). If so, it would tend to confirm suspicions about Crowley's activities in Mexico and bear on those coming in the First World War. However, there also has been speculation that Crowley was involved in a conspiracy to blackmail Martson by luring him into sexual rituals.[19] Writer Paul Newman finds nothing to support the accusation, but Crowley's proximity to an important naval officer might have attracted the notice of other parties. For instance, by claiming influence with or over Marston, the Beast might have made himself of greater interest to German intelligence.

From the intelligence standpoint, though, the most important of Crowley's associates in the A∴A∴ was Everard Feilding, or, to be exact, the Honorable Francis Henry Everard Joseph Feilding, second son of the 8th Earl of Denbigh and brother of the current Earl. Eight years Crowley's senior, Feilding was a fellow Cambridge-Trinity man and a former Royal Navy officer. Apparently leaving the Navy in the 1890s, Feilding prospered as a rubber planter in Malaya and attorney in the high financial, and High-Masonic, circles of the City of London. Like other friends of the Great Beast, Feilding took a strong interest in esoterica. A charter member of the elite Masonic Order of Christ (yet another group claiming direct descent from the Templars), Feilding was also a leading figure in the Society for Psychical Research. By 1907 he was its secretary. With the outbreak of war in 1914, Feilding quickly received a lieutenant's commission in the Royal Navy Volunteer Reserve (RNVR), a typical accommodation for intelligence operatives. As we shall see, his subsequent duties belonged to that realm. Feilding almost certainly maintained some connection with NID before the war.

The poet and A∴A∴ member Victor Benjamin Neuberg may have been innocently involved in espionage through his relationship with Crowley. London-born of German-Jewish parents, Neuberg was in his late 20s when he met the Beast around 1908 and became his lover, or at least a regular partner in homosexual (XI*) magical workings. During 1909–1911, the pair made frequent trips to North Africa, a place Crowley found particularly inspiring. There they used John Dee's "Enochian Aethyrs," and plenty of drugs, to invoke the spirits of the Abyss.

Much of their time was spent around Biskra and Bou Saada in northeastern Algeria. The area was not as desolate and remote as Crowley suggests. Both of those towns and other spots he visited "were on the standard tourist circuit of the day," enjoying a steady stream of European visitors.[20] Indeed, Biskra gained enough fame to later become the setting of Rudolf Valentino's *The Sheik*. The region also boasted important Sufi monasteries (zawiyas), which may have helped attract the Beast.

Algeria, of course, was under French rule, though Paris' control over various Berber and Saharan tribes was always tenuous. While the years leading up to the First World War were relatively tranquil, French authorities always cast a suspicious eye on foreigners and guarded against espionage. Again, despite the recent entente, the French regarded Britain as a dangerous rival in North Africa. According to Pierre Mariel, a writer who claimed connection to French intelligence, Crowley and Neuberg's activities drew the attention of the local police, the Services des Affaires Indigenes or "Blue Burnouses."[21] Following a "discreet" inquiry, they determined that the two Englishmen had come to the edge of the Sahara for more than occult illumination. The pair, or at least Crowley, was quietly gathering information for "l'Intelligence Service." If so, it was no different that what he had done in Yunnan.

Yet another possible player in Crowley's prewar intelligence gambits was the Australian-born A∴A∴ member Leila Ida Bathurst Waddell, who had been present at the Bartzabel ritual. The Mage met the thirty-year-old Waddell in London around 1910 and soon made her his new Scarlet Woman. Leila was a talented violinist, and Crowley wrote that her exotic looks (she was part Maori), musical ability, and her strong sexuality "appealed to [his] imagination."[22] A vague rumor holds that Waddell was married to or otherwise associated with a "naval intelligence officer." There is, however, no evidence that she ever was married to anyone.[23]

Among Crowley's literary output in the period was a volume of poetry, *The Winged Beetle*, published privately in 1910. He dedicated the book as a whole to J.F.C. Fuller, and each of the poems to some other friend or acquaintance. Among the select crew were Frank Harris, George Cecil Jones, Marston, Neuberg, and Raffalovich, as well as Crowley's wife and mother. The name of an up-and-coming politico, thirty-six-year-old Winston Churchill, is a puzzling name in this company. The poem dedicated to him is "The Jew of Fez," a brief ode to an unfortunate Hebrew who converted to Islam to get a red fez, only to be burned as an apostate for switching back to his yarmulke. This was, no doubt, an allusion to Churchill's 1904 defection from the Tories to the Liberals, in whose government he now served as Home Secretary. Crowley may have been commenting on Winston's apparent tendency to follow political fashion instead of ideological conviction. If so, he was again a prophet; fourteen years later, Churchill returned to the Conservative fold.

The naming of Churchill in *The Winged Beetle* raises the intriguing possibility of a personal link between him and Crowley, though there is no tangible evidence of such. Still, there had to have been some reason for the Beast to single him out. In 1910, Churchill was a Freemason (albeit a casual one), and a brother in such secret societies as the Ancient Order of Druids (the British parent organization of the German Druiden-Orden), the Independent Order of Odd Fellows, and the British Order of Ancient and Free Gardeners.[24] None of this proves a predilection for the occult, though Churchill entertained a certain curiosity about spiritualism, mysticism, and the like.[25] That might have made him curious about Crowley. Winston also evidenced admiration for such renegade and morally questionable figures as the Russian terrorist Boris Savinkov and the unscrupulous mercenary spy Sidney Reilly. Aleister Crowley would have fit right in. In any case, this will not be the only instance where Churchill's and Crowley's paths will seem to cross.

Also during 1910, Crowley became embroiled in two public scandals that would further blacken his reputation in the British press and public mind. The first was the so-called "Rosicrucian Scandal" that erupted in March when the Mage published supposed Rosicrucian secret rituals in *The Equinox*. According to him, the "Secret Chiefs" commanded it. More likely, it was part of his ongoing feud with former brethren of the Golden Dawn, particularly Macgregor Mathers. The Beast managed to fend off the resulting lawsuit, but his act of spite would cost him dearly. Beyond the offense he gave to Mathers *et al.*, Crowley's flagrant indiscretion offended the values and sensibilities of secret society members in general. These included hundreds of thousands of British Freemasons, many of whom filled the ranks of the Foreign Office and every other branch of the British Government. One person to enter the fray, though no friend of secret societies, was a self-appointed guardian of public morals named Horatio Bottomley. His paper and personal soapbox *John Bull* scolded Mr. Crowley for betraying his "solemn pledge," the opening round of a bitter personal vendetta against the Magician.[26]

The next flap arose in October, from Crowley's public performance of the "Rites of Eleusis" at London's Caxton Hall. While the name referred to the ancient Greek Eleusinian Mysteries, Crowley's extravaganza was really his homage to the seven planetary deities. The audience at the first, private performance was provided with a special treat, a mescaline cocktail to enhance their enjoyment. The Beast carefully observed the reactions. By the time they went public, the Rites, presumably minus the mescaline, had become a theatrical spectacle featuring Crowley's poetry and the musical talents of Leila Waddell. The attendees got their biggest shock when the theater lights unexpectedly went out for a brief spell.

Although pretty tame stuff by modern-day standards, the show was enough to offend some, and the Beast probably would have been disappointed if it had not. Leading the pack of the outraged was another newspaper man, De Wend Fenton, whose *Looking Glass* launched a series of scathing attacks on the performance and its mastermind. Fenton alleged that he had been kissed by someone—someone with a mustache—in the darkened theater, and he was determined to shut the whole thing down. Among other things, Fenton branded Crowley "one of the most blasphemous and cold-blooded villains of modern times."[27] The Beast preferred to dismiss Fenton as a cheap would-be blackmailer, but friends including Capt. Fuller and Raffalovitch pressed him to sue the *Looking Glass* for libel. After all, an attack on their guru was to some degree an attack on them, and by letting Fenton's insults go unchallenged Crowley could seem to be admitting their truth.

However, Feilding, a barrister, warned about the perils of such proceedings. Under British law, Fenton would be obliged to prove the accuracy of his statements to defend against a claim of libel, and even if he fell short of proving that Crowley one of the worst villains of modern times, he undoubtedly could dredge up plenty of dirt. That was the very trap Oscar Wilde had fallen into, a tragedy still vivid in the public memory. Thus Crowley might win the legal case but still lose in the court of public opinion. Sound legal advice, but perhaps Feilding had other things to consider. What if Fenton stumbled upon evidence of Crowley's work for His Majesty? That posed an intolerable risk of embarrassment for important people. So, Crowley declined to sue, and thus lost the confidence and friendship of Fuller, Raffalovitch, and others.

In its 17 December 1910 issue, *Looking Glass* took a final poke at the Beast, noting a recent report that he had "left London for Russia"—a most interesting allegation that raises the questions of just where he was and why. Doubly interesting is that on the same day Fenton's paper alleged Crowley's flight to Russia, London awoke to news of a horrendous crime the night before, one with its own Russian connection. A gang of "Russian anarchists," Latvians and Jews actually, were interrupted by police while trying to rob a jewelry store near Houndsditch. In the ensuing hail of bullets, three constables died, and the culprits fled to the teeming East End. Shortly after the New Year, authorities tracked some of them to a flat on Sidney Street. The man who took charge of the situation, grandstanding for all it was worth, was Home Secretary Winston Churchill. On his orders, troops in full battle gear surrounded the fugitives' hideout, and at least two of them perished in the resulting shoot-out and fire.[28]

Crowley's disappearance around the time of the original shootings would seem mere coincidence were it not for a later rumor that he was "more than acquainted" with the alleged mastermind of the same anarchist gang, the mysterious "Peter the Painter," a.k.a. Peter Piatkow.[29] While this allegation, like others, has to be taken with a large grain of salt, it merits a closer look. The Mage had long professed a fascination with Russia and, as we will see later, he was at least able to affect revolutionary sympathies. Cultivating contacts among the anti-Tsarist émigrés could have provided him with information of value to such worthies as William Melville (still very much in the spy business) or even Home Secretary Churchill. That alone could have motivated keeping a low profile in the wake of the Houndsditch Murders. Might he even have gone underground or abroad to help find the killers?

1910 also saw Crowley's first known brush with German intelligence, in the person of Theodor Reuss. About twenty years Crowley's senior, Albert Karl Theodor Reuss, also known as Willsson, Frater Peregrinus, and Frater Merlin, was a sometimes singer, druggist, and police spy. He also was involved with virtually every contemporary secret or occult society.[30] He started as a Freemason in 1876. In the 1880s, working for the Prussian political police, he infiltrated the Socialist League in London, a group of radical German expatriates surrounding Karl Marx's daughter Eleanor Marx-Aveling. Eventually uncovered and denounced as Bismarck's political agent, Reuss returned to Berlin, where he posed as a journalist.

As such, he roamed the Balkans and the Middle East, covered the Greco-Turkish War of 1897, and almost certainly continued to act as a German agent.

Around 1901 Reuss returned to London. By then he claimed to be the head of a revived Order of the Bavarian Illuminati, a high official of the esoteric Martinist and Swedenborgian Masonic rites, and a Rosicrucian magus. This brought him to William Wynn Westcott, a luminary of the Golden Dawn. From Westcott and others, Reuss would have heard plenty about Crowley's escapades.

Reuss' main achievement (with some help from the Austrian industrialist Karl Kellner) was the creation circa 1902 of the Ordo Templi Orientis (OTO), the "Order of Oriental Templars." Second only to the Illuminati, perhaps, the OTO has earned a reputation as a center of conspiratorial skullduggery and even the dubious title of "the World's Most Dangerous Secret Society."[31] As originally envisioned by Reuss, the OTO was to be an Academia Masonica that would unify assorted Masonic rites with other esoteric orders into an overarching occult organization. Reuss, who assumed complete control of the Order after Kellner's death in 1905, cobbled together assorted lodges, orders, rites, and "churches" into a nominal esoteric confederation.

The "great secret" of the OTO, and its main attraction for Crowley, was "sex magic." Roughly, this was based on the notion that sexual intercourse released profound spiritual energy. Through concentration and the proper rituals, an adept could harness and direct this energy and even generate a "magical child," a spiritual entity that would go forth and manifest the adept's will in the physical world. Crowley would become an avid practitioner of the technique.

Outwardly, the OTO seems to have remained rather small and exclusive, though Reuss tirelessly recruited, out of both spiritual zeal and vanity, but also to use the Order as a cover for German intelligence. It seems that Crowley first came to Reuss' serious attention as a result of the Rosicrucian Scandal. In spite of the Beast's flagrant violation of sacred oaths, Reuss recruited him. In 1912, in a Berlin ceremony, Reuss made Crowley the chief of the OTO branch in the British Isles, the Ordo Mysteria Mystica Maxima (MMM), a mandate later extended to English-speaking America. Thus he earned yet another magical name, Baphomet, after the mysterious idol allegedly worshipped by the Knights Templar.

Immediately after his initiation, Crowley drafted a Manifesto for the MMM, later adopted by the OTO as a whole.[32] In it, he listed some twenty organizations whose collective wisdom supposedly informed the new Order, among them the Illuminati, the Knights Templar, Knights of Malta, the Gnostic Catholic Church, and even, in the original edition, the Golden Dawn. He also offered an impressive, if improbable, list of mythical and historic members of the OTO's "constituent originating assemblies." Krishna, Lao-tze, Mohammed, and Moses were among those so honored, along with

Roger Bacon, John Dee, and Christian Rosenkreutz. Among the more recent and intriguing names Crowley added Cardinal Rampolla, the former Papal secretary of state who some years earlier had given his blessings to Ashburnham's Jacobites. Count Mariano Cardinal Rampolla del Tindaro had almost been elected Pope in 1903, only to see his candidacy undone by the fierce opposition of Habsburg Emperor Franz Josef. According to one version, Franz Josef's veto was stimulated by the revelation that the Cardinal was a secret Freemason.[33] Was that why Crowley later chose to list him among the OTO "saints"?

Was Reuss's recruitment of Crowley into the OTO also an attempt to lure him into the Kaiser's secret service? If so, were the Mage's British intelligence superiors aware of it? More to the point, did they encourage it? Notably, Crowley's association with Reuss occurred soon after a major reorganization of British intelligence specifically designed to counter the growing German menace. The old War Office Intelligence Division disappeared, replaced with two new agencies. One was a domestic counter-espionage section, the Secret Service Bureau, under Army Capt. Vernon G. W. Kell, and the other a Foreign Section led by Royal Navy Commander Mansfield Smith Cumming. In due course, Kell's outfit became the Security Service, and Cumming's the Secret Intelligence Service (SIS). Both secret organizations masqueraded as various subsections of military intelligence. During WWI, Kell's counter-intelligence service adopted the cover of MI5, while SIS became MI1c and later MI6.

Still, the Admiralty's NID, which liked to refer to itself as the "Intelligence Service," retained independence under the firm hand of Admiral W. Reginald "Blinker" Hall. The energetic, beak-nosed Hall was fascinated by "the world of spies, agents, deception, bribery, disinformation, destabilization, all that side of intelligence now stigmatized as the 'Dirty Tricks' department."[34] Hall also controlled the main communications interception and code-breaking section, "Room 40." Obsessed with secrecy, he routinely and unapologetically withheld information from other services.[35]

In 1911 Parliament approved a new Official Secrets Act (OSA), which remains, with various revisions, in force.[36] The heart of it was Section Two, which forbade anyone "who holds or who has held" a position under His Majesty, or simply contracted in any way with the government, from disclosing information about his or her work without lawful authority. Its most important aim was to keep intelligence operatives quiet— permanently.[37] The OSA was a sword hanging over the head of Crowley, or anyone else involved in covert activities, requiring great care in what was said or written.

During 1911–1912 Crowley kept himself occupied with writing and magical workings, including another sojourn to the Sahara with Neuberg. He also found time for a torrid fling with a rich American expatriate, Mary d'Esti Sturges. Through Sturges, he made the personal and carnal acquaintance of one of her close friends, avant-garde dancer Isadora Duncan. Duncan, in turn, may have offered some practical, or not so practical, tips for Crowley's next venture as a theatrical entrepreneur. In early 1913, he recruited Leila Waddell and six other young women to form the "Ragged Rag-time Girls." With Leila as the lead, the troupe played fiddles and pranced about the stage in scant costumes, the costumes probably being their chief appeal. After a brief and seemingly successful premier at London's Old Tivoli, in July Crowley took his performers to Russia with a contract to play Moscow's Aquarium variety theater.[38]

One might wonder why Crowley picked Russia of all places. The Tsar's domain presented a host of obstacles to foreign performers, such as the requirement of passports for the Beast and his charges, something not demanded of British subjects in most other places. Nor, to all appearances, was the six-week stay an artistic or financial success, and the Ragged Rag-time Girls disbanded as soon as they returned safely to England. The stint did, however, stimulate the Beast's creativity, and he poured out an impressive array of poems and other writings. He also had a brief affair with a masochistic Hungarian girl and ventured off on some interesting side-trips, including one to the famous Fair in Nizhni-Novgorod. He even wrote a poem about the experience, "The Fun of the Fair." In his notes to this, he reveals what really drew him there and to Russia itself. "Though little agitation was apparent in the general atmosphere of the Fair," he wrote, "the shrewd, astute, subtle, lynx-eyed, past master, analytical, psychic, eerie, hard-bitten Secret Service Chief could nose there was a certain discontent with the regime."[39] Russia might be Britain's new ally against Germany, but that did not make London's secret services blithe about what was going on there. In fact, Russia being an ally, its political stability was of greater concern than ever. An eccentric Englishman leading a troupe of dancing girls provided perfect cover for observing developments and contacting persons of interest.

Another sign of an intelligence angle to the Russian visit is the choice of theatrical agent, Mikhail Lykiardopoulos, the Anglo-Greco-Russian secretary of the prestigious Moscow Art Theatre. As a translator of many English works, "Lyki" probably knew something of Crowley through his writings. More significant, though, is his introduction of Crowley to the British commercial attaché in Moscow, R.H. Bruce Lockhart. "During the war," Lockhart later noted, "[Lykiardopoulos] ran our propaganda department in Moscow under my supervision—and ran it very well."[40] Thus, in short order, both men would be actively engaged in intelligence or para-intelligence work. One must wonder whether Lyki was not already so engaged in 1913. He would have been an ideal and invaluable contact for Crowley in Moscow. Lockhart, moreover, had clandestine contacts with members of the revolutionary underground, the very sort of people that the Beast would want to meet.

Crowley later mentioned other contacts with British consular officials in Russia.[41] These included Charles Clive Bayley, the vice-consul in Moscow. Bayley will later appear in New York.

Interestingly, Crowley's arrival in Moscow followed shortly after that of another mystic, George Ivanovich Gurdjieff. Unsurprisingly, Gurdjieff is also rumored to have had links to British intelligence. Most astounding is the claim that he started life as Frederick Dottle, a Cockney orphan from London's teeming East End.[42] After shipping out to the Russian Caucasus as a cabin boy, the story goes, he became the adopted son of the Greco-Armenian businessman Ivan Giorgiades, eventually drifted into the secret service of the Indian Government, and shifted to London's control around 1907. Whether this tale is fact or fantasy, in the two decades preceding the First World War, Gurdjieff traveled around the Near East and Central Asia and was poking around the borders of Tibet while Crowley was on K-2. However, there is no firm evidence that the two met before or during Crowley's 1913 Russian trip.

The final days of 1913 and the first months of 1914 were filled with more magical workings and initiations, mostly in Paris, with Walter Duranty playing his most prominent role. Crowley also made another mysterious visit to Stockholm, gateway to Russia, early in 1914. Spring saw the Beast return to his beloved Alps, where in June he tackled Switzerland's Jungfrau, near Interlaken. There he heard the ominous news of the assassination of the Archduke Franz Ferdinand on 28 June. War was on the horizon.

Crowley's recollections of the next few months are replete with details, but vague and even contradictory in chronology. He seems deliberately imprecise about what he was doing and where—perhaps with good reason. In *Confessions*, written in the late 1920s, he recalls a kind of panic that swept through the British community in Switzerland, inflamed by predictions that expedient transportation back to England might soon become hard to arrange. Many feared that the Swiss would join the fight on Germany's side.

Undeterred by such worries, Crowley simply boarded a train for Paris, where he lingered for a week admiring the sangfroid of the French as "they turned from peace to war."[43] That argues he was there when Germany declared war on 3 August, which conflicts somewhat with assertions that he was in London the very next day when Britain proclaimed war on Germany. In a later press article, he claimed that at the beginning of August he was in "a sick bed in Paris" laid up with phlebitis, an inflamed vein in his leg.[44] In Confessions, though, he speaks of phlebitis only after he reached England which supposedly left him bedridden there for six weeks during September and October. A diary entry pins down the onset of the malady as 7 September, the day after sex with a Piccadilly prostitute, which he blamed for the attack. This seems improbable, unless the bout aggravated an existing injury.

To add to the confusion, in a later interview given to an American paper, the Beast asserted that "at the outset of the Great War [he] was in the confidential service of the British Government [and] in this service he was shot in the leg…"[45] In a man of Crowley's age and physical condition, the usual cause of phlebitis is a penetrating injury, especially by a bullet. As for a climbing injury, the only recent one he mentions is a bruised toenail acquired on the Jungfrau.

It is unclear whether this story was mere braggadocio for a gullible American reporter or an important clue about Crowley's prewar secret service. The Mage may have been using his stay in Switzerland to collect information on the Republic's sizable population of exiled revolutionaries and related denizens. Perhaps he was following up on the Houndsditch/Sidney Street case. The alleged mastermind of that outrage, "Peter the Painter," had vanished, and was rumored to have sought refuge among the Alps with others of his ilk. Near the picturesque Swiss town of Lugano was the thriving commune of Monte Verita, the de facto capital of the European counterculture and a mecca for rebels of every political, spiritual, and sexual orientation.[46] Whether Crowley ever visited the place is uncertain, but it will figure prominently in Reuss' wartime intrigues.

According to the Beast, soon after his return to England, "I tried every means to get the Government to use me—without success."[47] What he meant was that they refused him any sort of official job. No doubt he felt he deserved one. As mentioned, his friend and adviser Everard Feilding had obtained a lieutenant's commission in the Royal Navy Volunteer Reserve, and through it Feilding soon joined the new Press Bureau as a naval censor. In fact, he was working for Hall's NID. "Blinker" dispatched men like Feilding to the censorship department to help in its work and to help maintain Admiralty control over the flow of information. The Press Bureau handled different functions, including the release of official information. A related Neutral Press Committee disseminated news to friendly and neutral nations, and a Military Room oversaw all press material other than cables. The NID exercised direct control of the latter. The line between intelligence and propaganda thus blurred from the outset.

The Mage may not have realistically expected to get a commission (though he counted his Carlist adventure as practical military experience), but in stressing to Feilding his knowledge of foreign languages, including Hindustani, and his expertise with cyphers, he clearly was making a pitch for a slot in the Press Bureau or the like. Another desirable slot was the War Propaganda Board, a.k.a. "Wellington House," which came together in September.[48] A hush-hush group, it recruited such well-known literary figures as Arthur Conan Doyle, J.M. Barrie, H.G. Wells, and G.K. Chesterton to churn out propaganda for domestic and foreign use. Chesterton, for one, was an admirer of Crowley's writing, but that sentiment likely was not shared by his superiors.

The great obstacle to any official post for Mr. Crowley was his reputation, so badly tarnished just a few years before. As the Beast recalled Feilding telling him, "you have a reputation for having committed every crime from murder, barratry and arson downwards. I am afraid there is nothing you could do."[49] Except, of course, what he had done already, unofficially. Crowley's talents, experience, and contacts had many uses, but none openly or in England.

Of all the neutral nations, the United States was of greatest concern to the Press Bureau and Propaganda Board. For reasons considered in the next chapter, they were extremely concerned about German activities there. Without offering any explanation of why or by whom, the Beast records that he suddenly "accepted an invitation to go to New York" on commercial pretexts—an odd undertaking for a man devoid of any practical business experience. Nevertheless, on 24 October, he boarded the Lusitania in Liverpool and headed west.

1   On Crowley's relationship with various branches of Freemasonry, see:
    Martin P. Starr, "Aleister Crowley: Freemason!," //freemasonry.bcy.ca/aqc/
    crowley.html.

2   *CAC*, 456.

3   *Ibid.* Re Crowley's views on invisibility, see also *Magick Without Tears*,
    Chapter XV, www.hermetic.com/crowley/met/mwt_25.html.

4   Daniel Yergin, *The Prize: The Epic Quest for Oil, Money and Power*
    (NY: Touchstone, 1992), 229–235.

5   Harry Thayer Mahoney and Marjorie Locke Mahoney, *Espionage in Mexico:
    Aztec, Spanish Colonial and the 1810 and 1910 Revolutions* (Privately printed,
    2001), 108–109.

6   For a general background, see: Peter Hopkirk, *The Great Game: On Secret
    Service in High Asia* (London: John Murray, 2006).

7   *CAC*, 491.

8   *CAC*, 489.

9   *CAC*, 490.

10 *Ibid.*

11 *CAC*, 500.

12 Crowley, "The Biter Bit" (c. 1917), www.hermetic.com/crowley/simon_iff/
    The_Biter_Bit.htm.

13 Ernest Jouin (ed.),), "L'OTO: Expulsion de Sir Aleister Crowley," *Revue
    Internationale des Societes Secretes* [hereafter RISS], (May 1929), 138.

14 J.F.C. Fuller, *The Star in the West: A Critical Essay upon the Works of Aleister
    Crowley* (London: Walter Scott, 1907).

15 *CAC*, 629.

16 UKNA, ADM 196/43.

17 Paul Newman, *Ancestral Voices Prophesying War: A Tale of Two Suicides*,
    unpublished ms, 7.

18 *Ibid.*, 21.

19 *Ibid.*, 31–32.

20 Dr. Ben Brower to author, 2 March 2006.

21 Pierre Mariel, *L'Europe Paienne du XX Siecle* (Paris: La Palatine, 1964), 49.

22 *CAC*, 629.

23 Obituary, "Miss Leila Waddell," *Sydney Herald* (14 Sept. 1932).

24 Yasha Beresiner, "Winston Churchill: A Famous Man and a Freemason,"
    www.freemasons-freemasonry.com/beresiner7.html.

25 For an interesting take on this see: D. Trull, "Winston and the Witch," www.
    parascope.com/articles/slips/fs23_1.htm.

26 "A Cat Out of the Bag," *John Bull* (2 May 1910).

27 "An Amazing Sect," *The Looking Glass* (29 Oct. 1910).

28 See: Donald Rumbelow, *The Houndsditch Murders & the Siege of Sidney*

Street (NY: St. Martin's, 1973).

29   Amado Crowley, *Secrets*, 174–175.

30   Ellic Howe and Helmut Moller, "Theodor Reuss: Irregular Freemasonry in Germany, 1900–23," *Ars Quator Coronatorum* [AQC] (16 Feb. 1978) at // freemasonry.bcy.ca/aqc/reuss/reuss.html. See also: Peter-R. Koenig, "Ordo Templi Orientis, Carl Kellner, Theodor Reuss: Once upon a Time on the Dark Side of the Moon," //user.cyberlink.ch/~koenig/reuss.html.

31   Craig Heimbichner, *Blood on the Altar: The Secret History of the World's Most Dangerous Secret Society.*

32   Reprinted in 1919, the Manifesto is also known as *Liber LII*: www.geocities. com/nu_isis/liber052.html#1. See also: RISS, "L'OTO," (May 1929), 137–145.

33   Craig Heimbichner, "Did a Freemason Almost Become Pope?: the Story of Cardinal Rampolla," *Catholic Family News* (Aug. 2003).

34   Patrick Beesly, *Room 40—British Naval Intelligence, 1914–1918* (San Diego: Harcourt, Brace, Jovanovich, 1982), 39.

35   Christopher Andrew, *Secret Service: The Making of the British Intelligence Community* (London: Heineman, 1985), 108–110.

36   This replaced an earlier Act established in 1889.

37   Notable examples include the Thatcher Government's efforts to prevent the publication of Peter Wright's *Spycatcher* memoir and the more recent travails of dissident MI5 man David Shayler and outspoken ex-MI6 agent Richard Tomlinson. See also: "The Troubled History of the Official Secrets Act," //news.bbc.co.uk/1/h/uk/216868.stm.

38   William Ryan, "The Great Beast in Russia: Aleister Crowley's Theatrical Tour in 1913 and His Beastly Writings on Russia," in *Symbolism and After: Essays on Russian Poetry in Honour of Georgette Donchin* (London: Bristol Classical, 1992), 137–162, 145.

39   *The Fun of the Fair* (London: Neptune Press,1971) [orig. printing 1942].

40   R. H. Bruce Lockhart, *British Agent* (New York: Putnam's, 1933), 75.

41   *CAC*, 711–717.

42   Peter Roberts, "Was Gurdjieff Really Irish?," www.promart.com/g.origins. html (1996).

43   *CAC*, 742.

44   "They Called Me a Renegade! [hereafter Renegade]," *Empire News* (17 Dec. 1933).

45   *The* [New York] *Evening World* (26 Feb. 1919).

46   Monte Verita lay above the small Ticino town of Ascona on the Lago Maggiore. It was founded in 1900 by eccentric Belgian industrialist Henri Oedenkoven and his feminist companion Ida Hoffmann as a utopian community devoted to vegetarianism, free-thinking and free love. There also was a strong Theosophist influence. In the years following it attracted a diverse array of short-and long-term visitors, including Crowley's

friend Isadora Duncan, Hermann Hesse, Carl Jung and Lenin. The grand old man of anarchism, Prince Peter Kropotkin, was another. By 1904, Monte Verita had become a gathering place for anarchists from around Europe and the world. See: Centro Stefano Franscini, "History of Monte Verita," www.csf.ethz.ch/about/history.

47 Renegade.
48 Jonathan Epstein, "German and English Propaganda in World War I," paper delivered to NYMAS, CUNY Graduate Center (1 Dec. 2000), //libraryautomation.com/nymas/propagandapaper.html.
49 Renegade.

CHAPTER THREE
~
An Irishman
in New York
~

ANYONE PAYING CLOSE ATTENTION to the passengers debarking from the *Lusitania* on 31 October 1914 might have noticed a well-dressed gentleman of about forty with a limp and an athletic build starting to go to flab. If he was hatless, a curious forelock on his otherwise bald head would have made him all the more noticeable. A closer look would have revealed large, soft fingers festooned with numerous strange rings.[1] The liner's passenger manifest listed him as Edward Alexander Crowley, Irishman.[2] No one would recognize the English magician Aleister Crowley—at least, no one who was not supposed to.

One must wonder if Crowley ascribed any significance to the fact that he landed in America on Halloween. He would remain there for five years despite, according to him, near constant penury and assorted other difficulties.

Why did he endure the hardships as long as he did? He had a job to do, one he did better than he later dared admit. Looming over every word he would write about his American adventures in years to follow was the Official Secrets Act. Crowley therefore pretended to have served his country "playing a lone hand," while hovering near the edge of destitution or worse.[3] The reality, as will be revealed, was something quite different.

The first problem the Beast encountered, right off the boat, was that the business "invitation" that had brought him there had somehow fallen through. He is, as usual, vague about the business, but his later reference to "the sinews of war" signals that it must have concerned war contracts.[4] He expected the deal to be worth "fifteen to twenty million dollars" (roughly $300 million today), though his end would have been only a modest commission. His likely role was as bag-man, conveying funds or financial instruments for contracts legal or not. If the latter, his status as a complete unknown in the commercial sphere would have been an advantage.

Crowley was operating against a backdrop of international intrigue and uncertainty in the opening phase of the war. As soon as war broke out, representatives of the European belligerents rushed to secure financing and war materials across the Atlantic, and American businessmen received them warmly. However Woodrow Wilson's pacifistic Secretary of State, William Jennings Bryan, chilled such plans by declaring that U.S. law prohibited Americans from providing loans or military goods to warring nations. President Wilson himself officially proclaimed America's neutrality on 5 August and the next day created a special Neutrality Bureau to police exports. As its head Wilson appointed an Irish-American attorney and Democrat Party hack, Dudley Field Malone, whom Crowley would later encounter.

Bryan's ruling did leave belligerent governments free to bring financial instruments into the U.S. or raise loans there. Perhaps aware that British interference could soon cut off access, the Germans were first to seek financing in America. In the second week of August 1914, a prominent banker from the Reich, Dr. Bernhard Dernburg, set out on an urgent secret mission to New York. Passenger records show that he accompanied another traveler under the name of Anton Mayer Gerhard.[5] In reality, this was an even higher personage in the German financial hierarchy, Max Warburg, head of the powerful M.M. Warburg Bank of Hamburg and a financial mainstay of the Kaiser's government. The Germans were carrying $175 million in German treasury certificates to market in the United States.

Dernburg and Warburg were headed for the New York City offices of Kuhn, Loeb & Co., a banking house closely linked to Warburg's. Indeed, two of his brothers, Paul and Felix, were partners therein. Felix was also the son-in-law of the firm's grand old man, Jacob Schiff. Schiff, the Warburgs, and the other leading lights of Kuhn, Loeb were all German Jews, most of whom maintained sentimental as well as financial ties with the Fatherland. One could reasonably expect that Schiff and his firm, reckoned the #2 financial house in America, would assist the needy Reich.

Schiff was glad to help set up a German war loan or purchasing credits but needed help from other institutions, most importantly Wall Street's foremost bankers, J.P. Morgan & Company. Ensconced at 23 Wall Street, Morgan was hostile to the German overture. The monetary and sentimental ties of the House of Morgan were firmly attached to London, and their clout on the American business scene made them hard to contravene. Morgan's allegiance ensured that Britain and her allies would enjoy access to America's immense financial and industrial power, and Germany would not. This ultimately drove a frustrated Reich to sabotage and submarine warfare to stem the transAtlantic flow of arms and munitions.

Britain, however, had another advantage in this clandestine battle, a spy inside Kuhn, Loeb. Otto Hermann Kahn, German-Jewish born like his colleagues, was also a naturalized British subject, a man later hailed by the #2 SIS officer in wartime New York as "whole-heartedly pro-Allied and especially pro-British," and a believer in the inevitability of Allied victory.[6] Kahn is a prime example of the main weapon British intelligence used against the Germans in America—the undercover agent inside the enemy camp. Crowley's ultimate mission in America would be the same. This does much to explain why he would later count banker Kahn among his "friends."

Max Warburg slipped back to Germany as quietly as he had arrived, but Dernburg remained to take on new tasks. Ostensibly, he ran the German Red Cross operation in New York. Actually, in close cooperation with Berlin's Ambassador Count Johann von Bernstorff, Dernburg also assumed control of the German Information Bureau on Broadway. The Bureau fronted for a secretive *Propaganda Kabinett* that counted Harvard Professor Hugo Muensterburg, writer and occultist Hanns Heinz Ewers, and German-American publisher George Sylvester Viereck among its members and resources.[7] Crowley would become intimately acquainted with all three. The basic aim of the *Kabinett* was to counter Allied propaganda and champion Germany's cause in America. Ultimately it focused on keeping the U.S. out of the war, just as the British tried ever harder to bring the Yanks into the conflict.

Meanwhile in New York, Washington, and London, interventionists and profiteers pressed for relaxed interpretations of American neutrality laws and nurtured the alliance between Morgan & Co. and His Majesty's Government. By the end of September, the likelihood of a long war had become obvious; hostilities would last for months, at least. A vast amount of money was at stake, and, as usual, what money wanted, money got. On 15 October State Department Counselor Robert Lansing, soon to replace Bryan as secretary, asserted the legality of selling war supplies to belligerents. The floodgates were open; it became a matter of managing the onrushing stream of orders. In mid-October two representatives of the British Treasury, Basil Blackett and statistics wizard George Paish, arrived at 23 Wall Street. empowered to offer all British war purchasing to a single firm—Morgan. Supplemental agreements extended the same authority over most French and Russian war purchasing.[8]

On 31 October, therefore, following fast on the heels of Blackett and Paish, came George Macauley Booth, a "man of push and go" who was not only a Bank of England director, but also soon to be Deputy Director of Munitions Supply.[9] He was close to the "sinews of war" and authorized to handle a deal as big as the one mentioned by Crowley. Booth, in fact, arrived on the *Lusitania* with the Beast, and this certainly was no coincidence. Crowley was to have been one of Booth's minions or cut-outs in arranging contracts, but the deal with Morgan, with Booth's immediate and enthusiastic support, obviated the Beast's services. Independent commercial agents were no longer wanted or needed; his "egg was addled," as he later put it.[10]

But if such had been Crowley's only business in New York, he would have hurried back to England at once. The war-contractor role, though, was never more than a convenient and potentially profitable cover for something else. Remember, every good spy needs a practical reason to be where he is. The Beast's employers back in London had other uses for him and did not leave him adrift. Despite later claims of near destitution, he was, in fact, far from penniless. By his own recollection, he arrived with some £50 worth of Yankee money in his pockets, about $5000 by 2007 standards. That would not last long in the Big Apple, but it does explain how Crowley could afford to take up residence at the St. Regis Hotel, among the most expensive in Manhattan. Moreover, within days of his arrival, he had a seemingly fortuitous meeting with an American "collector" who offered to buy some rare books. Crowley at once summoned these from England, which put another $500–700 ($10,000–12,000) in his hands.

The most important detail in this timely transaction is the identity of the collector. John Quinn, a second-generation Irish-American lawyer, was an influential figure both in local politics and in the art world. An avid bibliophile, Quinn also enthusiastically promoted the artistic avant garde.[11] That provided a credible—but false—pretext for his interest in Crowley. Quinn was an outspoken advocate of Irish liberty, specifically Home Rule, i.e. self government by an Ireland still firmly within the British Empire. In 1917, Quinn, Horace Plunkett, and George Russell wrote an Irish Home Rule Convention. While a moderate on the Irish Question, Quinn was also friendly with radical nationalists, most notably the firebrand Sir Roger Casement, Quinn's recent house guest.

Quinn was not just being hospitable, for his less obvious but no less important role was that of British agent. Casement and others among Quinn's Irish associates would have been shocked by the admiration he enjoyed at the British Consulate at 44 Whitehall Street. and the information he offered there about their activities. Sir Arthur Willert, chief correspondent of *The Times* in the U.S. during the war (later Secretary of the British War Mission) and an authority on British clandestine activities, praised Quinn as one of the "staunchest supporters that the Allies, especially the French, had among the Irish-American leaders."[12] Quinn himself later boasted that he had "given my time and my strength and my money to the pro-Ally causes of all nationalities."[13]

Quinn also had a long personal acquaintance with a past and future member of the British intelligence establishment, Claude Marjoribanks Dansey. In the years just before WWI, Dansey was the secretary of the exclusive Sleepy Hollow Golf Club, to which Quinn and many other New York luminaries belonged.[14] Upon the outbreak of war, Dansey dutifully returned to England and took a post in MI5. In that role he would return to New York in 1917.

Quinn's immediate role as regards Crowley, however, was that of temporary case officer. He saw the Mage regularly at least through early 1915, inviting him to dinners at his home as well as providing him with money and introductions. Quinn's reflections on this relationship show that he did not extend the helping hand out of genuine interest or affection. In letters to his friend William Butler Yeats, Crowley's old nemesis from the Golden Dawn days (and one wonders, what did Quinn know of that?), Quinn repeatedly complained that Crowley was always in need of cash. On 7 January, for instance, Quinn was obliged to pay or loan our man another $100. Quinn opined that aside from Crowley's love of drink, he could see "nothing wrong about him," but neither did he praise him. He found the so-called Great Beast rather dull company.[15] "Frankly his 'magic' and astrology bore me beyond words," Quinn added, and he complained that Crowley had "no personality." In place of a genius or even an amoral monster, Quinn saw only "a third or fourth rate poet." "I have …no interest or curiosity in what he is doing and have not taken up with him in any way," he wrote, concluding, "He is not my kind of person at all."[16]

Of course, Quinn may have been prevaricating in his letters to Yeats who, after all, was well-connected to Irish nationalist circles and bound to repeat what he heard. Practically speaking, Quinn had to keep his distance from Crowley in case the ties of either of them to British intelligence came to light. Thus, he may have tried to pass off their association as a disappointing indulgence of morbid curiosity. Certainly his comments about Crowley's poverty ring false. Not only did Crowley manage to maintain himself at the posh St. Regis for some weeks, but on 1 December he had the means to rent an apartment at 40 W. 36th Street. just off fashionable 5th Avenue.

Still, given Crowley's manifest inability to manage money, finances were a continual problem. That His Majesty's officials were willing to use Crowley as an operative did not mean they were willing to pay him, generously or directly. It would not do for him to be found, dead or alive, with a check or receipt from the British Consulate on his person, especially if he was involved in anything of dubious legality. Moreover, this was war, and a British subject was expected to do his patriotic duty, however he cared to define it, without expectation of personal gain.

Undoubtedly the first and most important bit of news Quinn passed to Crowley was that Roger Casement had gone. Casement may well have been the original object of the Mage's secret assignment in America. The Irish-born Casement was one of those charismatic and larger-than-life gentleman-adventurers who became national celebrities in Britain's imperial heyday. His sexual appetite was also large, but his promiscuous homosexuality was either unknown to or ignored by his admirers. In 1916, the same nation that knighted Casement would hang him as a traitor.

By summer 1914, the volatile Casement had become a convert to militant Irish republicanism and was in America raising money for the cause. The war, he believed, gave Irish patriots a heaven-sent opportunity to make a daring bid for Erin's freedom through an alliance with Germany. He secretly contacted German representatives in the U.S., including Ambassador Bernstorff and his military attaché Franz von Papen, and offered to form an Irish Legion to fight on Germany's side in exchange for Berlin's support for Irish independence.

On 1 October, Bernstorff told Berlin about Casement's proposal. Unknown to the Ambassador, Admiral Hall's NID had intercepted the message. Four days later, Casement sent a manifesto (also intercepted by NID) to his followers in Ireland urging them to make common cause with Germany. In London, Hall and others considered how to nip the danger in the bud. Quinn was one British agent put on Casement's case, and Crowley was another.[17] This explains why Crowley arrived in New York as an Irishman, ready to swear his life to Irish freedom. That sentiment and Quinn's ready introduction would have gotten him access to Casement. Casement would have appreciated Crowley as a man of adventurous reputation, apt for grand and noble enterprises. An added advantage was Crowley's real or assumed sexual proclivities. That the Beast, as alleged by at least one source, aimed to use "sexual advances to get close to Casement," is not out of the question.[18] Rumors about Casement's sexual preference already circulated in London, but lacked definite proof. If Crowley could get that evidence, one way or another, he would have the power to destroy Sir Roger's reputation and influence. The basic tactic was proven: a few decades before, another troublesome Irish politico, Charles Stewart Parnell, had been neutralized by the exposure of his adultery.

On 10 October, while Crowley was still in England, Casement and fellow rebels John Devoy, Joseph McGarrity, Daniel Cohalan, and others met in New York's German Club with Bernstorff, von Papen, and Dr. Dernburg. Devoy, a veteran of English prisons, the French Foreign Legion, and years of intrigue, backed Casement's arrangement with the Germans, though he questioned Sir Roger's ability to pull it off. Had he realized that Casement had been carrying on these traitorous negotiations virtually under the nose of a British agent (Quinn), his doubts would have been graver. As it was, they were to prove well founded.

Casement proved cleverer than Quinn and London thought.[19] Berlin jumped at Casement's plan and hastened to bring him to the Reich. Laying a false trail, he slipped out of New York on 15 October bound for Norway. Temporarily blinded by this disappearing act, the British and Quinn still believed Sir Roger to be somewhere in the U.S. when Crowley set sail on 24 October.

Casement duped the Lion but did not stay hidden long. On 28 October the British Consul in Oslo, Norway, picked up the trail when Casement's lover, Norwegian sailor Adler Christensen, appeared at the Consulate offering to betray him, or so British sources alleged. As Christensen later told the tale, it was the British who, perhaps desperate after the failure in New York, approached him offering money not merely to betray Casement, but to kill him.[20] Britain's representative in Norway,

Sir Mansfeldt Findlay, denied this emphatically. However targeted, Casement gave London the slip again and arrived safely in Berlin on Halloween, the very day Crowley walked down the gangplank in New York.

Quinn clearly was not cut out to be a spymaster, and with the flight of Casement, he lost most of his value to the Beast, and vice versa. Feilding remained Crowley's real controller, and behind Feilding, Admiral Hall and NID. Likely one of those two made the decision to keep the Mage in the States, necessitating a new and better-suited case officer. Forty-four-year-old Capt. Guy Reginald Arthur Gaunt was the British Naval Attaché in the U.S., and with the advent of the war he also became the representative of Hall's NID. Neither MI5 nor SIS would have any presence in America until early 1916. Gaunt, for the time being, was the ranking point man for British intelligence in the United States.[21]

The Australian-born Gaunt had no experience in intelligence work, but he took on the job with the same gung-ho attitude displayed in the rest of his naval career. Beneath his swashbuckling bravado, however, he was a bundle of prejudices and insecurities often masked with vicious snobbery. Gaunt's breezy sailor act proved a big hit with the Yankees, and he enjoyed the social limelight. The onset of the war obliged him to spend most of his time in the Big Apple keeping an eye on the Germans and overseeing the protection of vital supplies shipments. Gaunt quickly found himself saddled not only with counterespionage, but also with propaganda and public relations duties as well.

As a diplomatic officer, Gaunt could ill-afford to be caught doing anything unseemly or illegal, such as spying. The likely result would be his expulsion from the U.S. and the acute embarrassment of HMG. Nevertheless, the garrulous Gaunt simply was no good at keeping his clandestine role a secret. He complained of clueless society women who button-held him at public gatherings to pour out their concerns about real or imagined German intrigues, but he also relished their attention. Thus his German counterparts (von Papen, Naval Captain Karl Boy-Ed, Dernburg, and others) knew exactly what he was up to and did their best to try to discredit him or lure him into a compromising position.[22] Fortunately for Gaunt, they displayed even less talent for the game than he.

Gaunt and Crowley's meeting was delayed by the Captain's travels in late 1914 and early 1915. He was in Washington when the Beast first hit Manhattan, but in December Gaunt took a tour of the Caribbean, only returning to New York in early February. That likely explains the need for Quinn to play extended stand-in. Also, the visibility and vulnerability of Gaunt's position meant that he had to be extremely cautious about direct dealings with the likes of Crowley. Likewise, the latter's usefulness as an undercover operative would be blown sky-high should he be seen at Gaunt's office or any other place associated with British officialdom.

Such detachment suited Gaunt just fine. One need not imagine that their professional relationship, such as it was, necessitated any mutual respect or admiration; Gaunt would have despised Crowley, but orders were orders. When Gaunt later described Crowley to MI5 as a "degenerate…, age about 40; bald except for erect lock on hair of forehead; black eyes, athletic looking, but air of effeminacy; plump, soft hands; wears many rings," he probably summarized his own impressions accurately.[23]

When he also called our man a "pro-German propagandist," Gaunt was only admitting what seemed obvious, and the Captain also was performing his secret duty. Supplying such negative assessments to the Americans, even to other British agencies, was part of the game to maintain Crowley's cover. Except when absolutely necessary, one never reveals the identities of its agents, even to "friendlies." It is the basic rule of compartmentalization. As a basic precaution, one had to assume that the Germans had infiltrated MI5 and its sister agencies. However confusing such denunciations might be, they played a vital role in validating an undercover agent's story. Only a select few in New York and London had any business knowing Crowley's true allegiance and purpose.

This brings us back to the question of just what the Mage was supposed to be doing in New York. Casement was long gone, but there remained a dangerous Irish organization under such experienced conspirators as Devoy, ripe for exploitation by the Germans. Moreover, Indian seditionists also had allied themselves with the Kaiser. As a proclaimed Irish sympathizer, a speaker of Hindi and other Indian tongues, and an adept of an occult German lodge headed by one of Berlin's agents, Theodor Reuss, Crowley was much too valuable to send back to London. But how would he fit into Gaunt's apparatus?

A discreet distance from the consulate at 44 Whitehall, Gaunt ran his spy business out of the Biltmore Hotel. There he conducted the flow of information to and from his network of agents, a diverse group including a ring of Czech-Americans led by Emanuel Voska and a "volunteer secret intelligence organization" connected to the U.S. Army's Judge Advocate General's office in Washington, D.C.[24] The head of the latter was U.S. Army Maj. Herbert A. White, and his organization was the de facto investigative arm of the National Security League. Formed in late 1914, the NSL advocated "preparedness," including universal military service and a crackdown on anything deemed "un-American." It also was anti-German from the start, unsurprising considering that its financial mainstays included Frederic Coudert, T. Coleman Dupont, and most importantly J.P. Morgan, Jr. All were heavily invested in the Allied war effort.

Gaunt's dealings with White's outfit were a manifestation of his own alliance with, and dependence on, the Morganites, the single biggest American stakeholders in Allied victory. Gaunt later confessed to his SIS replacement, Sir William Wiseman, that one of his most fruitful sources of information was Martin Egan at the Morgan offices. Technically, Egan was the firm's "publicity chief," but he also was the liaison, or cut-out, between Gaunt and Morgan's private intelligence service.[25] The Morganites engaged a small army of private detectives who guarded ships, docks, and warehouses, but they used more sophisticated agents as well. High up in this clandestine array, and in contact with Gaunt, was a shadowy "Mr. Green."[26] Almost certainly the name was really Greene, and she was no mister.

Among a list of sexual partners Crowley dutifully recorded in his Magical Record appears "Belle Green." This was Belle da Costa Greene, "a truly remarkable woman of color."[27] Born Belle Marion Greener, she was the daughter of Richard Greener, the first African American to receive a degree from Harvard. Faced with the suffocating racism of her day, the bright, ambitious and well-educated Belle decided to deny her black heritage and venture across the "color line." Her light skin and green eyes doubtless aided this metamorphosis, as did a change in name that conjured a Portuguese grandmother to explain her exotic looks. Add to this her taste for flamboyant, if ever tasteful, dress and jewelry and a strong libido, and it becomes clear why she would have fascinated Crowley. For her part, Greene favored liaisons with wealthy and artistically-inclined men (J.P. Morgan, Sr. and art scholar Bernard Berenson were two), but we may guess that Crowley's artiness (among other things) offset his poverty. His carnal dealings with Greene do not seem to have been long or very satisfactory. Crowley found fault with her "manner," which probably reflects Greene's dignity, independence, and refusal to submit to any man, even the Great Beast 666.

In a note later expunged from Crowley's autobiographical *Confessions*, the Beast further identified Belle as "one of the first people I met in N[ew] Y[ork]."[28] La Greene was the manager of the immense Pierpont Morgan Library at 29 E. 36th Street. Crowley's new apartment was conveniently less than two blocks away. In 1905, J.P. Morgan, Sr. had hired the twenty-two-year-old Miss Greene to oversee his museum and its collections, a position she would hold for more than forty years. Under her hand, and with ample supplies of Morgan cash, the museum became an eminent repository of rare books and art. Locating desirable works, negotiating their purchase, and assuring their authenticity all called for intelligence, caution, and discretion, attributes applicable to other forms of "intelligence work." While she got along well enough with Morgan, Jr., he curtailed the large-scale acquisitions of his father and even contemplated selling off some the Library's holdings to finance British loans. Under such circumstances, it would have made sense for Greene to offer her services to the Allied cause. She was the ideal person to head a Morgan secret agency under cover of the Library. She already had experience in ferreting out and investigating artworks and their owners. The same nexus could be used to further Morgan's wartime interests— for example, by giving aid and cover employment to a British agent.

Greene's wide array of acquaintances notably included John Quinn; indeed, he was a friend and confidant. In 1915, Quinn convinced Greene to hire, albeit briefly, French avant-garde artist Marcel Duchamp. He could have interceded likewise on behalf of Crowley, whose wide knowledge of art and literature, particularly the obscure and esoteric, could have served the Library well. As a consultant to Greene, Crowley would have earned some money, kept in discreet contact with Gaunt and, of course, gotten to know Belle more intimately. The person who expressed interest in "a complete set of my works and also two or three hundred manuscripts," a deal from which Crowley hoped to reap a hefty reward, probably was Greene, not Quinn.[29] In any case, the prospective buyer reneged on the offer, just the sort of thing an ex-lover might do.

More telling, however, in the same deleted note, Crowley recalled making a very interesting proposal to Greene. "I should pose as an eccentric philanthropist of great wealth and collect indigent persons to found a new colony," he began. Next these volunteers would board a chartered ship. Once safely at sea, the "colonists" would transfer to waiting British warships and quietly be landed in some "secret place." In the meantime, the Royal Navy, using a captured German submarine, would torpedo the colonists' vessel and send it, and to all appearances its hapless passengers, to the bottom. The last step would be sinking the guilty sub "in very shallow water on the American coast so that the evidence of the German crime would be obvious." "The… passengers being American," he added, "the operation would have peeved the U.S.A."

The logical question is why the Beast would make such an outlandish suggestion to the director of a library. It makes perfect sense if he and Belle Greene were aware of their mutual connection to the British secret apparatus, and Crowley wanted her to approach Morgan about financing the operation. It would never do for the British hand to show itself openly. What makes the plan all the more intriguing is that it basically was a farcical version of the very real tragedy that would befall the *Lusitania* a few months down the road. That uncomfortable similarity likely lies behind the decision of John Symonds, Kenneth Grant, or someone else, to excise the story from *Confessions*.

Yet another clue to Crowley's clandestine connections in New York is his association with John O'Hara Cosgrave, another Irishman and the literary editor of the *New York World* and its *Sunday World Magazine*. "Cosegrave," as Crowley calls him, first sent a "sob sister" to interview him at the dock.[30] Over the next year or so, Cosgrave went on to entertain Crowley at his home and introduced him to the astrologer Evangeline Adams. On 13 December 1914, Cosgrave's *World Magazine* ran an article on Crowley's magical exploits. Whatever its accuracy, the piece served to advertise Crowley's presence in New York and firmly link him to the occult.

Strangely, while the Beast was openly pro-German, Cosgrave was a firm backer of the Allies. In fact, the *World* itself would become a semi-official fount of British propaganda.

Like Cosgrave, its foreign affairs editor, Frank Cobb, was a dogged promoter of London's interests and, as we shall see, a close personal friend of the future #2 SIS man in the U.S. Besides his duties at the *World*, Cosgrave was founder and editor of the muckraking *Everybody's Magazine*, also staunchly pro-British and interventionist from the first days of the war. Cosgrave and *Everybody's* had a cozy arrangement with London's secret Propaganda Bureau; the effusions of H.G. Wells, G.K. Chesterton, and other members of that select fraternity featured prominently in its pages. In light of that, Cosgrave's quiet patronage of another British asset—Crowley–makes perfect sense.

Much the same can be said for the Beast's relationship with Frank Crowninshield, editor of the tony New York *Vanity Fair*. Crowninshield first met our man at a party where Crowley amazed the multitude by accurately guessing their astrological signs.[31] He pretended to infer this solely from their appearance and manner, probably having peeked at the guest list in advance. Crowninshield took a shine to Crowley and paid him to write pieces for his magazine on such topics as Japanese poetry and motion pictures. The important thing, though, is that, like his good friend Cosgrave, Crowninshield was strongly pro-Allied. Also like Cosgrave, he was oddly unbothered by Crowley's writings for pro-German publications. Crowninshield's avid interest in modern art also linked him to Quinn and Greene.

By the close of 1914, with the subtle assistance of fellow British operatives Quinn, Gaunt, Cosgrave, and others, Aleister Crowley was positioned for his new mission. He would infiltrate the cabal of hostile forces busily plotting against the Empire in the security of neutral America. Indeed, he had already taken his first steps into the enemy camp.

Meanwhile, in Switzerland, an affair was unfolding that suggests the sort of thing Crowley's British controllers wanted him to explore. On 13 December, the *New York Times* reported that Swiss authorities had arrested James Meyer, a German-born American citizen, on charges of spying for Germany.[32] Evidence presented at a Swiss military tribunal showed that Meyer used his job as correspondent for a German-American newspaper to serve a German "espionage agency."[33] Using his U.S. passport, he had made several trips to France, where he collected information later turned over to his German employers. He was undone when he somehow left a package of incriminating documents on a train between Geneva and Basel. Some helpful soul turned it in to the proper authorities. That is a scenario we will see again.

The most significant detail for now, however, is that Meyer's employer was the *New Yorker Staats-Zeitung*, published by Hermann Ridder. Ridder was a close friend of Franz von Papen and George Sylvester Viereck and a loyal collaborator of the aforementioned *Propaganda Kabinett*. The Meyer case revealed a link between German clandestine efforts in Switzerland and America, something persons in London were eager to learn more about.

1   USNA, MID 9140-815/1, extract of British "Watch List", p. 106, entry #340, c. 1916.

2   This and other details concerning the arrival of persons in New York are gleaned from the searchable online passenger list records, c. 1892–1924, at www.ellisislandrecords.org [hereafter EIR].

3   *CAC*, 754.

4   *Ibid.*, 745.

5   EIR.

6   Norman Thwaites, *Velvet and Vinegar* (London: Grayson & Grayson, 1932), 255.

7   According to Viereck, Ewers and Muensterberg only attended the initial meeting of the *Kabinett,* but they certainly maintained an informal connection thereafter. Both supposedly elected to operate independently, though this also may have represented a practical compartmentalization of the German propaganda effort. See: Viereck, *Spreading Germs of Hate* (NY: Liveright, 1930), 51–52.

8   The final arrangement was worked out in London by Morgan partner Henry P. Davison who departed New York in late November. See John Forbes, *J.P. Morgan, Jr., 1867–1943* (Charlottesville, VA: Univ. of Virginia Press, 1981), 89–90.

9   On Booth see: Duncan Crow, *'A Man of Push and Go': The Life of George Macauley Booth* (London: Rupert Hart-Davis, 1965).

10 *CAC*, 745.

11 "John Quinn Literary Biography," www.bookrags.com/biography-john-quinn-dlb/index, and FAAC, "John Quinn," www.redflame93.Quinn.html.

12 Sir Arthur Willert, *The Road to Safety: A Study in Anglo-American Relations* (NY: Prager, 1953), 75–76.

13 Yale University, Sterling Library, Special Collections, Sir William Wiseman Papers (hereafter WWP), Box 5, File 140,[John Quinn], "In the Matter of Sir Roger Casement and the Irish Situation in America," 2 June 1916, 7.

14 Anthony Read and David Fisher, *Colonel Z: The Life and Times of a Master of Spies* (London: Hodder & Stoughton, 1984), 129.

15 Sutin, 243.

16 *Ibid.*

17 Tina Becker, "Weapon of Class War," *Weekly Worker*, #556 (9 Dec. 2004), www.cpgb.org.uk/worker/556/redscandals.htm.

18 *Ibid.*

19 WWP, 5/140, "In the Matter of Roger Casement…", 8.

20 UKNA, Foreign Office [FO] file 95/776 and MI5 [KV] 2/6.

21 Gaunt later recorded his experiences in *The Yield of the Years: A Story of Adventures Afloat and Ashore* (London: Hutchinson & Son, 1940).

22 Gaunt, 224–225.

23 USNA, MID 9140-815/1, p. 342.

24 Thomas Troy, "The Gaunt-Wiseman Affair: British Intelligence in New York in 1915," *International Journal of Intelligence and CounterIntelligence*, Vol. 16, #3 (2003), 448.

25 Troy, 448 and Ron Chernow, *The House of Morgan: An American Banking Dynasty and the Rise of Modern Finance* (NY: Simon & Schuster, 1991), 211, 315.

26 Troy, 448.

27 FAAC, Steve Jackson, "Belle da Costa Greene, www.redflame93/Greene2.html. For more on Greene see: Heidi Ardizzione, "*An Illuminated Life*: *Belle da Costa Greene's Journey from Prejudice to Privilege* (NY : W.W. Norton, 2007).

28 Special thanks to William Breeze for this information. The note originally applied to Crowley's comments about the "Unrestricted Submarine Campaign" that appear on p. 755 of the 1969 Symonds-Grant edition of *Confessions*. Breeze is currently working on an unabridged version of the book.

29 This amount would be equivalent to $80,000-$100,000 today—a tidy sum for Crowley.

30 *CAC*, 761.

31 *CAC*, 765, 825.

32 *NYT* (13 Dec. 1914), 1:6.

33 *NYT* (20 Dec. 1914), II, 2:3.

CHAPTER FOUR

~

SLEEPING WITH THE ENEMY

~

IN AUGUST 1914 AMBASSADOR BERNSTORFF'S superiors sent him back to Washington with the authority and money to conduct sabotage. The latter would become a vital part of Berlin's secret war in America. While Bernstorff was a conscientious diplomat who sincerely wanted to maintain good relations with the Americans, he also served his government loyally. He passed the dirty work on to his military attaché, von Papen, a lanky, officious Prussian and an eager, if inexperienced, conspirator. Crowley later offered that von Papen's signal trait was his "stultifying conviction that he was so much better than anybody else."[1]

The Kaiser's secret services were organized on a standard pattern. The main military intelligence agency was the German General Staff's *Nachrichtenabteilung* or *Nachrichtendienst*, most commonly known as *Abteilung* (Section) *IIIb*. For more clandestine duties the General Staff also organized a *Sektion Politik* or *Sabotage-Abteilung*. In the U.S., Military Attaché Franz von Papen was the nominal chief of all such activity. Not to be left out, the German Navy had its own *Nachrichten* or *"N" Abteilung*, whose American operations fell under von Papen's Navy counterpart, Capt. Karl Boy-Ed, whom Crowley called a "breezy naval ass . . . with the instincts of a gentleman."[2]

The *"N" Abteilung* maintained a close relationship with the giant Hamburg-Amerika (HAPAG) shipping line, which in turn employed its own security agents. Von Papen and Boy-Ed enlisted Paul Koenig, an experienced detective in HAPAG's New York office, to head a special "secret service bureau" charged with undermining the Allied war effort in North America.[3] Koenig's efforts commenced ineptly in September with a bungled an attempt to blow up Canada's Welland Canal. Undiscouraged, the Germans pressed on with other schemes.

Also stirring the pot of German intrigue was Berlin's Foreign Office, or *Auswärtiges Amt* (AA), which abetted Irish and Indian nationalists as well as an array of separatists and dissidents in the Russian Empire. On orders from Berlin, Bernstorff authorized von Papen and Boy-Ed to recruit Irish-Americans, Indians, and anarchists as agitators and saboteurs.

In Berlin, an "India Committee" appeared, headed by Virendranath Chattopadhyaya, which aimed to ignite a mass uprising against the British Raj.[4] The main launchpad for the insurrection was the neutral United States, whose West Coast Indian immigrant communities supplied recruits. The engine of this conspiracy was the Gadar or Ghadr ("Rebellion") Party. Violence erupted in October 1914, when John Hopkinson, a former Calcutta police inspector who was ferreting out sedition among Indians in Vancouver, BC, was shot dead by Mewa Singh, a young Sikh linked to the Gadar Party.[5]

To complement sabotage and subversion, the Germans planned an aggressive propaganda campaign aimed at Yankee opinion, led by the *Propaganda Kabinett*. The plan was to show the Americans the sound logic of strict neutrality and, failing that, to bully them into it. Crowley would conspicuously advocate bullying. Direction and funding of this "public relations" effort fell to Bernstorff's commercial attaché, Dr. Heinrich Albert.

However half-baked some of the German schemes and their architects, by early 1915 an Indo-Irish-German conspiratorial nexus was solidifying in America and threatening havoc there and throughout the British Empire. In response London formed a special Interdepartmental Committee to deal with the Indian revolutionary threat, including the chief of the Foreign Office's North American section, Rowland Sperling, MI5's Vernon Kell, and Admiral Hall's special representative, Commander Guy Rayment.[6] Rayment's name we will see again in a different role.

Admiral Hall was anxious about the mounting threat in America and convinced that neutralizing it would require more than just counterpropaganda. He argued that the best way to combat German intrigues in the States was to expose them to the American public and government, who would abhor the destruction of property and fomenting of rebellion on their soil.[7] Following Hall's logic, preventing German outrages was not necessary or even desirable. Far better was to let them happen and then expose them. In fact, it might even be necessary to give the enemy a little help. The beastlier the Germans, the better.

Hall communicated these ideas to Gaunt, who was more than willing to carry them out. Also drawn into the effort was the aforementioned War Propaganda Board. Its American Branch, run by Canadian-born Gilbert Parker, had the writings of "extreme German nationalists" such as the philosopher Friedrich Nietzsche and the military theorist Gen. Friedrich von Bernhardi printed in English and made available to American readers.[8] Crowley's activities would fit perfectly into Hall's scheme. Thus it seems reasonable to suppose that the Admiral was the ultimate authority behind the Mage's assignment in America. As noted, through his connection to the likes of Feidling, Marston, and others, Crowley's special relationship with NID probably predated the war.

Hall's strategy mirrors what Crowley later wrote about his own actions in America. "Statesmanlike sobriety was, in the peculiar temper of the American people at that time, highly dangerous to British interests," he wrote.[9] "I knew that the only way I could combat the influence of German propaganda in the States was to identify myself with it in every way, and by making it abhorrent to any sane being, gradually get the minds of the American public to react against its insidious appeal," he noted. "My real scheme," Crowley continued, "was to ingratiate myself with the other side that I should obtain their full confidence, and so be able to betray their plans to England." He insisted that he was "playing a lone hand" without direct authority from London, which may have been a crude version of the truth. As an undercover operative, Crowley inevitably worked more or less on his own. As we have seen, however, that did not rule out contact with other British agents or having to answer to authorities in London.

Crowley later attributed his penetration of the German clandestine apparatus to simple luck. Sometime in early January 1915, he wrote, he was riding a bus up Manhattan's busy Fifth Avenue. With seemingly nothing better to do, he pulled out clippings from the British press and began reading. Seated close enough to see the articles or overhear Crowley's comments was a man he later identified as "O'Brien." Sufficiently intrigued, or annoyed, O'Brien approached our man and asked if he was "in favour of a square deal for Germany and Austria."[10] Crowley vouched that he was, and identified himself as an Irish patriot. O'Brien, a man of strong Fenian sympathies, invited Crowley to continue the conversation at his office. The story, almost certainly, is bunk. One way or another, though, the Mage got the introduction he needed.

Upon visiting the address on O'Brien's card, the Beast found himself at the offices of *The Fatherland*, a weekly publication run by the aforementioned George Sylvester Viereck. Viereck greeted his visitor warmly and reminded Crowley that they had met once before, in the London offices of the *English Review*. One has to wonder whether the Mage had really forgotten that, and whether Viereck's presence in London also brought him into contact with Theodor Reuss. In any case, he and Crowley conversed vigorously about the war and attendant matters, and Viereck then and there offered him a job writing for the magazine. Crowley's first contribution, the first of roughly a dozen, was "Honesty is the Best Policy," a turgid attack on perfidious Albion that ran in the 13 January 1915 issue.[11]

During his chat with Viereck, Crowley later claimed, he realized that *The Fatherland* was "the headquarters of the German propaganda."[12] The English-language *Fatherland* was subsidized by Dr. Albert ($1500 per month) with the express aim of influencing American opinion. Beyond that, of course, Viereck was a leading light in the *Propaganda Kabinett*. Thanks to him, the Beast was now inside the enemy camp, and right where Hall wanted him.

The helpful "O'Brien" seems to have been a convenient invention; Crowley himself later used the pen name "Sheamus O'Brien" for a short piece on Sinn Fein written for Viereck.[13] More likely, his model was a real Irishman, Anthony J. Brogan. That Notre Dame graduate and fiery Irish partisan was a devotee of Casement, whom he recently had befriended in New York. Brogan also published a small radical paper, the *Irish American*, which in fall 1914 he sold to none other than Franz von Papen. Von Papen promptly handed over its assets to Viereck's *Fatherland*, including offices, probably the same ones that Crowley visited. British intelligence had been keeping tabs on Brogan through Quinn's pal Claude Dansey, but Dansey had returned to England.[14] It seems a good bet that Dansey left matters to Quinn, who pointed Crowley to Brogan, who, in turn, steered him to Viereck.

Crowley later gave intimates such as Norman Mudd a different and simpler version of his introduction to Viereck. In a 1924 letter to the FBI, Mudd wrote that the Mage encountered Viereck and his factotum, J. Bernard Rethy, in November 1914 "through some community of literary interest."[15] That might have been Quinn, or even Belle Greene. Crowley "at once seized on the opportunity of getting into their counsels." Fooled by his professed anti-Britishism, Viereck and Rethy "proposed collaboration."

Whatever his role vis-à-vis Viereck, the versatile Mr. Quinn had links to still other German agents. On 14 November 1914, Dr. Kuno Meyer of Berlin, one of the world's leading authorities on Celtic languages and Irish culture, reached New York on the Dutch liner *Rotterdam*. His ostensible mission in the U.S. was to legitimize German-sponsored Irish propaganda, but Meyer also took on a more secret role, that of the "German brain" directing conspiratorial collaboration with Irish and Indians on the West Coast.[16] On arrival in the U.S., Meyer gave his local address as that of his "friend," John Quinn.[17] Quinn would have passed on anything he gleaned about Meyer's mission.

Meyer also had an interesting occult connection. He was a member of the *Vereinigte Alte Orden der Druiden* ("United Ancient Order of Druids" or simply *Druiden-Orden*). This was the German branch of a British para-masonic body formed in the late eighteenth century, the same one Churchill joined in 1908.[18] The avowed purpose of the society was the study and practice of ancient Celtic mystical knowledge. By WWI, however, it also promoted a pan-German agenda, including an aggressive, expansionist foreign policy. Thus it was an ideal recruiting ground for Germany's cause.

Crowley's old acquaintance Frank Harris also helped him penetrate the German apparatus. The fifty-eight-year-old Harris was another Irish native who had taken the boat to America as a child. As an adult, he moved back to London, where he became a successful editor, first for the *London Evening News* and later for literary publications such as the *Saturday Review*. Harris had unconventional views and eccentric friends besides Aleister Crowley. An outspoken defender of Oscar Wilde during Wilde's travails, Harris also was a guest at Winston Churchill's wedding.

Literature and an interest in the metaphysical brought Harris the Beast together. As editor of the British *Vanity Fair*, he had published a few of Crowley's literary effusions.[19] Harris almost certainly was a brother in Crowley's private A∴A∴ sect and contributed at least one piece to its organ, *The Equinox*.[20] By the time war broke out, Harris had met legal troubles and served time behind British bars. That plus his Irish republican sympathies helped sour him on England, so he claimed, and he skipped back to the U.S. in fall 1914 as "Frank Vernon."[21] He and his mistress, Anna Strindberg, widow of the Swedish playwright, landed in Gotham barely a fortnight before Crowley.

Crowley met with Harris the day after arriving on the *Lusitania*. The two were bound to see each other, since Harris and his friend were at the same St. Regis Hotel. In the States, Harris, like Crowley, promptly proclaimed his sympathy for Germany. In an early 1915 report to London, British Ambassador Cecil Spring-Rice complained that Harris's writing evidenced "a profound detestation for England and a contempt for France."[22] Spring-Rice was certain that Frank Harris was "employed by the enemy." In 1916, Harris took editorial control of the foundering *Pearson's Magazine* and promptly turned it into a "radical, anti-war" publication, much to the irritation of British (and, later, American) authorities.[23] Harris also collaborated with the *Propaganda Kabinett*, which brought him into dealings with Viereck in early 1915, just when Crowley joined *The Fatherland*.

Harris, like Crowley, may have been secretly working for London, and his pro-Kaiserian blather, like our man's, a pose calculated to win the confidence of the Germans. Whatever the truth, Harris definitely was busy ingratiating himself with German operatives in the U.S. and making contacts that would be valuable to agent Crowley.

Crowley made other contacts during his first weeks in New York. During November, for instance, he established ties with George Winslow Plummer, an American veteran of various esoteric groups and current head of the *Societas Rosicruciana in America* (SRIA). Plummer granted Crowley admission to that society, and the Beast reciprocated by certifying Plummer as an honorary IX degree adept in the OTO.[24] The exchange shows that Crowley wasted no time exercising his authority as head of the OTO for North America, recently bestowed on him by Theodor Reuss. As Crowley himself later noted, Reuss barely escaped England along with the German Embassy staff when the war erupted.[25] This raises the possibility that he and the Beast bumped into each other, by accident or design, during those frantic August days. In any event Reuss promptly surfaced working for German counterintelligence on the Dutch border, no doubt trying to spot English agents he had identified during his time in London. He soon moved on to clandestine duties in Switzerland.[26] In recruiting Plummer and others into the OTO, was Crowley earning more points with the Germans by engaging them as agents for Reuss' operation?

The plot thickens further with findings by American investigators in 1917. A report issued by the U.S. Office of Naval Intelligence (ONI) names Plummer, Crowley, and another British "spiritualist," Holden Sampson, as members of an "occult German order ... undoubtedly that of the Rosicrucian."[27] Reuss did once proclaim that the OTO was "the exoteric front or showcase of a Rosicrucian order."[28] The report added, however, that Plummer, Crowley, and Sampson maintained some mysterious means of communication with their "chief in Berlin, Rudolf Steiner."[29]

At first glance, the order in question looks to be the Ordo Templi Orientis, but that is far from certain. Steiner certainly knew Reuss, and the latter had made him the head of a "subordinate chapter" of the OTO in Berlin called *Mystica Aeterna*. Nevertheless, Steiner's relationship to the OTO by WWI is uncertain at best. In 1912 Steiner had formed his own offshoot of Theosophy, Anthroposophy, and severed public ties to Reuss. Crowley later noted that Steiner had been "in relation to the OTO," whatever that meant.[30]

One explanation is that the mystery lodge was the Antient and Primitive Memphis-Misraim Rite of "Egyptian" Freemasonry, arguably the proto-organization of the OTO. Crowley and Steiner were both initiates, and at one point Reuss made Steiner chief of the M-M in Germany. The M-M, however, does not quite fit the "Rosicrucian" label. The Americans may have simply confused Steiner with Reuss, or been misled. Perhaps Crowley invoked Steiner's name as a means of masking Reuss' role. To add to the confusion, the same report states that Plummer, not Crowley, was the "representative in this country" of the order.

While Steiner had no outward association with German intelligence, a postwar British intelligence (SIS) report concluded that his religious training and initiation into occult secrets "were all preparing him for a career of subtle, underground political intrigue cleverly disguised under the cloak of religious illumination."[31] Where did they get that idea—from Crowley?

Steiner definitely had influence in high German circles. In 1914, for instance, he was spiritual guru to the Kaiser's mystically-inclined Chief-of-Staff, Feldmarschall Helmut von Moltke. Steiner also had connections to Berlin's Foreign Office and may have consulted for the secretive *Sektion Politik* on its subversive activities.[32] A hint of Steiner's possible involvement in German intrigues in America is the testimony of a Russian revolutionary in New York, Ivan Narodny. Avant-garde dramatist, student of mysticism, and spy, Narodny in 1914 was mixed up in a scheme to buy German rifles in the U.S. to aid an uprising against the Tsar. Among those involved in this murky plot was a German "noblewoman," Marie von Sievers.[33] She had the same name as Steiner's longtime secretary and recent wife, but whether they were the same person is impossible to determine. Crowley was to become acquainted with Narodny, so perhaps the Beast knew the answer to that mystery as well.

There must be a connection between the above ONI report and the later assertion by British espionage writer Donald McCormick ("Richard Deacon") that Crowley "ingratiated himself with a Hermetic Sect in order to expose its head to the Americans as a dangerous German agent."[34] Was that head in the U.S.A. or Germany, and was it Plummer, Reuss, Steiner, or someone else? This brings us back to Viereck and two other men closely associated with him and the *Propaganda Kabinett*, German writer Hans Heinz Ewers and Harvard professor Hugo Muensterberg.

George Sylvester Viereck was born in Munich in 1884, the son of Louis (Ludwig) Viereck, a one-time socialist who, after a term in the Kaiser's jails, renounced his Marxist ways and pursued a new life in America with his wife and son. Young George, or Sylvester as he preferred to be called, was a delicate only child. He grew up in an atmosphere of intellectual freedom, or perhaps indifference, which permitted him to indulge interests that ranged from classical mythology to sexology and to develop tastes that were at once refined, morally and sexually ambiguous, and a bit morbid. Viereck liked to describe his as the "temperament of a pagan."[35]

Also like Crowley, Viereck dabbled in poetry, and he shared with the Beast a common admiration for Swinburne and his ilk. In 1904, Viereck published his first volume of verse, *Gedichte* ("Poems"). The book earned praise from the German-American literati, including Hugo Muensterberg, who adopted the twenty-year-old Viereck as his protégé. By the time war engulfed Europe, Viereck had veered towards politics (he stumped for Theodore Roosevelt in 1912) and a blind, bellicose patriotism toward Germany. For that reason, in August 1914, his friend and mentor Muensterberg easily persuaded him to launch a magazine that would "counteract the expected onslaught of propaganda from England and France."[36] So was born *The Fatherland*.

In the decade before WWI, Viereck attained some fame as a poet, though his decadent style had fallen out of fashion by 1914. He also wrote the 1907 *House of the Vampire*, a novel of psychological horror with a psychic, as opposed to blood-sucking, villain and a clear homoerotic subtext. Later in life, Viereck "made no secret of his own bisexuality," and "from his youth onwards he had a fondness for orgies."[37] Such tastes suggest an affinity for the sex-magic practiced by the OTO. Did Crowley offer him initiation into that Order as he did Plummer?

Viereck took a lively interest in occult matters. Like his pal Muensterberg, he was a member of *Schlaraffia*, a German-speaking secret society with numerous lodges in the U.S.[38] Outwardly *Schlaraffia* seemed a harmless fraternity. Based in Hamburg, the self-proclaimed "humoristic" order attracted mostly artsy and academic types and lampooned aristocratic manners. While replete with Masonesque ritual and symbolism, it lacked heavy occult overtones. On the other hand, *Schlaraffia* shared membership with more esoteric groups such as *Sat B'hai* and the Royal Order of Sikha, the former one of the constituent orders of the OTO. So, there may have been more going on than met the uninitiated eye.[39] British and American intelligence identified *Schlaraffia* as a "Secret German Propaganda Society" that encouraged artists and writers to "spread German propaganda in a silent, secret way."[40] At the least, *Schlaraffia* provided a ready-made, secret, Germanophile organization with branches throughout the country—an ideal vehicle for espionage and other covert activities.

Crowley and Viereck had much in common. In his *Confessions*, the Beast discusses Viereck's character at length. Crowleyan analysis at once condemns Viereck as "mean and cowardly" and praises him as "one of the bravest of brave men."[41] It likewise calls him a writer of "great critical ability" and a crass opportunist. Suggestively, Crowley rejects Gaunt's view that Viereck was just "one of the lesser jackals of von Papen." More revealingly he cites Gaunt's contemptuous opinion from their "correspondence on that subject." Just when and in what context did they discuss Viereck?

Gaunt's memoirs mention a curious incident that may illuminate his dealings with Crowley and Viereck. Early in the war, Gaunt recalled that he was "being continually worried by a man in New York who professed to know all about German intrigues."[42] Gaunt tried to ignore him, but the man somehow managed to get in touch with Sir Edward Grey, the Foreign Secretary, who ordered Gaunt to see him. The reluctant Captain met the fellow in an antiane-and bric-a-brac-filled apartment in "a fashionable New York Hotel." Gaunt lightly dismissed what the man said, especially his seemingly absurd claim to be the "illegitimate son of the Kaiser," and reported back to London that the fellow was a "dud."

While Gaunt's memoir is full of erroneous and self-serving interpretations of people and events, he does not seem inclined to invent them out of thin air. One interpretation of Gaunt's tale is that the pest was Crowley. As noted, Gaunt would have been reluctant to deal with someone like the Beast and may have needed a kick in the pants from higher-ups. Gaunt freely tosses around names elsewhere in his book, so it is odd that he avoids giving one in this case. Crowley himself records that Gaunt "affected to ignore the importance of *The Fatherland*" and with it Viereck himself.[43] Did Crowley try to bring Gaunt and Viereck together, only to have Gaunt snub the "lesser jackal"?

More likely is that the man Gaunt interviewed was Viereck. For one thing, while George Viereck never claimed to be the Kaiser's son, he did boast of being the *grandson* of Kaiser Wilhelm I, a conviction he picked up from his father. Viereck even told this to Crowley, who does not seem to have taken it too seriously. Did Viereck do the same with Gaunt, only to have the Captain misunderstand the comment or later misremember it? If so, the implication is that Viereck offered to sell out his German brethren. Or was he trying to sell out Crowley?

Another, possibility is that Crowley had "turned" Viereck using bribery or blackmail.[44] That would explain why Viereck brought a British agent into the heart of the German apparatus and kept him there. Perhaps it also explains Crowley's ability years later to get Viereck to sign an affidavit that the Beast "had no trouble with authorities in the U.S.A." during WWI, i.e., that he had been loyal to the Allied cause.[45] That, however, directly contradicted what Viereck wrote in his 1930 memoir, *Spreading Germs of Hate*: that Sir William Wiseman, the SIS man who succeeded Gaunt, swore that Crowley had nothing to do with British intelligence.[46] As we will see, though, Wiseman was a master of disinformation, and denying Crowley was only proper procedure. Moreover to admit that the Beast had been in British employ would compromise Viereck's own judgment and loyalty.

Crowley was quite confident of his influence over Viereck. "I worked upon the mind of Viereck to such an extent," he later boasted, "that from relatively reasonable attacks on England, he went to the most stupid extravagances, with the result that he published the most futile rubbish from my pen."[47] Viereck claimed to accept Crowley as an authentic "black magician." He ran the Beast's work not just in *The Fatherland* but also in his monthly literary journal, *The International*, of which he eventually made Crowley editor.[48] One could almost imagine that the Magician had cast a spell over Viereck. Crowley later gloated of his ability to convince the gullible Viereck that a revised and blatantly anti-German version of "An Appeal to the American Republic," Crowley's polemic in the November 1914 *English Review*, was just more "camouflage" to deceive the bone-headed English.[49]

Viereck's basic flaw, Crowley felt, was his repressed homosexuality. While doubtless intelligent, he seemed to Crowley also plodding, oblivious, and gullible. Ultimately he found Viereck "not trustworthy enough to handle a propaganda involving the destiny of a people." There had to be "a man higher up," and the Beast was determined to find him.

One candidate for this role was Viereck's fellow propagandist, *Schlaraffia* brother, and "great friend," Hanns Heinz Ewers, the so-called "Edgar Allan Poe of Germany."[50] Ewers was a kind of Teutonic Crowley. His habitual monocle and a deep dueling scar across his cheek gave him the arrogant air of a Prussian officer, which he combined with the cultivated amorality of Nietzsche's *Übermensch*. In fact, he had only the briefest of military experience. His cosmopolitanism led one Allied report to note that Ewers "might pass as an Englishman."[51]

Early on, Ewers dedicated himself to being a "bad boy" of German literature. He deliberately sought to shock and appall decent society with tales steeped in blood, the supernatural, and moral depravity. His most famous work is the 1907 novel *Alraune* (the basis of several films). It told the eerie and sordid tale of a beautiful woman conceived by supernatural means to torment unfortunate mortals. Ewers created a literary alter ego in the character Frank Braun, a brilliant and callous adventurer with the unwholesome interests of an occultist and the clinical detachment of a scientist. Like his *Kamerad* Viereck, Ewers tried his hand at a vampire story. This was *Vampir*, in which the protagonist, based on Ewers himself, attacked women and drank their blood while in a mysterious trance. What should interest us, though, is that the book is set in WWI New York, where the "hero" is engaged in secret work for Germany. Some of its episodes were drawn straight from Ewers' own escapades.

Much like Crowley and Viereck, Ewers had an ambiguous sexual orientation, a keen interest in drugs (including hallucinogens like mescaline), and a more than literary curiosity in the blacker aspects of the occult—an attraction to evil that might explain his later gravitation to Nazism. Also like Crowley, Ewers traveled widely, visiting South and Central America, China, India, and other farflung places. Ewers possessed an alternate identity as Ernest Renfer, a Swiss, with whose passport he undertook wartime secret missions to Spain and Mexico.[52] He was almost certainly working for Germany well before 1914, and he likely had at least an acquaintance with Reuss.

Thus, it is not surprising that Crowley and Ewers developed a mutual admiration society. Ewers, for instance, was intrigued by Bert Reese, a Polish-born "mind-reader" then popular in New York. Crowley recounts an audience with Reese supposedly connected with some vague business deal.[53] Ewers may have sought Crowley's advice in evaluating Reese's psychic powers and the possibility of exploiting them for the German cause.

Ewers had other associations useful to Crowley. The German was socially and politically well-connected in both Berlin and New York. Ewers, for instance, enjoyed a personal pipeline to Ambassador von Bernstorff via mutual friendship with a Mr. and Mrs. Rachmann.[54] On occasion he even passed himself off as a relative of Bernstorff. Dr. Albert and other German diplomats seemed deferential to Ewers, perhaps afraid of his secret society and secret service connections. Ewers was not just a member of *Schlaraffia* but, according to a British intelligence report (possibly Crowley's), one of its key "directors" both in Germany and the U.S.[55]

Crowley actively courted Ewers by asking him to translate his Gnostic Mass, the OTO's "central ritual," a job that finally fell to Theodor Reuss.[56] This brings up another link between Ewers, Crowley, and Reuss. At 40 W. 36th, the same address as Crowley's flat, was the New York bureau of *The Continental Times*. This Berlin-based publication originally catered to Americans living in Europe. In 1914 the German Foreign Office appropriated the paper as a propaganda tool. Among other things, it was distributed to English-speaking prisoners-of-war, among them the ones Casement hoped to recruit. In Berlin, the official editor of the paper was "renegade Englishman" Aubrey Stanhope, but the real boss was Reuss.[57] Reuss even listed the paper's New York office as the American address for his *Oriflamme*, the "official" publication of the OTO.[58] He also had *Continental Times* reprint some of Crowley's pieces from *Fatherland* and *The International*. That Crowley and *Continental Times* shared the same Gotham address was no accident and must have been Reuss' design. As a native English speaker, the Beast was an ideal man to oversee the New York office.

Ewers, posing as a journalist, provided material to the paper.[59] More importantly, the *Continental Times* office helped him and other Germans get confidential communications and even money to and from Europe. Crowley was thus perfectly situated to monitor the transatlantic currents of secret information and funds. Still, Crowley soon concluded that Ewers was relatively unimportant. For one thing, his arrogance and disrespect irritated senior members of the German apparatus. At the initial meeting of the *Propaganda Kabinett*, he mocked the "bovine stupidity" of the Kaiser's officials, and Viereck considered him "too colorful" to work in that environment.[60] Moreover, despite his connections back home, Ewers lacked the credentials to influence German-Americans.

The man Crowley ultimately pegged as "the mastermind with whom [he] was to work, the secret director of German propaganda," was the highly-respected German-Jewish-

American academic, Hugo Muensterberg. It is easy to dismiss Crowley's claim as mistaken or malicious, reasoning that a man of Muensterberg's stature would never stoop to anything underhanded. Of course, anyone above suspicion is the perfect person for the job. Muensterberg undeniably belonged to (or at least associated with) the *Propaganda Kabinett* and vigorously supported the German cause up to his untimely and unusual death in 1916. Among other things, he personally lobbied his friend Theodore Roosevelt for Germany.

The professor was just what the Beast described. A native of the Prussian port city of Danzig, Muensterberg studied at Leipzig and Heidelberg and earned doctorates in medicine and philosophy. He is best known, however, as one of the fathers of modern psychology. William James helped entice him to Harvard in 1892 where, except for frequent visits to his beloved Germany, Muensterberg remained for the rest of his life. He took a special interest in behavioral psychology, which he applied to the classroom and the factory floor. His writings include a pioneering work on the influence of motion pictures on mass psychology.[61] As Crowley accurately points out, the Professor was "someone who had made a special study for years of the psychology of Americans," a man of "ripe, balanced wisdom," who as a teacher at Harvard had "acquired the habit of forming and directing minds."[62] Writing to a friend in early 1916, Muensterberg confessed, "day and night I work both before and behind the scenes almost entirely in the interests of the political struggle, and fortunately thus I accomplish much."[63]

Crowley was already acquainted with Muensterberg's less public and less scientific interests. The Beast calls Muensterberg an "old enemy" with whom he had quarreled concerning "philosophy and physics."[64] Muensterberg took a deep interest in paranormal phenomena, particularly the activities of mediums and psychics, most of whom he labeled frauds. In 1909, for example, Muensterberg debunked the Italian medium Eusapia Palladino. He thereby contradicted a previous study of Palladino by the British Society for Psychical Research.[65] Everard Feilding wrote the SPR report, which must have influenced the disagreement between Muensterberg and Crowley.[66]

Whatever their past differences, Crowley found a way to smooth over things with Muensterberg and influence him. Perhaps Herr Professor was not the skeptic he seemed. In any case, Crowley records that Muensterberg's Achilles heel was the "great German gift of Always being Right."[67] By constantly reinforcing to the Professor "how very right he was," our man helped nudge the increasingly frustrated Muensterberg to abandon rational argument for "violent and stupid" rhetoric—just what Admiral Hall wanted.

By the end of January 1915, Crowley was established in the offices of *The Fatherland* and the confidence of Viereck, soon followed by Ewers', Muensterberg's, and other German agents'. One secret job Crowley could have handled at *The Fatherland* offices was bugging. Electronic eavesdropping was in its infancy in 1915, but Viereck later recalled that the *Propaganda Kabinett* took active precautions against it. An engineer regularly searched meeting rooms for hidden microphones. Nevertheless, a long-standing bug turned up in a telephone in a supposedly secure meeting room.[68] Simply by observing the German precautions and noting where they looked and where they did not, the Beast could have offered Gaunt a valuable service indeed.

Crowley's presence surely did not bring the Germans good fortune. Viereck notes that German propagandists found it virtually impossible to keep their activities secret. "Every memorandum they ever made," he wrote, "seems to have fallen into the hands of the British Secret Service or the Department of Justice."[69] Nor was this the only thing to go wrong.

On 25 February, New York papers reported the arrest of three men for trying to fraudulently obtain U.S. passports: Richard P. Stegler, Richard Madden, and Gustav Cook. Facing the most serious charge, Stegler spilled his guts about a bigger plot involving Captain Boy-Ed, Viereck, and Ewers. Stegler, a German-American and reservist in the Kaiser's army, had approached Boy-Ed about returning to Germany or helping the cause abroad—for money of course. Boy-Ed, according to Stegler, offered to send him to England as a spy. For that Stegler needed an American passport in a new, non-Teutonic name (Madden's).[70] He received an introduction to Viereck, who directed him to Ewers. Viereck admitted meeting Stegler and giving him an introduction to Ewers, but denied any illicit activity. He had helped, he insisted, simply because "Dr. Ewers was interested in a psychological way in persons of peculiar characteristics, mental and otherwise."[71] Ewers, for his part, claimed that he spoke with Stegler to "humor" him and to get the bottom of what he suspected was a British trap.[72] The German response, therefore, was that Stegler was a nut-case, and any funny business he attempted with passports was his own doing. With only Stegler's word, prosecutors had no case against Viereck and the others. The publicity, however, eagerly exploited by Gaunt, further marred the German image. Ewers later incorporated the episode into *Vampir*. His character Frank Braun, besides blood-drinking, takes part in a German scheme to acquire U.S. passports.

American authorities were coy about how they had gotten the goods on Stegler. Officially they credited an anonymous female clerk in a photographer's studio who became suspicious of Stegler and his efforts to secure a passport.[73] Another possibility is that Stegler's lawyer, Mr. Griffiths, ratted out Viereck and the others in hopes of getting a better deal for his client. Ewers may have been on the right track by suspecting Stegler of being part of a British sting. Crowley was perfectly situated to spot Stegler visiting *The Fatherland* offices or even direct him there. Viereck and Ewers might have revealed the passport scheme to the Mage as a trusted associate. The Beast would then have passed word to Gaunt, intimate of American authorities. If nothing else, Stegler's aim of going to England to spy would have been of keen interest to "Blinker" Hall.

1   *CAC*, 749.

2   *Ibid.*

3   Frank Rafallo (ed.), *A Counterintelligence Reader: American Revolution to World War II*, Vol. I, Chapter 3, "Imperial Germany's Sabotage Operations in the U.S.," www.fas.org/irp/ops/ci/docs/ci1/ch3c.htm.

4   Nirode K. Barooah, "Har Dayal and the German Connection," *The Indian Historical Review*, Vol. VII, #s 1–2 (Jan. 1981), 185.

5   Robert Jarvis, "William Hopkinson: Spy, Patriot, Canadian Martyr," www.canadafirst.net/our-heritage/hopkinson/index.html. For additional background and somewhat different slant, see: *The History of Metropolitan Vancouver*, "Komagata Maru," www.vancouverhistory.ca/archives-komagatamaru.htm.

6   Richard J. Popplewell, *Intelligence and Imperial Defence: British Intelligence and the Defence of the Indian Empire, 1904–1924* (London: Frank Cass, 1995), 218.

7   Jonathan Epstein, "German and English Propaganda in World War I," p. 7, paper delivered to the NYMAS (1 Dec. 2000), //libraryautomation.com/nymas/propagandapaper.html.

8   For example, a translation of von Bernhardi's *Germany and the Next War* (orig. published 1912), with its "World Power or Decline" message, appeared in New York in late 1914.

9   Renegade.

10 *CAC*, 746.

11 From January 1915 through April 1917, Crowley contributed at least eleven articles to *The Fatherland* and may have prepared up to five others.

12 *CAC*, 748.

13 "Sinn Fein," *The International*, Vol. XI, #9 (Sept. 1917), 282.

14 Read, 129.

15 FBI, file on Edward Alexander Crowley, 61-2069 (FOIPA 229,138), Letter to New York Office, Department of Justice, 11 July 1924.

16 Matthew Erin Plowman, "Irish Republicans and the Indo-German Conspiracy of World War I," *New Hibernia Review*, 7:3 (Autumn 2003), 92.

17 EIR.

18 Hans Jurgen Glowka, *Deutsche Okkultgruppen 1875–1937* (Augsburg: Maro, 1981), 97, Hans Christoph Martens, *Geheime Gesellschaften in alter under neuer Zeit* (Leipzig, 1923), 196 ff., and Erich Hein, *Geheime Gesellschaften in alter und neuer Zeit, ihre Organization, ihre Zwecke und Zeile…* (Leipzig, Gerhard, 1913), 46–60.

19 *CAC*, 594.

20 "The Magic Glasses," *The Equinox*, Vol. I, #1 (1909), and CAC, 603.

21 EIR, Harris reached NYC on 17 October.

22 UKNA, FO 371/2570 Spring Rice cover letter to article 14/3/15.

23 USNA, MID 10110-1276, APL report, NYC, 20 March 1918, and Alfred Armstrong, "Pearson's Magazine," www.oddbooks.co.uk/harris/pearsons.html.

24 Peter Levenda to author, 1 Sept. 2005.

25 Thanks to William Breeze for this information.

26 Howe, "Reuss."

27 USNA, MID 9140-808, Biddle to Van Deman, 4 Aug. 1917 and NYPD to commander of Bomb Squad [Tunney], 19 Sept. 1917.

28 P. Koenig, "Ordo Templi Orientis, A.M.O.R.C.," //user.cyberlink.ch/~koenig/sunrise/amorc_en.htm.

29 USNA, MID 9140-808, Office of Naval Intelligence [ONI], "German Suspects," 10 July 1917.

30 Crowley to Jane Wolfe, 7 July 1919, quoted from Phyllis Seckler, Continuum. (Oroville CA), Vol. 2, #6 (1979), 23, in P. Koenig, "Veritas Mystica Maxima: Consider the O.T.O. Groups Non-Existant," user.cyberlink.ch/~koenig/consider.htm.

31 MID 9140-808, "Rudolf Steiner and the Anthroposophical Society," 21 April 1923.

32 See: T. H. Meyer (ed.), Light for the New Millenium: Rudolf Steiner's Association with Helmuth and Eliza von Moltke (London: Rudolf Steiner Press, 1998).

33 NYT (16 May 1918), 8:1.

34 Deacon, BSS, 310-311.

35 Neil Johnson, "George Sylvetser Viereck: Poet and Propagandist," Books at Iowa, #9, p. 2., www.lib..uiowa.edu/spec-coll/Bai/johnson2.htm.

36 Ibid., 3.

37 Kevin Coogan, Dreamer of the Day: Francis Parker Yockey and the Postwar Fascist International (NY: Autonomedia, 1999), 261.

38 Lennhoff, 748.

39 The totem animal of Schlaraffia was the great horned owl, oddly similar to the owl symbolism employed by the notorious Bohemian Club.

40 MID 10516-474/31, In re: Hans Heinz Ewers, 24 June 1918.

41 CAC, 749.

42 Gaunt, 194.

43 CAC, 751.

44 CAC, 747-748.

45 FAAC, "George Sylvester Viereck," quoting Crowley's 30 July 1936 diary entry, www.redflame93.com/Viereck.html.

46 Viereck, 51.

47 Renegade.

48 Viereck, 51.

49 CAC, 750.

50 Wilfried Kugel, Der Unverantwortliche: Das Leben des Hanns Heinz Ewers

(Duesseldorf: Grupello, 1992), 226.

51 USNA, MID, 9140-400, Inter-Allied Bureau, List #56, c. 1917.

52 MID, 10516-474/1WCD and attached, 18 Dec. 1917.

53 *CAC*, 683.

54 USNA, MID 10616-474/31, In re: Hans Heinz Ewers, 24 July 1918.

55 MID 10516-474/33, In re: Hans Heinz Ewers, Enemy Alien, 26 June 1918.

56 Kugel, 225.

57 Kugel, 227.

58 Peter Koenig to author, 20 Oct. 2005 and Kugel, 224–225.

59 Ewers also wrote for Hermann Ridder's *Staats-Zeitung*, the largest German-language paper in the U.S.: MID 10516-474, Summary, 8 June 1918.

60 Viereck, 51–52.

61 *The Photoplay* (1916)

62 *CAC*, 749–750.

63 William Stern, "Hugo Muensterberg: In Memoriam," p. 2, www.earlham.edu/%Edominel/obituary.htm.

64 *CAC*, 750.

65 "The Mediumship of Eusapia Palladino," www.fortunecity.com/roswell/seance/78/eusapia.htm#.

66 Another involved with this report was Crowley's friend Hereward Carrington.

67 *CAC*, 750.

68 Viereck, 58–59.

69 *Ibid.*

70 Kugel, 223.

71 *NYT* (28 Feb. 1915), 3.

72 *Ibid.*

73 *NYT* (20 March 1915), 8.

CHAPTER FIVE

~

RETURN TO THE LUSITANIA

~

ON 20 FEBRUARY 1915, THE ILL-FATED LUSITANIA brought Crowley a welcome face: Leila Waddell, his once and future Scarlet Woman. We last met Leila, erotic fiddle virtuosa, when she served as the star and den mother of the Beast's "Ragged Rag-time Girls" in Russia. She may have been privy to the Beast's intelligence duties in Russia. Whatever the case, now she was back in Crowley's sphere and soon enmeshed in his new intrigues. Her lodgings at Manhattan's Hotel Wolcott off 5th Avenue put her conveniently close to his lair on 36th Street. One of the first things she could tell him was what she saw or heard aboard the *Lusitania*.

The simplest conspiracy theory about the liner is that she was the victim of a German plot to destroy the pride of Britain's commercial fleet. A secondary aim was to teach a lesson to the Americans about the hazards of doing business with the English. From this standpoint, the subsequent German claims that the *Lusitania* carried concealed guns and a load of illegal munitions were just face-saving lies designed to excuse a terrorist assault on an unarmed passenger vessel. On the other side is the argument, advanced most forcefully by Colin Simpson in his 1972 *The Lusitania*, that the "*Lucy*" was the victim of a *British* conspiracy hatched within the Admiralty. Simpson pointed an accusing finger straight at First Lord Winston Churchill, along with Guy Gaunt and others. According to this theory, these men set up the liner for destruction in order to tar the Germans with the blame.[1] That does have a certain familiar ring. Besides a belly full of munitions, Simpson accepts the notion that the "*Lucy*" carried twelve six-inch guns in her forward compartments. The fact that the ship routinely carried crowds of Americans across the Atlantic was essential to the insidious plan, argues Simpson, because the sacrifice of the *Lusitania* was part of a larger plot to bring the United States into the war.

A few years after the appearance of Simpson's sensational work, Thomas Bailey's and Thomas Ryan's *The Lusitania Disaster* appeared with the evident aim of debunking Simpson's sensational charges.[2] Given that much of Simpson's evidence was circumstantial at best, Bailey and Ryan picked apart many of his arguments, though not all. The duo dismissed the secret guns and a hidden cargo of explosive powder, though they accepted that the *Lusitania* did carry millions of rounds of rifle ammunition, thousands of artillery shell casings, and other military-related goods. Given that alone, they acknowledged that the Germans probably had legitimate grounds to sink her. Nevertheless, they saw no credible evidence of a British plot to steer the liner toward harm.

In the early 1980s, veteran intelligence historian Patrick Beesly published *Room 40,* an examination of British naval intelligence and its chief, Admiral Hall.[3] Beesly found it suspicious that the Admiralty failed to assign escorts to *Lusitania* when she reached British waters. In essence, his conclusion was that if the Admiralty's leadership did not engineer the tragedy, they allowed it to happen and shamelessly exploited the result. Beesly accepts that the anticipated impact on American opinion explains the decision to leave her vulnerable.

In the absence of anything like a signed confession by Churchill or some other conspirator, it seems improbable that such allegations can ever be proven. Anyone devious enough to do such a thing surely would leave no paper trail. Whether German, British, or other conspiracy sank the *Lusitania*, Aleister Crowley had a part to play.

For reasons to be seen, the Germans sincerely believed that the *Lusitania* carried armament and munitions, and they made plans to destroy her well in advance of the fatal U-boat attack. Whether the guns or munitions were real is ultimately irrelevant. The Germans *believed* that the *Lusitania* was an important and viable target, and some of those who helped convinced them were British agents.

In his *Confessions*, Crowley boasted of having "proved that the *Lusitania* was a man-of-war" in a piece for *The Fatherland* published after the sinking. According to the Beast, Viereck, like other Germans, failed to see that the article was an "extravagance which achieved my object of revolting every comparatively sane human being on earth."[4] Crowley, aboard the *Lusitania* only a few months earlier, could credibly claim to have seen the guns himself. So could Leila Waddell.

Crowley elaborated in 1933 on his influence over Viereck and his *Kameraden*, asserting that he "gradually got the Germans to believe that arrogance and violence were sound policy."[5] Again, that was precisely what Admiral Hall desired. The Mage spoke more candidly about his wartime work for the "Naval Intelligence Service" to the French press. He admitted encouraging U-boat attacks against neutrals to draw the Americans into the fray. His accomplice and immediate chief in this endeavor, he added, was "capitaine Gount [sic]."[6]

Crowley confided even more to his friend George Langelaan, whom he met in the early 1930s. Langelaan is best known today as the author of the science fiction–

horror tale *The Fly*, but he also wrote numerous spy stories based partly on personal experience. Langelaan, like Crowley, enjoyed a relationship with British intelligence, and that may explain why the Beast opened up to him. Langelaan revealed nothing of this exchange until the 1960s, and then only in an obscure French journal.[7] Langelaan's revelations look like a response to questions about Crowley raised in another French magazine, *Planete*, a few months before. The *Planete* piece published anonymous allegations that the infamous Mssr. Crowley was "responsible for the torpedoing of the *Lusitania*."[8]

According to Langelaan, Crowley's influence reached to the top of the German clandestine and diplomatic hierarchies in the U.S. Through his connection to *The Fatherland* and the likes of Viereck, Ewers, and Muensterberg, Crowley rubbed elbows with Dr. Albert, Boy-Ed, von Papen, and even Ambassador Bernstorff. Thus he became more than a mere propagandist. Langelaan recounts that the Germans came to place great faith in the Beast's "intuition" and saw him as an indispensable guide to the mentality of the Americans and the British. He especially impressed them with his ability to predict the actions and reactions of the British. It was almost as though he could see into the inner sanctums of Whitehall.[9] The possibility that he was a British double agent plying them with disinformation apparently eluded them.

Why would the Germans have found this phony Irishman and affected fruitcake credible? The occult angle may explain it. Crowley's reputation as expert in supernatural methods and forces would have impressed many of his superstitious German collaborators and elevated their faith in him. These Germans would be neither first nor last in supposing such powers to have immense value in clandestine warfare. Then there was Crowley's position as American head of the OTO and his intimacy with Reuss, who had influential friends in Berlin.

As a result of this misplaced confidence, continues Langelaan, Crowley sat in at German strategy and policy meetings, including an intimate conclave hosted by the Kaiser's consul in Chicago, Baron Hans Kurt von Reiswitz. Just such a gathering did occur soon after the 3 March 1915 arrival in New York of another of Berlin's consuls, Franz Bopp, on his way to San Francisco. This war council provided an opportunity to allocate responsibilities and begin an expanded campaign of propaganda and sabotage. Reiswitz was a close collaborator of von Papen and up to his eyes in intrigues with Indians and others.[10] Bopp (discussed more in the following chapter) was to take up the same job once he returned to California.

At this or a similar gathering, Crowley allegedly offered that the greatest danger for Germany was America entering the war. After a suitable period of reflection, the Beast argued that the best way to keep the Yankees neutral was not by reason and concessions but by a display of *Schrecklichkeit* (fearsomeness).[11] America, a novice among the seasoned Great Powers, would be cowed. He advised an immediate coup that might pass as accident even as it showcased Germany's willpower and ferocity. Someone in America forwarded these ideas to Berlin. The result, says Langelaan, was the destruction of the *Lusitania* on 7 May.

In reality the Mage probably played only a supporting role in the fate of the *Lusitania*. Langelaan certainly misinterprets the Beast's role as that of an independent agent, likening him to a better-known British WWI operative, T.E. Lawrence. In fact, both Lawrence and Crowley were subject to the authority and scrutiny of higher-ups. However, the comparison is valid in the sense that each was a complicated and eccentric personality entrusted with a highly sensitive mission and inclined to act without or beyond standing orders. So, along with "Lawrence of Arabia," perhaps it is not unjust to speak of "Crowley of America."

Langelaan also links Crowley to a larger British psychological operation aimed at the neutral U.S. According to this, British writer Norman Angell (Ralph Lane) was Crowley's colleague in propaganda enticing America into the war.[12] This was an odd pairing even if neither knew of the other's mission. An outspoken pacifist, Angell had opposed Britain's entrance into the fray. He also was a leading member (along with Bertrand Russell) of the Union of Democratic Control, a left-leaning body that insisted the war be ended by a negotiated and "fair" peace.[13] Yet those same credentials made Angell an ideal crypto-propagandist, visibly distancing his views from those of the British Government. Likewise, few would suspect the notorious and bizarre Crowley of serving His Majesty's Government.

Langelaan errs on at least one detail: Angell did not accompany Crowley over on the *Lusitania* in late 1914. Angell did, however, show up in early 1915 for a speaking tour of the U.S. His views appeared prominently in the *New York Times* and other papers. The consistent thrust of his statements was that, while the war was a human tragedy and must end as soon as possible, the United States' immediate moral responsibility was to hasten that end by unreservedly supporting the Allies. As for the *Lusitania*, right after the sinking Angell argued for an impartial international court to investigate. In the same breath, though, he regarded Germany's guilt as given; the "court" would just determine its degree. Angell warned Americans that they must become aware of Berlin's methods of "inhuman warfare."[14] "I fail to see," he added, "how America can let this dastardly murder of its citizens pass." Thus, as Crowley goaded the Germans to ever greater aggression, Angell hectored America to do something about it.

To fully appreciate Crowley's role in the *Lusitania* affair, we need to examine some wider aspects. The Admiralty briefly considered using the "*Lucy*" as an Armed Merchant Cruiser and registered her as such on 17 September 1914. A refitting scheme called for mounting a dozen six-inch guns on her decks, but Navy authorities abruptly canceled the refit a week later. The official reasons were that the 32,000-ton behemoth burned too much coal and that it presented too big a target to be a fleet auxiliary.

There was, however, another sound reason to return her to commercial service. On 22 August, just before the *Lusitania's* removal from the auxiliary list, three Royal Navy cruisers (the HMS *Aboukir*, *Cressey*, and *Hogue*) had a fatal encounter with U-9 in the English Channel. The lone sub sank all three warships with torpedoes. Crowley took note of this, as did others.[15] A contributing factor to the loss of the cruisers was a common engineering feature—longitudinal bulkheads that allowed water to flood the length of the ship. The coal stored there made sealing them quickly impossible.

The *Lusitania* had the same weakness. If hit by a torpedo, she would begin to list immediately, complicating or preventing the launch of lifeboats. A large enough hole would sink her fast. In the event of a sub attack, therefore, the huge liner was a floating deathtrap. Churchill and others in the Admiralty knew of this compelling reason to pull her from active duty. Of course, by Colin Simpson's reasoning, one man's Achilles' heel is another's ace-in-the-hole.

Rumors that the Germans aimed to destroy the *Lusitania* surfaced as early as autumn 1914. In November, British author William le Queux, whose cash cow was pulp fiction about German intrigues, wrote to MI5 about his worries of enemy saboteurs planting bombs aboard the liner.[16] A more serious warning came shortly before the ship's sinking, in a letter from businessman-turned-politician Neville Chamberlain. He passed to "5" allegations that German agents planned to board the "*Lucy*" in New York with bombs, prime and plant them, and debark in Liverpool. The ship would sink in harbor with no passengers aboard.[17]

However Chamberlain came by the story, the fact was that German agents, and American ones, were working aboard the *Lusitania* during early 1915. Two of them were Kurt (or Curt) Thummel and Neil J. Leach. This duo play an important part in the conspiratorial tale spun by Simpson, because both later testified to the presence of concealed cannons on the Cunard liner. They were part of a plot, or plots, if not quite the one Simpson envisions.

Thummel, a.k.a. Charles E. Thorne, Chester Williams, and other aliases, emigrated to the U.S. about a decade prior to the war. His name, or names, later surfaced in connection with two sabotage cases, the Black Tom (1916) and Kingsland, New Jersey (1917) explosions. In 1933, American claims investigators questioned Thummel about his wartime activities.[18] Thummel was vague or misleading on several points, but the deposition offers a number of clues for us. From 1913 through May 1916, under the name of Charles Thorne, Thummel served in the U.S. Coast Guard, then a branch of the Treasury Department which also encompassed the Secret Service and the Neutrality Bureau.[19]

Thummel stated that during 1914–1915 he encountered a group of German agents in Baltimore. This was a local branch of Paul Koenig's and von Papen's organization run by Frederich Hinsch. Hinsch solicited Thummel to carry out clandestine work on behalf of his original Fatherland. Reluctant to admit to serving the Germans *while* in American uniform, Thummel told investigators he took Hinsch's offer only after his discharge. His secret assignment was to carry messages to German agents in Liverpool, the "*Lucy*'s" home port.

American interrogators pointedly asked Thummel if he had been "detained" by British authorities. Thummel answered "no," but cryptically admitted that he "came near being detained."[20] In fact, a few years earlier, the FBI had received an odd request for any records regarding "Charles E. Thorne alias Chester Williams," who "was arrested by British authorities as a German spy during the World War."[21] The FBI politely but firmly noted that information "contained in the Bureau files is considered strictly confidential and cannot be divulged."[22] There also may have been something to hide.

The truth was that Thummel undertook secret missions for Hinsch beginning in early *1915*, but he did so as an undercover agent of the U.S. Government. Evidence of this surfaced in his 1933 deposition, although it was conveniently ignored. Among Thummel's papers seized in 1917 was a letter sealed in an official War Department envelope. In it a Sgt. Ehrhart addressed a Sgt. Braun to say that the "bearer is a prospective recruit for regular service . . . he is looking for a special assignment."[23] Thummel simply denied that the letter referred to him or that he had any idea how it came into his possession. The investigators did not press the issue.

Recall that the Wilson administration created the Neutrality Bureau to police the shipment of war materials. Given concerns that the warring parties would try to break or bend the rules, the NB spun off a special "intelligence" section that extended its operations to Baltimore and aimed its attention almost exclusively at the Germans. As an employee of the Treasury and a native German speaker, Thummel made an ideal operative. His first assignment was to insinuate himself into Hinsch's confidence. Next, in January 1915, Thummel (then "Thorne") turned up in New York, where he signed on as a crewman aboard the Cunard liner *SS Transylvania* bound for Liverpool. He returned to Gotham aboard the *Lusitania* on 24 April 1915, using a new name. While in Liverpool, Thummel must have been nabbed by the British and saved his skin by revealing himself as an American operative. That would explain being "almost" detained. Thummel also could have revealed a German plan to plant bombs aboard the *Lusitania*, which would explain the rumor picked up by Chamberlain. Admiral Hall would not have been shy about enlisting Thummel for his own purposes.

On 26 April, soon after his return to New York, Thummel marched into Boy-Ed's office at 11 Broadway and added his voice to the charge that the *Lusitania* was carrying concealed armament. There were four guns, he insisted, and he gave a detailed description of their appearance and hiding place. He also got two other German seaman, friends Neil Leach and Gustav Stahl, to corroborate his tale. Crowley, of course, could have attested the same thing. Leach, an Irishman and British subject, had himself arrived from Germany in early March, a detail that may connect him to the Clan-na-Gael–Casement nexus and to Crowley. There even is a remote possibility that Leach, like Thummel and the Beast, was yet another British double. He was slated to ship out on the *"Lucy"* and would perish when the liner went down. Stahl seems to have been a mere patsy. Desperate to shore up German claims after the disappearance of Thummel and Leach, he too swore to having seen the guns when he helped Leach move his seaman's trunk aboard the doomed ship. When that same trunk mysteriously turned up back at Leach's old apartment (returned there by Thummel?), Stahl was forced to plead guilty to perjury.

The New York Germans, though they did not realize it, were the victims of a clever two-pronged con. On one side, Crowley, as devil in their ear, sowed rationalizations for destroying the *Lusitania*. On the other, Thummel conveniently turned up with more evidence of hidden guns, perhaps identical to that described by Crowley. This could have been enough to overcome any lingering inhibitions.

If there was a British mastermind in this affair, it was probably not Churchill (who may still have played an accessory role) but Admiral Hall, who "was prepared to use any methods [or persons] which seemed likely to achieve his objectives."[24] Hall's man in New York was Guy Gaunt, and Gaunt oversaw Crowley.

A instance of Gaunt and Crowley working hand-in-glove involves the warning that appeared in New York papers on 1 May, right next to announcements of the *Lusitania's* imminent departure. The notice cautioned that British vessels entering Germany's maritime "war zone" were subject to attack, so that Americans traveled on them at their own risk. The author of this warning was none other than the Beast's employer, George Sylvester Viereck. Crowley probably either encouraged him to write the notice or was looking over his shoulder when he did so. In the wake of the sinking, the letter was *prima facie* evidence of a premeditated attack. Next, on the morning of the *"Lucy's"* leaving port, at least nine telegrams came to the ship warning prominent passengers in terms almost identical to Viereck's notice. The telegrams had all come from the offices of the *Providence Journal*, a small New England paper. Although no one seems to have taken notice at the time, a close friend and collaborator of Gaunt, John Revelstoke Rathom, ran this newspaper.[25] Rathom and his paper were essential parts of the same British secret apparatus to which Crowley belonged.

As with any plot or con, the fate of the *Lusitania* depended on a certain amount of luck. If the U-20 had not been charging its batteries at just the right place and time, the liner might have sailed safely into Liverpool, but there would have been the next voyage and the one after that. . . . Sooner or later, the big ship was bound to come into a periscope's cross-hairs.

The plot sketched above arguably seems too cold-blooded, too devious, and involved too many people to be real. After all, what kind of men would willingly sacrifice not only a great ship but also the lives of hundreds of innocent passengers, mostly their own countrymen? A man like "Blinker" Hall for one. As for Aleister Crowley, he could have justified it all in Thelemic terms as an expression of raw, ruthless "will"—in effect, the same thing he was selling to the Germans. The war demanded huge, calculated, dispassionate sacrifices. Generals and admirals on all sides routinely made decisions that sent thousands and tens of thousands to their deaths. The objective in every case was to hasten victory and thus save hundreds of thousands. Mass civilian casualties were so much collateral damage and part of the price of victory. Crowley could have thought of it as the expression of the violent new age of which he was the prophet, the Aeon of Horus. Old notions of morality no longer applied. Perhaps he made that very argument to Viereck and others.

As for there being too many players to keep the conspiracy secret, only Hall needed synoptic knowledge of it. Crowley and Thummel, even Gaunt, need not have been aware of each other or of anything else outside their immediate mission. Such an arrangement would have nurtured Crowley's belief that he had been the prime mover all along.

Hall and his plotters could count on widespread condemnation of the unrepentant Germans' act. Whatever the logical or legal merits of their case, the Germans worsened the bad press with an ill-conceived propaganda gesture. The sinking of the *Lusitania* was touted as a triumph in the Reich, and a Munich artisan, Karl Goetz, took it upon himself to make a commemorative medal.[26] The obverse bore an image of the unlucky ship, complete with guns and even airplanes on her decks, going down, with the motto "No Contraband." The reverse featured a mob eagerly buying *Lusitania* tickets from the Grim Reaper, and the words "Geschäft über alles" (business above all). The general impression in Allied and neutral countries was of gloating and deliberate provocation of the Americans. The Beast hardly could have done better if he had designed it himself. Goetz may have intended to satirize both British and German policies, but the devious Admiral Hall saw another opportunity. His agents obtained one of the medals and struck 300,000 copies. These sold in Britain for £1 a piece and were held up, especially in America, as proof of German barbarism.[27]

Thus Aleister Crowley took part in one of the most successful psy-ops in modern intelligence, with weighty consequences for Britain, Germany, and the United States.

While the sinking of the *Lusitania* did not bring the U.S. into the war right away, it unquestionably had a profound pro-war influence on American opinion. The outrage gave the German cause a black eye from which it never recovered and was a critical step toward the eventual decision to intervene. Nevertheless, the American reaction to the *Lusitania* incident did nothing to undermine Crowley's credibility with the Germans. It probably strengthened it. While the Yankee press fulminated and Washington dispatched a series of angry notes to Berlin, Wilson did not declare war or even sever relations. Just as Crowley had predicted, it seemed, the Americans were too stunned and fearful to do more.

One little noticed but important repercussion was President Wilson's executive order, barely a week after the sinking, that established a special unit of the Secret Service charged with invigilating over German and Austrian diplomats and all their social contacts. No like measures were taken against British or other Allied representatives. In fact, British and American intelligence began then to act in close, if unofficial, concert. The chief of Wilson's Teuton-watchers was Frank Burke, whom Gaunt's "successor," William Wiseman, later praised for having always been "extremely helpful in checking the activities of the enemy in cooperation with British Military Intelligence."[28] What would a man like Burke make of a man like Crowley?

1   Simpson, *The Lusitania* (NY: Little Brown, 1973), esp. pp. 26–27, 78–101.

2   Bailey and Ryan, *The Lusitania Disaster: An Episode in Modern Warfare and Diplomacy* (NY: Free Press, 1975), esp. pp. 16–19, 70–82. See also: Keith Allen, "*Lusitania* Controversy," Sections III-V (1999), www.gwpda.org/naval/lusika00. htm, and Gaunt, 137–138.

3   Beesly, 84–122.

4   *CAC*, 752.

5   Renegade.

6   S. Lazareff and C. D'herelle, "Sir Aleister Crowley sera expulse de France demain," *Paris-Midi* (16 April 1929).

7   George Langelaan, "L'agent secret , fauter de paix," *Janus*, #2 (June-Sept. 1964), 49–53.

8   *Planete*, #16 (May-June 1964), 134.

9   Langelaan, 52–53.

10   "German Plots and Propaganda in America" (1918), www.oldandsold. com/articles26/world-war-one-15.shtml.

11   Langelaan, 53.

12   *Ibid.*, 52.

13   "Norman Angell," www.spartacus.schoolnet.co.uk.Jangell.htm.

14   *NYT* (9 May 1915), II, 8:2.

15   *CAC*, 755.

16   UKNA, KV 6/47, le Queux to MI5.

17   KV 6/47, Chamberlain, 30 March 1925.

18   USNA, MID 2801-199, appended deposition of Charles E. Thorne [Thummel] to U.S. Mixed Claim Commission, 25 Sept. 1933.

19   See: Darrel H. Smith and Fred W. Powell, *The Coast Guard: Its History, Activities and Organization* (Washington: Brookings Institution, 1929), 7, 64–66, 82, 90. Thummel/Thorne's original enlistment was with the Treasury's Revenue Cutter Service which became the basis of the new Coast Guard in February 1915.

20   Thorne deposition, 40.

21   FBI file on Curt Thummel, # 62-21551, Baltimore News to FBI, 28 May 1930.

22   *Ibid.*, J.E. Hoover , "Memorandum for Assistant Attorney General Luhring," 17 June 1930.

23   *Ibid.*, 45

24   Beesly, 38.

25   Rathom Obituary, "Milestones," *Time Magazine* (24 Dec. 1923). Rathom's

years wandering in Africa and the Far East probably involved him in some sort of prior intelligence work.

26 www.lusitaniamedal.com/description.htm.

27 The first edition of the medal incorrectly gave the date of the sinking as 5 May, a detail some took as further evidence of German premeditation.

28 WWP 3/84, "Suggestions as to Recognition of War Services Rendered by Persons in America," 22 Nov. 1918, 2.

~

CHAPTER SIX

A PARTY AT THE STATUE OF LIBERTY

~

AS THE FIRST RAYS OF DAWN TINTED THE JERSEY SKIES across the Hudson River on 3 July 1915, ten persons boarded a launch anchored at the public pier at the end of Manhattan's West 50th Street. Aleister Crowley led the party, projecting a quiet gravitas. Among his companions were Waddell (with violin), Joseph M. Dorr (an "Irish editor" said to have published in Ireland and England), and Patrick Gilroy (an "Irish agitator").[1] The rest, all said to be Irish to some degree, are unnamed. Crowley later offered that at least four of them were common drunks.[2] Also aboard, recording it all for posterity, was a reporter from the *New York Times*.

The journalist described Crowley as an "Irishman—poet, philosopher, explorer, a man of mystic mind—the leader of Irish hope."[3] He was "mild in manner, with the intellectual point of view colored by cabalistic interpretation." "He is said to be a close friend of William Butler Yeats," the article added, an ironic sign to anyone in the know, such as Everard Feilding, of how Crowley felt about the excursion.

The launch gently cruised five miles down river into New York Harbor and dropped anchor off Bedloe's Island, home of the Statue of Liberty.[4] The original intention was to land on the island and advance to the foot of Liberty, but an officious guard (the island then hosting a military installation) turned them away. Undeterred, Crowley and his companions remained on the boat a few yards from shore. At precisely 4:32 a.m., a time Crowley had determined to be astrologically auspicious, he faced west, invoked the "one true God of whom the Sun himself is but a shadow," and commenced to "swear the great oath of Revolution"—the Irish Revolution that is. Brandishing what he claimed was his British passport (actually an old envelope), he tore the "token of slavery" into pieces and renounced "forever all allegiance to every alien tyrant." In the next breath he swore to "fight to the last drop of my blood to liberate the men and women of Ireland" and called upon the freedom-loving Americans to support his noble struggle. "I unfurl the Irish flag," he went on, "I proclaim the Irish Republic. *Erin go Bragh*. God save Ireland!"

It was a fairly convincing performance from a man who later claimed to know "almost nothing about the Irish question" beyond its being "a devil of a mess and a devil of a nuisance."[5] Crowley did not stop there. He continued with an extended rant against England, "the enemy of civilization, justice, equality and freedom . . . and the human race," decried its numberless crimes against Ireland, and finished by proclaiming that "we do hereby declare war upon England" until Irish liberty should be achieved.

His Majesty's Government could have justifiably interpreted these words as treasonous. In early August 1914, just after Crowley returned to London, Parliament passed the Defence of the Realm Act (DORA) which gave the government sweeping powers of censorship and requisitioning and forbade a wide array of activities. Most relevant to the Beast, the Act criminalized anything "likely to cause disaffection to His Majesty." Declaring Ireland's independence and war on the British Empire would seem to fit the bill.

After the show at the island, the little crew, with Leila merrily fiddling some Irish tunes, sailed back to their starting point. Along the way they received enthusiastic greetings from sailors on the interned German ships lying off Hoboken. Once ashore, everyone headed to "Jacks," a rough-and-tumble all-night eatery. As they made merry with food and ample drink, some twenty miles away other events were unfolding that would crowd Crowley's grand gesture off the pages of the *Times* until ten days later.

In his declaration of Irish independence, Crowley claimed to represent "the Secret Revolutionary Committee of Public Safety of the Provisional Government of Ireland." He billed himself as member #418, while Waddell was #11. Both rankings were numerologically significant, 418, for instance, equating to the mystical ABRAHADABRA in the kabbalistic system.[6] Perhaps the Mage had slyly conducted some occult ritual before the great Goddess of Liberty.

According to Crowley, the mysterious Committee's immediate goals did not include armed insurrection, but focused on anti-British propaganda and a "secret effort to dissuade Irishmen from enlisting in the English Army." The *Times* reporter also interviewed an American "acquainted with Crowley's beliefs and intentions." This almost certainly was Frank Harris, who opined that while the "Committee sympathize[s] with Germany in the present war," active collusion with Berlin was a mere expediency. The Secret Revolutionary Committee is highly unlikely to have existed outside of Crowley's imagination, and he seems never to have mentioned it again.

Crowley later voiced "displeasure" that the *Times* had reported anything about the solemn events at Bedloe's Island, as though he had invited a reporter along expecting otherwise. Indeed, the Beast elsewhere contradicted this by claiming to have staged the event to get attention by doing "something more public."[7] The real audience for the stunt was not Irish militants or the American public but his German associates. "I did not feel that I was advancing in the confidence of the Germans," he later wrote, and as a result he had been getting "no secrets worth reporting to

London." There was only so much he could do as a phony propagandist. Crowley was auditioning for a bigger role.

London took notice of his antics. Crowley recalled a response in certain circles of "consternation," and, as noted above, for good reason.[8] He had neglected to clear his public performance before Liberty with higher authority. As a deep cover operative he was supposed to maintain a low profile, to work inside the enemy apparatus, not parade around with a gaggle of inebriates in front of the American press. His anti-British tirades in *The Fatherland* and like publications were not likely to draw widespread attention in Britain; Hall's censors and DORA could keep them out of the public eye. In any case, they could be explained away as the ranting in a pro-German rag of someone Gaunt dismissed as a "small-time traitor."[9] The political theater at Bedloe's Island was something else entirely.

Crowley soon heard from Feilding, who must have asked something along the lines of "what the hell were you thinking?" Crowley records that Feilding was still with "the Intelligence Department," i.e. NID.[10] According to the Beast, Feilding "understood and approved" the recent actions but also cautioned that he could not authorize anything further without approval from unidentified higher-ups. Feilding was soon to go to work for a branch of SIS in Greece, and later serve in the Middle East, but he would keep in touch with Crowley. The mysterious superiors would prove harder to convince. Whatever doubts they entertained about employing the Beast must have been exacerbated.

In response Crowley poured out his standard complaint that he could "find out exactly what the Germans were doing in America" if only given the "right sort of assistance."[11] That undoubtedly included more money, but he also was pleading for greater responsibility. His unique talents were being wasted, including not only his supposed magical abilities—hypnotism, divination, even invisibility—but also a growing body of experience with drugs. He emphasized having the "absolute confidence, years old, of a man high in the German secret service"—almost certainly Reuss. Crowley seems to have wanted to revive the Casement angle by offering to use his Irish cover to spy in Germany, a gambit in which the Reuss connection could have been critical.

The plan also may have included infiltrating Reuss' operation in Switzerland. Through his connection to the *Continental Times* and the German grapevine in New York, Agent Crowley doubtless had picked up hints of plots brewing among the Alps. In fact, a very dangerous one was taking shape during June–July 1915—a Berlin-sponsored conspiracy uniting Indian revolutionaries and anarchists to assassinate Allied leaders across Europe. Among the proposed targets were Lord Kitchener, the President of France, the King of Italy, and Allied and pro-Allied representatives in the Balkans.[12] British operatives, however, were able to penetrate and destroy the plot before it did any damage. One British agent who played a part in this was the

Mage's old acquaintance and antagonist, William Somerset Maugham.[13] Maybe he got the job Crowley was after.

The superiors decided that Crowley would stay right where he was. He could only express bewilderment at their "failure . . . to apply common sense to my proposals," but they may not have rejected all of them. [14] Crowley does seem to have gained approval for a wider range of action, beyond the streets and offices of New York.

As noted, the real audience for Crowley's recent histrionics was, of course, the Germans. By so publicly pulling the Lion's tail, Crowley hoped to convince any doubters in the German camp that he hated Britain, and there was nothing like publicly proclaiming himself a traitor to do that. Viereck, for one, seemed notably impressed by the little show. Still, some of the Beast's Teutonic associates must have wondered about the seeming indifference of the British to his baiting.

This insouciance of British officialdom sharply contrasts with the case of another anti-British propagandist then running around New York, Ignatius Timothy Trebitsch-Lincoln. Born Ignaz Trebitsch, the son of a prosperous and pious Hungarian Jewish trader, he is another enigmatic character whose bizarre and convoluted career can only be briefly sketched here.[15] He was at least as egomaniacal as Crowley, and far crookeder. Trebitsch also took an interest in things metaphysical and would reinvent himself as a Buddhist monk years later. French esoteric scholar Rene Guenon later described Trebitsch as a representative of dark occult influences with a close connection to Crowley.[16] Another French writer, Pierre Mariel, even insists that Trebitsch was a member of the OTO. [17] There is nothing tangible to support such claims, but New York may not have been the first or last place the pair's paths crossed.

About thirty-six in 1915, Trebitsch already had gone through a chain of metamorphoses—Talmud student, Christian missionary, British parliamentarian, oil speculator, swindler, and spy. He played at espionage in the pre-WWI Balkans, peddling information simultaneously to the Bulgarians, Turks, and Germans. Back in England by 1914, Trebitsch briefly worked as a censor for the War Office (a post similar to Feilding's) but aspired to bigger things. He apparently offered his services as a spy to the British and then, when they declined, to the Germans. He undertook a trip to neutral Holland that December, contacted the Kaiser's agents (was Reuss one of them?), and returned with what he said were German codes. He tried to hawk these to Admiral Hall, who was not fooled. The crafty Hall, in fact, had been watching Trebitsch, and warned him to get out of the country as soon as possible. That could suggest that Hall recruited Trebitsch as another double agent, or thought he had done so.

In a flash, Trebitsch was on a boat to America, where he arrived on 9 February 1915.[18] He soon penned a series of anti-British articles (most, oddly, appearing in the *New York World*) that boasted of his work as a German spy.[19] His actual dealings with the Germans in New York seem to have been limited. He visited the Consulate and *The Fatherland*'s offices, but was received with much suspicion, possibly stoked by Crowley.

Unlike Crowley's writing, Lincoln's insults, or failure to perform his double agent duties, provoked British authorities to action. Scotland Yard quickly dug up an old and outstanding forgery charge, and His Majesty's representatives dogged the Americans to arrest Lincoln, which they did on 4 August 1915.[20] London could easily have concocted similar grounds for arresting Crowley. For instance, a rumor that Crowley had been "chased from England where he fleeced some society women out of money" was still floating around New York Police circles in 1917.[21] That the Mage avoided Lincoln's fate, attests his relationship with influential persons in London.

As further evidence of his loyalty and utility to the British cause, Crowley may have helped set up a much more serious blow to Berlin's American organization. Recall that in May 1915 the Wilson Administration created a special section of the Secret Service to spy on the Germans and Austrians. The head of the hush-hush unit, Frank Burke, closely collaborated with Gaunt which directly or indirectly linked him to Crowley.

A major focus of Burke's attention was Viereck, whom his men watched continuously. In doing so, they could not help encountering the Beast. As Burke later told the tale, what ensued was pure luck. On 24 July, he and a subordinate tailed Viereck and an unknown German with saber-scars and a small, dark mustache. The latter was Dr. Heinrich Albert, the German secret paymaster. Burke and his companion followed the pair onto an uptown El-train. Soon after, Viereck got off at a stop very near Crowley's address. Burke decided to stick with Dr. Mustache. As the train rolled on, Albert dozed off. Suddenly awakened at his stop, he groggily stumbled out of the train, forgetting his briefcase. Burke seized the case and ran off with it. He immediately shared his swag with Gaunt. Inside the case was a trove of compromising documents, including a scheme for establishing a phony armaments company. Soon, with Washington's silent approval, Gaunt leaked excerpts from the Albert papers to the *New York World*.[22] Among the details revealed was Albert's financial and editorial control over Viereck's *Fatherland*. The resulting flap was the beginning of the end not only for Albert, but for von Papen and Boy-Ed as well.

Burke's story is unlikely the complete or true one. Years later, Emanuel Voska, the head of a Czech spy ring and one of Gaunt's key agents, took credit for stealing the briefcase.[23] Voska's involvement would imply that Burke was set on Albert by the British, who knew that the good *Doktor* would be toting around some juicy documents that afternoon. Who would have been in a better position to glean that information than the Beast? Albert's oversight is easy enough to attribute to the familiar devils of bad luck and bad timing. Still, it was awfully accommodating of him to nod off just when Burke sat behind him. Could hypnosis, drugs, or some other occult influence have been at work? Going back to the notion that Viereck was Crowley's willing accomplice, did he, perhaps, slip Albert some concoction put together by our man?

Crowley's contact with the Germans took a downturn with the departure of Ewers on a secret mission to Spain in mid-1915. One of Ewers' special connections was his intimacy with Ernst Franz "Putzi" Hanfstaengl, later a member of Hitler's inner circle. Although born in Munich, Putzi had an American mother and was a Harvard graduate, a detail that linked him to Muensterberg. One of Putzi's classmates, and a relation on his mother's side, was then assistant secretary of the U.S. Navy, Franklin Roosevelt. Another classmate was the journalist and future Communist gadabout John Reed. Putzi ran the Manhattan office of the family business, the Franz Hanfstaengl Fine Art Publishing House, at Fifth Avenue and 45th Street, not far from the Morgan Library. Indeed, J.P. Morgan Jr. and Belle Greene were among Hanfstaengl's regular customers.)

Putzi's association with Ewers went beyond common interests in art, literature, and the occult. Years later, Irish radical labor leader James Larkin fingered Hanfstaengl as a German operative during the war and a man "having general knowledge of the German sabotage work in this country."[24] Putzi was another part of Berlin's secret apparatus, a front for payments to Larkin and others, and one more source of information the Beast could have tapped through his association with Ewers.

Ewers' Spanish sojourns were carefully watched by British agents in Madrid. Again, Crowley was perfectly placed to tip them off. One British agent active in Spain was Crowley's former friend, brother-in-law, and Golden Dawn acolyte, Gerald Kelly. Kelly's case has some interesting parallels to Crowley's. When Kelly went to Spain in early 1917, his passport was provided by NID.[25] That suggests he was another of Hall's men but, as with the Beast, he never received an official commission in the RNVR or any other service branch. A complicating factor is that Hall ran the intelligence operation in Spain as a kind of franchise for Cumming's SIS. Thus, Kelly could have had a link to that quarter as well. Finally, Kelly sent back his reports on pro-Allied propaganda to John Buchan, then the chief of the newly formed Department of Information, successor to the War Propaganda Board.

Kelly's connections to Naval Intelligence and even his propaganda role roughly match Crowley's. Furthermore, Kelly was somehow aware of Crowley's activities in the U.S. When someone in London asked him about the dubious activities of his former in-law, Kelly "advised leaving Crowley alone," arguing that he was "an ineffectual tool in the hands of the enemy."[26] That almost exactly echoes Gaunt's comments and, of course, more or less describes Crowley's true role.

Crowley's biggest challenge with the Germans was new leadership and a shift in the methods and strategy of their clandestine operations. On 3 April, a Swiss traveler, "Emil V. Gasche," arrived in New York aboard the Norwegian liner *Kristianiafjord* (which may have carried more spies to and from America than any other ship). Gasche was really Franz Rintelen von Kleist, captain in the Imperial German Navy. He spoke perfect English, and his prewar career in investment banking gave him vital experience operating in the U.S. and Mexico. With his dark, refined features and cultivated manners, he looked and acted more like an Italian count than a German officer. Given the obvious failure of the Albert–Boy-Ed–von Papen triumvirate to staunch North American munitions to Germany's foes, *Abteilung IIIb* sent in Rintelen with orders to "do something positive" about the problem.[27]

With this authority, Rintelen diverted money from Albert's and the others' accounts to build up his own operations. These included the dummy armaments firm to tie up American production (revealed in Albert's briefcase) and a front organization called Labor's National Peace Council to recruit radicals to instigate strikes and agitate for a general arms embargo. Rintelen also joined forces with the "Wolf of Wall Street," rogue financier David Lamar, a bitter enemy of Britain's critical ally, Morgan & Company. Last, but not least, he embraced plain old sabotage, with the new twist of planting incendiary devices aboard munitions ships. Rintelen was probably the best agent Berlin had in America during the war, and his bold plans might have achieved much, given more time. He ran rings around Gaunt, who, while aware of Rintelen's activities, was unable to frustrate most of them.

Rintelen's downfall began with an order to return to Berlin on 6 July 1915. Using what he thought was the still secure identity of Gasche, he was nabbed in early August by Hall's men when his ship stopped for blockade inspection in Portsmouth. Rintelen later blamed his rival von Papen for the arrest, accusing the Military Attaché of stupidly (or deliberately) exposing his identity in cables intercepted by Hall's Room 40.[28] It could just as easily have been Crowley who ferreted out this precious information.

Crowley could not have overlooked the incident that precipitated Rintelen's abrupt recall. In fact, there is a strange synchronicity between it and his performance at the Statue of Liberty. That same morning, one "Frank Holt," pistol in hand and bombs in his pockets, forced his way into J. P. Morgan's palatial home on the north shore of Long Island. The Morgans, by another strange coincidence, were enjoying breakfast with their guest, British Ambassador Cecil Spring-Rice. It was never clear whether Holt's intention was to kill the financier, or Spring-Rice or, as he later claimed, to kidnap Morgan's children. In any case, he definitely came well-armed. The intruder managed to pump two bullets into Morgan before the burly banker tackled the smaller assailant to the floor. Although seriously wounded, Morgan survived; his attacker ended up in the nearby Mineola County jail. The resulting media frenzy, which went on for days, bumped Crowley's little escapade out of the limelight. If the Mage really had objected to press attention, he could not have conjured a better distraction.

Under questioning, the prisoner confessed that he was not Holt at all, but Erich

Muenter, a German-American fugitive wanted for the 1906 poisoning murder of his wife in Massachusetts. In another twist, the prisoner also confessed to having set off a bomb inside the U.S. Capitol the day before his attack on Morgan. Muenter had been a professor of German at Harvard and a friend and colleague of Hugo Muensterberg. Muensterberg later admitted recognizing "Holt" in news photos but insisted he did not see any responsibility to reveal the culprit's true identity to police. The Professor, though, was no disinterested party; he had been in secret communication with Muenter for years. After hiding out in Mexico for a while, Muenter had slipped back into the U.S. and as Frank Holt secured another teaching job at Cornell University. No doubt Muensterberg helped.

The immediate suspicion in Berlin was that Rintelen was the controlling hand behind Muenter's outrages. After all, before his recent crime spree, the would-be assassin had been quietly assembling time bombs for Rintelen's saboteurs. Should that link emerge in Muenter's questioning, there would be serious repercussions for Rintelen, not to mention further marring of Germany's image in American eyes. Thus, the wisest course seemed to be for Rintelen to become scarce. Rintelen and others must have given sighs of relief when on 6 July, the same day of Rintelen's recall, Muenter penned a farewell letter to his family, walked through his unlocked cell door, and leapt to his death off a jailhouse tier. So the local coroner concluded, anyway.[29]

However much Muenter's crimes might have compromised Rintelen, Crowley must have suspected another hand at work—"Moriarty" Muensterberg's. The Professor was Muenter's longtime confidant and knew of his former colleague's past crimes. That would have given Muensterberg plenty of leverage over the would-be assassin. Beyond that, Hugo Muensterberg was an expert psychologist. Who would have been better able to analyze and manipulate an unstable, homicidal personality? There is a suggestion in the Muenter case of the now all-too-familiar "lone nut," and what today might be termed a "programmed assassin." Crowley may have suspected something of the sort and wondered how Muensterberg had achieved his ends. Could hypnotic influences have been involved, or some sort of drug? As we soon will see, Crowley had his own expertise in that sphere.

Crowley's *Magical Record* diary details his experiments with "sex magick" and other occult doings, along with more mundane things. However, his extant diaries contain a major gap, from 16 June 1915 until 25 February 1916. A diary for this period certainly once existed, and it is suggestive that the entries for this period, and a later part of his American stay, vanished while others did not. The gap began just as Crowley was questioning his intelligence assignment and looking for new means to serve his country's clandestine needs. It largely obscures his journey across North America in fall 1915. This trip would signal a new and more active phase in Crowley's covert activities, one never intended for any record, magical or otherwise.

A major character in Crowley's coming adventure was a new love interest, Jeanne Foster (1879–1970).[30] He met her in June 1915 and soon was, he said, in love. The thirty-six year old Foster was a mature, brunette beauty, educated, artistic, and (as her interest in Crowley shows) a bit wild. She was also married. Born Julie Ollivier to a poor family in New York's Adirondacks, she made it to the big city through her marriage, at age seventeen, to a fortyish insurance executive, Matlock Foster. In the years to follow, Matlock seems to have remained oblivious or quietly tolerant of his young wife's marital indiscretions as she became first a popular model, then a journalist, and by WWI an aspiring poet. When Crowley met her, she was assistant editor of the influential *American Review of Reviews*. They shared a common acquaintance in John Quinn, and soon after dumping the Beast she became Quinn's devoted mistress. Another of her friends was Belle Greene.

In summer 1915, Crowley saw Foster as the perfect embodiment of the Scarlet Woman and was determined to sire by her the son prophesied by his guardian angel Aiwass in the *Book of the Law*. This naturally led to her initiation into the OTO as Soror Hilarion, and to regular sex-magic "workings." Crowley affectionately, and symbolically, nicknamed Jeanne "The Cat."

Crowley and Foster's relationship may have been partly professional. She had worked as a reporter for the *Boston American* and other papers, and during WWI she functioned as a "secret correspondent" for someone.[31] That hints at a link to intelligence—but whose? Her association with Crowley and Quinn suggests that she was another British asset, which might explain her accompanying Crowley on his coming mission. She might also have served Morgan's intelligence agency, reporting to Belle Greene, or Burke's outfit, or some other American agency. In any case, her job probably was as much to watch Crowley as to help him. There were those in both London and New York who trusted him little enough in their sight, and even less out of it. Perhaps Crowley meant this when he later lamented Foster's "falseness."[32] Still, she and her elderly husband would provide a handy cover for Crowley's adventure into the American hinterland.

For the trip Crowley acquired an alternate identity, further indication that he was planning more than a holiday. He later used the surname "Clifford," and must have had some identification to back it up.[33] He may have borrowed the identity of John Clifford, an Irish-born British subject living in New York as a respectable family man and banker. Clifford was the right age and, conveniently, yet another friend of Quinn's. Clifford's financial credentials, as we will see, could have come in handy.

Further indication of agitation in Crowley's affairs was his changes in address. At some point that summer, he quit the apartment on 36th Street and took up residence first in suburban New Rochelle and then in more distant Philadelphia. He then moved back to Manhattan and was living in rooms above the Alps Restaurant, a German hang-out on 57th Street, when he headed west. What drove these peregrinations is unclear. Maybe it was just money; maybe he was trying to obscure his whereabouts and connections, or find someone, or lose someone.

To understand what Crowley was about to jump into, we again need to pause to consider the larger picture and introduce a few new players. During spring and summer of 1915, the West Coast became a hotbed of German-inspired sabotage and subversion. At the end of June, for example, American authorities seized the schooner *Annie Larson* off the coast of Washington, loaded with arms intended for an uprising in India. The immediate oversight of this and other German schemes fell to San Francisco Consul Franz Bopp, whom Crowley had probably met in New York in March. Bopp assigned hands-on clandestine duties to his vice consuls, reserve army officers Wilhelm von Brincken and Eckhart von Schack. Von Brincken, for one, had close ties to Irishmen linked to Devoy's Clan-na-Gael. In May, von Papen traveled west to confer with German operatives in Seattle.

In addition to funneling money and guns to the Indians and Irish, Bopp and his underlings received orders from Berlin to sabotage munitions shipments and Canadian railways. In April, von Brincken paid a Dutch national, Henrickus van Koolbergen, to blow up rail tunnels in British Columbia.[34] Koolbergen, however, immediately betrayed the scheme to Britain's man in San Francisco, Consul A. Carnegie Ross, who wisely advised the Dutchman to remain in the Germans' confidence. To make Koolbergen seem worth his salt, Ross arranged to have fake stories about damaged rail lines planted in the Canadian press. Ross, though, was seriously outnumbered by an amateurish but still dangerous enemy cabal.

Bopp and his comrades employed other saboteurs. The most important of these was Charles C. Crowley. He was a former special investigator for the U.S. Attorney General's office in San Francisco turned private detective and general thug-for-hire. Beyond sharing a surname with the Beast, C.C. even bore a certain resemblance—sheer coincidence, but possibly useful. C.C. Crowley recruited an assistant of the same cloth, Lewis J. Smith, an ex-cop from Detroit. From late May through mid-July, Crowley and Smith took credit for destroying a load of explosives in Tacoma, Washington and more railway sabotage in the Canadian Rockies. In reality, they achieved nothing.

Another man mixed up in the plans to cut the Canadian Pacific, and the likely key link in Crowley's coming mission, was a tall, handsome German nobleman named Gustav Konstantin Alvo von Alvensleben.[35] Best known as Alvo, he was the wandering son of a Prussian Junker family. Landing in British Columbia around 1904, all but penniless, he rose from rags to riches in a few years. By 1914, he was a provincial celebrity and millionaire controlling huge investments in timber, land, and coal.[36] Much of Alvo's success stemmed from his secret role as front man for a syndicate of big German investors, among them Kaiser Wilhelm II himself.[37]

Alvensleben was also a prominent Freemason and *Schlaraffen*. It would not be at all surprising if he was OTO as well.

With the advent of war, Alvensleben's activities started to look suspicious to his Canadian neighbors.[38] He was fortuitously on his way back from Berlin when the war broke out and thereafter stayed safely on the American side of the border. Whether Alvensleben was part of a German plot to take over British Columbia is doubtful, but there is no doubt that he abetted Germany's secret activities on both sides of the 49th Parallel. Canadian authorities seized all of his known assets, and German victory was the surest way to see his property and position restored.

In spring 1915, Alvo brokered a secret meeting between Rintelen and the most important German saboteur operating on the West Coast, Kurt Jahnke.[39] Alvensleben also was among the men von Papen conferred with during a visit to Seattle. Alvo's business interests gave him access to numerous bank accounts and financial institutions, which he used to launder and move German funds. Chicago became Alvensleben's main base of clandestine operations, and he was a close friend of Chicago Consul von Reiswitz, who, according to Langelaan, invited Crowley to that special gathering at New York's German Club. Maybe Alvo was there too. Alvo even teamed up with a Lt. Baerensprung to arrange the dynamiting of railroad tunnels in B.C.[40] Baerensprung, in turn, linked back to the aforementioned duo of C.C. Crowley and Smith and Bopp's San Francisco cell.[41] Alvo was privy to almost every German secret work in North America.

There is no hard proof that Alvo and Crowley ever met, much less conspired, but an abundance of common links and opportunities makes it probable. Some years later, Crowley noted a "Frau von Alvensleben," presumably Alvo's Canadian-born wife, among his devotees.[42] It had to have been one of the Baron's relations. Crowley's coming travels gave opportunity for him to meet von Alvensleben and cajole his cooperation. In addition to lands and houses, Alvo had other assets in Canada: cash, bonds, and artworks that he dared not retrieve. Even his wife was too closely watched to make away with anything substantial. However, someone like Crowley, or rather Mr. Clifford, would not arouse suspicion. Crowley had OTO business in Vancouver which would provide excellent cover for being there and even accomplices if he needed them. With Alvo's directions, Crowley might be able to secure some loot and bring it safely to Seattle. A grateful Alvo could be very useful. With him and a little luck, Crowley might be able to expose the German network on the West Coast and pocket a little money in the bargain.

It would be interesting to know how much Crowley shared about his plans with those British superiors. His journey surely received some sort of official blessing. Just before his departure he noted receipt of a chunk of cash, by far the largest amount he had handled in some time. With "traveling money" in hand, he was set to go.

1   *NYT* (13 July 1915), 7, 10.

2   *CAC*, 753.

3   *NYT, Ibid.*

4   Renamed Liberty Island in 1960.

5   *CAC*, 750.

6   Steve Jackson to author, 22 Feb. 2006.

7   *CAC*, 753.

8   Renegade

9   Symonds, 199.

10   *CAC*, 753.

11   *Ibid.*

12   Nirode K. Barooah, *Chatto: The Life and Times of an Indian Anti-Imperialist in Europe* (London: Oxford Univ. Press, 2004), 134–135. See also: V. Chattopadhyaya, *Folkets Dagblad Politiken* [Stockholm] #237 (4 Oct. 1921), 4.

13   Maugham's story "Giulia Lazzari" was a fictionalized account of the British effort to neutralize Chatto. See: Maugham, *Ashenden, or the British Agent* (London: Heineman, 1928).

14   *CAC*, 754.

15   Perhaps the most thorough examination of Trebitsch's strange career is Bernard Wasserstein, *The Secret Lives of Trebitsch Lincoln* (New Haven, Yale Univ. Press, 1988). See also David Lampe and Laszlo Szenasi, *The Self-Made Villain: A Biography of I.T. Trebitsch-Lincoln* (London: Cassel, 1961). Trebitsch's own highly unreliable but often interesting story is *Autobiography of an Adventurer* (New York: Henry Holt, 1932).

16   Giorgio Galli, *Hitler e il Nazismo Magico* (Milano: Rizzoli, 1989), 5, Giuseppe Jerace, "Aleister Crowley," //xoomer.virgilio.it/gnscol/Varie/Crowley_biografia. htm, and Guenon to Rene Schneider, 13 Sept. 1936, as quoted in //elkorg-projects.blogspot.com/2005_07_01_elkorg-projects_archive.html. See also: Werner Gerson[Pierre Mariel], *Le Nazisme, societe secrete* (Paris: Productions de Paris, 1969), Annexe A, "Biographie de Trebitsch-Lincoln," 326–332.

17   Gerson, *Ibid.*

18   *NYT* (14 June 1915), 3:1, and (5 Aug. 1915), 1:2.

19   He later collected and expanded the articles into book, *Revelations of an International Spy* (NY: Robert McBride,1916).

20   *NYT* (5 Aug. 1915), 1:2.

21   USNA, MID 9140-808, NYPD Bomb Squad Report, 19 Sept. 1917.

22   The story, covering three pages, ran on 15 August.

23   FBI file on Emanuel Voska, #65-43505, Memorandum for Mr. E. A. Tamm, 14 Feb. 1941.

24   *NYT* (7 April 1934), 7:1. In a later deposition, Larkin recalled the German's name as "Umstangl" or the like. The fact that Larkin identified him as a prominent art dealer in New York during the war and recognized him as

a man "now said to be a close associate of Chancellor Hitler" leaves no doubt that it was Putzi. See also Hanfstaengl's FBI file, #100-76954, //foia.fbi. gov/hanfstan/hanfstan1b.pdf.

25   Tomaselli to author, 6 and 12 Dec. 2005, *in re* passport records.

26   Symonds, 199.

27   Barbara Tuchman, *The Zimmermann Telegram* (NY: Viking Press, 1958), 69–70.

28   Franz Rintelen, *The Dark Invader: Wartime Reminiscences of a German Naval Intelligence Officer* (NY: Macmillan, 1933), 115–116, and Henry Landau, *The Enemy Within: The Inside Story of German Sabotage in America* (NY: G.P. Putnam's, 1937), 48–49.

29   The coroner ruled on 4 August. Rintelen left New York the day before.

30   St. Lawrence County, NY Branch of the American Association of University Women, "Jeanne Robert Foster: Adirondack Poet," www.northnet.org. stlawrence aauw/foster.htm.

31   *Ibid.*, 2.

32   Aleister Crowley, *The Magickal Record of the Beast 666: the Diaries of Aleister Crowley, 1914–1920*, ed. by John Symonds and Kenneth Grant (London: Duckworth, 1972), 137–139.

33   Martin P. Starr, *The Unknown God: W. T. Smith and the Thelemites* (Bolingbrook, IL: Teitan Press, 2003), 37.

34   "German Plots and Propaganda in America," *Ibid.*

35   Ingrid Laue, "Gustav Alvo von Alvensleben (1879–1965), Ein Lebensbild," *German-Canadian Yearbook 5* (Toronto: Historical Society of Mecklenburg Upper Canada, 1979), 154–173.

36   Jan Peterson, *The Albernis, 1860–1922* (Lantzville, B.C.:–Oolichan Books, 1992), 236.

37   *Ibid.*, 237.

38   USNA, MID 9140-1421/18, DJ memo, 21 Dec. 1917, and /20, Treasury, 8 Feb. 1918; Peterson, 238-239, and "Spy or Casualty of War ?," *The* [Surrey] *Leader* (24 July 2005).

39   Reinhard Doerries, *Imperial Challenge: Ambassador Count Bernstorff and German-American Relations, 1908–1917* (Chapel Hill: Univ. of North Carolina Press, 1989), 177.

40   *Ibid.*, 180, 338.

41   USNA, MID 10108-69, DJ Nov. 1917, and 9140-5504, DJ memo quoting British War Office, 30 May 1917.

42   Crowley Diary entry, 6 Oct. 1931, quoted in David Scriven and Peter Koenig, "Caliphate Ordo Templi Orientis," //user.cyberlink.ch/~koenig/dplanet/ htmls1.htm.

~

CHAPTER SEVEN

THERE AND BACK AGAIN

~

CROWLEY AND THE FOSTERS ROLLED OUT of New York on 6 October. The sickly and sixtyish Matlock Foster must have been a drag on things, but he had at least one use. His presence reconciled the trip with the Mann Act, which made it a federal offense to transport a woman across state lines for any "unlawful" purpose, which in most places included adultery. Crowley and Jeanne would have ample opportunity to work on the generation of magick progeny while the old man was asleep or otherwise out of the way. As for "secret correspondent" Jeanne, presumably she was along for the ride for more than sex.

Crowley's later account of his journey back and forth across North America is episodic and vague. As for his reasons behind the trip, the most Crowley offers in *Confessions* is that he wanted to see the Pan-Pacific Exhibition in San Francisco and to "get first-hand facts about the attitude of the people [outside Gotham] . . . to the war."[1] As noted in the last chapter, San Francisco was the center of German intrigues on the West Coast, and gauging the mood of the American public was not something that would interest our man alone. A year later, Gaunt's replacement, William Wiseman, would dispatch another agent on a mission covering much of the same ground. That operative, British playwright Harley Granville Barker, sent Wiseman chatty reports on the public's mood and opinions about the war in each town he visited.[2] The Beast's secret agenda, however, involved much more than passive fact-finding.

Crowley's other confessed goal on the trip was to pay a visit on a small group of devotees in far off British Columbia. The roots of this went back to January 1915 when Crowley gave his blessing to the creation of an OTO lodge in Vancouver. At its head was Charles Stansfield Jones, a member of Crowley's A∴A∴ order and one of his prewar followers in London. The Mage knew that he could trust this devoted acolyte with a secret or two. Jones' local circle included another young Briton, Wilfred T. Smith, and from the prewar London scene the painter and dramatist Horace Sheridan-Bickers. Crowley also knew Sheridan-Bickers' wife Margaret "Betty" Dartnell-Bickers. In fact, he had enjoyed a brief affair with her some years earlier and was now suddenly keen to rekindle the flame. That, at least, was his explanation for some of what followed. Jones, Bickers, and the rest had contacts in the local Masonic community, which means one or more could very well have known Alvensleben—all the more likely if Alvo himself belonged to OTO.

Crowley may have had others to confer with in Vancouver. One was the local head of the Dominion Police, a no-nonsense Scotsman, Malcolm Nicolson Reid. Reid had assumed control over the network of Indian spies and informants created by the murdered Hopkinson. Unlike Hopkinson, though, Reid could not speak or read Hindi or other Indian tongues. Crowley, of course, did have such ability. Reid also happened to be the top Canadian cop looking for Alvo. On the other hand, for undercover operative Crowley, that could have made Reid someone to avoid.

In the roughly ten days en route to Vancouver, Crowley visited at least three American cities: Detroit, Chicago, and Minneapolis–St. Paul. His pressing errand in the Motor City was a visit to the Parke-Davis pharmaceutical plant. There the "rhythmical" mass production of pills and potions mesmerized him, but his real goal was scoring a big stash of pharmaceutically refined peyote, the psychedelic with which he had dosed audiences at the Rites of Eleusis. He appreciated the drug's ability to generate profound "altered states of consciousness" and must have been glad at the prospect of using it ceremoniously in Vancouver. But he may have had other uses in mind as well.

Eighteen years later, Nazi doctors at the Dachau concentration camp gave massive mescaline doses to prisoners in hope of achieving "chemical hypnosis." British interrogators dabbled with the same drug during WWII. The net result of these and like experiments was that the drug could amplify the effectiveness of interrogation techniques if properly administered. After WWII, the U.S. Navy's "Operation Chatter" continued to experiment with mescaline as a "speech-inducing agent."[3] The same and related psychedelics featured prominently in the CIA's secret MK ULTRA mind-control projects, which flourished throughout the 1950s and 1960s.

Crowley, circumstantial evidence suggests, was a pioneer in this bizarre field, and his groundbreaking work may have informed some of those later experiments. He once boasted, "I have myself made extensive and elaborate studies of the effects of indulgence in stimulants and narcotics," and produced "a vast quantity of unpublished data" on the subject.[4] Throughout his American stay, the Beast routinely administered mescaline or other drugs to willing and unsuspecting subjects (spicy curries were a favorite means), methodically cataloging the results.[5] These observations ended up in another of his journals, *Liber CMXXXIV, The Cactus*, which he described as an "elaborate study of the psychological effects produced by *Anhalonium Lewinii* . . . compiled from the actual records of some hundreds of experiments."[6] *The Cactus* vanished after the war.

When Crowley came to Detroit, Louis J. Smith was living inconspicuously as a Motor City auto worker. Recall that he and his partner C.C. Crowley had been Bopp's main saboteurs of Canadian railroads. Their ineptitude so disgusted Bopp that he cut the pair loose and banished Smith to the Midwest. Tipped off, agents of the U.S. Department of Justice's Bureau of Investigation, or BI (precursor of the FBI), were on Smith's trail. However much they suspected, though, the Americans had no hard evidence against him. Without that or, better yet, a confession, they could not arrest him.

Crowley later claimed to have worked with Washington's Department of Justice: "my services are contained in the records [of the DJ] to this day."[7] He lauded the Americans as more willing "to take advantage of my help" than the British and asserted that they "helped me to the fullest possible extent."[8] In a passage later expunged from *Confessions*, the Beast also commended the Yanks for having "brains, and they used them."[9] Asked to confirm Crowley's connection in 1924, the new FBI Director J. Edgar Hoover replied, "I find nothing in the Bureau files that any information was furnished to the Department by CROWLEY during the war, or any time subsequent thereto."[10] Indeed, there is nothing in the extant files for the FBI or the earlier BI to demonstrate any collaboration with the Beast.

But the files alone do not tell the whole story. First, the same U.S. Military Intelligence report that identified the Beast as an "employee of the British Government" shows that the Justice Department was aware of his status by 1918, possibly earlier, through the "British Counsel [sic], New York City," which had "full cognizance" of Crowley's activities.[11] The Consul Charles Clive Bayley, who had been vice consul in Moscow during Crowley's "Ragged Rag-time Girls" tour.[12] In New York, Bayley worked very closely with Gaunt, Wiseman, and other British intelligence officers in the loop about Crowley's secret activities.

Other marks of the Beast survive in American files. Crowley stated that his cooperation with the Americans took root in a mutual interest in Viereck. That is confirmed by the MID summary, which notes that Crowley had been "formerly investigated by the Attorney General Becker's office in connection with the activities of George Verick [sic] and the propaganda in New York City."[13] Becker ran a separate investigative bureau for the State of New York, which determined that the "British Government was fully aware of the fact that Crowley was connected with this German propaganda" and did not disapprove.

Alfred LeRoy Becker, an active Freemason, was a deputy attorney general for the State of New York. He worked very closely with BI and other Federal agents, sharing assets and information. Hoover knew this but perhaps conveniently chose to ignore it. On the day Hoover wrote the denial above, he had received from the FBI's New York office a report that Crowley had been "examined" at least twice by Becker's assistant in 1918–1919 and had "furnished certain information" about himself and his associations.[14] Crowley noted that he had no "official" position in the British secret service, but detailed his dealings with Gaunt. In 1919, the same Becker told a Senate investigating committee that he had personally interviewed Crowley and received from him examples of "German propaganda" produced by Theodor Reuss.[15]

Crowley's link to the Feds certainly predated his contact with Becker. In late 1915, the Bureau of Investigation was still a small and decentralized organization. Local chiefs could employ whom they pleased how they pleased without the approval or knowledge of Washington. The Mage also had Gaunt to act as middleman, and Gaunt had cultivated connections in every branch of American law enforcement. The Captain could have pointed Crowley toward the BI chief in Detroit, John Preston, who was hot on Louis Smith's trail and anxious to grab him. In keeping with Gaunt's behind-the-scenes tactics, Crowley might even have abetted Preston's efforts without his knowledge.

This brings us back to the Parke-Davis peyote deal. Coinciding with Crowley's Detroit visit, Smith and his wife started to suffer from chronic paranoia and hallucinations. They believed that they were being watched and followed (they were), and even thought that C.C. Crowley, or someone who looked like him, was spying on them. Smith, driven over the edge, finally went to the police.[16] Once in custody he talked nonstop and by 28 October had confessed to his work with C.C. Crowley for Bopp. Oddly, the Feds kept all this under wraps for the next month.[17]

Could Crowley have dosed the Smiths? A key could be Mrs. Smith. She was a "masseuse," a job which likely involved offering sexual services to certain customers. Crowley enjoyed that sort of thing, and it offered an opportunity to meet and charm her, and perhaps offer something exotic to liven up her hubby's food—or libido. Crowley also could have used casual conversation to ferret out details about the Smith's household and habits that allowed BI agents to drug them.

Whatever happened in Detroit, Crowley's next stop was the Windy City. There he met German-American publisher Paul Carus, "who received me royally and showed me around the city."[18] It was no casual meeting. Carus was an important member of Muensterberg's propaganda gang, and Carus' magazine *Open Court* had published Crowley's recent panegyric upon the Kaiser, which blasted King George V as an "obscene dwarf."[19] Moreover, Carus was a good friend of Berlin's local Consul von Reiswitz and of Alvo von Alvensleben. Alvo maintained his main business office in Chicago and was in town during or just after Crowley's visit. The photo archive of the *Chicago Daily News* holds a picture of von Alvensleben dated 6 December 1915, annotated: "Came from Vancouver, B.C. Reputed to be head of Espionago [sic] in Chicago."[20] As usual, the Beast was keeping very interesting company.

There could have been another covert reason for Crowley's stop in Chicago. In fall 1915, agents of the Russian *Okhrana* (secret police) in New York detected a German plot to mobilize "anarchists" to assassinate the Tsar's military representatives in the United States and impede Allied war orders.[21] Chicago was the central recruiting ground for this scheme, but its conspiratorial tentacles reached all the way to San Francisco, the Beast's declared destination. One prominent anarchist linked to the plot was the would-be assassin Alexander Berkman, the comrade and lover of "Red Emma" Goldman.[22] Berkman actually discouraged collaboration with the Germans, but he was making plans for his own trip to San Francisco, for reasons unknown.

At this very time British agents in Switzerland were smashing a more grandiose "anarchist plot ... financed from Germany, for the assassination of every one of the heads of the Allied nations."[23] As mentioned, Crowley probably knew about this through British channels, or through Reuss. This and other clues suggest that Crowley's westward journey and secret assignment was somehow linked to the Interdepartmental Committee on Indian Sedition formed in London almost a year earlier. The nominal chief of the murderous cabal in Switzerland was the Indian nationalist (and later Communist) Virandranath "Chatto" Chattopadhyaya, intimately connected to the Indian Committee in Berlin and Gadar conspiracies in North America.[24] Chatto teamed up with the Italian anarchist Luigi Bertoni, who had his own ties to revolutionary brethren in New York, Chicago, and other American cities. Robert Nathan, a veteran of counter-subversion work in India, uncovered and foiled the Swiss plot. Nathan and Crowley may have met during the Mage's past visits to India, where Chief Commissioner Nathan was then combating the seditious activities of men like that dubious Bengali doctor Crowley met in China. Thanks to Nathan, by the end of November 1915 Swiss authorities had put more than a hundred suspects "of various nationalities" in custody.[25] Soon after Nathan headed for America.

Crowley finally reached Vancouver, whence Alvensleben had so recently come, about 16 October. Along the way, he initiated himself into the OTO's 9=2 degree and adopted a new title, *To Mega Therion,* "the Great Beast" or "Master Therion." By the time he crossed into Canada, he was using his Clifford alias. Canadian records show no trace of him coming or going, so the subterfuge seems to have worked. It was a wise precaution. Under the Canadian War Measures Act, *The Fatherland* was a banned publication, and Aleister Crowley was a known contributor.[26] He would run into trouble if he tried to cross the border under his real name.

In Vancouver, the new *Mega Therion* was impressed by the local faithful, especially Jones, who had "splendidly drilled" his band of initiates.[27] He confided to the loyal Jones that he was traveling under the name Clifford and was only to be referred to as such. He also insisted that Lodge members stay absolutely mum about his movements. He declined the hospitality of his followers in favor of the Hotel Vancouver, securing further privacy.

All this secrecy was not just to conceal his liaison with Mrs. Foster; Jones and the others would have been little scandalized by adultery. It is not even clear whether the Fosters were with Crowley or had separated from him before reaching Vancouver. Maybe Crowley had gotten wind of Jeanne's double game, or he wanted to keep her out of possible trouble. The Beast also confided to Jones that he was involved in "a matter touching on the welfare of the Empire."[28]

Crowley's precautions indicate that he feared being recognized or followed, but by whom? He may have been trying to hide from German agents—he would later tell Viereck and others that he was somewhere else at the time. What if Alvo had eyes and ears within the ranks of the local OTO, and what if they detected him in contact with British officials? Another risk was some overzealous Canadian official connecting Crowley with German propaganda and nosing around.

When Crowley departed Vancouver on 21 October, Wilfred Smith jotted in his diary that "Brother Clifford, A.E.C., Baphomet, has left Vancouver for Victoria. But I am inclined to think somewhere else—first at least."[29] Canadian Pacific ran a direct steamer service from Vancouver to Victoria, but Crowley's likely stop on the way was Nanaimo, also served by a CP steamer, which lay some sixty miles north of Victoria, near von Alvensleben's old stomping ground around Port Alberni. As noted, Alvensleben had loot stashed in Canada that he was anxious to retrieve. Canadian authorities were on high alert, knowing that he lurked just across the border in Seattle. In Vancouver, wild rumors told of Alvo's clandestine visits to the city by airplane or in drag.[30] Local lawmen scoured his rambling Kerrisdale estate overlooking the Fraser River for clues, drilling into beautifully paneled walls after secreted documents or treasure. Alvo, though, had cleverer hiding places than his main residence.

On Vancouver Island, high on scenic Malahat Mountain overlooking Victoria, was another grand stone house, later said to have been built by a "German prince." If not Alvo's, the manse belonged to one of his well-heeled *Deutscher* cronies. Its relative isolation made it an ideal hiding place but also complicated recovery. Decades later, vague rumors still floated around Victoria to the effect that the Malahat property had been "Aleister Crowley's house."[31] Of course, the Mage never owned any house there or even visited the Island for more than a couple of days. Still, the stories may contain a tiny but important grain of truth.

Just a few miles from the Malahat mansion lay the little community of Shawnigan Lake, also on the rail line between Nanaimo and Victoria. Shawnigan Lake also was the home of Horace and Betty Bickers. Mr. Bickers was a journalist and aspiring dramatist, and, a noted, part of the local OTO scene. Crowley, recall, had determined to rekindle his romance with Betty and free her from her unworthy husband. Betty had not accompanied her spouse to Vancouver for his recent initiation.

Maybe Crowley really did want to rescue lonely Betty, or maybe he used his supposed passion as an excuse to go after Alvo von Alvensleben's money. From the Bickers' home in Shawnigan Lake one could easily slip off to the "German prince's" house and secure whatever was stashed inside. Crowley has virtually nothing to say about his foray to Vancouver Island other than that it was brief and that he failed to persuade Betty to come away with him. From Victoria, he claims, he took a boat to Seattle. Seattle immigration records show no trace of Clifford, or Crowley, or anyone remotely like him. He was as invisible leaving Canada as he was entering it.

The next place the Beast can be placed with certainty is San Francisco on 5 November. One of the few details he recorded about this visit was that he was invited to address "a semi-private gathering" soon after his arrival.[32] Were the attendees drawn by interest in the OTO, or was something else on the agenda? The most intriguing detail, however, is his lodging, the Palace Hotel—the same establishment used by Bopp, von Brincken, and the other German conspirators as their base. Did

Viereck tip him off to that, or Alvensleben? A larger question is whether he revealed his presence to the Germans or watched them secretly.

In San Francisco, Crowley could have provided local British operative A. Carnegie Ross with any information he had gleaned about Alvo and German funding. Ross would have passed on that to U.S. officials, including the local BI branch. As the Americans later admitted, information provided by British agents, was absolutely essential in making the case against Bopp and his associates.[33]

Another man Crowley may have been looking for in San Francisco was Kurt Jahnke.[34] Alvo, former middleman between Jahnke and the ill-fated Rintelen, could have provided the introduction, especially if he had reason to trust our man. A big, pock-marked Prussian whose calm manner masked a cunning and mercenary mind, Jahnke was one of the greatest double, triple, or even quadruple agents of the twentieth century. By 1915 his colorful résumé included stints with the Chinese Customs Service (an early link to Crowley?), the U.S. Marine Corps, and smuggling everything from opium to Chinese corpses. He also found time to act as the lead agent in America of German naval intelligence, which mobilized him for sabotage service at the outset of the war, making him an unofficial advisor to Bernstorff and Boy-Ed.[35] Jahnke's present cover was to work for a Bay Area private detective firm, the Morse Patrol, which gave him access to the docks and even American Navy facilities. Jahnke worked with, though never really under, Bopp and his crew. He had collaborated with Louis Smith and C.C. Crowley in the February 1915 destruction of a barge of Russian explosives near Tacoma, Washington and knew all about their antics.

In fact, Jahnke's loyalty to the Kaiser was doubtful and definitely for sale. He had at least one other job, informer to the Americans. There are repeated references to Jahnke serving in the American "Customs Service" or "Secret Service" before the war, and that relationship continued in some form.[36] Jahnke seems to have had a connection with the Yanks much like that of fellow German double-agent Thummel/Thorne, from the *Lusitania* affair. Just before Crowley's arrival in San Francisco, and again soon after he left, Jahnke appeared in the local Bureau of Investigation office. His ostensible purpose was to report suspicious activity by German agents at the nearby Mare Island Navy Yard. That facility soon was the target of sabotage, an outrage the devious Jahnke later claimed for himself. Other American investigators were puzzled by the failure of the San Francisco BI office to pounce on Jahnke before or after the fact.[37] Of course, since he was one of their confidential informants, that was unnecessary. The versatile Jahnke would have unhesitatingly given information to a British agent, especially one on good terms with the BI. Along with knowing everything that Bopp was up to, Jahnke had useful connections to Indian nationalist circles and the Irish, including an "Irish Secret Lodge."[38]

Crowley's presence in town also coincided with a strange act of sabotage by Jahnke. In early November, Bopp ordered Jahnke to blow up a factory he believed to be secretly making munitions for the British. Bopp was mistaken; the business manufactured nothing more dangerous than cast-iron window sash-weights. As a result, the furious Bopp refused to pay Jahnke the full amount for the job, something that doubtless further undermined his loyalty to the Consul.[39]

The sash-weight fiasco was not the worst result of the Crowley curse, if such it was, to befall Bopp and his associates. On 26 November, shortly after the Beast had gone south, Federal agents swooped down. They first grabbed C.C. Crowley, using the information earlier extracted from the hysterical Smith, perhaps supplemented by Jahnke's. At almost the same instant, on the other side of the country, Gaunt's mouthpiece *The Providence Journal* ran a full exposé of Smith and C.C. Crowley's nefarious activities and their ties to Bopp. In short order, the Americans rolled up the whole German organization. By mid-December federal indictments loomed over C.C. Crowley, von Brincken, and others. The *Providence Journal* added more fuel to the fire by publishing double-agent van Koolbergen's confession, which implicated even more of the Kaiser's officials. Indictments rained down on Bopp and his *Kameraden* into early 1916. The worst was yet to come.

The German apparatus in America was falling apart in late 1915. British propaganda relentlessly kept the pressure on von Papen, Albert, and the rest of the East Coast leadership. On 8 December, President Wilson finally demanded Berlin's recall of Papen and Boy-Ed, and both were gone by the beginning of the New Year.[40] The Americans grabbed head saboteur Paul Koenig ten days later. The Germans were down, but not quite out.

Interestingly two figures, Viereck and von Alvensleben, escaped unscathed. So did Jahnke, with his preternatural slipperiness. Again, Viereck was less likely Crowley's dupe than his collaborator. The Beast may have likewise corrupted Alvo. The latter was, after all, a businessman, and if the Germans could not help him preserve his wealth, perhaps the British could. Crowley could have brokered a deal through which von Alvensleben quietly got back some of his moveable wealth for helping to bring down Bopp and friends.

After San Francisco, Crowley dropped out of sight for while—a smart move. He did not go far, however; his presence or advice might be needed. His refuge was quiet, scenic Santa Cruz, just south of the Bay Area, where he was reunited with Jeanne Foster. After a round of magick couplings with *Hilarion* beneath the redwoods and an inspired outburst of poetic exultation, the Mage's next known stop was Los Angeles. He found the place teeming with "the cinema crowd of cocaine-crazed, sexual lunatics, and the swarming maggots of near-occultists."[41] Perhaps Crowley was among those who took in the spectacle of the faux Babylon D.W. Griffith had constructed for his epic *Intolerance*, then in production. One person the Beast may have encountered during his brief stay was an aspiring actor and writer named Carl de Vidal Hundt (or Hunt). Among other things, Hundt was a friend of Bopp's underling von Brincken. As we will see, Crowley and Hundt were destined to meet in a very different time and place.

Leaving L.A., Crowley pushed on to San Diego where he paid a visit on the "Raja-

Yoga Academy and Temple of Peace" at nearby Point Loma. This was the Theosophical Society's American headquarters, run by Katherine Tingley. Crowley was repelled by the place's "nauseating atmosphere" and offended by Tingley's curt refusal to see him. His interest in her operation may have stemmed from more than curiosity.[42] Tingley was a bitter rival of another Theosophist luminary, Annie Besant. Besant was an outspoken proponent of Indian freedom and was suspected in London of using her movement to provide aid and comfort to "seditionists." Crowley's visit was an opportunity to see if any threads of the "German-Hindu Conspiracy" led to Point Loma or whether Tingley's hostility toward Besant could be exploited to serve the Empire.

After San Diego, Crowley's route becomes very hazy, possibly by design. He notes only two more stops: "Tia Juanta" [sic], Mexico, which he glowingly described as an oasis of "brothels, drinking saloons and gambling hells," and the Grand Canyon, where he briefly stretched his alpinist's legs. Thereafter he made his way back to New York by "short stages," without further details.

About a hundred miles east of Tijuana, along Crowley's route to the Canyon, lay another border town, Mexicali. It was the capital of a quasi-independent regime under Baja California's governor, Col. Esteban Cantu. He supplied regular reports to the BI and other American agencies about "German activity in Mexico."[43] Cantu was also a pal of Kurt Jahnke. Crowley could have expected a warm and informative reception from the Colonel. There was, after all, much going on south of the border to interest him and persons in Washington and London. Assuming he passed through the Southwest during late November and early December, Crowley had opportunity to make personal observations along the turbulent border.

The day after Christmas, the Beast surfaced in an interview in the *Washington Post*. This noted his presence in D.C. only a few days before.[44] The article presented him as an occult scholar dedicated to reconciling science and magic, but embedded in the piece were some revealing comments about the OTO and his labors on its behalf. Crowley said that he recently had founded "several lodges" on the Pacific Coast and that another was now "in process of formation in Washington." He characterized the Order as a "semi-Masonic organization" that "follows Rosicrucian lines," which makes it sound like that mysterious German order with a secret chief in Berlin. The stopover in Washington also gave Crowley a discreet opportunity to confer with Gaunt or others at the British Embassy.

At the end of December the Beast at last came to rest back in New York, where he took up temporary lodging at the Harvard Club on 44th Street. Beginning on December 29, *The Fatherland* ran his two-part article "Behind the Front," describing a recent incognito visit to France and England.[45] In this he mocked British censorship and vividly portrayed London as battered and demoralized by zeppelin raids. In an apparent sardonic jest, he generously provided the address of his Aunt Annie's house in Croydon so that the German bombers might be sure to hit her in their next raid. To anyone aware of how fond he was of this woman, as Feilding and a few others undoubtedly were, this joke revealed the piece for the fakery it was. Of course, Crowley had been nowhere near London or Paris in the preceding weeks, but might have convinced some of his German friends otherwise. In the wake of recent events on the West Coast, Crowley had reason to obscure his presence there.

In January 1916, Viereck's *International* ran another article by the Mage. The subject was a British nurse, Edith Cavell, whom the Germans had executed in Belgium the previous August for abetting the escape of Allied POWs. This act of apparent Hunnish brutality earned Berlin more bad press in the U.S. and elevated the martyred Miss Cavell to near sainthood in Britain. Crowley's little article, provocatively titled "The Crime of Edith Cavell," branded her a common spy, something the Germans alleged but never actually charged her with. According to the Mage, she got what was coming to her, although he regretted that the Kaiser missed the opportunity to garner Yankee goodwill by pardoning the wretch. Recently released British documents show that Nurse Cavell really was a spy, an SIS operative no less. Was Crowley's story a mere flight of fancy, or did he know the truth? Did he pen the deliberately inflammatory article on Gaunt's or Hall's secret orders in order to discredit by association the Germans' accusation of espionage?

Crowley arrived back in Manhattan just a week or so after Hanns Heinz Ewers, traveling as Ernest Renfer, returned from Spain. Ewers soon was off on another secret mission for the Kaiser in northern Mexico, near where Crowley had been roaming so recently. Ewers' mission there was to convince the volatile Mexican rebel leader Pancho Villa to turn his hostile attentions on the Americans. This, it was hoped in Berlin, would divert energy and armaments from the war in Europe. The Wilson Administration had recently bestowed de facto recognition on Villa's rival in Mexico City, Venustiano Carranza, and cut off the guns and money flowing to Villa.[46] Pancho was out for revenge. Ewers' labors paid off spectacularly. In January 1916, Pancho demonstrated his displeasure by murdering sixteen (or seventeen) American miners in the Chihuahuan town of Santa Isabel. In March, he took the fight to American soil in a daring but costly raid on Columbus, New Mexico. Wilson rushed General John J. Pershing and an expeditionary force to the border, and for the next year the U.S. and Mexico hovered on the brink of war.

How much Ewers confided about his activities to friend Crowley, and how much the Beast passed on to his British superiors, we can only guess. At this time the American press was full of stories about German intrigues to sow conflict between the U.S. and Mexico. Unsurprisingly, Gaunt and Hall were the source of many of these revelations.[47]

Another German agent working on Villa and well-known to Ewers was Arnoldo Krumm-Heller (a.k.a. Arnold Krumm).[48] A one-time Theosophist, esoteric freemason, and founder of his own Rosicrucian order, *Fraternitas Rosicruciana Antiqua* (FRA), Krumm had been a pupil of both Theodor Reuss and Don Jesus de Medina. There is no evidence that Crowley and Krumm met at this time, which is not to say that they were unaware of each other. Krumm was one of Berlin's most important agents in the pro-German Carranza's entourage. A grateful Presidente made Krumm an honorary lieutenant colonel on his general staff.[49] In addition, in early 1916 Carranza appointed Krumm military attaché to Berlin. That spring, on his way to the Reich, Krumm stopped near New York, waiting to catch a Danish steamer. He kept a low profile and traveled under the alias Dr. von Carey. Ewers, however, knew of his presence, something he easily might have let slip to Crowley. Somehow American and British authorities got wind of Krumm's visit and destination.

Soon after, at the Scottish port of Kirkwall, where Krumm's ship stopped for blockade inspection, British authorities grabbed him. Scotland Yard chief Basil Thomson recalls the episode in his memoirs, including Krumm's odd behavior. Although the German insisted that he was a Mexican citizen and the emissary of a neutral country, Thomson knew that his real mission was "propaganda." Moreover, Thomson knew that Krumm was carrying a secret letter from von Bernstorff to Berlin. When Krumm's protests fell on deaf ears, he offered to cut a deal by revealing "a new German plan and would thus save the Allies thousands of lives."[50] Could this have been Crowley's "turncoat spell" at work again? In the end, according to Thomson, Krumm had nothing to offer, and the British put him on the next boat back to Mexico.

Another character who drew the attention of the entire British apparatus in New York in January 1916 was the troublesome I.T. Trebitsch-Lincoln, who escaped American custody. To say the British were angered and dismayed by this development is an understatement. Although a U.S. court had approved his extradition to England the preceding fall, the wily Trebitsch delayed his departure by ingratiating himself with his American captors. He convinced the head of the Bureau of Investigation in Gotham, William Offley, that he could break German codes and help uncover Berlin's intrigues, including the passport fraud case that involved Viereck and Ewers.[51] If nothing else, this suggests that Offley would have gladly accepted a like overture from Crowley, with or without the British Consul's or Washington's approval. Trebitsch similarly solicited the British, but Consul Bayley quickly determined that he was faking his expertise. Frustrated and alarmed, Bayley and others would have welcomed the application of the Beast's special talents in the effort to recapture the fugitive.

The Americans proved gullible, in several ways. Trebitsch got out of lockup regularly to "work" at the nearby federal building and even wangled evening furloughs for dining, drinking, and skirt-chasing. He so beguiled the federal marshal assigned to watch him that one evening he simply walked away. Trebitsch remained a free man for thirty-five days before being caught casually strolling down Broadway by BI agents. He was planning to board a ship to the Far East a day or so later. The Bureau's success was not blind luck: they had been tipped off to Trebitsch's whereabouts and new appearance by unnamed informants who included "naturalized citizens of German birth."[52] That could have included Viereck and behind him, Crowley.

1   *CAC*, 767.

2   WWP, 6/161, Granville Barker to Wiseman, 20 Nov. 1916.

3   Martin A. Lee and Bruce Shlain, *Acid Dreams, The Complete Social History of LSD: The CIA, the Sixties and Beyond* (NY: Grove Press, 1985), 5–6.

4   *CAC*, 490.

5   At one such gathering, probably in spring or summer 1915, Crowley dosed Theodore Dreiser with the drug. See: Oliver Marlow Wilkinson, "Aleister Crowley Rest In?," in Colin Wilson (ed.), *Men of Mystery* (London: W. A. Allen, 1977), 98.

6   Steve Jackson to author, 13 July 2003.

7   Renegade.

8   Renegade.

9   Thanks to William Breeze for this information. The passage originally was appended to p. 754 of the Symonds-Grant edition.

10 FBI, file 61-2069 (FOIPA 229,138), "Crowley, Edward Alexander," Hoover to Brennan, SCA New York, 1 Aug. 1924. The author of the original query, clearly from one of The Beast's followers, was most likely Norman Mudd. Special thanks to Martin Starr for the information.

11 USNA, MID 10012-112/1, "General Summary," 23 Sept. 1918, 4.

12 *CAC*, 716.

13 USNA, MID 10012-112/1, *Ibid.*

14 Crowley FBI file, Brennan, Memorandum for Mr. Hoover, 1Aug. 1924, 2–3.

15 Sixty-Sixth Congress, U.S. Senate, Subcommittee on the Judiciary, *Brewing and Liquor Interests and German and Bolshevik Propaganda*, Vol. 2, (Washington, 1919), 2027–2028.

16 *NYT* (15 Dec. 1915), 3.

17 *NYT* (28 Nov 1915), 3, and (3 Dec. 1915), 3.

18 *CAC*, 751.

19 *Open Court* (Aug. 1915), and *CAC*, 751.

20 "Alvo von Alvensleben," *Photographs from the Chicago Daily News, 1902–1937*, //memory.loc.gov.

21 Hoover Institution Archives [HIA], Stanford, Paris Okhrana Collection, file, XXVb, 2, "Note," 5 Feb. 1916.

22 In 1892, Berkman shot steel magnate Henry Clay Frick. Frick survived and Berkman spent fourteen years in prison.

23 "Secret Service Work in the War: Sir R. Nathan's Work, *The Times* (28 June 1921), 10.

24 Barooah, *Chatto*, 133–137.

25 *NYT* (12 Sept. 1915), 3:2 and (28 Nov. 1916), II, 2:7.

26 National Archives of Canada, RG 6, Secretary of State, series E, Vol. 596, File 269-118 re *A Prophet in His Own Country* and RG 18, Records of the Royal Canadian Mounted Police.

27 *CAC*, 769.

28 Starr, *Unknown God*, 37.

29 *Ibid.*, 39.

30 Jo erg Nagler, "Enemy Aliens and Internment in World War I: Alvo von Alvensleben in Fort Douglas, Utah, a Case Study," *Utah Historical Quarterly*, Vol. 58 (1990), 392–394, and Terry Reksten, "Alvo von Alvensleben—Kaiser's Secret Agent?," *The Illustrated History of British Columbia*, at //archives. rootsweb/com/th/read/GERMAN-NOBILITY/2002-10/1033695058.

31 Steve Jackson to author, 5 Sept. 2003.

32 *CAC*, 804.

33 WWP, 6/161, Wiseman to Chief, 6 Sept. 1918.

34 On Jahnke, see: Richard Spence, "K.A. Jahnke and the German Sabotage Campaign in the United States and Mexico, 1914–1918," *The Historian*, Vol. 59, #1 (Fall 1996), 89–112.

35 USNA, MID 10541-268 and KV 2/755, Extract S.F. 1/8b, 26 April 1918.

36 UKNA, KV 2/755, Schellenberg Report, 23 Aug. 1945 and *Ibid.*, Extract from G.F.K. Kraft, 24 Oct. 1917.

37 MID 10541-367, DS report re Jahnke, C.A., 19 March 1918, quoting 9 Feb. 1916 report by BI Special Agent in Charge, Rathbun.

38 Spence, "Jahnke," 98-99.

39 FBI, file on Kurt Jahnke, #62-5394-2, Memorandum for Mr. Hoover, 30 April 1923.

40 Papen departed on 21 Dec., Boy-Ed on 1 Jan.

41 *CAC*, 770.

42 *CAC*, 771.

43 Mahoney, 270.

44 *Washington Post* (26 Dec. 1915), 2.

45 *The Fatherland*, Vol. III, #21 (29 Dec. 1915) and #22 (5 Jan. 1916).

46 For background, see: Friedrich Katz, *The Life and Times of Pancho Villa* (Palo Alto, CA: Stanford Univ. Press, 1998) and Katz's *The Secret War in Mexico* (Chicago: Univ. of Chicago Press, 1984).

47 *NYT* (8 Dec. 1915), 1.

48 Peter Koenig, "Baphomet and Rosycross, *Fraternitas Rosicruciana Antiqua*: Biography of Arnoldo Krumm-Heller," //user.cyberlin.ch/~koenig/fra.htm.

49 *Ibid.*

50 Basil Thomson, *Queer People* (London: Hodder & Stoughton, 1922), 199–200.

51 *NYT* (20 Feb. 1916), 1:6.

52 *NYT* (21 Feb. 1916) 3:2.

~

CHAPTER EIGHT

SHIFTING SANDS

~

WHILE CROWLEY WAS AWAY FROM NEW YORK, the British intelligence array in North America was changing. Shortly before the Beast arrived in San Francisco, two British businessmen disembarked in New York. Forty-four-year-old Sydney Mansfield and thirty-year-old Sir William Wiseman were really intelligence officers dispatched from London. Mansfield had been hand-picked by Lord Kitchener, and Wiseman by Commander Mansfield Cumming, chief of the Secret Intelligence Service (SIS), then operating as MI1c.

Gaunt was not at all happy to see them. The Captain mobilized the support of his friends at Morgan & Co. to resist the unwanted intrusion of the "secret service" into "our organization" and even sought the intervention of Ambassador Spring-Rice.[1] Gaunt later gloated that he quickly sent the "gumshoe merchants" packing back to England.[2] He had won the skirmish, but he already had unwittingly lost the war.

The appearance of Mansfield and Wiseman indicated growing concerns in London. Gaunt's role as spymaster was, after all, not part of the legitimate duties of a naval attaché, all the more because it was general knowledge to the enemy and most everyone else. His overextension threatened to compromise him and his government just as von Papen and Boy-Ed had done.[3] The second concern related to Gaunt's handling of expenses, especially those related to Morgan's protection of munitions ships. Gaunt had persuaded the Morgan-contracted Dougherty Detective Agency to reduce some of its exorbitant charges, all billable to His Majesty, but overcharging and outright fraud were still rampant.[4] Unsurprisingly, neither the Captain nor 23 Wall Street welcomed outsiders poking their noses into the matter.

In January 1916, Wiseman returned to Manhattan and, with the full backing of Cumming and the Foreign Office, set up what he termed "MI1c, Section V" in the Consulate at 44 Whitehall Street. His broad mandate included "Contre-Espionage" and the investigation of Irish and "Hindu" sedition in the U.S.[5] It also came to include a good deal of propaganda activity and even more secretive and sensitive black ops.

A hereditary baronet (which also stuck in Gaunt's craw), Wiseman was a banker by profession. More recently he was an Army captain wounded in Flanders, which left him with impaired eyesight and led to his reassignment to intelligence work.

In contrast to the big, brash, and flamboyant Gaunt, Wiseman was a small, plump, soft-spoken, and scrupulously polite young fellow whose pencil mustache struggled to give gravitas to a round baby face. His disarming appearance disguised a subtle and cunning mind, much abler than Gaunt's for spy work. Gaunt insisted later that Wiseman did nothing but "play a very small part under me," but the reality was something else entirely.[6] Slowly but inexorably, Gaunt was marginalized and finally wholly displaced by Wiseman's operation.

Wiseman's job required him to wear a number of hats, all kept neatly compartmentalized as befitted a master conspirator. While he continued Gaunt's policy of close cooperation with the Americans, he confided to London that the Yanks had never known "the details and extent of our organization" and never would.[7] He also organized a separate "political and Secret Service organization" that he ran all by himself.[8] This doubtless was connected to Wiseman's most confidential mission, as an agent of influence on the Wilson Administration with the aim of bringing the U.S. into the war.[9] That certainly gave him something in common with Crowley, who had labored in the same vineyard for some time. Something else that Wiseman and the Beast would come to share was a postwar charge of treason.[10]

Two more experienced operatives arrived in early 1916 to support Wiseman. Major Norman Graham Thwaites, an ex-journalist who became Wiseman's right-hand man, had many old acquaintances in New York, such as Crowley's friend Cosgrave. The other man was Robert Nathan, the veteran Indian Civil Service officer who recently had been battling assassination plots in Switzerland.[11]

Interestingly, the only known SIS document about Crowley to see light of day is a brief report from "Contre-Espionage, New York" (Wiseman's outfit) dated 8 March 1916 that somehow ended up in a French intelligence file.[12] It looks like a response to a query from London, and indicates copies sent to NID, Military Intelligence, and MI5. The document is little more than a summary of articles about Crowley that had appeared in the American press, including the *World* piece of December 1914. Most attention focuses on the *New York Times* coverage of his performance at the Statue of Liberty and his membership in the supposed Irish "Secret Revolutionary Committee." Based on this, the report identifies Crowley as "an Irish agitator" but makes no reference to his many German connections nor does it make any definite statement regarding his loyalty. This contrasts tellingly with notices sent out by MI5 about the same time unequivocally identifying our man as a "pro-German propagandist" and "degenerate Irish journalist" who was to be "searched and sent [to] Metropolitan Police, London" if apprehended in a British port.[13] Thus, Wiseman or Thwaites acknowledged nothing that was not already public record. The report indicates no interest in investigating Crowley further.

Wiseman and Thwaites behaved precisely the same way toward another doubtful character and British operative running around wartime New York—Sidney Reilly. Reilly's and Crowley's paths had crossed before, from Victorian London to prewar Russia, though whether they had met is unknown. Nevertheless, both ended up in the service of British intelligence. Reilly arrived in the States in January 1915 in the guise of a war contractor for the Russian Government. In New York, he insinuated himself into the affairs of the corrupt and spy-infested Russian Supply Committee, turning his influence there into a small fortune. At the same time, like Crowley, he assiduously cultivated contacts with the Germans, including those involved in propaganda and sabotage.[14]

Norman Thwaites later devoted a whole chapter to Reilly in his memoirs, in which he praised Reilly's "valuable services" to British intelligence.[15] Nevertheless, Thwaites—and Wiseman—spun a very different story to American investigators during the war, denouncing him as probably an enemy agent. They deliberately withheld information about him and his activities from MI5. This is an example of one intelligence section concealing its assets from an allied agency. The same standard operating procedure was used to obscure Crowley's roles.

Gaunt, as might be expected, was never so clever or discreet. In 1917, hoping to embarrass and compromise Wiseman, he denounced Reilly to the Americans as an enemy agent.[16] Gaunt could not make a similar fuss about Crowley, because that would implicate him as well. The Mage's name did come up during Gaunt's visit to London in November 1916. On that visit, he had his "long talk" about Crowley with Scotland Yard chief Basil Thomson. Gaunt later recounted the incident to John Symonds, to whom he also supposedly characterized Crowley as a "small time traitor." Gaunt told Symonds he "preached" to Thomson to "Let [Crowley] alone, I have a complete line on him and also *The Fatherland*."[17] Why would Gaunt have thought it necessary to intercede on behalf of a traitor, even a petty one? More likely, what he really told Thomson was that he had a complete line on *The Fatherland* *through* Crowley. Gaunt simply interceded to protect a useful asset.

Gaunt's postwar recollections about Crowley may have been tainted by lingering bitterness toward Viereck and Wiseman. In a 1929 article in the *Saturday Evening Post*, Viereck accurately portrayed Wiseman as the real brains of British intelligence in wartime America and included a rather uncomplimentary portrayal of the jaunty Australian.[18] This insult must have stung all the more if, as surmised, Viereck also had been one of Gaunt's informants. Gaunt seethed about Viereck's "gross libel" for the rest of his life, and it fed his vendetta against Wiseman. Gaunt raged that he knew enough about Viereck "to hang him" but insisted that he had "arranged" with Admiral Hall to leave him alone because it was "better [to] have a devil one knows all about than perchance get a stranger one knew nothing of."[19] Crowley could have convinced him of that. If so, Gaunt may have thought the Beast an accomplice in Viereck's libel. In Gaunt's mind, which appears to have become a bit unstable in his declining years, maybe Crowley really did become a "traitor"—to him.

Basically, Crowley came back to New York to find British intelligence under new management. Like any employee in that situation, he had to wonder where that left him. One effect was probably financial: Crowley was on a leaner budget after his return and would remain so for some time. Of course, that may have been his fault. Never one to travel on the cheap, he likely spent every penny he had received. That left him with what Viereck paid him plus money from freelance writing. Wiseman, who knew a thing or two about finances, kept a tight rein on accounts. Plus, there may have been some questions about just what Crowley did in Canada and whether he had thereby enriched himself. Wiseman and his Section V routinely shared information with "Canadian Police and Military authorities."[20] Perhaps this is why Crowley later complained that because the Germans paid him, "the British Government decided to pay me less."[21]

Wiseman had no personal experience with Crowley and good reasons to regard him with caution. To exacerbate the uncertainty, Crowley's old ally and controller, Feilding, left London and NID for the Eastern Mediterranean Special Intelligence Bureau (EMSIB) in January 1916.[22] Because of Wiseman's paramount political duties, the day-to-day operation of Section V more and more fell into the hands of Norman Thwaites, a man more likely than Wiseman to have viewed Crowley with favor, or at least curiosity. For one thing, Thwaites took a keen interest in the paranormal and the occult. He was familiar with, and possibly a member of, Feilding's Society for Psychical Research. Moreover, the EMSIB, to which Feilding now belonged, was the Middle Eastern branch of SIS. This common connection explains Feilding's ability to maintain contact with the Beast while stationed in the Near East.

In his memoirs, Thwaites recounts a peculiar episode in which he and some New York friends used a Ouija board and a medium to ferret out a German-Indian plot involving stolen passports.[23] It is quite possible that the Beast played a part in the case. About this time the Mage took a new interest in the oracular board. Thwaites further mentions that he had an agent, "#27," with contacts inside the German Consulate, who presented his boss with a copy of a German surveillance report detailing Thwaites' own movements.[24]

Crowley's return to New York coincided with the arrival of another traveler from abroad, Paul Marie Bolo Pasha. Like the Mage, Bolo had been lurking in Switzerland when the war started. In the interim, he had become the personal agent of the exiled Khedive of Egypt, hence his "Pasha" title. Bolo also became a willing tool of the Germans and the point man in a scheme to sow defeatism in the French press. That connected him to a corrupt French politician, Joseph Caillaux.[25] The plan called for the German funds to be laundered through the Guaranty Trust Company in New York with help from one of its employees, Jacques Minotto.[26] Minotto was friends with von Bernstorff, Dernburg, Viereck, and most of the rest of the New York German crowd. He also had ties to Chicago, which, along with his banking expertise, suggests a link to von Alvensleben. Once more, Crowley was well-placed to discover some secrets. French authorities got wind of the plot, arrested Bolo Pasha in fall 1917, and shot him the following April. About the same time, the Bureau of Investigation arrested Minotto as a German agent.

One thing that did not long survive the Beast's return to New York, if it made it that far, was his romance with Jeanne Foster. He seems to have taken her "betrayal" hard, but wasted no time finding solace elsewhere. There was still loyal Leila, of course, but during April Crowley began simultaneous affairs with two other women. In both cases more was involved than sex and magick.[27]

The first was Gerda Maria von Kothek, identified as a German prostitute and the "brilliant young angel of Revolution."[28] Her real name was Gerda Schumann and she was around nineteen when she met the Beast. Not long after, possibly even before, Gerda married another German immigrant. Dr. Rudolf Gebauer, and the pair took up residence in Passaic, New Jersey. A chemist employed at a nearby plant, Gebauer shared his wife's radical sympathies, but he had other interesting connections. First, he had ties the main German radical organ in Manhattan, the *New Yorker Volkszeitung*, run by veteran socialist Ludwig Lore. Clandestine threads tied Lore's anti-war publication to the *Propaganda Kabinett* and German Consulate.

The Bureau of Investigation took an interest in Gebauer in April 1917. An unnamed source claimed that he was in league with von Bernsdorff, von Papen, Koenig and other German plotters, but a brief investigation turned up no tangible evidence.[29] Might Crowley have provided such information in the hope of getting the good doctor out of the way? One more thing that could have attracted the Mage's attention was Gebauer's membership in the German University League. A leading member of the same body was Hugo Muensterberg. Berlin's agents cultivated radicals not just as assassins, but also as saboteurs, instigators of plant and dock strikes and anti-war agitators. A chemist could have all manner of uses. As Gerda's lover, Crowley had yet another means to monitor such intrigues.

Gerda may be the same "German prostitute" linked to the second new woman in Crowley's life, Alice Coomaraswamy, better known by her stage name, Ratan Devi. The Yorkshire-born Devi, who "possessed a strange seductive beauty and charm," had mastered the intricacies of Indian singing and was the wife of the Anglo-Indian critic and writer Ananda Coomaraswamy.[30] The pair landed in New York not long after Crowley returned from his travels. Coomaraswamy, according to Crowley, shared his interest in "Asiatic religion and Magic," but it was Devi who fell madly in love with the Beast.[31]

Unsurprisingly, Crowley later voiced contempt for the man he cuckolded. He expressed special disgust with Coomaraswamy's creation of a *ménage à trois* which compelled his wife to share a bed with the "German prostitute" he had taken in.[32] There was more to this than sex. The two women swapped confidences about Coomaraswamy, and both would have been willing to share the same with the Mage, especially if they both were sleeping with him, too. By seducing Coomaraswamy's wife and planting another girlfriend in his bed, Crowley could keep tabs on everything Coomaraswamy did and everyone he met. The Beast had his reasons.

Crowley's animus toward Coomaraswamy went beyond jealousy or contempt for a cad. He ultimately declared the Eurasian nothing less than a "Black Brother," i.e. a member of the sinister Black Brotherhood, adept of the dark arts and a servitor of the German cause.[33] Coomaraswamy definitely had Indian nationalist sympathies and consorted with that circle in New York. His Indian associates included Sailandranath Gose, the man Wiseman later stood accused of conniving with. From the British standpoint, Coomaraswamy wanted careful, discreet watching.

The man who would have been most interested in anything Crowley obtained from Coomaraswamy was Robert Nathan. In May 1916, Nathan embarked on his own cross-country trip that closely followed Crowley's earlier route. He headed to Vancouver and then to San Francisco, where he revitalized and expanded the covert campaign against the Indians, Irish, and Germans with the willing cooperation of local authorities. Among Nathan's informants in New York was one known simply as "C" who did much to illuminate the doings of the Indo-Irish-German nexus.[34] One theory pegs "C" as Chandra Chakravarty, another nationalist who enjoyed the confidence of German officials.[35] However, given the connections noted above, it is just as possible that "C" stood for Crowley.

In the meantime, American authorities, egged on and assisted by British agents, kept up the hunt for German plotters and saboteurs. A leader in this campaign was Inspector Thomas Tunney, chief of the NYPD's crack Bomb Squad. He also was an old pal of Thwaites, who later praised Tunney as a man who "has been of great service to the British Authorities here."[36] On 10 April 1916, Tunney's men arrested Karl von Kleist, who was mixed up with a New Jersey bomb factory run by another German, Dr. Walter Scheele. Its explosive devices reached German agents as far away as New Orleans. Tunney's men managed this coup by convincing von Kleist that they were working for yet another of Berlin's operatives, Wolf von Igel, Papen's former secretary.[37]

Kleist ended up betraying Scheele, and his confession had a familiar twist; he claimed that the Americans had drugged him—perhaps Crowley had come to the rescue with a dose of tongue-loosening peyote.

Meanwhile a much bigger game was afoot in New York and off the stormy west cost of Ireland. Breaking Kleist helped Tunney close in on von Igel, whom the Americans nabbed on 18 April. A search of von Igel's office turned up documentation of a conspiracy linking John Devoy and Clan-na-Gael with compatriots in Dublin and Roger Casement in Berlin. Their aim was an Irish insurrection that the Germans had pledged to support with guns and ammunition.[38]

Included in Igel's papers was a cipher message mentioning a shipment of German arms already on its way. On 21 April, British naval forces intercepted the Norwegian merchant ship *SS Aud Norge* off the Irish coast. The *Aud*, in reality a disguised German vessel, was carrying 20,000 rifles, ten machine guns, and millions of rounds of ammunition intended for the doomed uprising later known as the Easter Rebellion (24 April–1 May).[39] The *Aud's* nervous skipper scuttled the ship and surrendered with his crew. For the Irish rebels the disaster was compounded by the almost simultaneous capture of Casement, who had arrived by U-boat on a beach near Tralee.

Devoy blamed the Americans for the fiasco, because they revealed his cipher message to the British. This caused some concern and head-scratching in Washington. State Department intelligence insisted that the *Aud* was undone by "the British Naval Intelligence Service" with no official help from U.S. authorities.[40] It did appear, however, that "the information was given probably informally by American secret agents to the British Service."[41] Another document pointed to unnamed "Justice's agents" as the most likely to have been involved.[42] In reality, the British picked up information about the Easter Conspiracy from a variety of places, but New York was one. With his connections to the BI and British intelligence (especially NID), Crowley would have been a reliable and deniable conduit for passing information between them.

The Beast certainly followed these Irish events and tried to exploit them for propagandistic effect. On 12 May 1916, the *Washington Post* ran a letter from him in which he claimed that his earlier declaration of Irish independence had been the inspiration for the recent uprising.[43] "I begat the Irish republic on Great Mother Time," he wrote, "in due course the first born has come to light." He went on to urge all true Irishmen to forgive England for its sins and for both nations to approach each other in a spirit of equality and reconciliation. Of course, unless London granted independence, he also predicted further bloodshed.

It is even possible that Crowley played a subtle role in sealing the fate of Roger Casement, who stood trial for treason on 26 June 1916 in London. The court handed down a verdict of guilty three days later. Casement's treason was not in question; the only issue was whether or not he would hang for it. He was still a highly respected figure, and many voices called for clemency, among them John Quinn's. However, the release of the "Black Diaries," which vividly detailed Casement's homosexual promiscuity, silenced most of these pleas. He died on the gallows at Pentonville Prison on 3 August.

Interestingly, Gaunt's name crops up in connection to the "leaking of the Casement homosexuality scandal."[44] There were, and still are, questions about the authenticity of the incriminating diaries. Gaunt's task was to dredge up supporting evidence from Casement's time in New York. Since Quinn dismissed the homosexuality charge, who would have been better suited to collect or concoct such dirt than Crowley?

Crowley records that "during this time [spring 1916], I was often away in Washington."[45] As usual, he offers no particular reason why, but he was not shy about advertising his presence in the American capital. On 30 April (Beltane), the *Washington Post* ran a short article by him commenting on a recent sensational murder case involving New York dentist Dr. Arthur Warren Waite (no relation to A.E. Waite of the Golden Dawn).[46] Waite had killed his in-laws and tried to kill his wife with arsenic and germ cultures. Crowley's comments were reserved for Waite's claim to have been driven to the deed by demonic forces, something the Mage considered entirely possible.

Next, on 26 May, the Beast appeared at D.C.'s National Press Club, where he lost a series of games against chess whiz Norman Tweed Whitaker.[47] The real purpose of Crowley's trip to the capital was his affair with "Stuart X." This was the pseudonym of Henry Clifford Stuart, an eccentric economist who hired Crowley to introduce and edit his rambling essays on politics and culture into a self-published book titled *A Prophet in His Own Country*.[48] This book, incidentally, was censored by Canadian (but not British) authorities because of Crowley's involvement.

Outwardly, the Beast's participation in the project was a purely mercenary arrangement, perhaps an act of financial desperation, but this does not rule out other angles. Stuart intended the book as propaganda for his challenge to Woodrow Wilson in the upcoming presidential election. That made Stuart a potentially useful tool for German propagandists, such as Crowley ostensibly was. Moreover, Stuart was familiar with at least two passionately pro-German members of the American literati, Theodore Dreiser and the "Sage of Baltimore," H.L. Mencken, both of whom also knew Crowley.[49] If nothing else, this explains how Crowley and Stuart met.

The arrangement with Stuart gave Crowley a legitimate reason to visit D.C. and an opportunity to learn about the region's Germanophile nexus. That could have been very valuable from the intelligence perspective. Expulsions and arrests had shattered the German secret apparatus in New York, and the East Coast center had shifted to Baltimore and the ring run by Thummel's old friend, Frederich Hinsch. In fact, Hinsch and his comrades were now involved in a disturbing escalation of the sabotage campaign.

In the quiet Washington suburb of Chevy Chase, only five miles from Stuart's home, German agents were hard at work making biological weapons. The head of this diabolical enterprise was a thirty-one-year-old American-born physician, Anton Dilger. Raised and mostly educated in Germany, Dilger had volunteered for the Kaiser's army in 1914 but was mustered out after suffering some physical or mental breakdown. Still, he was determined to aid Germany's cause. Dilger had made a detailed study of *Bacillus anthracis*, better known as anthrax, and related pathogens. In October 1915, he returned to the U.S. (using his American passport) with cultures of anthrax and glanders. With the help of his brother Carl, he set about mass-producing the organisms in a home lab. He then supplied disease-laden vials to Hinsch's operatives in Baltimore and elsewhere to infect horses and other animals being shipped to Allied countries.[50]

Dilger's activities may throw light on Crowley's sudden interest in the similar methodology of Dr. Waite. Rumors of Dilger's operation had leaked out by the spring of 1916, possibly via Ewers, who knew Dilger through connections in Spain and Mexico. Spurred by clues from Ewers, Crowley's visits to D.C. may have aimed to sniff out Dilger's lab. Perhaps he thought the Waite article would smoke out some information. If so, he failed, because Dilger's germ factory continued to crank out pathogens until he returned to Germany in the coming autumn.

Crowley also made a quick trip in mid-May 1916 to Philadelphia, where he had briefly stayed a year before. This was to visit another old acquaintance from England, novelist Louis Wilkinson, husband of the American poet Frances Gregg. Wilkinson shared an interest in magic and was one of a few who remained a friend of the Beast to the end. Wilkinson had no evident connection to intelligence matters, but Crowley arrived in the City of Brotherly Love the day after Hinsch's men destroyed the Dupont munitions plant in nearby Gibbstown, NJ.

Frances Gregg did not share her husband's enthusiasm for Crowley. In fact, she feared and loathed him as a kind of evil spirit who haunted her for the rest of her life. She later confided to her son, Oliver Wilkinson, a disturbing incident during the war. Walking into a room of her home that she had every expectation of finding empty, Frances was shocked to find "a bald man at the table."[51] As she watched, "the man put on his hair, and turned into Crowley." She claimed that Crowley carried a case full of wigs. Gregg also was disturbed by his peculiar efforts to hide himself, or literally make himself invisible, in restaurants and other public places. These weird incidents convinced Mrs. Wilkinson that her husband's friend was some sort of "master criminal" involved in sinister conspiracies. The Beast tried to convince

Wilkinson that his wife was crazy, and Gregg probably was overly imaginative. Along with her instinctive dislike of the man, however, another explanation may be that she had encountered and misread aspects of Crowley's clandestine work. He had always enjoyed disguises, and they would have been useful in undercover duties. Something Gregg may not have appreciated was that her husband could have been a willing accessory to such activity.

Crowley made another short trip at the end of April to Bronxville, a quiet Hudson Valley town just north of Manhattan. It, too, was close to New Rochelle, which he had visited months before. This somehow connected to his relations with Winslow Plummer and the Rosicrucians. Maybe it involved the secret communications with the Berlin head of their "German order." Crowley later told Attorney General Becker that Reuss had paid a secret visit to the Bronx. Did he mean Bronxville? The Beast also said that he had reported this to officials of the Bureau.

It was through Plummer that Crowley met Henry Christopher Watts. The Welsh-born Watts was secretary of another esoteric religious order, the Society of Atonement, which was based further up the Hudson in Garrison, New York. The avowed goal of the Society was the reunion of the Anglican Church with Rome.[52] That was identical to the aspirations of some of the Jacobites Crowley had associated with back in the 1890s. Watts, however, had another job, as agent for London's Department of Information, later the Ministry of Information. This was run by John Buchan, the same man to whom NID operative Gerald Kelly reported.

British archives once contained four files on Watts and his activities. Like Crowley's, all have vanished. From the few traces remaining, Watts worked as a propagandist feeding articles to Catholic papers in the U.S., as a counter to German and Fenian influence. A 3 November 1917 letter from Watts to the Foreign Office shows that he was familiar with Crowley and his associates. In it Watts linked John Devoy, Frank Harris, and Viereck to each other and to Crowley, and all to German propaganda. He called our man a "renegade Englishman . . . , a mystic and Rosicrucian," who of late had taken a strange interest in becoming a Roman Catholic.[53] In pursuit of that goal, seemingly an odd one for the Beast, Crowley used one of his women (Leila? Gerda?) to approach a "well-known Catholic poet" at the *New York Times*, apparently without result. Watts was certain that Frank Harris was in the thick of whatever was going on. Crowley's Roman gambit may have been connected to a recent Papal peace initiative and resulting efforts by Germany and the Allies to exploit it to their advantage.[54] The Vatican's actions threatened to affect Catholic opinion in the U.S., not least among the Irish. Watts is another fine example of one British agent not recognizing another, perhaps just as it was meant to be.

Another recent arrival from Europe must have piqued Crowley's interest. She was "Baroness" Ida Leonie von Seidlitz, a longtime Berlin operative who had most recently tried her hand in lobbying members of the Tsar's Government to seek a separate peace. In spring 1916, she ran a neat little operation out of her rooms at the Waldorf-Astoria. She recruited a stable of attractive young women whom she maneuvered into relationships with targeted men. One of her protégées was the Russian ballerina Tamara Svirskaya, who ended up the bedmate of the local Russian Consul General, Dmitrii Florinskii.[55] Yet another intimate of the Baroness was Rozika Schwimmer, the Hungarian-Jewish pacifist (and reputed Austrian agent) who had persuaded Henry Ford to mount his abortive "Peace Ship" effort in late 1915.[56]

British intelligence soon caught on to the Baroness' game, and someone kept Gaunt and Thwaites up to date on her intrigues.[57] Von Seidlitz dabbled in Irish plots and maintained a secret line of communication to Ambassador von Bernstorff through the avant-garde French composer Edgard Varese.[58] Varese and the Baroness both had a strong interest in the occult, which afforded the Mage a means to infiltrate their circle. An "ardent Theosophist," von Seidlitz claimed psychic powers and reigned as high priestess over séances and like mystical gatherings.

Wittingly or not, Frank Harris played a part in Crowley's ongoing penetration of the German secret apparatus. Back in summer 1915 Ambassador Spring-Rice had forwarded to London an anonymous letter (likely from Watts) that blasted Crowley and Harris as dangerous "German agents."[59] By 1916, as editor of *Pearson's Magazine,* Harris polished that reputation with a steady stream of anti-war, anti-Allied articles.

Through Harris, Crowley reunited with another old fellow student of the occult, George Raffalovitch, whom Harris gave a cover job on his magazine. A onetime contributor to *The Equinox* and member of Crowley's elect A∴A∴, Raffalovitch had parted ways with the Beast over the prewar Rites of Eleusis flap. Raffalovitch, born in France and a naturalized British subject, came from a distinguished Russian-Jewish family. He was a nephew of Arthur Raffalovitch, the longtime "financial agent" of the Tsarist Government in France and a confidant of the Rothschilds. Shortly before the war, George R. embraced Ukrainian nationalism and came to head a "Ukrainian Committee" in London. The catalog of old Foreign Office correspondence reveals that the British had a dossier on Raffalovitch c. 1916, but it, too, was "not preserved."

After 1914, Raffalovitch's nationalism led him to the Germans, who offered support to Ukrainian nationalists as they did to the Irish and Indian. Raffalovitch's subsequent appearance in New York was to rally Ukrainian-Americans to the cause, though he denied that Berlin was behind this. Raffalovitch claimed to be a secret agent for mysterious persons inside Russia, probably anti-Tsarist groups. He may also have been a double agent for Russian intelligence. Whatever the case, he afforded Crowley further access to intrigue-infested Russian circles in New York, from Baroness Seidlitz's occult salon to revolutionary cells plotting in Greenwich Village basements.

Raffalovitch had yet another role. According to the Bureau of Investigation, he was "paymaster of German agents" in New York, dispersing some $18,000 each month.[60] The source of this information was an informant dubbed "A-139," "who appear[ed] to have a private connection to the British Consulate."[61] A-139 was very well-informed about Raffalovitch's past activities in Britain. A further clue is A-139's contact at the Consulate: Royal Navy Lt. Henry Fitzroy. Fitzroy showed up at 44 Whitehall in July 1916 and took over "military control" and passport duties. His secret responsibilities included counterespionage and "tracking enemy agents."[62] Technically, he was Gaunt's subordinate, but Thwaites and Wiseman also claimed him, and he reported to both.[63] Fitzroy is the man would have handled routine liaison with Agent Crowley.

In early 1916 Crowley met Evangeline Adams, astrologer to the rich and famous. She was taken with him, for a while at least, and engaged him to ghost-write a tome on astrology. Crowley and Adams encountered one another at a soirée hosted by the now familiar *World* editor John Cosgrave, another helpmate of British propaganda. Cosgrave too was a friend of Norman Thwaites, who may have been at the same gathering. In any case, the Beast's presence at Cosgrave's table shows that their relationship continued, a strange association for a supposed pro-German propagandist and a pro-Allied editor.

In the end, Adams never paid Crowley for his work, but she did put him up. Crowley had moved again, to Broadway and 52nd Street, but Adams offered him the use of her cabin on the shores of New Hampshire's scenic Lake Pasquaney (Newfound Lake today). He was settled in there by mid-June and would spend the summer enjoying a "magical retirement" in this bucolic setting far from the madding crowds and intrigues of New York—most of them, anyway. He craved rest and seems to have been undergoing a genuine personal crisis. The Beast hoped to renew and strengthen his connections with spiritual forces and vowed to stop degrading himself "by working at anything whatever."[64] He put his labors for Stuart X, *Vanity Fair*, and even Adams in that despised category. More stress doubtless stemmed from his double life on the undercover front. At the Lake, he devoted himself to meditation, writing, and the ritual crucifixion of the occasional toad, fueling his visions with abundant use of mescaline and ether. Keeping body and soul together was far cheaper in the New Hampshire woods than in Manhattan. The move even let him wriggle out of his relationship with the now pregnant and increasingly clinging Ratan Devi.

This does not mean that he entirely abandoned intelligence work. In the course of the summer, Crowley found opportunities to visit Boston, only a few hours away by train. His diary records trysts with a French-Canadian prostitute and a couple of anonymous homosexual encounters all, apparently, connected to magick operations. But he cannot have overlooked the fact that Cambridge was the home of his nemesis, Dr. Muensterberg, who was still fully engaged in his pro-German machinations. A rustic hideaway with easy access to Boston afforded Crowley ideal means to keep an eye on the Professor's activities.

It was during his Pasquaney idyll that Crowley formulated ideas for a cycle of stories featuring his Sherlock Holmes-esque sleuth, Simon Iff, genius at deduction and master magician. As with most of his fiction, Crowley based characters and plot elements on real persons and events. Three of these Iff tales merit special attention, because they derived at least part of their inspiration from the author's clandestine escapades.

The most important is "The Natural Thing to Do," which has Simon Iff and his plucky Watson figure, Dolores Cass, battling a gang of German conspirators bent on crippling America's shipping industry and "cut off England from American supplies."[65] Iff admits, "I'm here on a special mission for the British Admiralty," and in one episode ponders:

> Wouldn't everybody be surprised if they knew just what the British Government had sent him to do in America? If they knew what was in a certain paper at the bank, a casus belli, no less? But with whom? Aha—there was the secret! And wouldn't everybody be amazed if they knew just what he knew about a certain subject that he wouldn't mention, not he?

Was this a veiled reference to the *Lusitania* or some other secret? In the end, Iff distracts his enemy by revealing "a dozen secrets, any one of them enough to shake the world." Among the story's characters, "my good friend Lascelles, of the Royal Navy," fits Gaunt or Fitzroy; the American "Commissioner Teake, head of the New York Police," is Tunney, and "Col. Blagden" of the Secret Service stands in for Frank Burke. On the other side, allied with the Germans is one "Berkeley," a disgraced English gentleman turned enemy spy. One must wonder if he, too, had his counterpart in the real world. The mastermind of the German villains, "Prince Joachim von Ararberg, . . . a mathematician of the highest rank, a physiologist of extraordinary distinction . . . who had become a specialist in psychotherapeutics," can only be Muensterberg.

On 16 December 1916, Hugo Muensterberg, age fifty-three, dropped dead while lecturing to a class at Radcliffe, then Harvard's "women's annex." The German cause lost its "Moriarty." Family and friends were stunned by his unexpected passing, but Muensterberg had been under much strain. Crowley was far, far away in New Orleans, a journey we will look at more closely in the next chapter. Did he invoke a voodoo curse from the sanctuary of the bayous?

The answer may be more mundane. Hints can be found in the two other Simon Iff stories. In "A Sense of Incongruity," Iff is up against another nefarious plot, a Japanese one to surreptitiously poison prominent politicos. Written right after Muensterberg's death, the story may indicate what was on Crowley's mind. More revealingly, in "The Pasquaney Puzzle," the Magician's young partner in detection, Dolores Cass, first appears as a Radcliffe student and pupil of the occult who mystifies her family with a clever *Doppelgänger* experiment. The Mage identifies her as a student of Hugo Muensterberg.

Dolores Cass must have had her own flesh-and-blood model(s). Crowley had the opportunity to meet many young women like her during his summer on the lake, and he did have a way with women. His familiarity with drugs and magical concoctions equipped him to pharmacologically induce a fatal heart attack or stroke. The tricky part was dosing the victim. That is where "Dolores" from Radcliffe could play her femme fatale part, maybe as simple as spiking a glass of water on a podium. If the Beast had the satisfaction of disposing of "Moriarty," it was another secret that "he wouldn't mention—not he."

1   Gaunt, 172.
2   *Ibid.*
3   Willert, 22–23.
4   Troy, 448 and WWP, 6/166,Gaunt to Wiseman, 12 April 1917 and Wiseman to Gaunt, 17 April 1917.
5   WWP, 6/174, Memorandum on the Scope and Activities of M.I.1.C. in New York, 27 April 1917.
6   Gaunt, 172.
7   WWP, 6/171, Memo sent to Col. Murray…, 6 Sept. 1918.
8   WWP, 6/172, American Section M.I.1.c., Oct. 1917.
9   On Wiseman's political role, see Wilton B. Fowler, *British-American Relations, 1917–18: The Role of Sir William Wiseman* (Princeton, NJ: Princeton Univ. Press, 1969), and on the intelligence angle see Richard B. Spence, "Englishmen in New York: The SIS American Station, 1915–21," *Intelligence and National Security*, Vol. 19, #3 (2004), 511–537.
10 USNA, Department of State [DS], U-1, Counselor's Office, CSA 215, Sharp to Bannerman, 13 Dec. 1924 and Sharp to Kinsey, 13 July 1925.
11 Popplewell, 248–249.
12 This two-page report became part of French military intelligence (*Deuxieme Bureau*) file An Z 7633 which later became Delo 5314/36457 of Fond 7, Opis 2 of the Soviet *Tsentralnyi Gosudarstvennyi Arkhiv SSSR* ("Special Archive") and returned to France in the 1990s as part of the *Documents Repatriees*, Carton 1298.
13 USNA, MID 9140-815/1, Extract British Black Book, p. 106, entries dated 21 and 29 January 1916.
14 Spence, *Trust No One*, 110–169.
15 Norman G. Thwaites, *Velvet and Vinegar* (London: Grayson & Grayson, 1932), 181–182.
16 USNA, Department of Justice, Bureau of Investigation [BI] Investigative Case Files, 1908–22, Old German [OG] file 39368, Agent Perkins to BI, 3 April 1917.
17 Symonds, 199.
18 "One of the Propagandists" [Viereck], "War Propaganda," *The Saturday Evening Post*, (29 June 1929, 21, 174. Viereck basically repeated the same story in his 1930 *Spreading Germs of Hate*.
19 WWP, 14/23, Gaunt to Wiseman 10 Oct. and 1 Dec. 1949.
20 WWP, 6/173, Notes on the Work of Section V. in U.S.A., c. 1917.
21 Amado Crowley, *Secrets*, 107.
22 Yigal Sheffy to author, 13 July 2002.
23 Thwaites, 233–240.
24 *Ibid.*, 153.
25 Caillaux ended up on trial for treason in 1919. See: Severance Johnson, *The Enemy Within* (London: Allen & Unwin, 1920).

26 Antony Sutton, *Wall Street and the Bolshevik Revolution* (Morley, Australia: Veritas, 1981), 66–69.

27 Crowley records the beginning of his affair with von Kothek on 12 April and Devi on 15 April.

28 Crowley, "The Gospel According to St. Bernard Shaw," (1916), typescript (c. 1953), University of Texas, Austin, Harry Ransom Humanities Research Center, Aleister Crowley Collection, 1/8.

29 BI, 8000-10653, German Activities, In Re: Dr. Rudolf Gebauer, 25 April 1917.

30 *CAC*, 772

31 *Ibid.*

32 *CAC*, 773.

33 Crowley, *Liber LXXIII*, "The Urn" [Diary], 13 Jan. 1917, p.s., www.rahoorkhuit. net/library/lib-0073.html.

34 Stephen Hartley, *The Irish Question as a Problem in British Foreign Policy, 1914–18* (New York, 1987), 46.

35 A.C. Bose, *Indian Revolutionaries Abroad, 1905–1922* (Patna: Bharati Bhawan, 1971), 255.

36 WWP, 3/84, "Suggestions as to Recognition of War Services Rendered by Persons in America," 22 Nov. 1918.

37 On Tunney's exploits see his *Throttled!: The Detection of the German and Anarchist Bomb Plotters* (Boston: Small, Maynard & Co., 1919).

38 USNA, MID 9771-56, "Synopsis: Irish Agitation in the United States," 1 June 1918, 8, and 9771-56, "John Devoy."

39 The Irish had hoped for 200,000 rifles.

40 USNA, MID 9771-56, L. Winslow to M. Churchill, 30 July 1919.

41 *Ibid.*, M. Churchill to L. Winslow, 5 Aug. 1919.

42 *Ibid.*, L. Black to M. Churchill, 24 April 1919.

43 *The Washington Post* (12 May 1916).

44 Troy, 459.

45 *CAC*, 773.

46 "Dr. Waite's Wicked 'Man from Egypt'," *Washington Post Sunday* (30 April 1916).

47 *The Washington Post* (28 May 1916) and Robert T. Tuohy, "Crowley Versus Whitaker 1916: Rediscovered!," www.chessville.com/misc/History/PastPawns/ CrowleyVsWhitaker1916Rediscovered.htm

48 Crowley, "Introduction" to A Prophet in His Own Country: Being the Letters of STUART X," *Thelema Lodge Calendar* (Aug. 1996), www.billheidrick.com/ tlc1996/tlc0896.htm.

49 FAAC, "Henry Louis Mencken," www.redflame93/Mencken.html, and Louis Marlow [Wilkinson], *Seven Friends* (London: The Richards Press, 1953), 57–58.

50 H.P. Albarelli, Jr., "The Secret History of Anthrax, " *World Net Daily* (6 Nov. 2001), www.wnd.com/news/printer-friendly.asp?ARTICLE_ID=25220,

and "Anton Dilger," www.biocrawler.com/encyclopedia/Anton_Dilger.

51 Oliver Wilkinson, 94.

52 The heads of the Society of Atonement were Father Paul James (*né* Lewis Wattson) and Luranna White.

53 UKNA, FO 395/83, Watts to FFO, 3 Nov. 1917; see also Hutchinson, 154–156.

54 On 1 August 1917, Pope Benedict XV proposed a peace based on compromise and mutual, limited concessions. The general view in Allied countries was that the proposal was inspired by Berlin but there was concern that it could influence Catholics worldwide. The Germans showed more interest and offered a formal, if very reserved, response in September.

55 FBI, Voska file, 62-21551, Memorandum for Inquiry at the Justice Department, 13 Jan. 1929, 1, 3.

56 HIA, Russia, Posol'stvo, U.S.A., File 370-12, Nekrasov Report, 9.

57 *Ibid.*, 10–12

58 Landau, 197–198.

59 Hutchinson, 138–139. The letter, dated 13 July 1915, is noted in the pre-1920 index to Foreign Office correspondence.

60 USNA, BI, OG 39583, In Re: George Raffalovitch, 2 Aug. 1917 and 24 Aug. 1917 and MID 9140-1226, 2 Oct. 1917.

61 *Ibid.*, 2 Aug. 1917.

62 *Ibid.*

63 WWP, 6/171, Wiseman to Chief, 6 Sept. 1918.

64 *Liber LXXIII*, 13 July 1916.

65 Crowley wrote this and other tales under the pseudonym "Edward Kelly," a tip of the hat to Dr. John Dee's Elizabethan sidekick in magic and espionage. Online copies of this and other "Simon Iff in America" stories may be found at www.hermetic.com/crowley/simon-iff/The_Natural_Thing_To_Do.htm.

Crowley at Cambridge. (Courtesy Ordo Templi Orientis)

Expelled from Paris, 1929 (Courtesy Ordo Templi Orientis)

(facing page) The Explorer, 1906 (Courtesy Ordo Templi Orientis)

(this page) Crowley in Masonic Regalia, New York, 1916
(Courtesy of Ordo Templi Orientis)

(facing page) Imitating Churchill, c. 1940 (Courtesy of Ordo Templi Orientis)

Hounding the King of the Devi[l]

Barred From England, Raided in Italy, the Beast 666 Bobs Up in Paris--- and Gets Yawns Where Once He Thrilled and Horrified

By NIGEL TRASK

PARIS.

ALEISTER CROWLEY is back again, a fatter, balder, older, sadder but apparently no wiser man. This high priest of dark devil cults, once hated and feared by Parisians, he who mysteriously disappeared from America, was driven from London and hounded from Sicily, returns to the boulevards like a figure from his own fantastic pages on black-magic. Thereby hangs an amazing tale.

Last year they said Crowley was dead, murdered by other demonologists in the high places of ancient Thibet. Now the Parisians assert he sent out this story himself to protect himself from his sworn enemies.

If that is true, Crowley might have saved himself the trouble. The most tragic thing that could happen to the Beast of the Apocalypse has happened —he has become old-fashioned, he is no longer feared, he is considered just a mild, harmless, slightly eccentric, elderly Englishman, not rich and not at all terrifying.

The celebrated basilisk stare that made scores of women his love-slaves doesn't seem to work any more, the mumbo-jumbo of his paganistic rituals calls forth laughter.

The other day I talked to a charming blonde, blue-eyed American flapper, aged 22, who had met Crowley at the Cafe du Dome

Crowley in full regalia as King of the Devil cults

Left, Crowley when he was a boy, and, above, as an aesthete of the nineties

the day before. She could hardly describe the incident for pent-up giggles.

"Of course I have heard of Aleister Crowley," began Miss 1928. "Mamma used to know him, and every time she mentioned him he was so dark, dangerous and handsome, and he had those hypnotic eyes. He was so mysterious, daring and evil. Of course I wanted to meet him.

"Well, it happened, and he was a shock, but not in the way he expected to be. He grabbed my hand, just like any Yale man on his best

Aleister Crowley as a boy of sixteen

Love is the law, love under will,

Yours ever,

The Beast 666.

Reproduction of the signature to one of Crowley's letters written to a friend in America. He proclaimed himself the Beast of the Apocalypse and King of the Devil Cults, using this signature instead of his name

night club behavior, but with a difference in results, drew me over to him, and began to yodel sotto voce: 'Do what thou wilt shall be the whole of the law!'

"Can you imagine! I learned afterward that that is always his opening line. It's part of his funny pagan ritual. Then he began working his eyebrows fast, just like old ———— that may have got results in the naughty nineties, but it seemed just a wee bit ham to me.

"Then he told me that I was Nuit, his lady of the starry heavens, that I should take my fill of love, that my ecstasy was his, and his joy was to see my joy. I was simply aghast, but I let him carry on just for the fun of the thing. Then when he came up for air I answered:

"'Listen,' I said, 'you ought to see Jung. He does a lot for cases like you. You have a complex or something. Any behaviorist could tell at a glance you haven't been properly conditioned. Your reactions are dated, and your manifestations of ego show a desire to escape from actualities. Besides, your chemistry is different from mine. I don't like you.'"

I really think that pretty Miss 1928 is a little hard on the famous Aleister Crowley. I have known him for years, and have often found him a delightful companion. He is a man of tremendous energy, mountain climber, explorer, novelist, painter as well as King of the Devil Cults. He is also a poet of some distinction.

But the reaction of this 22-year-old child shows why Crowley's astonishing power has fled, why he is no longer feared. The world has advanced and he has grown older. His dark, mysterious power—and he undoubtedly had it—fades before the shibboleths of the new, materialistic generation. Jung, Freud, Adler and the behavioristic psychologists, which Miss 1928 drew on so amusingly by way of reprisal, have done for him.

Those who hated and hounded him around the globe, called him monster, Satanist and Sadist, now snap their fingers in derision. The king is deposed!

Crowley still has his followers in Paris, who tried to give the Beast a welcome on his return, but their number has dwindled to a pitiable few. Yet this bald-headed man with the hypnotic eyes was only a few years ago the self-proclaimed Anti-Christ, the head of the celebrated O. T. O. cult, with secret branches all over the world. Many people, including Crowley himself, believed he could perform miracles.

He first became widely known in the London of the nineties as a brilliant young poet. You will find a number of his poems in the Oxford Book of Mystical Verse. His friends were the most distinguished writers, artists and diplomats of the Yellow Book days. Then he turned to mysticism as a cult, and to drugs, but was never enslaved by them.

Crowley never did anything half way. His researches in ancient religious and mystical beliefs consumed years. He probably knows as much about these subjects as any man living to-day. He emerged from these studies to found the cult of O. T. O. based on the ancient practices of the Rosicrucian Order and the Gnostics.

But Crowley was not satisfied with the teachings of books; he went among people. He lived for three months among Hindu religious fakirs and starved himself as they did. He walked across China, he studied the Mayan and Aztec religions in Mexico.

ENGLAND'S PUNCH AND JUDY SHOW

(facing page) The Many Faces of the Beast: American Press, 1920s
(Courtesy of Ordo Templi Orientis)

B. I. Modèle 1 — Crowley Aleister — [Bureau Am]
Nom et prénoms
Surnoms ou alias
Sexe M — Nationalité d'origine Irlandais — Naturalisation

RÉFÉRENCES.
Am
Z 7637

Né le — à — en
Fils de — Nationalité
et de
Époa de
Domicile
Résidence actuelle
Adresse commerciale Fulham Rd Studios
Adresses anterieures Fulham Rd London S.W
Profession
Services militaires
Papiers d'identité
Remarques Agitateur irlandais dont les excentricités
ont attiré l'attention de la police. Le but du
"Comité secret révolutionnaire, auquel il appartient est
d'empêcher les Irlandais de s'engager dans l'armée anglaise.
Il se propose également de faire proclamer la République
en Irlande après la guerre   9/3/16

(this page) a. The Well-Dressed Beast
in London, 1934
b. Index card to Crowley's
Deuxieme Bureau File

(facing page) The English Gentlemen
(Courtesy of Ordo Templi Orientis)

(facing page) Rudolf Steiner

(this page) Kurt Jahnke

(facing page) Hanns Heinz Ewers by Trevor Brown from the collection
of C. Laufenburg (H. H. Ewers Society)

(this page) Karl Germer [Courtesy of Ordo Templi Orientis]

CROWLEY, ALEISTER. Real name EDWARD
ALEXANDER CROWLEY. (M.) **340**

Class—IJ. *Source*—A.

8 Mar 16, believed in New York. Irish. Journalist. *Aunt, Mrs.
Annie CROWLEY, lives Eton Lodge, Outram Road, Addiscombe,
Croydon.* Explored in Kashmir 1902 under auspices of Austrian
Geographical Society. Claims to have travelled in India, Persia
and Thibet. Lived Fulham Rd. Studios, London, S.W. Went
Paris. Arrived New York about Dec 1914.
 Height 5 ft. 11 in. (1. 80m.); age about 40; bald except for erect
lock of hair on forehead; black eyes; athletic-looking, but air of
effeminacy; plump soft hands; wears many rings.

I.—21 Jan 16, pro-German propagandist, United States; wrote
offensive article in "*Open Court*," *Chicago periodical.*
Proclaimed 3 July 15 at Statue of Liberty, U.S.A., the
Independence of Ireland; is member of "Secret Revolu-
tionary Committee" to procure establishment of Irish
Republic after the war and dissuade Irish from enlisting.

J.—29 Jan 16, degenerate Irish journalist, pro-German, signalled
British ports concerned to be searched and sent Metropolitan Police, London.

(*5 June* 16. *Reference M.I. 5/P.F.* 1943 *and* 2573.)

(this page) a. George Sylvester Viereck, 1917
(Courtesy, George Sylvester Viereck Papers,
The University of Iowa Libraries, Iowa City, IA)
b. Crowley's 1916 Entry in the MI5 "Black Book"

(facing page) Leila Waddell
(Courtesy Ordo Templi Orientis)

The Classic Beast
(Courtesy Ordo Templi Orientis)

CHAPTER NINE

~

THE WANDERING MAGICIAN

~

CROWLEY'S SUMMER IDYLL ENDED in early September. Back in New York, restless and at loose ends, he was, as usual, short of cash. His *Confessions* skips abruptly from the shores of Lake Pasquaney to New Orleans, ignoring the intervening months. He does mention various magical operations, most with an ether accompaniment, and he had at least one late September rendezvous with Gerda von Kothek, the "Angel of Revolution." She sent notice by wire that she was arriving, which signals some urgency.

One or two matters in this period merited his interest. The first centered on George Vaux Bacon, a young American journalist and sometime writer for *Photoplay Magazine*. British authorities arrested Bacon as a German spy in November 1916; he had been collecting information under the guise of researching wartime conditions in England.[1] Bacon had signed on as a German agent in New York. His key contacts there were Charles "the Dynamiter" Wunnenberg, one of Paul Koenig's recruiters, and Albert Sander, another journalist and the head of the German-American Literary Defense Committee. Sander was another intimate of Viereck's and the *Propaganda Kabinett*'s circles, and his job as drama critic for the Hearst-run *Deutsches Journal* linked him to Ewers. As usual Crowley had a good vantage to study Sander's intrigues, including the recruitment of Bacon. Certainly Hall's men and MI5 were put on Bacon's trail by tips emanating from Wiseman's New York section. Sentenced to death in early 1917, Bacon turned on Wunnenberg and Sander to save himself. William Offley's New York BI swooped down on that pair in February 1917, and soon the whole gang was in the federal pen in Atlanta.

In the wee hours of 1 November, another event began to unfold. In the pre-dawn darkness, the German merchant submarine *Deutschland* pulled up to the Connecticut State Pier in New London, about 120 miles northeast of Manhattan.[2] Among the small crowd gathered before dawn to welcome her stood sabotage kingpin Frederick Hinsch, acting as director of the German-run Eastern Forwarding Co.

This was the big U-boat's second American voyage; its first had been to Baltimore during Crowley's New Hampshire retreat. This time the 750-ton submarine carried a valuable cargo of chemical dyes, medicines, and gems, plus packets of confidential mail for Ambassador von Bernstorff, and maybe some fresh cultures for Anton Dilger's germ lab in Maryland. The *Deutschland* was no threat to Britain's control of the seas, but her ability to slip in and out of American ports was bad PR for London. The boat's commander, Capt. Paul Koenig (another one), and his crew were fêted as heroes by the locals, and their arrival made the front page of the *New York Times*. The Admiralty made a priority of destroying or capturing the sub. A few days before its appearance at New London, Gaunt "prophesied" her arrival on 1 November.[3]

During the *Deutschland*'s twenty days in port, rumors spread of British warships lurking in ambush just outside the three-mile limit. Meanwhile the submarine hosted a steady stream of visitors, including Bernstorff and Viereck. Viereck easily could have arranged a glimpse for Crowley and undoubtedly gabbed about what he saw. The Germans were on guard for mischief. Koenig foiled one attempt by a "crank plotter" to damage his boat, but on her first attempt to leave on 17 November she struck a harbor tug, which sank with five men, Hinsch alone surviving.[4] The *Deutschland* sustained only minor damage, but investigation and litigation threatened to keep her tied up in New London indefinitely. British agents quietly encouraged these entanglements. Koenig and his vessel at last made it safely out of port on the night of 21 November and back to Bremen with a load of rubber and nickel. The *Deutschland* would never return to America.

Besides using his German contacts to spy on the *Deutschland*, the Beast may have had more ambitious designs. In "The Natural Thing to Do," Simon Iff speaks of returning to England "by the *Deutschland*." In the story the vessel is a liner, but no passenger ship had borne that name since before the war, and he wrote the tale soon after the real *Deutschland*'s appearance. Back in Germany, Capt. Koenig revealed that there had been some talk of bringing back an unnamed passenger or two from America.

Crowley had not long before expressed his desire to "go to Germany . . . and report on the conditions of the country," an offer rejected by those "unimaginative" British officials.[5] Maybe the coming sojourn to New Orleans was a substitute for this much bolder mission.

Crowley was as coy about his reasons for going to the Crescent City as about most of his travels. According to his diary, it was all a "desperate magical effort."[6] On 12 November, however, he recorded "receipt of the largest sum of money I have handled in twelve months," that is, since his last road trip.[7] He also notes that his original destination, as of early November, was Texas. The pretext for this was a visitor he had received a little earlier, Professor Lindley Miller Keasbey of the University if Texas at Austin. Keasbey was interested in starting a branch of the OTO, and Crowley, as American chief of the Order, thought he would lend a personal hand. Then again, maybe there was more to it.

Keasbey has some familiar traits. The scion of a wealthy New Jersey clan, he graduated from Harvard and Columbia. He also studied in Germany, where he met and became good friends with Hugo Muensterberg. When the war broke out, Keasbey advocated stridently for Germany. The Muentersberg connection may also provide a link between Keasbey and Morgan's assailant, Erich Muenter. As a fugitive, Muenter had visited Texas and studied in Austin. Keasbey could have had some unwitting part in a Crowley scheme to undo Dr. Muensterberg.

As if his pro-Germanism was not enough to arouse trouble, Keasbey held a "socialist revolutionary" political position. Perhaps that gave him connection to Gerda von Kothek. He bitterly opposed the Wilson Administration and its drift toward intervention.[8] Whether he actively abetted his German friends is uncertain, but U.S. and British authorities found him a person of interest. Keasbey definitely had links to German networks in New Orleans and Mexico. By the time of Crowley's departure, Keasbey's controversial views had attracted such trouble that it doubtless seemed wiser to stay clear.

Given his interest in the OTO, Keasbey also could have figured in Crowley's ongoing dealings with Reuss. By late 1916, that worthy had shifted his base of operations to Monte Verita, the eccentric Swiss enclave mentioned in Chapter Two. The mood there was overwhelmingly anti-Establishment and anti-war. Reuss hoped to maneuver the resident radicals, pacifists, and occultists into an openly pro-German stance and exploit them for propaganda. To this end, on 22 January 1917, Reuss announced the creation of the Anational Grand Lodge and Mystic Temple of the Ordo Templi Orientis and Hermetic Brotherhood of Light. This was the first step towards an "Anational Congress" at Monte Verita that coming summer. The gathering would bring together like-minded folk from across war-torn Europe and elsewhere to lay the foundations of "new ethics, a new religion, a new social order" based on vaguely communist principles.[9] Reuss noted two "neutral centers" of the Order, in Monte Verita and New York. The latter was in the hands of the Beast. Crowley's name and works figured prominently in the literature and rituals of the new Lodge, including the Gnostic Mass. In January, Reuss unveiled a revised constitution for the OTO, the same one Crowley was working on in early October.[10] The *Deutschland* could have carried back a copy in its bag of special mail.

Crowley left New York about 4 December and rolled into the Big Easy five days later. He remained there for about eight weeks. His rooms at 3402 or 3403 Dauphine St. were convenient to the Old Absinthe House and the notorious red-lit Storyville, both of which he patronized frequently. Its tolerance of vice made New Orleans one of the few places dear to Crowley in America. Its atmosphere unleashed an "ecstasy of creative energy" leading to a string of Simon Iff tales and the beginnings of a novel tentatively titled *The Butterfly Net*—eventually to become *Moonchild*, Crowley's *roman à clef* of wartime occult battles between the White and Black Lodges. Among things real and fanciful, it featured his old mentor and enemy MacGregor Mathers as a German spy.[11]

The Black Lodge and its schemes seemed much on Crowley's mind. In mid-January 1917, he received a letter from Ananda Coomaraswamy in New York. Why they remained in contact is a puzzle. Something in Coomaraswamy's letter convinced Crowley that the Eurasian was a true "Black Brother."[12] Did the letter, perhaps, betray to Crowley the movements of other German agents, such as Hanns Heinz Ewers?

Crowley bemoaned his chronic lack of funds. At one point, he claimed to have a mere 70 cents to his name, although he somehow could afford shelter, sustenance, and ether.[13] Financial frustration finally provoked him to go "on strike" against the spiritual, and perhaps human, powers that controlled his fortunes. Accumulated resentment over the stinginess of His Majesty's representatives could have led him to withhold reports as well as rituals and invocations.

However distracted and distressed Crowley may have been with literary and monetary matters, he had to have noticed the arrival of Ewers, and their overlapping presence in New Orleans was more than coincidental. Ewers materialized in the Crescent City fresh from secret missions in Spain, Mexico, and the Caribbean, which naturally attracted the interest of British intelligence. Among other things, the German had spent time in Haiti investigating voodoo and the methods of Haitian sorcerers, or *bokors*, renowned for their ability to turn persons into zombies. This power, as explained by more recent investigations, was no mere superstition. Using powerful natural toxins and assorted herbs and compounds, the magicians could send victims into a death-like stupor, or simply kill them. A common element in these diabolical recipes was powdered human remains, probably to divert attention from a more secret ingredient.

While in New Orleans, Ewers robbed a grave for such ritual purposes.[14] In the aftermath, he came down with a persistent and disfiguring case of what seemed to be psoriasis on his hands, and thought it supernatural retribution. The affliction could have had a more natural cause. A few years later, during the Irish "Troubles," British agents used the powerful caustic in mustard gas to identify IRA activists.[15] Latches and doorknobs at a suspect locale were doctored with the sticky liquid which gave any who touched them telltale lesions on their hands. Perhaps the Beast played a like trick on Ewers.

A closely related application for "corpse powder" was in the concoction of goofer dust, a common weapon in the African-based magic practiced in New Orleans.

Dusting the victim's residence or person would cause misfortune, illness, or even sudden death. This brings to mind the unfortunate Dr. Muensterberg, who died not long after the Mage arrived in New Orleans. Could the Mage have mailed something to an accomplice to be administered to the Professor unawares?

A 2 February note in Crowley's Record is significant. It reads, "My 2¼ years' work crowned with success; U.S.A. breaks off relations with Germany."[16] He was a little prescient; Washington formally severed relations with Berlin the next day, although it had become inevitable when the Germans proclaimed the resumption of unrestricted submarine warfare on 1 February. Crowley made this notation to himself and his gods; whatever his actual influence in bringing about this event, it establishes that he had been working to that end.

Barely a week later, with no explanation, Crowley bolted from New Orleans and headed east to tiny Titusville on Florida's Atlantic coast. Here lived his cousin, Lawrence Bishop, who hosted Crowley until the end of March. He did not tarry with the Bishops because of the amenities or warm reception; Crowley complained of ill health and Mrs. Bishop's surliness. Mooching off relatives saved money, but some other reason must have delayed to return to New York. Was he waiting for something, or lying low?

He was not incommunicado. On 28 March, Crowley received a letter from Frater Fiat Pax, a.k.a. George Macnie Cowie, financial trustee of the OTO lodge in London. Whatever the letter contained enraged and/or frightened the Beast and resulted in a break with Cowie. As the war progressed, recalled Crowley, Cowie became "violently anti-German" and started to "intrigue against me."[17] Cowie had come to believe reports (whose?) about his master's pro-German activities and had decided he could no longer serve such a blackguard. The deciding factor may have been Reuss' recent manifesto, which Cowie must have seen. Whatever the exact cause, Cowie had gone the authorities which stirred up a wave of trouble that reached all the way the Washington.

Also at issue was money. According to Crowley, Cowie refused to send him much needed funds, including money from the recent sale of the Boleskine property. Part of the problem was that depressed wartime prices and the many mortgages Crowley had piled on the place left little profit. Nevertheless, the Beast seemed most upset that "the stupid's [sic] have misinterpreted my whole attitude and raised trouble."[18] It was serious enough for him to hasten to Washington the next morning to "straighten this out."[19] That meant meeting with British officials, always a risky move. But Crowley was in a desperate state of mind. Referring to His Majesty's men in D.C., he vowed that "if I fail this time to get them to listen to sense, at least I can go up to Canada and force them to arrest me. My hand is therefore at last on the lever."[20] He was threatening to blow his cover and provoke an embarrassing situation unless demands (undoubtedly including money) were met. One way or another, he seems to have gotten what he wanted.

This crisis and what soon transpired at the London OTO lodge at 93 Regent Street must be related. One morning, Scotland Yard detectives raided the premises, guns drawn. Inside, according to the amused Mage, were "a dozen mild old people trying to browse on the lush grass of my poetry."[21] The officers arrested one of them, "a motherly old fool," for fortune-telling. Officially, the incident had absolutely nothing to do with Crowley. That did not stop him from making "a wonderful show scene of indignation in the office of *The Fatherland* which helped me quite a little on my weary way."[22] Crowley later admitted that the whole purpose of the raid was to "help me consolidate [restore?] my position with the Germans by heating the branding irons of infamy for me in the fire of publicity." It also was an excellent way to get back at Cowie and other perceived traitors.

The Beast also alleged that Fielding helped choreograph the London stunt. At first glance, this seems doubtful. Feilding was in Cairo working with the Arab Bureau as liaison to Naval Intelligence and the EMSIB, and thus hardly situated to arrange police raids in London. In the Cairo post, however, Feilding worked closely with the NILI spy ring of Zionist Jews working for Britain against the Turks.[23] The NILI group had political allies and financial connections to the same Zionist circles in New York that were working closely with Wiseman and Section V. Thus Crowley and Feilding had a confidential means to stay in touch. Feilding's intervention in the London flap removed any need for direct communication between Crowley and persons there. In any case, the ploy seems to have worked. Viereck and others were reassured (if Viereck needed any) of Crowley's pariah status among the British. In July 1917, Viereck even named Crowley editor-in-chief of his monthly *International.*

Meanwhile, U.S.-German relations continued to deteriorate. Fresh U-boat attacks enflamed the situation, as did the 1 March publication of the Zimmermann Telegram, intercepted and provided to Washington by Admiral Hall's Room 40. In it German Foreign Secretary Zimmermann advocated a German-Mexican-Japanese alliance against the U.S. On 6 April, with Crowley back roaming the streets of New York, Washington declared war.

Immediately most of the remaining German agents, including Dilger, Hinsch, and Jahnke, made tracks for Mexico, where they continued their plotting, albeit feebly. Nevertheless, the outspoken German propagandist Aleister Crowley suffered no problems, nor did his boss, George Sylvester Viereck. He simply changed the name of *The Fatherland* to *Viereck's Weekly* and maintained its publication uninterrupted. This did not fool the BI and MID, but they let the magazine and Viereck go on unmolested, despite ample evidence of his continued association with suspect persons.[24] Oddest of all, in early 1918 American investigators actually consulted Viereck on Ewers' doings.[25]

But new players were on the scene. Baron Georg von Polenz, an intimate of Viereck, entered the U.S. legally in mid-1916, having been released from internment by the Canadians. Ambassador Bernstorff personally arranged this in exchange for the release of a Canadian prisoner by Austria-Hungary. Von Polenz's value in the exchange remains a mystery, but he also was closely connected to von Alvensleben.[26] Von Polenz set up shop as a New York stockbroker with an office on Broadway and an abundance of capital. Later investigation revealed that he was involved in fraudulent stock schemes, but he also was the secret patron of *Viereck's Weekly*, which continued to "indirectly [promote] German propaganda with money furnished by the German Government."[27]

Alvo von Alvensleben remained free until 10 August 1917, when BI agents, answering local complaints, arrested him in Portland, Oregon. From there he went to the internment camp at Fort Douglas, Utah. The only evidence the Americans ever offered against Alvo was a report "provided to the Justice Department by British intelligence" before the American declaration of war.[28] Alvo's name headed a list of "dangerous" German agents received from Horace D. Nugent, the British Consul in Chicago. Nugent got it from an unnamed British operative—perhaps Crowley.

As for Hanns Heinz Ewers, the Americans monitored him throughout 1917 and early 1918 but held back, perhaps at British suggestion. The Yanks consulted Norman Thwaites, who offered that Ewers had been on "the British Black List for some time" but did not urge his seizure.[29] Was that because he was of more value to Cowley at large?

When the order for Ewers' arrest finally came on 13 June 1918 (he was taken into custody on 27 June), officers got right to work ransacking his apartment. Their subsequent report mentions two interesting letters found among his papers. One, dated 16 August 1917, from Otto Kahn, the banker and British asset inside Kuhn, Loeb, pertained to financing of Ewers' plays, and showed Kahn to have been one of his longtime backers. The other letter was from Aleister Crowley. No date is given, but Crowley's indicated address was 64-A West 9th Street, which suggests sometime during October 1917–June 1918. The report says nothing about the letter's contents other than that it "appears to have been written by someone mentally weak."[30] In any event, it shows the two occultists to have been in contact at least to late 1917 and perhaps right up to the time of Ewers' arrest.

America's entry into the war had serious implications for British intelligence in the States. What had been heretofore a clandestine and technically illegal operation now emerged from the shadows, partly. Collaboration with American authorities became formalized and subject to official scrutiny. Furthermore, the Americans took charge of combating German intrigue, while British agents would merely advise, at least in theory. This ignited a fresh debate about which of London's agencies should handle intelligence liaison with the new ally. Vernon Kell insisted that everything should rest with MI5. The situation came to head in April 1917 when Kell's man Claude Dansey (John Quinn's old friend) landed in Gotham. Wiseman expected Dansey to take over.[31] In the end, though, for reasons neither Sir William nor Dansey ever discussed, the turnover did not happen. MI1c's Section V retained its independence and pre-eminence on the American scene.

This is not to say that nothing changed. Wiseman, now at President Wilson's side, was more and more consumed by political duties. That left Section V in the expert hands of Norman Thwaites. Meanwhile Gaunt's role withered to insignificance, and soon he was headed back to England for good.

A shift in authority to MI5 certainly would not have boded well for Crowley; that agency regarded him as a disloyal subversive who merited immediate arrest. In any event, his relationship with British officialdom appears to have become increasingly strained in 1917. He had long complained that they needlessly subjected him to repeated, pointless "tests," but that summer insult was added to injury when "our Secret Service" sent a "Temporary Gentleman" (wartime officer) to deal with him.[32] In the standard version of *Confessions*, the man's name is given as "H…d," but in the original it is "H…l" and further identified by a handwritten notation as "Hall." This pegs him as Frederick Hall. Posing as a journalist, Hall arrived in New York on 1 September and promptly joined the Thwaites-Wiseman crew at 44 Whitehall. Wiseman's papers show that he was assigned to "general work" connected with personal contacts (informants) in the American press and intelligence bodies.[33] Crowley told him about his special relationship with "a man high in the German Secret Service" and of his willingness to go to Germany and report on conditions there. In response, Hall seemed untrusting and infuriatingly dense. Most likely, the Beast's pride was hurt by being subjected to questioning by a low-ranking nincompoop.

But the Beast was not wholly dependent on British largesse. In the wake of America's joining the war, his collaboration with the Yankees increased, or so he claimed. In another passage later deleted from *Confessions*, he boasted that the "Department [of Justice] used me to the full" and "helped me in every possible way, and to my astonishment (almost amounting to collapse!) they were even grateful to me for what I did to help them!"[34] Supposedly he cadged enough money out of the Americans to pay off debts.

As opposed to the Department of Justice proper, it is possible that his actual work was performed for the American Protective League. That also could explain the dearth of records in Bureau files. This ostensibly private, patriotic organization became a de facto arm of Justice and the BI. It raised a 250,000-strong army of citizen spies to root out subversion and disloyalty from every facet of American life. While APL operatives were mostly true-blue Americans, Crowley could easily have joined up in cosmopolitan New York. As noted, the Gotham APL included an informant, A-139, who provided regular, detailed reports on the activities of Frank Harris and Raffalovitch and had a "private" channel to Lt. Fitzroy and the British Consulate.

Immediately after his return to New York, Crowley moved into a studio on Fifth Avenue run by Leon Engers Kennedy. A fellow Brit, Kennedy was another member of OTO and A∴A∴. He painted the portrait of the Beast dressed in a red robe that later graced the cover of the revived *Equinox* and other works. From mid-1917, Crowley also focused on magical pursuits and writing. In August, he recorded no less than ten "operations" in twelve days, all or most involving sex and drugs.[35] On 14 June, Crowley recorded an entry that summed up his recent experiences or at least tried to explain them: "All my sympathies are profoundly with the Allies; but my brain refuses to think as sympathizers seem to; so in argument I often seem 'pro-German'; hence constant muddle not in myself but in others who observe me."[36] In the same entry he noted his inner conflict of a "socialistic, anarchistic brain" and an "aristocratic heart."

New magical-sexual partners came and went. In August he met Anna Miller, with whom he briefly shared a new flat on Central Park West at 110th Street. La Miller, of German extraction, soon proved another unstable drunk. By October there was Roddie Minor, a married woman, also of German extraction, with supposed psychic talents. He proclaimed her the newest incarnation of the Scarlet Woman, and the two took up cohabitation on West 9th Street in Greenwich Village.

Among his "lesser" initiates and sexual partners were actress Eva Tanguay and an eighteen-year-old Russian, Marie Lavroff (Maria Lavrov), later named Marie Roehling. Lavroff was connected to Apollonarii Semenovskii, an official of the Russian Provisional ("Kerenskii") Government recently assigned to Petrograd's consulate-general in New York. He and Marie, his ward and perhaps mistress, arrived in America on 4 November, three days before the German-backed Lenin seized power in Petrograd. Among Semenovskii's friends and colleagues at the Russian Consulate was Lev Arkadievich Shumatov, a devotee of the mystic (and possible British agent) Gurdjieff.

The atmosphere in the Russian Consulate and its satellite commissions became one of utter confusion as Soviet agents, Provisional regime officials, and Tsarist reactionaries vied for control. Back in Russia, Semenovskii had been linked to Col. B.V. Nikitin, the head of the Provisional Government's counterintelligence service. Nikitin had tried but mostly failed to expose Bolshevik-German collusion, and

Semenovskii may have been assigned such investigations in New York. Thus Crowley's dalliance with Lavroff could help keep him apprised of Russian intrigues.

Another local Russian whom Crowley must have met was the pale, effeminate, and sinister Boris L'vovich Brasol.[37] After brief service at the front and a stint in London, Lieutenant Brasol came to the U.S. in summer 1916 as a special legal representative of the Tsarist Government. Among other duties, he served on the Inter-Allied Board and the Anglo-Russian [Supply] Subcommittee, where he rubbed elbows with British officials. Brasol's secret task was ferreting out enemy agents and subversives among the local Russians. He zealously pursued radicals while ignoring German intrigues, which raised suspicion about Brasol's own loyalties. For instance, he effectively quashed an investigation into German corruption of Russian officers. This so-called "Nekrassov Affair" involved characters already known to us and Crowley.[38] Among them were the Theosophist Baroness von Seidlitz and the Russian revolutionist Ivan Narodny, mentioned earlier in connection with Marie von Sievers and Rudolf Steiner. Also mixed up in the business were Gaunt and Thwaites.

Brasol fancied himself literary and adored Edgar Allen Poe, whom Hanns Heinz Ewers also passionately admired. In fact, Ewers wrote an essay on Poe in 1916 that Brasol added to his library. Beyond that, Brasol took a discreet but intense interest in the supernatural, which offered another point of connection with not only Ewers but also Crowley. Brasol's greatest passion, however, was his anti-Semitism, a subject revisited in the next chapter.[39]

In America one effect of Bolshevism's ascendance in Russia was a frenzied reaction against all forms of radicalism as subversive tools of German militarism. In New York City, Alfred Becker led the attack—a man also destined to become Crowley's closest American contact and sometime guardian angel. It probably was with Becker's and others' encouragement that the Mage would firmly establish himself in Greenwich Village, the capital of radicalism and bohemian culture in the U.S.

One notable visitor to the Village in early 1917 was Leon Trotsky, soon to become Lenin's second-in-command. Crowley was in New Orleans and Florida at the time, but his friend Frank Harris interviewed Trotsky. Ivan Narodny, the anti-Tsarist émigré mentioned above, was also interested in Trotsky.[40] An active revolutionary and fierce enemy of Berlin and the Bolsheviks, Narodny shared Crowley's interest in art and the metaphysical. Both frequented the soirées of another of the Beast's New York friends, the eccentric artist Robert Winthrop Chanler.[41] These swinging get-togethers provided an excellent means to sow and reap information.

Soon after the Bolsheviks came to power, Crowley wrote to Trotsky to praise the Revolution and offer help in ridding the Earth of the scourge of Christianity.[42] So far as can be told, Trotsky never responded to the overture—wisely so. Everything in Crowley's modus operandi suggests his display of radical sympathies was a new twist on his old game: agent provocateur.

Crowley could have pointed to his affiliation with Reuss and the "Anational Congress for Re-Establishing Society on Practical Cooperative Lines" as proof of his bona fides to the Bolsheviks and their friends. That body finally convened during 15–25 August 1917 at Monte Verita. While not expressly communist, the temper of the Congress was openly collectivist and anti-capitalist. Crowley did not attend, of course, but Reuss openly touted Thelema as the official religion of the coming revolutionary epoch.

During early 1918 Crowley's attention was consumed by one of his biggest magical efforts, the Alamantrah Working. Also involved were Roddie Minor, in the key role of medium, along with Marie Lavroff, Eva Tanguay, and other devotees. The aim was to open a doorway to the astral realm and contact its denizens. Crowley reckoned it a great success. For our purposes, the significance of the Alamantrah Working is that Crowley's efforts to capitalize on its results dominated the remainder of his stay in the U.S. and sent him on two more Magical Retreats, both with underlying intelligence agendas.

As usual, Crowley's finances were precarious. Viereck sold *The International*, and there went his regular paycheck. He also griped, "the British would not employ me," and while the Department of Justice remained "warmly appreciative of my work," their warmth fell short of generosity.[43] On the other hand, paychecks from both governments probably could not have kept up with Crowley's prodigality.

Meantime, German clandestine activities were still alive, if weakened. In March 1918, just as the Alamantrah Working was winding down, events in New York cried out for agent Crowley's special touch. They centered on the Americans' pursuit of a group of female agents working for Germany and its allies. One of these dubious ladies was twenty-something Despina Dawidovitch Storch. She claimed Turkish origin but was in fact Russian Jewish.[44] Sophisticated, beautiful, and able to lie in many languages, she materialized in Paris before the war to wed the unfortunate provider of her best-known surname. In 1913, in London, she briefly had another husband, British Army officer James Hesketh. A year later, Despina was back in Paris as the mistress of a dissolute French nobleman, Baron de Beville, restyling herself "Baroness de Beville." She spent part of 1915 in Spain, when Ewers was roaming about there. Her description closely matches that of a mysterious *femme* connected to him, and Ewers probably accompanied her and the Baron back to the Americas.

In New York, Storch, Beville, and another shady couple with aristocratic affectations lavishly entertained their way into Gotham social circles. These included Chanler's gatherings and the occult salon run by von Seidlitz, who introduced

Storch to the same gang of corrupt Russians as were being spied on by Narodny and Lavroff's friend Semenovskii.[45] The aim of Storch's ring, American investigators found, was intelligence on munitions production and shipments, "transmitted to Berlin through channels which are not open to inspection by Allied censors."[46] That sounds curiously similar to the communication "without the use of either the telegraph or cable systems" allegedly used by Crowley and Plummer.[47]

The BI and Secret Service offices in New York discovered Storch's operation in late 1917, immediately after the Mage began consorting with Marie Lavroff. Having infiltrated her circle, the Americans picked up Storch and her accomplices on 18 March 1918. She confessed with surprising alacrity (peyote again?), but to the consternation of her captors the seemingly healthy young woman suddenly died of what looked like acute pneumonia. Some suspected the Spanish flu, others foul play, but nothing could be proved.

Despina Storch did reveal enough to help put two of her sister spies behind bars, Baroness von Seidlitz and a more recent reinforcement, Maria de Victorica. The Americans arrested both in late April. Maria de Victorica, a.k.a. Maria von Kretschmann, Mlle. Vussiere, and other aliases, was one of the few female agents to meet Hollywood standards.[48] About forty when she arrived in New York aboard a Norwegian steamer on 21 January 1917, she was an erudite cosmopolitan whose "blonde, bold attractiveness" had seduced her Chilean husband into spying for Berlin, as it had many others.[49]

Her assignment in the States was to "carry on German and pacifist propaganda through the Catholic Church and to assure Irish revolutionaries of the backing of Germany."[50] The Catholic angle may mesh somehow with Crowley's interest in that faith as noted by Watts. Beyond that, through her collaboration with Clan-na Gael and allied Irish groups, Victorica certainly met people Crowley knew, if not the Beast himself. Her grander aims were to initiate a fresh sabotage offensive against British ships (to coincide with the renewal of unrestricted submarine warfare) and to drum up support for a new uprising in Ireland.[51]

Obviously, British intelligence had reasons to watch her. Once more, the Americans found Victorica's trail in November 1917 through information provided by the "British Secret Service."[52] Crowley was an ideal source. Handling the case for the BI was Superintendent Charles de Woody, who was close to Attorney General Becker. Like Storch, Victorica ended up at the presumably secure military jail on Ellis Island. Her severe morphine addiction complicated questioning. Given his pharmacological savoir faire, Crowley could have advised on how best to exploit Victorica's cravings. Withdrawal aside, Victorica fell ill with symptoms identical to Storch's, and American authorities now feared that some sort of "scientific murderer" was at work.[53] Whether or not her affliction was scientifically or magically caused, she recovered and went on to give damning testimony in several espionage and sedition trials.

In mid-1918 Frank Harris introduced Crowley to another American writer and journalist, William Seabrook, who described the Mage as reminding him of "a nursery imp masquerading as Mephistopheles."[54] Fascinated by all things occult and grotesque (he boasted of having once eaten human flesh), Seabrook formed an immediate bond with Crowley. Another dimension to their relationship probably remained invisible to Seabrook. His employer, press mogul William Randolph Hearst, had used his newspapers to promote a strongly anti-British and anti-interventionist stance, much to the annoyance of His Majesty's officials in New York and London. Hearst corresponded with Viereck, and according to the Bureau of Investigation, "there was no other man whose attitude was so friendly to Germany during the war."[55] Crowley's friendship with Seabrook fit a now familiar pattern, cultivating a source of information inside the enemy camp.

Crowley later described the summer of 1918 as "uneventful."[56] On 17 July, however, our man was summoned to the Murray Hill Hotel which housed the offices of Attorney General Becker, where Crowley was quizzed about his work for the Germans and the British "Secret Service."[57] At the meeting, Becker's agents (though not Becker himself) probed the Beast about the activities of Edward Rumley, the pro-German editor of *The New York Evening Mail*.[58] Rumley was a friend of Viereck and suspected of taking German money. He also was part of the spy ring set up by Victorica. What Crowley had to say about Rumley and friends unfortunately is not revealed.

Two days after the meeting, the Mage borrowed some money from Seabrook and headed up the Hudson River in a leaky canoe. His purpose, he claimed, was a magical retreat on Esopus (Aesopus) Island, a rocky, uninhabited speck between Poughkeepsie and Kingston.

Crowley paddled north past the small town of Garrison and the Society of Atonement's nearby Graymoor Manor. Near Newburgh a violent storm forced him ashore, where he found unexpected hospitality from an English gentleman acquainted with Crowley's Aunt Annie. It was a one in a million chance, or no chance at all. The gentleman was Jonathan T. Whitehead, a wealthy British businessman who had a summer house there. Perhaps he and the Master Therion had met before. Doing business in the City, Whitehead was very familiar with the British Consulate and its officials. If Crowley needed a cut-out to stay in contact with New York, Whitehead fit the bill perfectly. Whitehead later paid at least one visit to the Mage's Esopus camp—on the pretext of answering Crowley's prayers for fresh prawns.[59]

Crowley made a spectacle of himself on the island, writing "Do What Thou Wilt" and other slogans on the surrounding cliffs with the gallons of red paint he had brought along. His spiritual exercises often compelled him to sit motionless in the same spot for hours, which naturally intrigued the locals. Still, his magical and physical needs required a female presence. Mrs. Minor paid a few visits, but when the already tattered relationship disintegrated for good, Crowley was temporarily hard up.

He found a remedy during a brief return to Manhattan on 19 August. The main purpose of the visit was "OTO business," but he also visited Becker's office. On this errand, Crowley encountered a friend of Seabrook, the artist and puppeteer Tony Sarg, who knew just the girl willing to give it up to a stranger on a deserted island.[60] The arrangement certainly was not so accidental, contra Crowley. The young woman was the aspiring actress Madeline George, a twice-divorced, petite brunette whom one ex-husband described as "very erratic and an adventuress" and capable of just about anything.[61] Anything may have included espionage. Madeline had recently attracted the attention of British intelligence by entertaining a string of officers in her Montreal hotel room. The British shared with the Americans their suspicion that La George was playing Mata Hari, a suspicion supported by her contact with real or supposed German agents such as Baroness von Seidlitz and Edward Rumley.[62] Becker's men likely tapped Crowley to turn the tables on the wily Madeline and seduce secrets from her.

As the Beast later told it, after leaving a note at George's hotel, he returned to his island lair and offered prayers for her swift arrival. The next day, Crowley received a wire from Madeline asking him to meet her at the station nearby in Hyde Park. There he noticed "a tall, distinguished, military-looking man, who seemed to be eyeing me strangely."[63] This was Maj. James B. Ord, the MID's resident officer in West Point, who kept an eye on the lower Hudson Valley. According to Crowley, the Major approached him and explained that his presence on Esopus had provoked much concern locally. Upon querying New York, however, Ord was surprised to learn that "[Crowley] was . . . working for the Department of Justice."[64] Crowley happily confided to the Major that the DJ (more probably Becker) "had instructed me to keep my eyes open for any suspicious incidents." Like Simon Iff, Crowley helped Ord clear up a minor mystery involving strange lights and troop trains and even reported on a couple of doubtful nocturnal boaters—or so says Crowley.

Crowley's version of events is basically true but also misleading. The other side of the story is in Ord's report to his MID superiors in Washington. Ord wrote that Crowley interested his office because of his connection to Madeline George and her trip to the Island. Making inquiries with the New York BI, specifically de Woody, Ord learned that Crowley served the British and had been investigated and "cleared" by Becker. Still, Ord was not altogether convinced. "In view of the information that has been gathered within the past two months [August-September]," he noted, "it may be possible that Aleister Crowley is double crossing the British Government . . . the case has not been completed as yet."[65] The Major apparently kept the Beast under surveillance and was not reassured by what he found out. The dossier gives no further details.

Expurgated passages from Crowley's later account provide a few more tantalizing clues. First, he had a gun with him, which suggests that he was anticipating some sort of trouble. In his absence, Madeline discovered it hidden among his bedding and threw it in the bushes. That argues she was not quite so trusting after all. Also, according to the Beast, she feared that he was going to lead a "squad of secret-service men" back to the island, presumably to arrest her.[66]

Extraordinary coincidences surround Crowley's Esopus adventure. On 4 July 1918, a British traveler, Guy Varley Rayment, arrived in New York on Admiralty orders. Rayment was an NID officer and Admiral Hall's representative to the Interdepartmental Committee on Indian sedition. He stayed at the Brevoort Hotel, unseemly lodging for a naval intelligence officer. On the edge of Greenwich Village, the Brevoort was a popular watering hole for the local radical and Boho-literati crowd, among them Crowley's friend and mescaline guinea pig Theodore Dreiser. Crowley dined there often as it was barely a block away from his rooms on 9th Street.

Rayment remained in the U.S. for three months, covering the time Crowley was at Esopus. During this same period, Assistant Secretary of the Navy Franklin Roosevelt made a special trip to Europe, and Rayment had some role in arranging details. FDR sailed from New York aboard a U.S. Navy destroyer just five days after Rayment's arrival. Upon reaching England, Roosevelt received an especially warm greeting from Rayment's and Crowley's boss Admiral Hall, who gave the Secretary a tour of Room 40. As discussed further in the following chapter, FDR was fascinated by cloak-and-dagger affairs and ran his own special unit of naval intelligence. The future president also took a lively interest in the occult.

Roosevelt had cooperated closely with Gaunt, Thwaites, and other British operatives well before the U.S. officially joined the war. FDR later liked to boast that his pro-Allied activities earned him the #2 spot on a secret German list of troublesome Americans "to be eliminated." [67] The common assumption is that this was one of FDR's fantasies, but British agents may have planted the idea to flatter and manipulate him.

Esopus, recall, was near Hyde Park, which lay in the county where Robert Chanler had been (or still was) sheriff. Close to Hyde Park was Springwood, the family home of Franklin Roosevelt. Did mere chance put the Mage at this spot, or was he directed there by Rayment or Becker? Becker knew Roosevelt well via New York State politics and may have felt a special obligation to the Navy Secretary. One concern, given the alleged German threat against FDR, could have been a Meunter-style assault on the Roosevelt household in FDR's absence. Crowley might not have been much of a deterrent to any physical attack, but he could keep an eye out for suspicious characters. Moreover, the Storch and Victorica cases had raised real concerns about the enemy's use of "occult" methods, and who was better prepared to deal with something like that?

On 11 October, soon after he returned to New York, Crowley was summoned again to Becker's office, presumably for debriefing about his recent adventures up the Hudson. This time he spoke with Becker himself, and passed what he described as a "delightful evening, telling my tale." The Beast added that Becker was "vastly amazed" and a bit aghast that some of his best operatives had "spent weeks of painstaking strategy on the trail of a man from the department next door."[68] According to Becker's side of the story, he quizzed his guest on "his knowledge of German propaganda."[69] Much of the discussion focused on Theodor Reuss and the OTO. Crowley provided Becker with a copy of Reuss's 22 January 1917 proclamation. According to Becker, "Mr. Crowley has characterized the circular . . . as being German propaganda."[70] He reminded Becker that Reuss may have come to the U.S. during the war and that he had "previously informed the Bureau" of that.[71] He also asserted that Reuss had "some considerable official position in Germany."[72] In later testimony before the U.S. Senate, Becker admitted that "Aleister Crowley and his organization may be classified as a dubious proposition," but he denied that the Mage had been a German tool. Crowley's group, opined Becker, was merely a "pacifist affair."[73]

1   Details of Bacon's case can be found in USNA, KV2/4-5. See also Landau, 88,150. For contemporary press accounts, see *NYT* (20 Feb. 1917), 1:7, (22 Feb. 1917, 2:5, (15 March 1917), 3:3 and (27 March 1917), 15:2.

2   Dwight Messimer, *The Merchant U-Boat: The Adventures of the Deutschland, 1916–1918* (Annapolis: Naval Institute Press, 1988).

3   *NYT* (1 Nov. 1916), 1:5 ff.

4   *Ibid.,* (14 Nov. 1916), 2:6.

5   *CAC,* 754.

6   *Liber LXXIII,* 15 Dec. 1916.

7   *Ibid.,* 12 Nov. 1916.

8   In 1917, Keasbey was one of the main organizers of the Peoples' Council of America, "one of the more radical antiwar groups." The University of Texas summarily dismissed him from its employ in July 1917. See: www.ardisnet.com/personal/DaveAllerdiceSr/Keasbey.htm.

9   Reuss, "Manifesto," 22 Jan. 1917, in Peter Koenig (ed.), *Ordo Templi Orientis: Theodor Reuss,* //user.cyberlink.ch/~koenig/tituals.htm.

10 *Liber LXXIII,* 6 Oct., 1916.

11 *CAC,* 776.

12 *Liber LXXIII,* 13 Jan. 1917, p.s.

13 *Ibid.,* 27 Dec. 1916.

14 Stephen E. Flowers, 'Introduction," H.H. Ewers, *Strange Tales* (Austin, TX: Runa-Raven Press, 2000).

15 Bis-(2-chloroethyl) sulfide.

16 *Liber LXXIII,* 2 Feb. 1917.

17 *CAC,* 855–856

18 *Liber LXIII,* 29 March 1917.

19 *Ibid.*

20 *Ibid.*

21 *CAC,* 756.

22 *CAC,* 757.

23 For background, see Yigal Sheffy, *British Military Intelligence in the Palestine Campaign, 1914–1918* (London: Frank Cass, 1998).

24 USNA, MID 10175, Viereck reports, 1917.

25 *Ibid.,* 10516-474/33, In re: Hans Heinz Ewers, Enemy Alien, 26 June 1918.

26 *Ibid.,* 10516-282, 6,7, 18 Dec. 1917.

27 *Ibid.,* BI, OG 39583, Burleson, Postmaster General note, 8 Feb. 1918.

28 Nagler, 393, quoting BI Investigative Case Files, "British suspect list," reel 1877, 9-19-1880-0. See also, BI 8000-2500.

29 MID, 10516-474/20, In re: Hans Heinz Ewers, 15 June 1918.

30 *Ibid.*, /18, 15 June 1918.

31 WWP, 6/171, Wiseman to Chief, 6 Sept. 1918.

32 *CAC*, 754 and William Breeze.

33 WWP, 6/173, "Office Personnel," c. March 1918.

34 Thanks again to William Breeze for this deleted excerpt.

35 *Liber LXXIII*, 28 Aug. 1917.

36 *Ibid.*, 14 June 1917.

37 In Russian, *Brazol.*

38 Thwaites also showed no interest in investigating the affair because it threatened to expose British double agents like Reilly. See: HIA, Posol'stvo, U.S., 370/12, "Nekrassov," 12, and USNA, DS, 861.202 11/5, Bakhmeteff to Polf, 12 Oct. 1917.

39 See: Norman Hapgood, "The Inside Story of Henry Ford's Jew Mania," *Hearst's International*, Vol. 41 (June 1922), 14-18 and Vol. 42 (July 1922), 14-18, 106.

40 UKNA, KV2/502, Division of Special Intelligence Report #654, 26 Aug. 1917.

41 "When the Sheriff Heard about the Soprano's Divorce!," *Athens* (Ohio) *Messenger* (11 Sept. 1927).

42 Colin Wilson, *Aleister Crowley: The Nature of the Beast* (Wellingborough: Aquarian Press, 1987), 137.

43 *CAC*, 836.

44 *NYT*, 31 March 1918, I 16:3

45 M.I. Gaiduk, *Utiug: Materialy I fakty o zagotovitel'noi deiatel'nosti russkikh vooennykh komissii v Amerike* (New York, 1918), 80.

46 *Ibid.*

47 USNA, MID 9140-808, Re: W. Plummer, etc., 19 Sept. 1917.

48 Landau, 90.

49 *NYT* (13 Aug. 1920), 24:1.

50 USNA, MID 9771-56, "Irish Agitation in the United States," 10 March 1919, 9.

51 *Ibid.*, 6, 9.

52 Landau, 90–91

53 *NYT* (13 Aug. 1920), 24:1.

54 William Seabrook, *Witchcraft, Its Power in the World Today* (NY: Harcourt Brace, 1940), 217.

55 W. A. Swanberg, *Citizen Hearst* (NY: Bantam Books, 1967), 377.

56 *CAC*, 783

57 BI, file 365985, Agent O'Donnell Report, 30 July 1919.

58 *Ibid.*, "Memo for Mr. Hoover," 7 Jan. 1920, and Crowley FBI file 61-2069, Brennan to Hoover, 1 Aug. 1924, 2–3, quoting 19 July 1919 report of Agent O'Donnell.

59 *CAC*, 784.

60 *Ibid.*

61 BI, Case file 181633, "In re: Madeline George," 23 April 1918.

62 USNA, MID 10012-112/1, 23 Sept. 1918.

63 *CAC*, 785.

64 *Ibid.*

65 USNA, MID 10012-1121/1, *Ibid.*

66 Thanks to William Breeze.

67 Joseph Persico, *Roosevelt's Secret War* (NY: Random House, 2002), 8. The first name on the alleged list was Frank Polk, chief of the State Department's Bureau of Special Intelligence and a close pal of Norman Thwaites.

68 This comes from another deletion in *Confessions*. Thanks to William Breeze.

69 BI file 365985, "Memo for Mr. Hoover," 7 Jan. 1920.

70 Sixty-Sixth Congress, *Ibid.*, 2027.

71 BI, file 365985, Agent O'Donnell Report, 30 July 1919, and FBI file 61-2069, *Ibid.*, 3.

72 *Ibid.*

73 Sixty-Sixth Congress, *Ibid.*, 2028.

CHAPTER TEN

~

AMERICAN END GAME

~

THE ARMISTICE OF 11 NOVEMBER 1918 ENDED THE WAR but brought neither peace nor security. Old conflicts continued and new ones erupted as the diplomats gathered in Paris. Fighting would drag on for months or years in Russia, the Middle East, and Ireland. The spread of Communism fueled new hopes and fears, igniting a worldwide secret war to advance or contain it, one in which Crowley would play his part. Still, in America, the situation seemed bright and clear. Germany and her allies were beaten, their intrigues *kaput*. Britain and the U.S. glowed with mutual admiration, and British intelligence could roll up its tent and go home.

The reality was starkly different, especially behind the public display of affection between London and Washington. Britain had gone to war against Germany as against the Empire's primary naval and commercial rival. With the Reich's defeat, the United States assumed both positions. As long as London's and Washington's policies harmonized, peace would prevail; if not, armed conflict could easily erupt. Even before the war was over, Wiseman warned his chief, Mansfield Cumming, that the American establishment was full of persons "afraid of the influence of the British Navy" and "still afraid of George III."[1] Likewise many in the British Admiralty, Crowley's employer, saw American naval power as a greater menace than Germany's had ever been. The U.S. was simply a bigger, stronger, and (thanks especially to war profits) richer nation. It also was one to which Britain was deeply in debt. Just as the Germans had, the Americans now merited careful watching.

While many American officials continued to help to their British colleagues, some grew suspicious. In late 1918, Justice Department officials began to balk at sharing information with the British. For example, Nathan's demand to see all reports on Irish agitation sparked strong objections.[2] Part of this reluctance came from new officials at Justice and its BI, among them Wilson's Red-hunting Attorney General A. Mitchell Palmer. At Palmer's side was his hand-picked chief of the Radical Division, the punctilious and suspicious young John Edgar Hoover. Hoover suspected the

British not only of general bad faith, but also of manipulating the radical movement for their own obscure purposes. He was correct on both counts. As one Bureau report put it, "the British have better information concerning radical activities in this country and it is known that to secure this information they must have a very efficient force in operation."[3]

This shift inevitably affected Crowley's relationship with American agencies. His German intrigues had afforded him many links to the radical underground, as had Greenwich Village's bohemian circles. Among his Village neighbors, for instance, was anarchist firebrand Emma Goldman, then running a massage parlor off 17th Street. The voluptuous Beast is sure to have enjoyed a good rub there. As noted earlier, Red Emma was the comrade and paramour of anarchist Alexander Berkman. Like Crowley both were friends of Frank Harris. A few years later in Paris, the Beast tried to cadge money out of Goldman, an overture arguing some prior acquaintance. Crowley's movements at the end of his American stay are also strangely synchronous with Berkman's and Goldman's.

The end of the war also weakened but did not end Crowley's relationship with British intelligence. It first seemed that Section V would shut down completely. William Wiseman, now full-time "Liaison Officer between the British War Cabinet and Washington," was consumed by the upcoming Peace Conference. Before the year was out, however, he informed subordinates in New York that, while the SIS station would be scaled back, Cumming was determined to maintain a British intelligence presence.

Postwar intelligence work for the British in America focused on the "Irish Problem." This escalated in January 1919, when Sinn Fein parliamentarians proclaimed independence in Dublin. Guerrilla warfare and bloody reprisals spread across the Emerald Isle. Indian nationalist unrest likewise continued. Disturbingly, in place of Berlin, Irish and Indian dissidents found a new champion—Red Moscow.

In February 1919, control of the reduced SIS station at 44 Whitehall Street. passed to the able hands of Robert Nathan, aided by the trusty Norman Thwaites. Although his primary focus was the Irish case, Nathan broadly scrutinized radical activities in New York and around the country. He and Thwaites "recovered and re-organized a number of useful informants" to keep tabs on "Bolshevists, I.W.W., trouble-makers, Anarchists, etc."[4] Nathan did not overlook an experienced asset like Crowley, with his links to American counterintelligence, the Irish and Indian spheres, and New York's radical demimonde.

The Beast had something more in common with a mysterious figure that joined the British operation in March 1919 and eventually took control of it. This man variously styled himself "Ronald Strath" (apparently his true name), "Dr. Alexander

Edmund Strath-Gordon," "Captain James," and "Charles Fox." The forty-six-year-old Strath was born in Dublin, studied in Edinburgh, and served in the Boer War. Later he was a medical officer ministering to the Cree Indians in remote northern Manitoba.[5] There he took an interest in shamanistic medicine, an early example of his esoteric and occult studies. A theosophist, or at least strongly influenced by Theosophy, he later founded the Atlantean Research Society, which sought to recover and apply the secrets of the legendary lost civilization. It almost goes without saying that Strath was a 33rd-degree Mason.

In WWI, Strath joined the Canadian Army Medical Corps, but ultimately found himself in MI5, probably recruited by Nathan. Captain Ronald Strath joined the British Mission in New York in March 1919 and worked there through 31 August. A U.S. naval intelligence report identifies "Captain Strath-Gordon" as the man who relieved Thwaites of his post in March.[6]

Nathan left for England by August, and Thwaites soon after. At the same time, Ronald Strath vanished from MI5's roster, and "Captain James" appeared as head of the SIS section concealed within the New York Consulate's Passport Control Office.[7] Thereafter identified as the "head of the British Secret Service force in the United States" with "charge of all operatives," James received agents at his home in Elmhurst, Long Island, where "a great many secret meetings are held."[8] As alter ego "Charles Fox," Strath communicated with other agents through a post box in Manhattan's City Hall Station. City Hall Station was close to Crowley's new abode on Greenwich Village's Washington Square.

The new intrigues in New York picked up some threads from 1917. During 29–31 October of that year, the "League of Small and Subject Nationalities" held its opening congress at Manhattan's McAlpin Hotel. At the conclave, representatives of some twenty-five national and ethnic groups, including Albanians, Assyrians, Koreans, Serbs, and even Swedes, called for recognition or independence.[9] Anti-militarism and anti-imperialism were the leading themes, and Irish and Indians predominated among attendees, generating a strongly anti-British mood.[10] There also was a strong undertone of radicalism; the gathering included many anarchists and socialists, and quite a few future communists. Even Crowley's old comrades the Jacobites sent a representative, the soi-disant Chief of Clann Fhearghuis of Stra-Chur, who spoke for Scotland. Was the unnamed Chief a disguised Beast reprising his role as a Highland laird?

At the head of the League stood Dr. Frederic C. Howe, the commissioner of immigration for the Port of New York and a former Wilson loyalist alienated by that President's interventionist and "repressive" policies. Howe's right-hand man was former Assistant Secretary of State Dudley Field Malone, a fellow leftist and disgruntled Wilsonite who had recently resigned as Collector of Customs. We have encountered him before in connection to the *Lusitania* and the operations of the U.S. Secret Service. Malone would go on to serve as attorney for German spy Maria de Victorica and the "Soviet Government Bureau" that appeared in New York in early 1919.[11] During 1919, he took over the above League and retooled it into the openly pro-Bolshevik "League of Oppressed Peoples."[12] That body was linked to a Soviet-backed one of the same name in Berlin.

To no surprise, British intelligence spied on Malone. In July 1919, Wiseman, back in New York on ostensibly private business, wrote to Prime Minister David Lloyd George's office, "Our friend Dudley Malone has come out as a regular socialist revolutionary leader. He spends his time trying to keep the Bolsheviks out of jail [but] he is still a most delightful companion and sends you his love."[13] Was Malone also a British asset? If so, did Crowley know?

Of more interest to us is the claim that "Aleister Crowley, the well-known Satanist, who was then working in the United States for Germany, was connected with this [League of Oppressed Peoples] through one of its agents in America. . . ."[14] So asserted Nesta Webster, a pioneer of conspiracy theory, unreserved British-imperialist, anti-radical, and anti-Semite. Despite her own fascination with spiritualism and reincarnation, Webster constantly fretted about the nefarious doings of secret societies, especially Freemasons and their kin. She was certain that Aleister Crowley was an instrument of the Powers of Darkness.

While Webster's interpretation of data frequently veered off into the bizarre and obsessive, she also dredged up weird but verifiable details. She suggests that the same individual who connected Crowley to the Leagues also got him to write "an obscene libel on the King," which sounds like a reference to the Beast's 1915 piece for *Open Court*. That points to Viereck, who knew Malone and many others involved. Yet another Crowley link to the Small and Subject Nationalities realm was former acolyte turned German paymaster George Raffalovitch.

The tale of the Leagues gets curiouser. According to Webster, the American-based League of Oppressed Peoples was taken over and moved to Berlin by "a mysterious American, subsidizer of a defeatist paper in Switzerland, acting under the direct orders of a powerful pan-German secret society—the Druidenorden [sic]."[15] There is at least some truth in this. The American was John Wesley De Kay, a prewar entrepreneur in Mexico whose crooked financial dealings forced him to flee U.S. justice to Europe. Early in the war, he engaged in shady arms deals for Pancho Villa and other Mexican factions as a front for the Germans. The French later arrested him for defrauding the Belgian Army. In 1917, he took refuge in Switzerland, where British intelligence identified him as "chief of the sabotage and murder section of the German [Secret Service]."[16] De Kay also wrote and subsidized publications promoting social revolution and pacifism, guided at first by the "extreme Junker party in Germany" and later by the "Propaganda Section of the Communist International." His wartime activities in Switzerland display a strong similarity to those of Reuss, and some connection surely existed. So, it is not hard to see how Crowley, or at least Crowley's name, could be roped into this nexus.

During 1919, the busy Mr. De Kay collected funds from both the Soviets and a continuing "German Secret Bureau" to form a new society to "unite all the Revolutionary Parties of different countries to further the mutual cause". [17] A prime goal of this organization was the destruction of the British Empire. De Kay created a true secret society, sealed with oaths of grisly death to traitors. The precise relationship of this body to the League of Oppressed Peoples (*Vereinigung Vergewaeltister Voelker*) in Berlin and Malone's like-named New York group remains vague, but there were common conspiratorial threads. British sources, which may have included the Beast, reported that De Kay was "endeavoring to link up" his society with Malone's.[18]

British intelligence also identified one of De Kay's key backers and his secret society's #2 as Count Ernst zu Reventlow. This German naval officer, a militant expansionist, earned the nickname "High Priest of German Frightfulness" for his unrelenting advocacy of U-boat warfare and other hard-nosed policies.[19] The Count loathed England, which he saw as Germany's most dangerous enemy. In the postwar environment, this drew Reventlow to those reactionary Germans who allied themselves with the Bolsheviks to continue clandestine war against Perfidious Albion.

Since the Count's bloodthirsty sentiments exactly matched the line Crowley was pushing on the Germans in the States, mutual admiration blossomed. In February 1917, the Beast's piece "Delenda est Britannia" ran in *The Fatherland*. It was a glowing review of Reventlow's recent book *The Vampire of the Continent*, a vituperative assault on Britain and all it stood for. Crowley's personal copy came over on the *Deutschland*. He proudly recalled the article as one of his best "counter-propaganda" efforts, and that it helped to persuade Bernstorff to support unrestricted submarine warfare even as it reached new heights of absurdity by advocating England's reduction to "a German colony."[20]

Another conspicuous detail is that Reventlow's sister, the writer and "Cosmic Countess" Franziska zu Reventlow, was a luminary of Monte Verita during the war.[21] She knew Reuss well, and one of her last stories, *Wir Spione*, dealt with accusations of espionage among residents of a neutral "health resort."

Like nearly everyone linked to Crowley, Reventlow was fascinated by the occult, and he belonged to the shadowy *Druiden-Orden*. Also, De Kay's and Reventlow's European supporters included Hungarian statesman and Rosicrucian adept Count Alfred Apponyi, said to have fraternized with the Golden Dawn years earlier.[22] The Beast was one of the very few operatives who could have recognized and pieced together these tangled threads.

In 1917 William Wiseman began a special operation of his own. Soon after the fall of the Tsar, he decided to "guide the storm" in Russia, using money, secret propaganda and hand-picked agents.[23] Doing this from New York, he believed, would obscure the British hand. One of Wiseman's most important agents in this gambit was Crowley's old antagonist, Somerset Maugham. The latter popped up in Gotham after his stint for British intelligence in Switzerland helping Nathan chase down Indian seditionists and anarchist assassins. Maugham and Crowley maintained their enmity, but could not have ignored each other's presence in New York, especially since they had the same boss.

In getting the Russian mission from Wiseman, Maugham may again have bagged a job that Crowley wanted. The Mage, unlike Maugham, actually had some experience in Russia. Wiseman described one part of his plan as "endeavor[ing] to do in Russia what we have done successfully elsewhere; namely to place Germans who are working for us among the real German agents . . . ," and use persons who "have special facilities for getting into the confidence of German agents."[24] One of Wiseman's concerns was that "the Germans have managed to secure control of the most important secret societies in Russia."[25] "It is necessary that this German influence should be exposed," he noted, "and counter-Societies organized, if necessary." Crowley would seem ideal for such duty, but Wiseman perhaps decided that the Master Therion was more useful where he was, cultivating the likes of Lavroff, Narodny, and Brasol.

Another gap in Crowley's *Magical Record* lasts from early September 1918 through the rest of his American stay. He remained at 1 University Place until January 1919, moving then a few blocks away to 63 Washington Square South. There he lived with a new lady-love, Swiss-American Leah Hirsig, whom he dubbed "Soror Alostrael" and "The Ape of Thoth."[26]

On 26 February 1919, the *Evening World*, again at British collaborator Cosgrave's instigation, ran an article lauding Crowley as "Greenwich Village's latest sensation."[27] The emphasis was on his recent and moderately successful exhibition of "Dead Souls" paintings. The article drew an un-Bohemian portrait of the Mage, noting his well-tailored clothes and proper manners, both more befitting a Wall Street banker than a Village artist. It also observed that his roomy, well-furnished apartment was atypical for the neighborhood. Obviously, he no longer was in the poorhouse.

By far the most interesting thing about the article is that Crowley was unusually candid about his service for Britain. He confessed to having been in the "confidential service" of the British Government before the war and to have been shot in the leg in the line of duty. "He then came to this country, in late 1915 [sic, 1914]," the article read, "on a special mission for the British, and later became editor of *The International*, a radical magazine published in Greenwich Village." He did not come right out and say that he was a British spy, and he sidestepped his labors for the Germans. Spinning *The International* as a radical rag was clear pandering to the pro-Bolshie crowd. He played to the same audience by drawing special attention to one of his paintings, *Young Bolshevik Girl with a Wart Looking at Trotsky*. Crowley also pointed out that one of his favorite Dead Soul portraits was that of the actress Madame Yorska. The Madame was an intimate of Hanns Heinz Ewers, who in June 1918 had offered to betray him and his accomplices to the Bureau of Investigation.[28] Was Crowley's portrait intended as a reproach, or a commendation?

Aside from his new Scarlet Woman and his painting, Crowley's chief preoccupation during early 1919 was arranging publication of a new, third volume of the OTO's *Equinox*. Despite the assistance of Charles Stansfield Jones, whom the Mage embraced as his "spiritual son," it proved hard going. Crowley blamed the "dishonest intrigues of the people in Detroit" who handled the money end.[29] These were a gaggle of wealthy "high grade freemasons" headed by millionaire publisher Albert W. Ryerson, a star in Detroit's "bohemian colony" whose "palatial home in aristocratic Grosse Pointe" was a gathering place for that ilk.[30] The *Equinox* business was part of Crowley's bigger aim, to enlist Ryerson and friends in creating a "Supreme Grand Council" of Masonry. This body would "reorganize" Masonic rites, with the ultimate aim of subordinating them to the OTO.[31] The Beast spun visions of a luxurious temple that would make Detroit the Midwestern Paris of esotericism.

Like most of Crowley's schemes, this fizzled. Still, hidden agendas lurked in his dealings with the Detroit brethren. Ryerson's contacts in the "bohemian colony" included members of the local radical crowd. Along with New York and Chicago, the Justice Department regarded Detroit as a prime center of revolutionary activism. Dealing with Ryerson afforded the Mage a cover for his ongoing work as snoop and informant.

Ryerson's social contacts also included the towering figure of Motor City Masonry, Henry Ford. While nothing directly ties Ford to the *Equinox* affair, the Masonic nexus afforded Crowley a conduit to the Great Man. Ford was a devout Freemason, an avowed believer in reincarnation, and (like his friend Thomas Edison) intrigued by the mysteries of Theosophy.

Ford's politics were as irregular as his metaphysics. When not too busy union-busting in his plants, he hobnobbed with avowed socialists (e.g., Rozika Schwimmer), subsidized quasi-radical causes (e.g., the abortive Peace Ship) and took an active interest in revolutionary Russia. In 1918, for instance, Ford backed a press syndicate whose correspondents included a strange Russian, Boris Leonidovich Tageev, a.k.a. Colonel Roustam Bek. This former Tsarist officer, a veteran of the revolutionary agitation, aligned himself with the Bolsheviks after the October Revolution. Tageev met several times with Ford after his arrival in the States, and in early 1919, while Crowley was busy in Detroit, Tageev became military advisor to the new Russian Soviet Government Bureau in New York. That, moreover, put him in the same circle as Dudley Field Malone.[32] The Soviet Bureau courted commercial deals with American businessmen, and Ford was a prime target. Naturally the Soviet Bureau also engaged in propaganda and espionage. Tageev may have played another role as the mysterious "Colonel Malinowsky," head of the "Bolshevik Secret Service in the U.S.A."[33]

The Jewish Question that vexed Ford may have given Crowley another angle to exploit. The Flivver King was convinced that German-Jewish bankers were the invisible hand behind the World War. In early 1919, he found further fertilizer for his conspiracy theory in the infamous *Protocols of the Learned Elders of Zion.*[34] Boris Brasol, the Russian who put an English translation of *Protocols* in Ford's hands, we have met before. Brasol was now a special informant to American Military Intelligence. His Jew-baiting reports often fell on deaf ears, but he found Ford receptive. In July 1919, Ford gave an interview to the *World* in which he openly denounced the "International Jew" as the arch-instigator and profiteer of wars and revolutions.[35]

Crowley's attitude towards Jews was, typically, contradictory, and he was certainly capable of telling the likes of Ford and Brasol what they wanted to hear. Basically, the Beast held that Jews were inherently decent folk, but that centuries of relentless persecution had exaggerated their "worst qualities."[36] Thus he could proclaim that Jews in Eastern Europe practiced human sacrifice and that "Israel has corrupted the whole world, whether by conquest, by conversion or by conspiracy."[37] In 1922 he proposed a convenient means for Jews to regain their true will and destiny—the adoption of Thelema as the foundation of a new Israel.[38]

British and American intelligence reports in this period contain many references to the Russian Revolution and Bolshevism as the handiwork of Jewish conspiracy. In early 1920, even Winston Churchill publicly attacked the insidious work of "international . . . atheistic Jews," whom he distinguished from good "nationalist" (i.e., Zionist) Jews.[39] Closer to Crowley, New York's Section V received and circulated many reports describing the insidious collusion of Jewish revolutionaries and bankers. In March 1917, for instance, Wiseman himself cabled to London that Trotsky was about to sail for Russia backed by "Jewish funds . . . behind which are possibly German."[40] Later dispatches from Russia, including Maugham's, described "Jewish socialists" as the main tools of German intrigue in Russia, financed by Jewish financiers such as Max Warburg.

In New York, much suspicion centered on Warburg's friend and ally Jacob Schiff and the two Warburg brothers he employed. Recall that British intelligence generally, and Crowley personally, had a friend inside Schiff's firm, Otto Kahn. In April 1919, Robert Nathan (himself Jewish) sent a "Bolshevist Report" to London that warned of "wide and violent" Soviet propaganda in America and of the Wilson administration's dangerous "leniency and even sympathy" toward Bolshevism.[41] A few months later, a similar report arrived from London's agent Ralph Isham, who headed "A-2," a secret anti-Bolshevik unit in the British Army. Visiting the U.S. that summer, Isham compiled a report that accused Jacob Schiff of being pro-German during the war (basically true) and a secret benefactor of the Soviet regime.[42] Tangled in the same net of intrigue was our old friend the Baroness von Seidlitz, ex-Tsarist officials, German revanchists, and, for good measure, Dudley Field Malone. Crowley could have briefed Isham on many of these tidbits.

Also, the Flivver-King maintained his own secret service, manned by ex-APL, BI, and other government agents, some of whom our man may have known. From an office at Manhattan's 20 Broad Street, Ford's detectives carefully watched prominent Jews, radicals, and anyone else who raised their suspicions.[43] Tapping into this network would have helped British intelligence discreetly collect and disseminate information, and disinformation.

One propaganda gambit that allegedly received Crowley's special touch was the "British Secret Document" that surfaced in New York in June 1919. This purported to be a letter from Sir William Wiseman to Prime Minister Lloyd George outlining an insidious British scheme to turn American citizens into loyal subjects of His Majesty. The letter detailed a systematic campaign of subversion of everything from the White House and Congress to American religion, press, and popular culture. It was a gross parody of what British propaganda actually had done to shape American opinion, and written by someone familiar with that effort.

The document's *reductio ad absurdum* recalls Crowley's calculated ludicrousness on the pages of *The Fatherland*, etc. For example, the author notes that the "anglicization" time for the average American had been reduced from 104 days to a mere "29 days, 3 hours, 16 minutes" at the low, low cost of only $0.53 per "colonist."[44] Snide references to the "traditional ignorance" of most Americans and their tendency towards homogeneity, covetousness, and pride echo Crowley's own observations. Someone noticed the similarities. After consulting with the chief of the U.S. Secret Service in New York, a BI agent reported to Washington, "It is believed that Crowley may be the author of said paper."[45]

The publisher of the tract, a small firm with Irish Republican connections, attributed the document to an anonymous source. Improbably, an unsigned carbon-copy supposedly was found lying on the sidewalk near Wiseman's former address. As though that were not fishy enough, analysis by U.S. Naval Intelligence discovered enough errors and inconsistencies to prove the document a fraud. Still, only someone with inside knowledge of British intelligence personnel and operations could have concocted it. The letter, for instance, identified Gaunt and Nathan's clandestine "affiliations with the American Secret Service."[46]

Ten years later, Dr. William Maloney stood up to take credit for the document, which he claimed was a "lampoon" of British propaganda. Maloney was a veteran Irish activist and die-hard admirer of Roger Casement. Back when the Document appeared, however, the Bureau of Investigation knew Maloney as something else, a "British agent."[47] The reasonable conclusion is that Maloney and Crowley concocted the Document together, at Wiseman's behest, to discredit Irish criticism of British influence.

Crowley came again to the attention of American authorities in 1919 through a 4 June letter to U.S. Attorney General A. Mitchell Palmer. Its anonymous author declared, "If you desire to find the mastermind that is secretly directing the bomb outrages . . . look into the doings of Aleister Crowley, 1 University Place."[48] It accurately pointed out the Beast's role as an Irish agitator and his connection to *The Fatherland*, describing the Mage as "clever and cunning" and the "directing and planning mind behind men of lesser intelligence." "[He] is more shrewd than any living being," the letter warned, "[and] a real power of evil among men." The writer concluded, "I know absolutely whereof I speak."

Assuming the letter was not Crowley's own perverse self-promotion, someone had it in for him who knew about his recent activities. Unfortunately, nothing else in the files offers a clue to the writer's identity. The letter struck a raw nerve in Washington. At the beginning of June, mail bombs exploded or were disarmed in eight U.S. cities—one addressed to Attorney General Palmer, and all sent from the main post office in Manhattan.

Then on 9 June the Department of Justice received a letter form Joseph W. Norwood of Louisville, Kentucky. Norwood was secretary of the Louisville-based International Magian Society, who described themselves as "freemasons concerned with combating pro-German, Bolshevist and radical propaganda."[49] Norwood was a self-proclaimed expert on Masonic symbolism and a student of Oriental occultism. According to Norwood, Crowley had recently contacted his organization offering confidential information and other services. The Beast billed himself as "a member of the British Mission to the United States" and confessed that in the employ of His Majesty's Secret Service "my main object [was] to bring America into the war."[50] Norwood, suspicious of this strange Englishman, asked Justice to share any information it had on him.

The BI, as usual, politely declined the request, but in evaluating it, they apparently discovered gaps in their files about this peculiar and possibly dangerous man. One wonders, had someone been systematically removing anything related to him? In New York, BI agent O'Donnell got the job of gathering what information he could. This led him to Becker's Bureau, which admitted to having "a more or less extensive file on the subject."[51] Becker's men claimed a hard time locating the file, and it took weeks for O'Donnell to get it, or some redacted version. What O'Donnell saw detailed Crowley's claims to have worked for British interests by goading the Germans into "mak[ing] asses of themselves . . . until even the Americans kicked."[52] He also found the comments of an unnamed British official (certainly Guy Gaunt), dismissing the Beast as a "harmless neurotic" who was "never taken seriously."[53] Crowley may reasonably have assumed that Becker naturally shared all information about him, and his assistance, with the Feds. In that he was clearly mistaken.

The sudden scrutiny by the federal authorities may have helped Crowley conclude that he needed another magical retreat. So he left Manhattan and "spent the summer in a tent beyond Montauk at the extremity of Long Island."[54] In the years since, Montauk Point and its associated military installations have acquired a lively reputation for strange phenomena, and the Great Beast's sojourn there is cited as evidence of the high weirdness that permeates the place.[55] Crowley's declared purpose at Montauk was to build on the success of his recent Workings. But if untroubled mystical contemplation and cool ocean breezes were his goal, Long Island afforded much more secluded spots. Like Esopus Island, his encampment at Montauk was for more than spiritual exercises.

Crowley pitched his tent near one of the most militarized spots on the East Coast. U.S. military presence around Montauk dated back to the Spanish-American War. In 1904, the Navy chose the Point for one of its first maritime wireless stations.[56] During WWI, the Army conducted training nearby while the Navy's outpost grew into a full-fledged Naval Air Station, equipped with seaplanes and the latest communications equipment. The Army had mostly pulled out by the time Crowley showed up, but the Navy station was still manned and operating. Indeed, Montauk

Naval Air Station was still running as late as November 1919, well after Crowley's visit, with a complement of at least a hundred men. Questioned about the slow demobilization, the Navy would only say that the men were staying of their own accord.[57] In reality the Station was a secret experimental base for hydrophone and ground radio devices, torpedoes, and perhaps other things.[58]

The British Admiralty had a division interested in such technologies, the Board of Inventions and Research (BIR). In 1917, the BIR had established a presence within the British War Mission to the U.S. under the direction of Commander Cyprian C. D. Bridge.[59] He was Assistant Secretary of the BIR and the namesake of Admiral Sir Cyprian Bridge, a past Director of Naval Intelligence. The younger Bridge returned to service in 1914 as a naval censor, which put him in the same branch as Feilding. Bridge moved to the BIR in 1915 and ended up in its Section II, which dealt with submarines, wireless telegraphy, telephony, and electrical gizmos, such as the U.S. Navy was developing at Montauk. Bridge had good reason to support Crowley's trip to Montauk, where the Magician might get a hint of what Britain's new naval rivals were up to.[60]

Other business at the Point included a plan by the American military and private concerns for a huge maritime terminal to relieve congestion in New York Harbor. One of the key firms involved was the British Cunard Steamship Line, which, of course, had close ties to the Admiralty. Curiously, Cunard abruptly dropped its Montauk scheme in July 1919, not long after Crowley arrived.[61]

Crowley's presence at Montauk may link him to a wizard of a different kind, Nicola Tesla. Tesla, the epitome of the eccentric scientific genius, invented alternating current, as well as other ideas that challenged prevailing notions of physics and outstripped the technological means to realize them. Perhaps Tesla's greatest unfulfilled project was the huge tower at Wardenclyffe near Shoreham, Long Island, roughly halfway between New York and Montauk. Tesla saw the 187-foot-tall, mushroom-shaped structure as a first step in a worldwide communications system and, most importantly, a system to generate unlimited, free electric power by tapping the Earth's own electrical currents. The "free" part eventually discouraged his financial backers, among them J.P. Morgan. As a result, Tesla was pushed to the edge of financial ruin.

When the war started, Tesla had just managed to save Wardenclyffe from foreclosure by making a deal with his landlord, hotel manager George Boldt. Boldt, though, was associated with a more powerful player, blue-blood real-estate mogul (William) Vincent Astor. Astor, furthermore, was a friend and kinsman of Crowley's frequent host Robert Chanler, and both were relations of Assistant Secretary of the Navy Franklin Roosevelt. Moreover, Astor was an officer in the U.

S. Naval Reserve and (thanks to cousin Franklin) a member of a special branch of the Office of Naval Intelligence.

Astor's outfit got its start in 1916, when Roosevelt directed their mutual Ivy League pal, Lt. Commander Spencer Eddy, to set up a super-secret operation in New York that would report directly to FDR. SIS man Norman Thwaites counted Eddy among those Americans who worked "in close co-ordination and co-operation with the British Military Intelligence" and who had "taken up with enthusiasm any cases presented to him."[62] So, when a broke Tesla finally handed over Wardenclyffe to Boldt in 1916, control really ended up with ONI officer Astor.

ONI and the British had good reason to be curious about Tesla. In late 1915, he announced to the press that he was working on a "destructive invention" that would revolutionize warfare by destroying entire fleets with immense bolts of electricity.[63] The weapon, he claimed, could be operated by a single man "in a tower on Long Island." With Tesla's track record as an inventor, men in Washington, London, and even Berlin could not have failed to take notice.

An ethnic Serb, Tesla was born in Austria-Hungary, Germany's ally. Although the inventor is not known to have waxed patriotic about his native land or Germany, he had long-standing business connections in Berlin and many Germans among his associates, including his personal secretary George Scherff, a close friend of Viereck. Tesla eventually befriended Viereck as well, having probably met him during WWI.[64] Here was a source of information for Crowley, or even a pathway into Tesla's circle. Like Edison, Tesla was intrigued by Theosophy and, like the Beast, he was an admirer of the Hindu mystic Swami Vivekananda.[65]

Astor's ONI group, and perhaps the British as well, may have schemed to take the Wardenclyffe tower from Tesla out of fear that the Germans would get hold of it or its secrets. Since the U.S. government took control of the big *Deutsche Telefunken* antenna at Sayville, Long Island, in 1915, German agents in the States had been without a secure wireless link to Berlin. Wardenclyffe offered a viable substitute. In July 1917, the Navy supervised the demolition of Wardenclyffe on the grounds that "German spies were using the big wireless tower" to communicate with submarines and Germany itself.[66]

Could Crowley and Plummer have used Tesla's tower to communicate with Steiner "without using any cable or telegraph system in public use"?[67] Revealing this to the Americans would have demonstrated Crowley's good will to ONI, a chip to be cashed in when he camped at Montauk. The first reference to Crowley's and Plummer's alleged communications with Berlin appears in an ONI memo dated 10 July 1917, exactly when the Navy moved in on Wardenclyffe.

Crowley departed Montauk by the end of August. He blamed the place for nasty plantar blisters that plagued him for months to come. The stay also convinced him "that the current [presumably the magical one] was exhausted. . . . I had finished my work in America and began to prepare my escape."[68]

Still, he seems to have been in no rush. The following month, he again quit New York and headed south to spend six weeks with his friends Willie and Kate Seabrook on their farm near Atlanta, Georgia. Both the Mage's and Seabrook's recollections indicate an entirely personal agenda for the visit, which included sex-magic workings between Crowley and Kate (Willie liked to watch). Close by, though, lay the forbidding grey edifice of Atlanta Federal Penitentiary, temporary home of Franz Rintelen, Karl von Kleist, and other German operatives. Another recent inmate, released just a few days before the Beast's arrival, was Emma Goldman's lover, Alexander Berkman.

While at the Seabrooks', the Mage was interviewed by the Hearst-controlled *Atlanta Journal Sunday Magazine*.[69] Its editor, Angus Perkerson, emphasized Crowley's esoteric side, labeling him "an authority on occultism" who could teach anyone "how to become a magician," and evidently took the whole thing rather lightly. The piece resembled the earlier *Evening World* item, with one notable exception: it did not mention Crowley's past work for Britain or anyone else.

From Atlanta, the Beast sped north to Detroit for more haggling with Ryerson about *The Equinox*. The Motor City was then a focus of anti-radical raids launched by Palmer's Justice Department. One target was Alexander Berkman. Detroit also was home to Parke-Davis, Crowley's peyote connection, where he could stock up on *Anhalonium* for his next diversion, a trip into Kentucky's spectacular Mammoth Cave. That was not far from Louisville, making it easy to commune with Norwood and the International Magians. Crowley's overtures to Norwood and friends look like an attempt to hedge his bets with the Ryerson gang or perhaps rope the Magians into his grand Masonic Plan.

During late November and early December, the Master Therion was again back in Detroit for more dickering with Ryerson. *The Equinox* was going badly, and in the end it proved an utter fiasco for everyone, Ryerson above all. He sank about $35,000 of his and others' money into the project. Beyond this, the "lewdness" of the publication aroused the hostility of local and federal authorities. Later scandals generated by Ryerson's serial divorces included lurid public testimony about OTO rituals and led to the utter collapse of the Detroit chapter.

The Mage's last visit to Detroit coincided with a local lecture tour by Berkman and Goldman. Thanks to the relentlessness of Palmer's underling, J. Edgar Hoover, that pair and scores of other radicals now faced deportation. When Crowley sailed from New York Harbor, he must have cast a glance at Ellis Island, where Berkman and Red Emma awaited a slow boat to Russia.

Those two were not Palmer and Hoover's only concerns. In mid-December, the BI received disturbing intelligence from Detroit that members of the radical Industrial Workers of the World, including many auto workers, were arming themselves against expected "interference in their activities by the American Legion."[70] Crowley could have tapped Ryerson's bohemian contacts, or Ford's people, to investigate the rumors.

In *Confessions*, The Mage recalls reaching home "a few days before Christmas," and that is confirmed by a diary entry placing him at his Aunt's house in Croydon on 25 December.[71] About the timing and method of return, however, he is artfully vague. The Atlantic crossing generally took at least a week, often longer in winter. Relatively few passenger ships were sailing from New York to British ports at this season, and only two fit Crowley's timeline: the *Imperator* and the smaller *Lapland*. The first ship left Gotham on 11 December; the *Lapland*, two days later. Both reached England on 21 December.

Crowley probably took passage on the *Imperator*. Not only did it offer better accommodations, no small issue to the Mage, but it also was faster. The liner's history also may have piqued Crowley's curiosity or perversity. The *Imperator* was German, a former flagship of the Hamburg-America Line. Having sat out the war mired in a north German estuary, she was requisitioned by the Americans to bring soldiers home. In August 1919, Washington turned the liner over to the British shipping board, which then handed it to Cunard as a replacement for the long-sunk *Lusitania*.[72] Crowley, having come to America on that vessel, returned to Blighty on her replacement. Neither Crowley's name nor any obvious alias appears on the *Imperator*'s manifest. The *Lapland*'s is lost, and no trace of him appears on any passenger list bound for Britain that December.

Again, he was using some alias. The 1916 MI5 notification to all British ports that he be "searched and sent Metropolitan Police, London" might still cause him trouble. On the other hand, Crowley's name is absent from an MI5 blacklist compiled in 1918. Had Kell's people been warned off? The nosy press were a bigger worry. Crowley and his employers had good cause to keep his name out of the papers. The likes of Horatio Bottomley could be counted upon to raise holy hell if they caught scent of the Beast, now that he had added cheerleading for Germany to his already appalling résumé.

To get quietly into England, Crowley needed help. His 1914 passport had expired, and wartime regulations still in effect demanded he have one. Thus, he must have carried a new passport or visa. The only place he could get one of those was the Passport Control Office in New York. Of course, he had connections there.

Also attesting to the secrecy of Crowley's exit is that in January 1920 American officials still believed him to be on their soil. A 7 January memo to BI's J. Edgar Hoover assured that Crowley was still in the U.S.A.[73] This was based on the promise, attributed to unnamed British officials, that the Beast would be arrested and prosecuted the moment he set foot in England. On 30 January, John Hurley of the State Department wrote to the BI chief in New York asking for news of Crowley's plans to return to the U.K.[74] Hurley believed that Crowley was hiding in the States to avoid certain prosecution, and he thought it best to find him and "keep an eye on him." By this time, however, Crowley was long gone from America, and from England as well.

1 WWP, 6/172, New York, October 7, 1917," 2.

2 MID, 9771-56, "My Dear Churchill," c. Oct. 1918.

3 MID, 9944-A-178, "British Espionage…," 15 Feb. 1921, 3.

4 WWP, 9/211, M.I.1.C. Report, 22 March 1919.

5 Strath-Gordon Obituary, *The Oregonian* (18 Jan. 1952). Thanks also to Vance Pollock and John White.

6 U.S. Senate, 71st Congress, Senate Investigating Committee on Alleged Activities at the Geneva Conference, Exhibit #125, "Memorandum for the Director," 9 Feb. 1929, 683.

7 USNA, MID, 9771-145/42, "British Activities," 17 Nov. 1920.

8 MID, 9771-145/45, "British Secret Service Activities in This Country," 2 Nov. 1920, 3, and 9944-A-178, "British Espionage in the United States," 15 Feb. 1921, 12.

9 Swarthmore College Library, Peace Collection, "League of Small and Subject Nationalities, First Congress," program, Oct. 1917.

10 Leading the Irish representatives was Hanna Sheehy-Skeffington, the wife of Easter Rising martyr, Francis Sheehy-Skeffington. The Indian cause was represented by Lala Lajpat Rai, the "Lion of the Punjab" who headed the Indian Home Rule League office in New York.

11 Sixty-Sixth Congress, 2nd Session, Subcommittee on the Committee on Foreign Relations, U.S. Senate, "Russian Propaganda," (Washington, DC, 1920), 42. Perhaps Malone's proudest moment came years later when he got to portray Winston Churchill in the pro-Soviet film *Mission to Moscow.*

12 Michael G. Malouf, "With Dev in America: Sinn Fein and Recognition Politics, 1919–21," *International Journal of Post-Colonial Studies,* Vol. 41, #1 (April 2002), 22–34

13 WWP, 1/27, Wiseman to Drummond, 3 July 1919.

14 Nesta Webster, *Surrender of an Empire* (London: Boswell, 1931), 132.

15 *Ibid.,* 133.

16 UKNA, FO 371/5266, "John Wesley de Kay," c. Feb. 1923.

17 *Ibid.,* FO 371/3799, "John de Kay," 2 March 1920, 1.

18 *Ibid.,* 4.

19 "Collapse of the Old Regime, " *The Age* (12 Nov. 1918).

20 *CAC,* 755.

21 The Countess zu Reventlow had been a leading light of Munich's bohemian society before the war. She died at Monte Verita in 1918 due to complications following surgery.

22 UKNA, FO 371/3799, *Ibid.*

23 WWP, 10/261, "Intelligence and Propaganda Work in Russia, July to December 1917."

24 WWP, 10/255, "Russia," 18 May 1917, 3.

25 *Ibid.*, 2.

26 Crowley had first met Leah and her sister Alma (a.k.a. Renata Faesi) the preceding spring.

27 "Painting Dead Souls with Eyes Shut Easy for Subconscious Impressionist...," *New York Evening World* (26 Feb. 1919).

28 USNA, MID 10516-474/28, 18 June 1918.

29 *CAC*, 793.

30 "Latest 'Black Magic' Revelations about Nefarious American 'Love Cults'," *Helena Daily Independent* (27 Nov. 1927).

31 Starr, *Freemason!*.

32 V.V. Abramov and V.N. Frolov, "Tageev: Voennyi uchenyi-vostokoved ob'ezdil polmira, a rasstrelian v Moskve," *Voenno-Istoricheskii Zhurnal*, #4 (2002), 79.

33 Yale Univ., Sterling Library, Special Collections, Ralph H. Isham Papers, "Information Gathered in America and the Sources of Such Information," July 1919.

34 Neil Baldwin, *Henry Ford and the Jews: the Mass Production of Hate* (New York, Public Affairs, 2001), especially 59–85.

35 Max Wallace, *The American Axis: Henry Ford, Charles Lindbergh and the Rise of the Third Reich* (St. Martin's Press: New York, 2003), 7. For a detailed account of Ford's anti-semitism see Baldwin, *Henry Ford and the Jews*.

36 *CAC*, 469.

37 "A Gentile" [Crowley], "The Jewish Problem Restated," *The English Review* (July 1922), 28–37.

38 *Ibid.*

39 Churchill, "Zionism vs. Bolshevism...," *Illustrated Sunday Herald* (8 Feb. 1920).

40 UKNA, KV2/502, #625, New York, 22 March 1917.

41 WWP, 9/211, "Recognition of the Government of the Russian Soviet Republic, 11 April 1919.

42 Isham, "Information Gathered...".

43 Norman Hapgood, "The Inside Story of Henry Ford's Jew-Mania: Henry Swallows Old Bait," *Hearst's International* (Sept. 1922), 45–48, 133–134.

44 Seventy-First Congress, U.S. Senate, Investigating Committee on the Alleged Activities at the Geneva Conference, Exhibit #125, "British Secret Document," 685.

45 BI, file 365985, "Radical Activities," 24 July 1919.

46 Seventy-First Congress, *Ibid.*, 689.

47 USNA, MID 9944—A-178, "British Espionage," 10.

48 BI, file 365985.

49 *Ibid.*, Norwood to "Chief of Intelligence Bureau," 9 June 1919.

50 *Ibid.*, "Memo for Mr. Hoover," 7 Jan. 1920.

51 *Ibid.*, "In re: Aleister Crowley," 28 July 1919.

52 *Ibid.*, "Memo...," 7 Jan. 1920.

53 *Ibid.*, "In re ...," 28 July 1919.

54 *CAC*, 793.

55 E.g., Preston Nichols and Peter Moon, *Montauk Revisited: Adventures in Synchronicity* (NY Sky Books, 1993) part of multi-book series on Montauk and its mysteries.

56 Capt. Linwood S. Howeth, *History of Communications-Electronics in the United States Navy* (1963), 554–556.

57 *NYT* (8 Nov. 1919) 23:3 and (16 Nov. 1919), IX, 6:2.

58 "The Coast Artillery at Camp Hero," www.skyfighters.org/camphero/indexp.html, and H. Winfield Secor, "America's Greatest War Invention," *Electrical Experimenter* (March 1919), 787–789, 834–835.

59 *Who's Who in the British War Mission, 1917*, attached chart.

60 The BIR technically dissolved in 1918, but practically morphed into the new Directorate of Experiments and Research. Bridge's service record, however, shows him serving in the BIR to 1919. Thanks to Phil Tomaselli for this information.

61 *NYT* (29 July 1919), 27:4.

62 WWP, 3/84, "Suggestions as to Recognition...," 22 Nov. 1918.

63 *NYT*, "Tesla's New Device Like Bolts of Thor" (8 Dec. 1915), 8:3.

64 G.S. Viereck and Nikola Tesla, "A Machine to End War," *Liberty* (Feb. 1937).

65 Vivekananda (b. Narandranath Dutta) was head of the Vedanta Society.

66 "U.S. Blows up Tesla Radio Tower," *The Electrical Experimenter* (Sept. 1917), 293.

67 USNA, MID 9140-808, ONI, "German Suspects," 10 July 1917.

68 *CAC*, 793.

69 Angus Perkerson, "Poet-Painter Who Studied Magic under Indian Savants Visits Atlanta," *Atlanta Journal Sunday Magazine* (c. Oct, 1919), 1.

70 USNA, MID 10110-KK-2/2, "Subject: I.W.W. Detroit, Michigan," 19 Dec. 1919.

71 *CAC*, 794.

72 Later renamed *SS Berengaria*.

73 BI, file 365985, "Memo...," 7 Jan. 1920.

74 *Ibid.*, Hurley to Burke, 30 Jan. 1920.

~

CHAPTER ELEVEN

THE UNWELCOME GUEST

~

ON CHRISTMAS DAY 1919, CROWLEY BEGAN A NEW DIARY WITH A DESCRIPTION OF HIS HOLIDAY REPAST, complete with plum pudding and brandy, at Aunt Annie's house in Croydon. Fortunately, German zeppelins had not acted on his suggestion to bomb it. This cheery gathering shows that he still had friends in England, and that his homecoming was known to a few. The Beast remained, lying low, for about two weeks, then quietly slipped across the Channel to France.

Meanwhile he had busied himself (he claimed) trying reorganize OTO affairs in London. The main aim was to get his hands on any remaining funds. As ever, he protested poverty, but just as usual he managed to pay for travel and amenities. For instance, while in London, he visited a Harley Street doctor to secure a prescription for heroin. While he had used heroin and other opiates ritually or recreationally, he now sought the drug to alleviate his asthma that flared up during the last months in America. Heroin helped the ailment, but at the price of turning the *Mega Therion* into its slave.

Outwardly, British officials completely ignored the Beast's return. Crowley insisted that he went straight to Scotland Yard and proclaimed, "here I am—if you have anything against me, I am perfectly willing to meet any charges. They simply laughed at the idea."[1] This contradicts the later account of French writer Pierre Mariel, who asserts that Crowley faced a "long interrogation" upon his arrival.[2] Both could be versions of the truth. One purpose of Crowley's brief and discreet visit must have been a debriefing, and that doubtless involved lengthy questioning. But he faced no charges or apparent reprimand for his actions in America. On the other hand, neither did he receive public acknowledgment or reward for his loyal service.

Crowley's treatment again contrasts starkly with that of fellow British subject and pro-German propagandist I.T. Trebitsch-Lincoln. Hauled back to England and tossed in jail, he got out in 1919 only to face immediate expulsion from the country. The lion did not forgive or forget. Even Frank Harris fared worse than our man. Harris' Germanophile effusions excited public condemnation during the war, while Crowley's writings, at least as provocative, elicited almost no mention in the British press. Likewise, while Crowley met no official obstacles to his presence in postwar England, Harris felt *persona non grata* and never set foot there again.

Some, of course, were not so indulgent of Crowley's indiscretions. A few days after he left London, his old enemy Horatio Bottomley learned of his presence in France and launched an attack in the pages of *John Bull*. During the war, Bottomley had wrapped his pugnacious moralizing in a thick layer of jingoism, lambasting anyone he deemed less devoted to King and Country than himself. He also pursued profitable sidelines—lucrative lectures, for example, and shady bond schemes. Bottomley, despite his police and intelligence connections, had no inkling that Crowley had already come and gone.

In "Another Traitor Trounced," which ran on 10 January, Bottomley railed against that "traitorous degenerate, Aleister Crowley," who was "anxious to sneak back to the land he has sought to defile." The piece lumped him with Frank Harris and made special note of Crowley's association with Viereck, "one of Dernburg's agents." Thus Bottomley revealed some acquaintance with Crowley's German associations and treasonous prose. He took particular offense at the *International* article praising Reventlow's *Vampire of the Continent*. "Can such a dirty renegade be permitted to return to the country he has spurned and insulted?," Bottomley asked, demanding "assurance from the Home Office or the Foreign Office that steps are being taken to arrest the renegade or prevent his infamous feet ever again touching our shores." Crowley and Harris, Bottomley concluded, were "dangerous firebrands," and their presence in England or Ireland "would involve perilous consequences." It was "the duty of the Government [to] . . . take effective action" against these miscreants. The Government obviously ignored Bottomley's advice, but the diatribe must have convinced some that Crowley had best remain scarce. The Mage would not again return to England until Bottomley was safely disgraced and headed for jail.

When Bottomley's attack appeared, Crowley was sitting in Paris, awaiting two important reunions. His faithful and very pregnant Scarlet Woman, Leah Hirsig, was coming from Switzerland, where she had been staying with family. The Beast had packed her off to Europe shortly before his own departure, possibly as a diversion. The other meeting was with Everard Feilding, back from the Middle East and now involved in sensitive negotiations about that volatile region. Feilding also stepped back into his role as Crowley's intermediary with higher-ups in London. No doubt he offered the Beast a helping hand and, above all, kept him quiet.

French occultist Georges Monti, later known as "Count Israel," also appeared at Crowley's side soon after his arrival in France. Monti had been secretary to the late and venerable Josephin Sar Peledan, a leading light of French Rosicrucianism and the Gnostic Catholic Church. Peledan knew Reuss and had some dealings with the OTO, and Monti apparently wanted to pick up where his master left off. In years following, Monti formed his own order, the *Groupe Occidental d'Études Ésotériques*, but he also claimed to be Crowley's special "French representative."[3] On the other hand, Monti had a reputation as a charlatan and liar. It was even rumored that Monti, a serial joiner of esoteric societies, was someone's spy. French intelligence could have used him to feel out or watch Crowley.

Another accusation is that Monti was an agent of Jesuits.[4] As we will see, persons connected to that Order would take a special interest in the self-proclaimed Great Beast. Monti definitely was linked to two secretive Catholic societies, the *Solidatium Pianum*, a kind of counter-subversive service, and the mysterious *Hieron du Val d'Or*. *Solidatium Pianum* theoretically ceased to exist around 1921, but *Hieron* lasted longer. Its chief aim was a "reconciliation" between the Church and Freemasonry or, perhaps more accurately, the infiltration and reorganization of Freemasonry for Rome's benefit.[5] This smacks a little of Crowley's dealings with Ryerson and the Detroit Masons and his strange wartime interest in Catholic conversion. Stranger still, both *Hieron* and Monti connected to a later secret society, the shadowy and controversial Priory of Sion. They even had links to extreme rightist groups such as *Action Française* and assorted Gallic fascists. At the very least, Monti was a trafficker in information, a useful sort for Agent Crowley to know.[6]

Bottomley's insults, coming from a man the Beast despised as a crook and poltroon, got under Crowley's skin. What most bothered him was being unable to respond. He recalled conjuring up a lengthy retort to Bottomley's smear but decided, likely on Feilding's advice, not to publish it.[7] He also compiled a list of persons who could be summoned as character witnesses to rebut Bottomley's libels. These included Feilding, John Cosgrave, Somerset Maugham, John Quinn, and other intelligence-related contacts.[8] Not long after, the Beast began a first draft of what would become "The Last Straw," a meandering account of his time in America that eventually became an appendix in *Confessions*.

Crowley explained his willingness to submit in "silence" to Bottomley's calumnies because he hoped "to make myself again useful to England in a similar capacity if certain eventualities, which I then thought not impossible, should materialise."[9] In other words, he was anticipating a new mission that might require the same treasonous façade.

"Eventualities" probably alluded to events brewing in Germany. There the fledgling Weimar Republic struggled to hold power in the face of violent opposition from Moscow-backed Communists and revanchist proto-Nazis. The only question seemed to be which band of extremists would seize control first. Mixed up in the chaotic and murky plotting were the familiar American occultist-financier John de Kay, the anglophobe Count Reventlow, inveterate conspirator Trebitsch-Lincoln, and even Berlin's former chief saboteur in North America, Kurt Jahnke. Crowley, thus, could be a potentially useful asset to toss into the fray. Such a mission also would conform to the Mage's long-standing desire to work in Germany. For whatever reasons, that did not happen.

Perhaps things simply moved too fast. The German unrest flared up in March 1920, when right-wing *Freikorps* troops seized Berlin in the abortive Kapp Putsch.[10] British agents hovered around these events, including Gaunt and Norman Thwaites.[11] The latter kept a watchful eye on Trebitsch, now press secretary of the putschists.

The Beast spent the next couple of months cooling his heels in Fontainebleau, just south of Paris. He set up a cozy *ménage-à-trois* with Leah and a young French woman, Ninette Shumway, and their two young sons. Ninette took on the role of nursemaid when Hirsig gave birth to a baby girl, Anne Leah or "Poupée," in late February. Fontainebleau, especially the nearby *forêt*, had a long association with witchcraft and black magic. Soon after Crowley moved on, Russian mystic George Gurdjieff chose Fontainebleau for his new headquarters.

During these weeks Crowley got the idea of establishing his own "college of occult knowledge." For its campus he looked to warmer climes, and on 1 March, the *I Ching* directed him to sunny Sicily. Traveling via Naples, Crowley and Ninette arrived in the sleepy seaside town of Cefalu, about fifty miles east of Palermo, at the beginning of April. Dominated by dramatic rock outcroppings, the place had little to recommend it besides good weather and cheap living. Crowley proclaimed it his New Jerusalem. Leah and Poupée arrived in mid-April. As "Countess Lea Harcourt" and "Sir Alastor de Kerval," she and Crowley signed a lease on the Villa Santa Barbara, a vacant farmhouse outside town. Whether this masquerade was a playful joke or a serious attempt to disguise themselves is unclear. Crowley dubbed the six-room house the "Abbey of Thelema" and envisioned it as a utopian community of students and adepts that would spread his teachings across the globe. The actual result was a hippie commune ahead of its time, complete with free love, abundant drugs, and poor sanitation.

Undoubtedly factors other than an *I Ching* hexagram influenced the choice of Cefalu. Sicilians had abounded in Crowley's beloved New Orleans, many from Cefalu.[12] Intelligence considerations played their part as well. According to one dubious story, Crowley's relocation to Cefalu followed an agreement with the French secret service to keep a watch on Italian naval movements.[13] If the Beast had been put on the shelf by London, a deal with the French might have made sense, especially with a growing household to support. The Abbey afforded an excellent view of local waters and easy access by train to Palermo and its naval base. That base would have been a main staging area for any Italian naval operation in the Mediterranean, especially against nearby French-controlled Tunisia. Like Germany, postwar Italy was politically volatile, seething with resentment over the postwar division of spoils.

Crowley's skimpy *Deuxième Bureau* file provides no clues about whether the French engaged him as an agent. It contains only the previously noted 1916 British report on Crowley's pro-Irish (but not his pro-German) antics and two extracts from the French press about his 1929 expulsion. Those articles do mention his work for the Germans in wartime America, but they also include his claim to have been working for England. A copy of the original French index card attached to the file merely describes the Beast as an "Agitatuer irlandais."[14]

French intelligence should have had much more information on such a controversial figure and longtime resident of France. The dossier might once have been fatter. In 1940, the invading Germans took all the French intelligence files they could get their hands on, including Crowley's, to Berlin. When Berlin fell to the Red Army in 1945, the victorious Soviets stashed the same files as war booty in Moscow's "Special Archive." There Crowley's file remained until repatriated with many others in the 1990s. The French, the Nazis, and the Soviets had ample opportunity to remove or lose material from the file.

However, Crowley was most likely spying at Cefalu, not for the French, but *on* them, and for the British. He also kept tabs on the Italians. Feilding's was the guiding hand that steered Crowley to where he could pursue his mystical designs and still be of use to His Majesty. Before returning to Europe in mid-1919, Feilding had been in Syria, a territory recently handed over to French administration. The Anglo-French division of the Middle East was fraught with suspicion on both sides, and London was particularly concerned about the French military resources pouring into Syria. From his base in Sicily Crowley made regular trips to French-controlled Tunisia, the main staging area and logistical hub for French forces in the Levant.

While at Cefalu, Crowley started work on a new novel, *Diary of a Drug Fiend*. Among its characters was a British consul in Naples, a fair-minded, "tall, bronzed Englishman" who helps the protagonists out of a jam with local authorities. His inspiration was Walter Alexander Smart, a career diplomat who served at the Consulate-General in New York from early 1917 to summer 1919. Smart also worked in a vague capacity at the Foreign Office during 1915, possibly intelligence-related. Most of his career had been spent in North Africa and the Middle East, experience that meshed with Feilding's. Smart took a new post in French-controlled Damascus not long after Crowley set up camp at Cefalu. French writer Xavier de Hauteclocque, who had close ties to Paris' secret services, identified Smart as the British agent who later instigated the anti-French uprising of Syrian Druze tribesmen.[15] Any information Crowley picked up in Tunis or Palermo about the strength and deployment of French forces would have keenly interested Smart and others.

Crowley's enemies in the British press inadvertently revealed another link in this nexus, the Beast's association with His Majesty's Consul in Palermo, Reginald Gambier MacBean. Their acquaintance predated the War. The Consul's occult affiliations most notably included Annie Besant's wing of Theosophy and its attendant Order of the Star of the East. MacBean's devotion to Besant, an outspoken proponent of Indian freedom, created ripples in the Foreign Office. In 1917, MacBean nearly resigned after he inappropriately sent a letter praising Besant through the diplomatic post to a "friend" in America.[16] That friend was probably Crowley.

MacBean also was the newly-minted Grand Master of the Antient and Primitive Rite of Memphis-Misraim for Italy.[17] The Memphis-Misraim order suddenly reappeared in Italy in 1921, perhaps midwifed by Crowley in Cefalu. Memphis-Misraim being a constituent of the Ordo Templi Orientis, MacBean's familiarity with Reuss and Crowley suggests that he may have been OTO too. Beyond this, Crowley was an honorary member of the *Rito Filosofico Italiano*, another fringe Masonic group to which MacBean belonged. Thus the Consul and Crowley had a wide basis for collaboration, and the Palermo Consulate was an ideal information conduit to Feilding, Smart, and London.

The Crowley-MacBean connection had other advantages. Like any diligent totalitarian, Mussolini disliked secret societies, and in late 1922 he began to crack down on everything from the Masons to the Mafia. The antipathy was mutual. Italian Masonic and Theosophist circles teemed with informants and operatives hostile to the Fascist regime, and collecting information from them was part of Crowley's job.

Pierre Mariel, a longtime collaborator of the French Army's intelligence arm (the *Service de renseignements*) also alleged espionage by Crowley in Sicily.[18] Mariel claimed to have seen a file unflatteringly detailing the Mage's activities as a secret agent. London, he said, had deemed Crowley a "rather inept" agent whose chronic inability to manage money and "moral corruption" necessitated "the very greatest caution" if he was to be used.[19] Again, there may be more than a grain of truth to that.

Over the next year, the little colony at Cefalu attracted such acolytes as Crowley's Cambridge friend, the mathematician Norman Mudd, and a minor league American film star, Jane Wolfe. Ninette Shumway's two sisters, Helene and Mimi, also joined the faithful. The truth about the Abbey fell somewhere between Crowley's idealized portrait of it as an almost puritanical assembly of spiritual seekers and the cesspool of blasphemy, depravity, and drug-crazed licentiousness later portrayed in the press. Drugs abounded, and the Mage's and Leah's heroin use mushroomed into full-blown addiction.

Things at the Abbey started to take a bad turn as early as October 1920 with the death of Crowley's and Hirsig's infant daughter, Poupée. Both parents took the loss hard, but Leah's miscarriage a few days later pushed her into a deep depression and further under the spell of the needle. Crowley escaped on trips to Naples, Tunis, and Paris, staying in the City of Light during February–March 1921. That trip included an early attempt to wean himself from dope.

In February 1922, Crowley, with Leah in tow, began an extended vacation from the growing mess at the Abbey. They first ensconced themselves in a small hotel in Paris's Montparnasse, where they struggled to kick their habit. The Beast, however, was very anxious to get to London, as if summoned there. His first attempt to go, on 14 February, ran into a strange obstacle. French authorities in the Channel port of Boulogne stopped him on the alleged suspicion that he was a fugitive English businessman, Mr. Bevan. Crowley later passed off the incident as simple mistaken identity. Others have claimed it was a ruse by the French secret service so they could consult with him discreetly about Italian matters.[20] That seems unlikely, but there definitely was more going on than met the eye.

The elusive Gerard Lee Bevan was a prominent London stockbroker who had fled to France to escape financial ruin and accusations of embezzlement. As yet, however, Bevan faced no formal charge, was not a fugitive, and was not missing. The day Crowley was stopped, *The Times* noted Bevan's presence in Paris and predicted his imminent return to London. The French had no charge against Bevan, and the British police had every reason to want him back home. Bevan, however, had made noises about going "south." Several days later he vanished from Paris, soon reappearing in Naples, a short journey by boat from Cefalu.[21]

This raises the possibility that the French police or Scotland Yard smelled collusion between Bevan and Crowley. The Beast, as ever, was short of money. The stockbroker might have tried to buy sanctuary at the Abbey, and Crowley's journey to London could have been a scheme to retrieve some of Bevan's valuable artworks, much as he may have done for Alvensleben.

A more likely explanation, however, is that Scotland Yard used the French to turn Crowley back toward Paris to spy *on* Bevan. The latter was a sibling of Edwyn Bevan, an acquaintance of Crowley's old chum Commander Marston (who carried on an affair with Edwyn B.'s wife). So, it is possible that the Beast and fugitive Bevan had met before. In any case, after briefly returning to Paris, Crowley proceeded unmolested to London.

Crowley remained in Britain for several months, keeping a low profile and causing no hue or cry in the press or elsewhere. He used the time, in part, to work on his American memoir, "The Last Straw." His old tormentor Bottomley recently had been convicted and, like Bevan (who perhaps not coincidentally knew Bottomley), was prison-bound. Still, Bottomley was not the only enemy of the Beast, and his visit must have had some measure of discreet official protection to go without protested

In London, Crowley reconnected with an old acquaintance, Austin Harrison, editor of *The English Review*. The Beast pseudonymously contributed some pieces to it, including "The Jewish Problem Restated." Crowley's renewed interest in the Jewish Question happily coincided with his reunion with another friend, New York financier Otto Kahn. He was offering his backing to a plan to merge the financially troubled *English Review* with another publication and proposed to send Crowley back to Gotham to run it.

That scheme fell through, but Crowley's encounter with Kahn may hint at some larger design. Kahn had come to dominate the formerly Germanophile Kuhn, Loeb upon Jacob Schiff's recent death. Furthermore he had recruited none other than Sir William Wiseman into the firm, and Wiseman had accompanied Kahn to London. All in all, it was quite a little reunion. Wiseman's new job was arranging loans in restive Central Europe. As his chief troubleshooter, Sir William employed yet another former (?) British operative, Sidney Reilly. SIS had formally dumped Reilly and supposedly viewed him as untrustworthy and dangerous.[22] Similar doubts shadowed Wiseman.

About this time, a "reform element" in British intelligence, suspicious of Wiseman's wartime activities and loyalties, was secretly investigating him.[23] At the same time, SIS began poking into Reilly's wartime activities, especially his relations with German firms and agents.[24] The suspicion was that Reilly and Wiseman, as agents for New York bankers, were working against British interests, perhaps channeling money to the cash-hungry Soviets and bankrolling political unrest from India to Italy.[25] Was Kahn eyeing the Beast for some part in this, or was the "reform element" using Crowley to probe the Kahn-Wiseman circle?

If the latter, "Blinker" Hall likely had a hand in it. After the Armistice, Hall resigned his post as Director of Naval Intelligence but continued clandestine work. Hall and Basil Thomson, chief of Scotland Yard, were obsessed with the Communist menace and unsure of MI5's inability to deal with it.[26] Hall offered his expertise to right-wing groups such as the British Empire Union and the Economic League to wage clandestine war on the Reds. Close to Hall personally and politically was yet another of Crowley's old intelligence bosses, Guy Gaunt. Like Hall, Gaunt had officially retired from naval service, but his name continued to pop up in intelligence matters.[27] To round out this cabal, Norman Thwaites also collaborated with Hall while running his own private intelligence bureau.[28]

Two new figures involved with this right-wing nexus were Col. John Filis Carre (J.F.C.) Carter, Assistant Commissioner of Scotland Yard's Special Branch, and an up-and-coming young spy, Charles Henry Maxwell Knight. Both would come to know and use Crowley some years later, which does not rule out an earlier introduction. The Master Therion would have fit right into Hall's operation—as always, unofficially and as an informant and provocateur among the Reds.

In July 1922, Crowley finally finished *Diary of a Drug Fiend*, which he counted on for much-needed revenue. It disappointed in that regard, but it did ignite a fresh anti-Crowley frenzy in the British press. In September, the *Sunday Express* fired the first salvo against the book and its author. By November, the *Express* was calling for the banning of the book, and it savaged Crowley's character with the article "Orgies in Sicily."[29] Castigating him as a ringmaster of "pagan orgies" and corrupter of morals, the author took a cue from Bottomley by raking up Crowley's pro-German writings in America, the Rites of Eleusis scandal, and even his alleged bilking of a female devotee. For good measure, he added the falsehood that Crowley had penned a "defeatist manifesto" circulated in France in 1915. The author, the *Express*'s straitlaced literary editor James Douglas, expressed his amazement that the villain had been living in London, skulking among a "small circle of initiates."

Crowley missed the story, having hurried back to Sicily in October at the urging of "friends." Rather than catch a boat from Nice or Marseille, he took the train straight through Italy, then on the edge of revolution and civil war. Fascist strongman Benito Mussolini had marshaled his Blackshirts and was threatening to march on Rome. The Beast just happened to be on hand when the King and his ministers caved in to Mussolini's bullying and named him to lead a new Government. Our man also had a front-row seat when the triumphant Il Duce marched into the Eternal City on 30 October.

While Crowley made occasional approving sounds about Fascism, he despised Mussolini as a bombastic opportunist who sold his soul to the Catholic Church.[30]

Still, Crowley and his little band of foreign eccentrics hardly constituted a threat to Il Duce. Or did they? Two fresh faces at the Abbey in fall 1922 were the poet Frederick "Raoul" Loveday and his lover Betty May. Betty instantly disliked the place and its fat, bald master, but Raoul lapped it all up, ultimately too eagerly. May later said that he died from drinking cat's blood in some obscene ritual. The apparent cause of Loveday's death in February 1923 was cholera, contracted from the local water. The same bacterium also laid Crowley low.

Returning to England, Betty raised a new alarm about the beastliness going on in Sicily. About the same time, Ninette Shumway's sister Helene turned up at the British Consulate in Palermo spinning more tales of depravity at the Abbey. In London, *John Bull* leapt to virtue's defense in early March with the polemics "The King of Depravity," "A Wizard of Wickedness," and the classic "The Wickedest Man in the World."[31] The series was a lurid and largely imaginary exposé of Crowley's exploitation of women and children and his "cesspool of vice" in Cefalu. The paper insinuated that the Beast had corrupted Italian officials and the British Consul in Palermo, and demanded that the Home Office or Rome prosecute the scoundrel and snuff out his "contaminating influence." The final installment on 24 March boasted that "it is understood that the Italian Government are resolved to put an end to Crowley's career of vice. . . ." A month later, Italian authorities presented the Abbey's master with a notice of expulsion.

The common assumption has been that, if the Loveday scandal and the press attacks did not force Mussolini to eject Crowley, they helped. Crowley later claimed that "no reason was given, no accusations made" by the Italians.[32] He suspected "backstairs intrigue," but does not name any suspects. Writer Marco Pasi suspects British authorities, including Consul MacBean, of actively encouraging the expulsion.[33] Some were surely eager to see the embarrassing Crowley leave, but fellow Mason MacBean actually seems to have tipped off the Beast to the imminent arrival of Italian authorities. Certainly someone did.[34] A contributing factor may have been the expected arrival in Cefalu of Monsignor Roncalli, the future Pope John XXIII.

A dossier in the Central State Archive in Rome yields intriguing details about Crowley's expulsion.[35] Inquiries about the suspicious Englishman commenced in July 1922, months before the Fascists came to power. The expulsion order applied to him exclusively and came from the Ministry of Internal Affairs on 13 April 1923, to take effect on 1 May. Its official justification was Crowley's "obscene and perverted" sexual activity, including polygamy. The others at the Abbey were free to remain and continue their orgies; the Italians were not bothered by the alternative lifestyles, just by Crowley. Mussolini's men believed that he was up to something besides mere vice, but they could not prove it.

The key likely was a Sicilian nobleman and prominent politician, Giovanni Antonio Colonna, Duca di Cesaro, then a non-Fascist member of Mussolini's cabinet. He also was an enemy of Il Duce, who would boot Cesaro from the Government in 1924. Cesaro also was deep into the Italian occult scene. He was a Theosophist, a follower of Rudolf Steiner, and associated with various esoteric Masonic groups.[36] He knew MacBean well and would not have ignored the presence in his backyard of a man like Crowley. The merest suspicion that the English Magician and the dissident Duke were in cahoots would have moved Mussolini to act. The British moral panic merely provided a handy excuse.

In 1927, Il Duce's new political police (OVRA) revisited the Crowley case in response to one of the many attempts to assassinate Mussolini. The would-be killer, who only managed to graze the Dictator's nose, was an Irish-British woman, Violet Gibson.[37] Italian authorities eventually deemed her deranged and deported her to Ireland, but suspicions lingered that she had been a pawn in some larger plot.

According to Italian author Claudio Mauri, she was, and the conspiracy involved a murky cabal of occultists and spies.[38] Violet Gibson was another Theosophist and, like Crowley's friend MacBean, a devoted follower of Annie Besant. Among her Italian acquaintances was the Duca di Cesaro. These connections were enough to excite the suspicions of any decent policeman. Mussolini's cops hauled in Cesaro for questioning, but he steadfastly denied any involvement. It seems possible that Gibson was acting on post-hypnotic suggestion, and Crowley, in league with Cesaro, may have had a hand in preparing her.

The London-based Tavistock Clinic, or Tavistock Institute of Medical Psychiatry, might have figured in such a conspiracy.[39] Founded about 1920, it generally focused on the treatment of shell-shock and related psychological damage from the World War. Tavistock's methodology embraced Freudian and Adlerian psychoanalysis. We will learn about Crowley's admiration of Alfred Adler a bit later. Later rumors held that Tavistock had a more secret and sinister function, as a laboratory for brain-washing and mind-control research serving the intelligence and military branches.[40] If it did, the Beast's experience with psychoactive drugs would have been invaluable. What, after all, became of *The Cactus*, Crowley's lost dissertation on the wonders of mescaline? The Mage was supposed to be living quietly in Paris at the time or Gibson's attempt, but he could easily have slipped back to Rome using old tricks and new documents.

French mystic Rene Guenon believed that the Theosophists served British intelligence, and some in OVRA seem to have believed the same. Papers seized by the Italians at the Abbey showed that it had been used as a center for propaganda against Fascism and Italy. More importantly, OVRA identified materials from the "special espionage service (*servizio speciale di spionnagio*) of the British Foreign Office."[41] The Beast had been up to his old tricks. It appeared that someone, most likely MacBean, was *supplying* him with information to guide his inquiries and observations.

Perhaps there were other spies among the devout at Cefalu. Crowley casually mentions the arrival of two Oxford men at the Abbey, Pinney and Bosanquet, the day before he received the expulsion notice.[42] In any case, for the Mage or anyone else to leave intelligence-related materials lying about for the Italians to find was a serious breach of tradecraft, one that might account for the "inept" label Mariel says he saw. Perhaps Crowley expected other operatives to tidy up and carry on the secret work, or maybe he was just too stoned to notice or care.

Some blame may rest on the slim shoulders of Ninette Shumway. Next to Leah, who accompanied Crowley into exile, Ninette was an old and presumably trustworthy associate. Since the Italians were unlikely to notice her, she had safe pockets for secret papers. However, abandoned by the Beast and destitute, she ultimately may have surrendered the papers or bartered them for a ticket home.

Meantime, back in England, others were looking at Crowley with the blackest suspicion. At the center of this was George Makgill, a friend of Bottomley and a fellow super-patriot. Makgill ran a private intelligence outfit, Section D, for the British Empire Union and the Economic League.[43] That endeared him to Scotland Yard, MI5, the British Fascisti, and even Admiral Hall. In addition to battling subversives, Makgill "also devoted a considerable amount of time to unmasking the cult of evil of which Aleister Crowley, alias 'The Beast', was the centre."[44] He linked Crowley to "international traffic in drugs and the traffic in women and children." One of Makgill's agents, designated "H," allegedly "uncovered a blackmail plot, involving two well-known politicians, connected to Crowley's activities in the island of Cefalu [sic]."[45]

By 1922–1923, Makgill had gotten close to members of Britain's budding Fascist movement. One of these home-grown Blackshirts was Capt. Arthur L. Rogers, OBE, a former intelligence officer in the Middle East and a self-proclaimed expert on "Black Magic and extreme left-wing activities."[46] Another of this set was the previously cited Nesta Webster, a close friend of both Makgill and Rogers. Her 1923 opus *Secret Societies and Subversive Movements* includes a thinly disguised attack on Crowley and his influence.[47] Also, one of her brothers was Edwyn Bevan who was, as noted, connected to Crowley's friend Guy Marston. Bevan also served as a wartime Propaganda and Ministry of Information officer and may have been able to provide sis a little inside information. Her other brother was Gerard Lee Bevan, the very man

Crowley was "mistaken" for in 1922.

For the most part, Makgill's obsession with the Mage was a personal affair. Around 1923, however, a curious note appears at the bottom of an MI5 report on a British Fascist informant inside the Soviet mission: "note for Don on A. Crowley."[48] It could refer to another A. Crowley, but that seems very doubtful. "Don" doubtless refers to Makgill's son, Donald, closely linked to the Fascists.

It might seem inconsistent for Crowley to be under acute suspicion by a collaborator of Admiral Hall, if the latter had the Beast in his employ. Actually it would have been a repeat of the wartime situation, in which Crowley's true allegiance was known only to a privileged few. Just as a general belief that he was a German tool made him all the more convincing to the Germans, the conviction of Makgill and his ilk that Crowley was a depraved and seditious monster insulated him against other doubts.

The months following Crowley's departure from Sicily were a low point in his life, and arguably the beginning of a long, irreversible decline. He and Leah first ended up in Tunisia, where they wasted months shooting dope while the Beast worked on *Confessions* and cooked up the occasional magical working. Obviously he had some means of support. It may be significant that he sought refuge on French territory and would mostly remain in France for some time thereafter, not setting foot in England for some years. Perhaps his failure in Sicily made him *persona non grata*; or perhaps he had committed some other sin.

At the close of 1923, the Beast and Leah surfaced in Paris, broke and strung out. Truly destitute, Crowley got help from his old friend in magic and conspiracy Frank Harris, who had likewise drifted back to Paris. He mooched off Harris for weeks, but eventually found a new meal ticket and Scarlet Woman, the rich American expatriate Dorothy Olsen (Soror Astrid). Poor Leah he cruelly cast adrift to find her own way in the world and out of addiction. Through late 1923 and early 1924, the Beast returned to writing and magic with something like his old vigor. He even dragged the hard-drinking Olsen back to Tunisia on a couple of ill-conceived expeditions.

During 1924, Crowley suddenly reappeared in Fontainebleau, where he had holed up with Hirsig and Ninette Shumway after his return from the States. The attraction was the presence of Gurdjieff and his "Institute for the Harmonious Development of Man." After fleeing the Bolsheviks to Constantinople, the wily Gurdjieff made his way to France, where he now ran a more successful version of Crowley's Abbey. Once again allegedly guided by the *I Ching*, the Beast paid one "brief, unwelcome visit" on Gurdjieff's domain.[49] "How he gained entry," writes Gurdjieff's biographer James Moore, "is a mystery." In any case, Gurdjieff soon sent the "noxious guest" away, and that, so far as Moore and most others are concerned, was the end of the matter.[50]

As with Cefalu, there was more to Crowley's appearance at Gurdjieff's door than the *I Ching*. Gurdjieff has been alleged to have had his own ties to London's secret services. One of his key lieutenants at Fontainebleau was John Godolfin Bennett. When Gurdjieff arrived in Constantinople in 1921, Bennett was there as a British officer assigned to "special duties."[51] He offered his help to Gurdjieff and soon became a trusted devotee. Bennett was undoubtedly an intelligence officer, but whether he served the military, SIS, or some other entity is unclear; nearly every type of British spook was active in Constantinople at the time. By the time the Beast appeared at Gurdjieff's door, however, both the Foreign Office and MI5 had soured on Bennett. They viewed him as a shady character mixed up with the late Turkish Sultan and with a familiar schemer, John De Kay. In fact, Bennett was married to De Kay's secretary. MI5 believed Bennett to be in league with the Turkish secret service and, more ominously, "to be violently anti-British and have communist associates."[52] Crowley's errand at Fontainebleau likely included sniffing around for what Gurdjieff and his pal Bennett were up to. Did someone in London put him up to it, or was he spying on speculation in hopes of restoring himself to good graces? If Bennett or Gurdjieff guessed his true intentions, it would explain the cold shoulder.

The Beast seemed to be waiting for a call, and at last it came, from Germany. Shortly before the end of the war, Theodor Reuss had abandoned his Anational Lodge. He was still a *Propagandachef*, however, and in July 1920 he attended a "World Federation of Universal Freemasonry" in Zurich.[53] So did the ubiquitous John De Kay. By the early 1920s, Reuss' failing health arguably led him to issue some questionable degrees and charters. Crowley pounced on this as evidence of Reuss' foundering judgment. Our man also slammed Reuss as the representative of "a beaten and disintegrating nation."[54] Their relationship grew more and more strained until Reuss expelled Crowley from the OTO 1921.[55] Not to be outdone, the Beast brazenly informed Reuss that he was assuming the mantle of Frater Superior and "Outer Head" (OHO) of the Order. The dying Reuss' failure to respond convinced Crowley that he was now the Order's master, a position he claimed until his death. Reuss' passing in October 1923 seemed to seal the deal.

However, according to Karl Germer (whom we will meet shortly), Reuss and the Beast patched up their differences before the former's death and met for one last time in Palermo, Sicily sometime in 1922.[56] This must have occurred just prior to or soon after Crowley's trip to England. Reuss recently had attended another Masonic congress in Switzerland where his plan to establish the Gnostic

Mass as the ritual for a "unified world Masonic federation" received a rude rebuff. Where the Palermo meeting left the matter of leadership over the OTO is unclear.

Other brethren, including the man Reuss had named OTO chief in Germany, Heinrich Traenker, challenged Crowley's succession, and the Reich was still the main center of the Order. In early 1925, however, a fresh "revelation" convinced Traenker that the Secret Chiefs really did want Crowley at the helm. He invited the Beast to an upcoming gathering that would resolve the question once and for all.

The Weida Conference, held around the summer solstice in the little Thuringian town of Hohenleuben, ended up splintering the OTO. Crowley had the support of Olsen, old devotees such as Norman Mudd, and a forgiving Leah Hirsig, along with a German faction led by the above Karl Johannes Germer and Martha Kuentzel. Traenker, after another change of heart, rejected Crowley's authority and left with his own followers. In the middle was a third German group headed by Eugen Grosche, a former socialist commissar. Grosche and his devotees, who eventually dubbed themselves the *Fraternitas Saturni* ("Brotherhood of Saturn"), acknowledged the Beast's spiritual guidance but elected to govern their own affairs.[57]

The Weida gathering was Crowley's first visit to Germany since before the war, and a long-sought opportunity to connect or reconnect with persons and currents there. Of course, occult assemblies provided excellent cover for a little reconnaissance and recruitment. From that perspective, his most important contact was Karl Germer. In 1914 Germer had been the Berlin representative of Alfred Herbert, Ltd., a British machine-tool firm based in Coventry with many Royal Navy contracts—a perfect job for a German spy. Germer's sales territory included European Russia, and he was there when war erupted, narrowly avoiding internment. During the conflict, he spent much of his time on the Eastern Front, where he served in military intelligence. For his "special services," Germer received the coveted Iron Cross First Class.[58] He may have maintained a connection to German intelligence after the war, or, as a distinguished veteran, he may have been on the lookout for a new employer. Be that as it may, in the years to come, Germer would become one of Crowley's most loyal followers and a vital financial prop.

About a year after meeting Crowley, in spring 1926, Germer and his wife journeyed to New York. Mrs. Germer hoped that the change of scene would free her husband's mind from esoterica and the influence of the "international crook" Crowley.[59] She was disappointed. Soon after their arrival, Germer took off for Chicago to meet a mysterious "brother of the Order" on the Beast's orders.[60] The unnamed brother may have been Crowley's magical son, C.S. Jones, but Alvo von Alvensleben was still living in the U.S. and doing business in the Windy City. Alvo was a fellow German, well connected in America and the Reich. Did the Beast have some new or unfinished business with him? Germer disappeared for almost two years before finally reappearing in Boston. Meanwhile, his exasperated wife had returned to Germany and filed for divorce.

On the surface, the situation in Germany was very different from what it had been a few years before. The Weimar Republic seemed to have weathered its early crises and be on a path to peace and prosperity. Fall 1923 witnessed the Communists' last failed attempt at armed revolution and a smaller abortive insurrection in Munich by a band of Fascist imitators, the National Socialists. Their leader was a preternaturally charismatic ex-corporal and former army spy, Adolf Hitler.

The occult certainly influenced Hitler and the Nazi movement, mainly through "Ariosophist" groups (a racialized mutation of Theosophy) such as the *Germanen Orden* and, most infamously, the Munich-based *Thule Gesellschaft* (Society). The extent of such influence continues to be debated, especially where Hitler himself is concerned.[61] As the following chapter will discuss, Crowley has been invoked as a guiding influence on the future Führer. That is doubtful, but he definitely took an interest in Hitler and tried to approach him with the aim of promoting Thelema. Those overtures may have had an ulterior motive.

At or right after the Weida Conference, the Mage encountered one of Hitler's recent co-conspirators in the Beer-hall Putsch, General Erich Ludendorff. All but dictator of Germany in the final years of the war, Ludendorff had drifted into mystical right-wing extremism and saw Germany's defeat as the work of sinister "occult forces," namely Jews, Jesuits, and Freemasons.[62] The antidote, Ludendorff argued, was the revival of German paganism, which would replace enfeebling "Jewish" Christianity. This view gave him some common ground with Crowley and also formed the basis of his loose alliance with the Nazis. Crowley recalled that he and Ludendorff discussed "Nordic Theology," including the occult symbology of the swastika. He later spun this into the claim that he, through Ludendorff, convinced Hitler to adopt the swastika as his Party's talisman. The kernel of truth may be that the Beast was trying to use Ludendorff to contact, or simply collect inside information on, the rising Nazi leader.[63]

More generally, Ludendorff was a valuable source of information about occult influences on the German Right. He was friendly with Dr. Karl Haushofer, a Bavarian officer, scholar, and mystical adept who also was sympathetic with Nazism, or at least with some Nazis. Haushofer claimed membership in the so-called Vril Society or Luminous Lodge, another body which sought contact with spiritually and technologically advanced beings (another twist on the Mahatmas or Secret Chiefs) dwelling somewhere in *or under* the vastness of Central Asia.[64]

After the war, Haushofer held a professorship at the University of Munich, where he expounded his "geopolitics," a key point of which was the need for more *Lebensraum* (living space) for the German *Volk*.[65] He was surrounded by a coterie of admiring students, among them the eager young Rudolf Hess, Hitler's bosom friend and right-hand man.

At the same time Crowley cultivated connections in the German Right, he also tried to win friends among the Bolsheviks. Early in 1925, he drafted a manifesto and accompanying essay advocating a new religion for Soviet Russia, an "orgiastic" faith "based upon sound science," which would provide a needed spiritual basis for the Revolution. He even proposed a non-Russian "Savior" as the personal focus of this new faith. To no surprise, the religion was Thelema, and the savior, Aleister Crowley. "This new rite," he argued, "will produce in Europe and America the utmost religious consternation, and the old faiths will crumble into dust. . . ."[66] Thelema would become the vehicle of World Revolution—or vice versa.

The recipient of this modest proposal, written in English, was one of two old friends of Crowley then in Paris, both with high-level connections in Red Russia. One was dancer Isadora Duncan, just back from a not altogether happy stint in Moscow. A much more likely intermediary was the mutual friend of Duncan, Crowley, and Willie Seabrook, newspaperman Walter Duranty, then in Paris recuperating from injuries received in a train wreck. As Moscow correspondent for the *New York Times*, Duranty had become de facto dean of Western journalists in the Red capital. He had privileged access to Soviet leaders, the ability to move freely in and out of the Socialist Motherland, and even a reliable supply of heroin for his junkie wife (and Crowley's erstwhile lover), Jane Cheron. The amoral Duranty earned these perks by acting as a tool and apologist for the Soviet regime and probably informer.[67] He was the perfect person to carry Crowley's manifesto back to Russia and put it before the right people.

Occult influences flourished in the Soviet realm, albeit less obviously than in Germany. The Masonic and other secret societies that permeated pre-revolutionary Russian society did not disappear after 1917, but adapted and spread their influence into the Soviet government and secret services.[68] A key figure in this was Dr. Aleksandr Vasil'evich Barchenko, longtime student of the esoteric and paranormal, and de facto "Bolshevik professor of the occult."[69] A Martinist Freemason, Barchenko was a one-time student of Gurdjieff's teachings and seems to have maintained some connection to that master at Fontainebleau. In that regard, it is worth remembering the alleged Soviet connections of Gurdjieff's man Bennett. Like the Theosophists, Haushofer, and many Nazis, Barchenko also believed that dwelling in their sanctuary of Shambhallah

(Shangri-La, or Agartha) somewhere in Central Asia were powerful adepts who held the knowledge of a lost civilization. However, in the version promoted by Barchenko, instead of being a survival of ancient Aryan Thule, these Ascended Masters were the original Communists.

During the 1920s, Barchenko touted his ideas to members of the Red hierarchy. The most receptive was Gleb Ivanovich Bokii, chief of the "Special Department" (*Spetsotdel'*) of the Soviet secret police (the dreaded Cheka, later OGPU, NKVD, and eventually KGB). This was an ultra-secret section that handled codes and ciphers, and even the personal dossiers of the Soviet leaders. Bokii himself was a Martinist, a Rosicrucian, and a reputed devotee of Tantric sex rituals.[70] Surely Crowley would have fascinated him. Bokii put Barchenko in charge of a special laboratory within the Moscow Institute of Experimental Medicine to study hypnosis, telekinesis, remote viewing, ESP, etc., with the aim of harnessing them for intelligence purposes.

Bokii and Barchenko even formed an occult lodge, the innocuous-sounding United Labor Brotherhood (*Edinoe trudovoe bratstvo*), with veteran occultists and secret police operatives among its members. The Brotherhood survived until Stalin liquidated the lot during the late 1930s. Interestingly, the main charge leveled against Bokii, Barchenko, and friends was that their occult activities were a cover for treasonous contacts with British intelligence in the Far East.[71]

Barchenko and Bokii were behind the OGPU's effort to exploit the mystic, artist, and explorer Nikolai Roerich (or Rerikh). Roerich, too, was an ardent believer in mysterious and wonderful Shambhallah and a willing tool in Communist intrigues around the world. In 1925, he embarked on an expedition into the Himalayas with a retinue including OGPU agents disguised as religious pilgrims. Roerich's stated aim was to contact Tibet's Dalai Lama. More secretly and importantly, Bokii's men were seeking the Mahatmas of Shambhallah.

Later, Roerich set up shop in India, where his presence caused concern among officials who suspected that he had been "'illuminated,' under duress as to the excellence of the Union of Soviet Socialist Republics."[72] In July 1928 a flap occurred in London when the Explorer's son, Sviatoslav Roerich, applied for a British visa to visit his father. The India Office's query to the Foreign Office for more information fell to a former Army and RAF officer turned diplomat and SIS agent, Arthur Vivian Burbury. Burbury recently had returned to London from a three-year posting as third secretary with the British Legation in Moscow. There his secret intelligence duties focused on Soviet intrigues in Asia.[73] In reply to the IO request, he noted:

As to possible sources of information about Roerich—his connection with Russia, Thibet . . . Theosophists . . . and various 'secret' organizations . . . leads me to think that information as to him might be obtained from an (undesirable) Englishman who has had curiously intimate knowledge of all these things. His real name is Aleister Crowley. . . . I could endeavor privately to have him sounded [out] if it were thought desirable. He is a rascal and dare not show his face in England; but his knowledge of oriental evil is very deep.[74]

Mr. H.L. Baggallay of the FO warned in response that it would be "deplorable if it became known that the FO had any communication, however remote, with Aleister Crowley . . . who would at once go to prison if he set foot in this country." Baggallay's colleague C.M. Palairet cautioned more strongly, "Whatever happens, do not let us approach, however remotely, Crowley."[75]

Burbury supposedly received his introduction to Crowley from Lance Sieveking, a BBC journalist based in Paris, but a connection seems to have predated this. How, for instance, did intelligence officer Burbury learn about the Beast's expertise on "oriental evil?" Cleary, Burbury knew how to contact him. Our man therefore was not entirely cast adrift, though evidently viewed in a highly negative light. Burbury's recent service in Russia and his special interest in Asiatic intrigues logically included Barchenko's and Bokii's schemes, and possibly the doings of Bennett, De Kay, and Gurdjieff as well.

The theme of Asian intrigue also crops up in Rene Guenon's discussion of Crowley's dealings with another British officer in the 1920s, "Colonel Ettington."[76] Guenon was rightly convinced that the Beast was an asset of the "British secret service."[77] The man in question actually was Percy Thomas Etherton, an Indian Army man who had spent much of WWI in Egypt and other parts of the Middle East where he met Feilding. During 1918–1924 Etherton was His Majesty's "political resident" in Kashgar, a remote caravan town in westernmost Chinese Turkestan, conveniently and perilously close to the Soviet frontier.[78] From Kashgar, Etherton gathered intelligence on the Reds and ran agents such as the swashbuckling Frederick Bailey and L.V.S. Blacker. He continued to dabble in intelligence matters after his return to Delhi and London, and took at least a casual interest in Theosophy. Etherton would have been keen to learn all he could about the Soviets' plans to reach Tibet and Shambhallah.

In spring 1929 Crowley's life seemed to be going smoothly. He had a comfortable flat on the Avenue Suffren and had resumed writing, preparing *Magick in Theory and Practice* and the long-delayed *Moonchild* for publication. He had also acquired a devoted secretary in a young Jewish-American, Francis Israel Regardie (1907–

1985), and a fresh Scarlet Woman (and soon-to-be wife), Maria Theresa Ferrari de Miramar, a thirty-something Nicaraguan voodoo priestess.

Then his spying past came back to haunt him. Crowley had lived in Paris for nearly six years without the least molestation from French authorities despite his flagrant drug use, sexual deviations, and well-known association with Black Magic. So it was a surprise when on 9 March the French suddenly suspended his residency permit and demanded that he leave the country. He had to clear out by 17 April, and take Regardie and Miramar with him.

Crowley wrote to the Embassy demanding (and fully expecting) intercession on his behalf by His Majesty's Government. The original correspondence in the case was, typically, "not kept," but the registry index of the Foreign and Commonwealth Office preserves a brief summary. It reads: "[T]he Embassy are unable to intervene with the French authorities on his behalf. Has ascertained that Mr. Crowley has been asked to leave French territory exclusively on moral grounds. Proposes therefore to take no action on his behalf."[79] As Crowley later put it, "the British Embassy has left my case severely [alone] and has absolutely refused to help me."[80]

What "moral grounds" justified the expulsion? The Mage mentions that the French officials who came to see him were very curious about drugs, even wondering if his coffee mill might be a "machine for cocaine," and a press report mentions police suspecting him in an *affaire de cocaine*."[81] These suspicions could have arisen from Crowley's recent involvement with a dubious Spanish nobleman. Don Louis Ferdinand de Bourbon-Orleans, a member of both the Spanish and French royal houses and cousin to King Alfonso XIII, had been frequently accused of "questionable conduct" in France and elsewhere. Don Louis's first run-in with the law came in 1924 and led to his expulsion from France on criminal charges probably involving narcotics. He moved to Portugal, but in 1926 customs officers on the Portuguese-Spanish border arrested him for drug smuggling. A year later, the French again kicked him out, permanently this time, for assorted criminal infractions and all-around bad manners.[82]

Don Louis may have been one of Crowley's heroin connections. In any case, it is not hard to see why French authorities would have found their relationship questionable. The Beast insisted that he had "never met or corresponded with [the Spaniard] in any way," but that does not rule out entanglement in Don Louis' affairs. Those notably included the Don's proposed marriage to a rich American widow living near Paris, Mabelle Corey. Since Louis could not enter France, these negotiations had to be conducted by proxy. The Don's representative was Carl de Vidal Hundt, a German-American actor and occult-dabbler who had been in Hollywood when Crowley passed through in 1915. Hundt was in and out of Europe after the war where he pursued his acting career with little success. By the late 1920s, he was earning his crust as a publicist and press agent. Crowley himself engaged Hundt to promote his books and polish his image. Mabelle Corey's reputed fascination with the occult probably motivated Hundt to enlist the Beast's help in the Don Louis scheme. Then again, Crowley may have volunteered his services, hoping for a share of the payoff.

Whatever the case, the Don Louis flap sounds more likely a handy pretext than a pressing reason to expel the English Magician. Suspicion of espionage almost certainly was the real reason. French authorities never accused him publicly, but the press was more outspoken. One example was the conservative Catholic, conspiracy-mongering *Revue Internationale des Societes Secretes*, which had long painted Crowley as a knave and pernicious influence.[83] Curiously, the Soviets also later concluded that he had been kicked out "for espionage and the good of France," though just what they based this conclusion on is uncertain.[84]

If Crowley was engaged in espionage, who was he working for? And what or whom was he spying on?

1   Renegade.

2   Mariel, 56.

3   Robert Richardson, "The Priory of Sion and the Da Vinci Code," www.
    alpheus.orr/html/articles/esoteric_history/richardson4.htm, and Societe
    Perillos, "The Priory of Sion.com/pos1-2.html. See also Richardson's book,
    *The Unknown Treasure; The Priory of Sion and the Spiritual Treasure of
    Rennes-le-Chateau* (Houston, TX: NorthStar, 1988).

4   Richardson, "Priory of Sion and the Da Vinci Code."

5   *Ibid.*, and Pierluigi Zoccatelli, "Notes on Unpublished Correspondence
    between Rene Guenon and Louis Charbonneau-Lassay," //www.cesnur.
    org/testi/bryn/br_plz.htm#Anchor-46919.

6   Robert Richardson, "The Priory of Sion Hoax," www.jungcircles.com/muse/
    mason.htm.

7   *CAC*, 741.

8   *Ibid.*

9   *Ibid.*

10 Also known as the Luettwitz-Kapp Putsch. Wolfgang Kapp, an East Prussian
    civil servant, was the nominal leader, but the real muscle was provided by a
    Freikorps commander, Gen. Walter von Luettwitz. The short-lived coup began
    March and collapsed five days later.

11 Thwaites, 261–266.

12 The *Societa Italiana de Mutua Beneficenza Cefalutana* formed in New Orleans
    in 1887 and still exists.

13 Amado Crowley, *The Riddles of Aleister Crowley* (Leatherhead: Diamond
    Books, 1992), 130–131.

14 France, Documents repatriées, Carton 1298, index card An Z 7633.

15 Xavier de Hauteclocque, "L'Intelligence Service et ses mysteres," *Le Crapouillot*
    (Nov. 1931), 70.

16 UKNA, FO 371/3067.

17 Denis Laboure, "Petite Histoire (Vraie) des Rites Maconniques Egyptiens,"
    //membres.lycos.fr/cirem/travaux/histmis.htm, and P.R. Koenig, "Ancient
    and Primitive Rite of Memphis-Misraim: Historical Notes," //user.cyberlink.
    ch/~koenig/sunrise/mm1.htm.

18 The SR handled intelligence and counterintelligence duties and passed on
    information to the analytical and archiving *Deuxieme Bureau.* Richard
    Deacon, *The French Secret Service* (London: Grafton Books, 1990), 107–108.

19 Serge Hutin, "Les annees d'enfance et de jeunnesse d'Aleister Crowley,"
    EzoOccult [webzine] (Dec. 2004).

20 Amado, *Riddles*, 131.

21 *The Times* (25 Feb. 1922), 123 and (27 Feb. 1922), 10a. The British Consulate
    in Naples seized Bevan's passport, but he again gave them the slip only to be

arrested in Vienna some four months later.

22 Spence, *Trust No One*, 351.

23 USNA, DS, CSA, Sharp Bannerman, 13 Dec. 1924, 4, and Sharp to Kinsey, 13 and 17 July 1925.

24 SIS/MI6, File CX 2616, Reilly Report, 13 Feb. 1922.

25 For background, see Sutton's *Wall Street and the Bolshevik Revolution*.

26 Mark Hollingsworth and Charles Tremaine, *The Economic League: The Silent McCarthyism* (London: National Council for Civil Liberties, 1989), 5.

27 Spence, *Trust No One*, 432.

28 *Ibid.*, 363 n9.

29 *Sunday Express* (26 Nov. 1922).

30 *CAC*, 912.

31 *John Bull* (10, 17, 24 March 1923).

32 *CAC*, 920.

33 Marco Pasi, *Aleister Crowley e la tentazione delle politica* (Milano: FrancoAngeli, 1999), note, p. 41.

34 Mauri, "Aleister Crowley in Italia," 6.

35 Italy, L'Archivio Centrale della Stato a Roma (ACS), P.S., AA.G.R, 1903–1949, R.G., b. 1, fasciolo 20 as published in Pasi, 175–176, 196–199.

36 Claudio Mauri, "Tre Attentati al Duce: Una Pista Esoteria," *Esoterismo e Fascismo*, 14–15.

37 *Ibid.* On Gibson, see also: Richard Oliver Collin, *La donna che sparo a Mussolini* (Milan; Rusconi, 1988).

38 See: Claudio Mauri, *La Catena Invisibile: il giallo del fascismo magico* (Milan: Mursia, 2005).

39 Claudio Mauri, "Aleister Crowley in Italia," in G. de Turris (ed.), *Esoterismo e fascismo* (Rome: Edizioni Mediterrannee, 2006), 11. On the Clinic see: Eric Trist and Hugh Murray, "Historical Overview: The Foundation and Development of the Tavistock Institute to 1989," www.moderntimesworkplace.com/archives/ericsess.tavis1/tavis1.html.

40 E.g., Dr. Byron T. Weeks, "Tavistock—The Best Kept Secret in America," www.rense.com/general12/twaa.htm. More on the alleged conspiratorial role of Tavistock can be found in John Coleman's *The Conspirator's Hierarchy: the Committee of 300.*

41 Pasi, *Ibid.*, citing "Nota #500/5883, 27 June 1927."

42 *CAC*, 920.

43 Hollingsworth, 8–10, and Mike Hughes, *Spies at Work* (1994), Chapters 1 and 3, //www.1in12.go-legend.net/publications/library/spies/spies.htm.

44 Hughes, Chap. 3.

45 *Ibid.*

46 UKNA, FO 371/28896.

47 Webster, *Secret Societies and Subversive Movements* (London: Boswell, 1924), 314–315.

48 UKNA, KV 3/57, Note from General Winter re agent in ARCOS.

49 James Moore, *Gurdjieff: A Biography, The Anatomy of a Myth* (Rockport, MD, Element, 1991), 219–???.

50 *Ibid.*

51 UKNA, WO 339/21087, Capt. J.G. Bennett, and FO 371/15232, containing a summary of Bennett's activities through the '20s.

52 *Ibid.*, noting MI5 summary.

53 Glowka, 67.

54 William Breeze to author, 30 Jan. 2008.

55 Peter Koenig, "Introduction to the Ordo Templi Orientis," //user.cyberlink. ch/~koenig/intro.html.

56 Breeze to author, *Ibid.*

57 Glowka, 69–74.

58 Koenig, "In Memoriam: Fra ∴ Saturnus, Karl Johannes Germer," //user. cyberlink.ch/~koenig/metzger.htm.

59 Translation of Germer divorce decree, 25 June 1929, at: /bbs.bapho.net/bbs/I-drive/mags/lodge/tlc.0798.nws.

60 *Ibid.*

61 Probably the most scholarly and conservative work on the subject is Nicholas Goodrick-Clarke, *The Occult Roots of Nazism: Secret Aryan Cults and Their Influence on Nazi Ideology* (New York: New York Univ. Press, 1985). In much the same vein is Reginald H. Philips, "Before Hitler Came: Thule Society and Germanen Orden, *Journal of Modern History*, #35 (1968), 245–261. The notion of much wider, even paramount, occult influences on the Nazis is promoted in works like Dusty Sklar's *The Nazis and the Occult* (New York: Dorset Press, 1977), Louis Pauwels and Jacques Bergier's *The Morning of the Magicians* (New York: Ace Books, 1968), Giorgio Galli's *Hitler e il Nazismo Magico* (Milano: Rizzoli, 1989), Peter Levenda's *Unholy Alliance: A History of Nazi Involvement with the Occult* (New York: Continuum, 1995) and Trevor Ravenscroft's *The Spear of Destiny* (Boston: Weiser Books, 1982). Also of interest in this regard is Stephen E. Flowers and Michael Moynihan, *The Secret King: The Myth and Reality of Nazi Occultism* (Los Angeles: Feral House, 2008).

62 Robert Boucard, *Les Dessous de l'Espionnage Allemand* (Paris: Editions Documentaires, 1931), 12–13.

63 Sutin, 377.

64 All of this seems to have started with the late-nineteenth-century appearance of Sir Edward Bulwer-Lytton's (a Rosicrucian, among other things) *The Coming Race* (Edinburgh, Blackwood, 1871), which spun the tale of

subterranean super-beings possessing mysterious and terrible "Vril" power.

65 Sklar, 62–72.

66 Ryan, "The Great Beast in Russia," 156.

67 S.J. Taylor, *Stalin's Apologist: Walter Duranty, the* New York Times's *Man in Moscow* (NY: Oxford Univ. Press, 1990), 172–173, 249–250. Duranty most infamously helped cover up the disastrous famine in Ukraine in the early 1930s.

68 For background see: Viktor Brachev, *Chekisty protiv okkul'tistov* (Moscow: Eksmo, 2004), Oleg Shishkin, *Bitva za Gimalei* (Moscow:Eksmo, 2003), and Oleg Platonov, *Istoricheskii slovar rossiiskikh masonov XXVII-XX vekov* (Moscow, 1996).

69 The most thorough work on Barchenko and his connection to Bokii is Aleksandr Andreev, *Okkul'tist strany sovetov* (Moscow: Eksmo, 2004). See also Paul Stonehill and Philip Mantle, "The KGB, Tibet and UFOs," *Fate* (Sept. 2002).

70 Alexander Berzin, "Russian and Japanese Involvement with Pre-Communist Tibet: The Role of the Shambhala Legend," www.berzinarchives.com/kalachakra/russian_japanese_shambhala.html.

71 Andreev, Bokii Interrogation, 360–361.

72 Phil Tomaselli to author, 18 Dec. 2005, citing July 1928 correspondence between India Office and Foreign Office Library.

73 Vladislav Minaev, *Podryvnaia deiatel'nost' inostrannykh razvedok v SSSR* (Moscow, 1940), 89.

74 Tomaselli to author, *Ibid.*

75 *Ibid.*

76 Jerace, "Aleister Crowley." Guenon also linked Ettington/Etherton to Trebitsch-Lincoln who was up to his tricks in China at the same time.

77 Rene Guenon, *Il Teosofismo* , Vol. 1 (Torino: Delta Arktos, 1987), 39–40.

78 Etherton recounted his adventures in *The Heart of Asia* (London: Constable & Co., 1925).

79 British Foreign and Commonwealth Office, Registry Index, Treaty File notes concerning "Expulsion of Mr. Crowley from France."

80 "Black Magic Denied: Former Spy's Exploits," *The Star* [Auckland] (22 June 1929).

81 *Ibid.*

82 *NYT*, obituary (23 June 1945), 13.

83 "L'O.T.O., Expulsion de Sir Aleister Crowley," RISS, (May 1929), 134.

84 Cover sheet to *Tsentral'nyi Gosudarstvennyi Osobyi Archiv SSSR*, Fond 7, Opis 2, Delo 5314/36457.

ONE OF THE PRESS EXTRACTS PRESERVED in Crowley's Deuxième Bureau file cryptically attributes to the English Magician "certain suspect relations with the intelligence services of foreign countries."[1] Pierre Mariel also notes a piece in the 14 April 1929 edition of *Paris-Midi* that specifically charged that the Beast "had been proven to be a secret agent in the service of Germany."[2] French press coverage of *l'Affaire Crowley* almost never failed to mention his work for Berlin in wartime America. Of course, the same articles colorfully labeled and mislabeled him a *Mage Noire*, the *Raspoutine anglais*, and "Sir Crowley."[3] Similar allegations appeared in the *New York Times* and even in papers as far away as New Zealand. Interestingly the British press largely ignored the affair, although one minor paper repeated the accusation that the infamous Mr. Crowley had been booted from France because he "has been acting as a secret agent for Germany."[4]

The Mage fought back as best he could, pointing out that his wartime service to the Germans had been under the supervision of the "Naval Intelligence Service," or simply *"l'Intelligence Service anglais."*[5] He bragged about inciting the Germans to provoke the Americans, and singled out Admiral "Gount" as a man who could vouch for his loyalty to England.[6] Crowley actually cabled Gaunt to request a letter attesting to his true colors, but the Admiral, like the rest of His Majesty's officials, discreetly ignored the embattled Beast. The invocation of Gaunt and British intelligence was a desperate attempt to leverage help from London, but there was only so far he dared go. Saying too much could result in far worse repercussions than deportation from France.

A connection between Crowley and German intelligence may not have been a fantasy spun by the Gallic press. We have already noted that his key devotee in Germany, Karl Germer, had at least a past association with Berlin's secret services. Despite the official détente created by the Locarno Treaty (1925) and like diplomatic niceties, France remained Germany's mortal enemy. French troops stayed in the Rhineland long after the Americans and British had pulled out, and Paris was loath to abandon its huge reparations claims. Moreover, Berlin had a keen interest in French aeronautical developments. So did London.

But would the Germans have been desperate or foolish enough to trust a man who openly admitted gulling and betraying them during the Great War? That was then, this was now. If Crowley had deceived them, it proved his qualification for the job of deceiving others. After all, Kurt Jahnke, the *éminence grise* of German intelligence in the 1920s, insisted that "the full value of a Secret Service always depended on the number and standard of Double Agents."[7] For the Germans, as for the British, the crucial question about Crowley was not whether he could be trusted, but whether he could be *useful.*

Weimar intelligence and security agencies were a more tangled mix than most. At the top was the Military Intelligence Service (*Deutscher Militärischer Nachrichtendienst*—DMN), the remnant of the wartime *Abteiling IIIb*. Under the Versailles Treaty, the Allies allowed the Germans only *defensive* intelligence capability, so in 1921 the DMN became a much scaled-down *Abwehrgruppe*, later plain *Abwehr*. It remained a shoestring operation until 1923, when the French invasion of the Ruhr triggered its expansion. Many old agents, including Jahnke, and maybe Germer, returned to the fold. Versailles Treaty or no, the Germans resumed aggressive intelligence abroad, mostly against France and Poland.

The Weimar Republic also had its equivalent of MI5 or Special Branch. Up until 1928, when leftist pressure forced its dissolution, this was the *Reichskommissariat für die Überwachung der öffentlichen Ordnung* (Commissariat for the Protection of Public Order). A secretive inner core stayed busy even after the official dismantling. RÜöO comprised two agencies, *Abteilung 1A*, which operated in the Berlin Police Presidium, and the ultra-secret *Centrals Staatspolizei* (Central State Police). The embryo of the future *Gestapo*, the Staatspolizei oversaw the security of Germany's secret re-armament programs and the attendant collaboration with the Soviets.

The German military initiated collaboration with the Red Army in 1921, and it soon grew to include Russian-based plants producing planes, tanks, and poison gas.[8] This collusion was of great interest to British intelligence, and anything Crowley could find out about it would have been welcome, even if that necessitated his doing a little dirty work for the Germans against the French. Nations, it is said, do not have friends, only interests.

Government agencies were only a part of the picture. Even before they came to power, the Nazis had their own intelligence–counterintelligence bodies. In 1932, "Blond Beast" and future Holocaust mastermind Reinhard Heydrich created the *Sicherheitsdienst* (SD, Security Service) inside the SS (*Schutzstaffel*), Heinrich Himmler's black-uniformed corps. The SD was to ferret out and destroy Hitler's (and Himmler's) enemies, including those within the Party itself. Not to be outdone, the intra-Party rivals of the SS, the brown-shirted SA (*Sturmabteilung*), maintained an "information service" run by a half-Scottish political adventurer, Georg Bell.[9] Bell also served as a confidential agent for Anglo-Dutch oil tycoon Sir Henri Deterding, which raised suspicions that he also had links to British intelligence.[10]

Then there was our friend Kurt Jahnke. Around 1924, Jahnke set up an ostensibly private agency, the "*Jahnkebüro*," which operated from the seclusion of his Pomeranian estate.[11] Jahnke was with a close friend of Franz Pfeffer von Salomon, chief of the SA from 1926 to 1930, and he knew Georg Bell. Most importantly, Jahnke's organization worked hand-in-glove with the *Abwehr* and the Soviets.[12] In the early 1920s, Jahnke had continued to act as double agent for the Americans by supplying information to the U.S. Army's military observer in Berlin, and he probably did likewise for the British. For Jahnke, Crowley would have been a handy, discreet, and familiar contact. The connection might have been made stronger by a common interest in the occult. Jahnke was an intensely private man, and the doings at his estate were the source of dark rumors.

Weimar Germany still roiled with Communist intrigues. Besides the local Reds—the KPD—and their *Geheimapparat* (Secret Apparatus), Moscow's OGPU, military intelligence, and the Comintern (Communist International) all maintained a major presence that linked up with Communist and Red-inspired activities in other countries.[13] As it happened, the French broke up a big Soviet spy ring shortly before the Beast's expulsion. Moreover, during 1928–1929 Crowley had cultivated the acquaintance of a colorful Hungarian in Paris, Louis Gibarti (real name Laszlo Dobos), a veteran Comintern and OGPU agent, about whom more in the next chapter. For now, suffice it that Gibarti was the right-hand man of the Comintern's chief agent in Western Europe, the German Willi Münzenberg.[14] French authorities kept a watchful eye on Gibarti and would not have have overlooked his association with the curious Englishman. That can only have added to their discomfort about Crowley's residence.

Crowley's contact with Gibarti, like his dealings with the German services, took place with the tolerance and probable encouragement of persons in London. To the extent the Beast was spying in France, he ultimately was doing so for dear old England. London, as noted, had ample reason to mistrust and snoop on its dubious ally. During the 1920s, British intelligence developed a pro-German stance, at least where France was concerned, and France was on the lookout for Anglo-German collusion. They found plenty of it. The late 1920s saw two sensational spy cases involving British subjects. At the end of 1925, the *Sûreté* arrested three Britons and two French accomplices for espionage. A French court convicted the lot of spying on air fields and naval facilities.[15] At the head of the ring was Captain John Henry Leather, an officer attached to British military intelligence and probably affiliated with SIS.[16] In addition to serving Britain, Leather and his crew passed much the same information to Germany.

In late 1926, French authorities arrested another former British officer, Vivian Stranders, for supplying secrets to Berlin. The French were convinced that Stranders also was spying for his native country. In order to dispel this notion, MI5 was planning to seize him on its own charges.[17] After two years in a French prison, Stranders bolted to Germany just before Crowley's expulsion. Crowley's PR man, Carl de Vidal Hundt, also took an odd interest in Stranders' case, which doubtless raised Gallic suspicions. In the Reich, Stranders became a German citizen and later a fervent Nazi. He also may have had contact with Soviet agents. London wanted him watched.

One person who may have had a bearing on Crowley's relationship with British intelligence in early 1929 was a mysterious Mr. Stratford. According to Francis Dickie, a Canadian journalist in Paris, Stratford suddenly popped up at the Beast's side that spring as part of a bizarre plot to fake Crowley's death. They tried to enlist Dickie in the scheme (about which more later). Stratford, he recalled, was "a dubious character, everyone in the little café-world around Montparnasse knew, and wondered how he made a living."[18] Stratford claimed to be an old Cambridge classmate of the Mage, but no one believed that, either. Others thought he must be a spy. Crowley himself apparently never mentioned him. Were it not for Stratford's implied age (any Cambridge classmate of the Beast would have had to be in his fifties), he might have been one of two other men in Crowley's life around this time.

One of these we have met before: George Langelaan, who recounted Crowley's confessions about his WWI undercover work and the *Lusitania*. Langelaan placed his first meeting with Crowley "about 1930," but it must have been in early 1929, shortly before the Beast's ouster.[19] Although born to British parents, Langelaan had lived most of his life in France, which helped to equip him for intelligence work. It is unknown whether Langelaan, later a WWII Special Operations Executive (SOE) officer, had links to London's secret services when he met the Beast. In any case, young Langelaan found his way into Crowley's confidence. He recalls watching the Mage take on chess master Savielly Tartakower at the Paris British Chess Club, convinced by what he saw that Crowley used hypnotism as part of his strategy.[20] There is no entry of any such encounter in Tartokower's official game record, but he was in Paris at the time. Langelaan also had sporadic encounters with Crowley during 1930–1932. That coincides with Crowley's stay in Germany, but whether the meetings took place there or elsewhere is uncertain.

The second man was Gerald Joseph Yorke, a.k.a. "Frater Volo Intelligere." He met Crowley in 1927, having flown to Paris in a flush of enthusiasm for the Beast's writings and wisdom. At least, that was how he later explained it. Gerald Yorke came from a wealthy Midlands family not at all pleased by his hobnobbing with the infamous Wickedest Man in the World.[21] A Cambridge graduate and a lieutenant in the Territorial Reserves (2nd Royal Gloucester Hussars), Yorke was personable but secretive, perhaps to conceal his alleged homosexuality, his interest in the occult, his intelligence work, or all three. He confessed to being a member of Crowley's A∴A∴, but denied having anything to do with the OTO or being the Beast's "follower" *per se*. Nevertheless, he readily assumed the role of Crowley's "financial organizer and ombudsman."[22] Yorke respected Crowley the magick adept, but not especially

Crowley the man, being appalled by the Beast's cavalier treatment of women and recklessness with money.

The real key to their relationship may be that Yorke was the *Mega Therion's* assigned case officer. If so, which branch of spookdom did he serve? His profession or cover was that of a freelance journalist and correspondent for Reuters. That and his later work in China all point to SIS, but the lines separating the various aspects of British intelligence were especially vague in this period.

Another hint of an SIS connection is Yorke's intercession in late 1928 with an intelligence worker mentioned in the last chapter, Arthur Burbury. The latter, recall, had touted the Beast as an expert on "oriental evil" and Soviet intrigues in Asia. Yorke was the probable intermediary. The new matter at hand was Crowley's effort to get his book *Magick in Theory and Practice* published in Britain. Standing in the way was the blue-nosed Home Secretary William Joynson-Hicks. Joynson-Hicks, or "Jix," was a bosom friend of James Douglas of the *Sunday Express*, a paper that had done more than its share to blacken Crowley's name. In hope of getting around the "Jix" obstacle, Crowley sent Yorke and another young former officer, Lance Sieveking, to see Burbury at the Foreign Office. Crowley's secretary Israel Regardie believed that this really had something to do with Burbury's connections to the "secret service."[23] It would not have been the first time the Beast had used his intelligence contacts to circumvent or neutralize opposition from another branch of British officialdom. The effort succeeded; *Magick in Theory and Practice* appeared in print the next year.

Yorke also connected Crowley to a cabal of occultist-literary types centered on the Mandrake Press, a small publishing house that would bring out some of Crowley's works, including *Confessions* and *Moonchild*. Besides Yorke, the outfit's directors included a pro-fascist Australian, P.R. "Inky" Stephenson. During 1930, Stephenson, with help from Regardie, published *The Legend of Aleister Crowley*, part of Crowley's new offensive to redeem his public image. Other directors were a mysterious Major J.C.S. MacAllen and an ex-RAF officer, Robin Thynne, who, as we will see, had shadowy ties to the intelligence realm. Another of Mandrake's authors was a Crowley acquaintance, the composer Peter Warlock (Philip Heseltine), whose lover was another composer, Elizabeth Poston. Warlock died in 1930, but in the coming war Poston ended up working for British intelligence.[24] Thus, in his dealings with Mandrake Press, the Mage found himself in the familiar situation of being surrounded by past, present, and future spies. Mandrake, however, proved a financial bust and collapsed amid accusations of malfeasance and incompetence.

After he quit Paris, the Beast holed up in the Hotel Metropole in Brussels. Regardie and Crowley's fiancée, the exotic Miss de Miramar, had tried to enter England but were turned back by His Majesty's officials. Technically, this was due to their lack of visas and other documents. Crowley seems to have been surprised by the rebuff, and worried that it meant an equally hostile reception of him. Had he revealed too much to the French press? Belgian authorities made clear that they did not welcome his presence. Crowley once again turned to his friend and "employee of the Intelligence Service," Gerald Yorke.[25]

Shortly after Crowley's exit from France, Yorke received a call from Scotland Yard's Col. J.F.C. Carter, mentioned in the previous chapter, the boss of Special Branch and an avid Red-hunter. A few years later, Crowley would write half-jokingly, "legend says that my dossier at Scotland Yard fills a whole room."[26] Roomful or not, Carter had ample sources at his disposal about the Beast's history; his long association with George Makgill and Nesta Webster doubtless versed him well in the sins of Aleister Crowley, real and imaginary.

However, as a former Indian police official and a wartime member of MI5's section G, Carter had also known Robert Nathan (d. 1921), who could have offered a very different view of Mr. Crowley. The same may have been true for Burbury. Burbury, Carter, and Yorke all shared a Masonic allegiance, which might have included more occult ones. According to Yorke, Carter wanted to know "what magical potions Brother V.I. [Yorke] had been brewing recently with Britain's Worst Man," which shows that Carter knew about their connection. [27] Carter may have smelled a link between such activity and Crowley's trouble in France. Yorke simply offered that "the Beast was not as beastly as he was made out to be," whereupon Carter asked to meet him.

In late May, Carter handed Yorke enough money to arrange the Mage's travel to London.[28] On 11 June, Crowley recorded in his diary that he had dined with Carter and that the upshot of their meeting was "All clear."[29] Years later, Yorke assured a curious American that Crowley "was never in any difficulties or trouble with the Home Office"—at least, not with Col. Carter.[30]

Carter's support was vital to getting Crowley back into the country without hassles or invasive scrutiny, and he did not proffer this help out of kindness. If the Colonel went out of his way for Crowley, he expected something in return. He may have received quiet encouragement from another interested quarter. The Yard and its Special Branch were supposed to be concerned with *internal* security, not foreign espionage. In reality, it had run agents abroad since Melville's time. Likewise SIS, despite its foreign intelligence mandate, ran its own domestic anti-Communist section. That did not sit well with Kell's MI5, the agency formally charged with internal security.

What all these entities shared in the late 1920s was an overriding concern with Communist subversion. Special Branch's main Red-hunter then was Guy Maynard Liddell, so any reports Crowley filed with the Branch would have ended up in his hands. As head of Special Branch, Carter also oversaw two sections, SS1, the liaison with SIS, and SS2, which handled coordination with MI5. As noted, everything about Yorke smacks of SIS, making him a likely liaison to Carter from that agency. This suggests that the Beast became a shared asset, with Col. Carter acting as a cut-out to mask SIS' involvement. Curiously, SIS' list of Crowley "Press References" stops dead in 1929 with a single article on the French expulsion, resuming only in 1947 with a brief announcement of his death.

During 1929, Communist activity seemed especially dangerous in Germany. While the Great Depression was still around the corner, the Reich was already astir with economic unrest, which helped to inflame the Communist and Nazi movements. Hitler's Party and the Reds were bitter rivals, but they shared a common determination to topple the Weimar Republic. Crowley's array of connections gave him access to elements in both camps, and soon, on Carter's orders, he would be off to Germany again.

First, however, Carter may have looked to Crowley for help with another matter. In the summer of 1929, expatriate Italian anarchists were plotting another attempt to kill Mussolini.[31] The center of the conspiracy was Brussels, where Crowley had just been cooling his heels. Given his reputation as a victim of Il Duce's persecution and his rumored connection to the 1926 plot, Crowley was ideally suited to gain the confidence of the anarchists and ferret out details. It recalled his days in New York. Whether or not Crowley lent a hand, Carter penetrated the plot and passed the necessary information to Mussolini's secret police.

On 2 July, the tabloid *Daily Sketch* noted Crowley's presence in London "after a long absence." The brief article slants noticeably in favor of the prodigal son. Calling him "one of the most interesting and talked of men in Europe," it pooh-poohs "exaggerated and ridiculous" stories circulated about him. "Actually, he is a very brilliant and interesting man," it continued, "who has traveled all over the world observing religious practices and philosophy." It even plugged his forthcoming Mandrake titles. This puffery's timing with the Beast's meeting with Carter is telling. The *Daily Sketch* was run by Lord Rothermere (Harold Harmsworth), a close friend of Carter who had done his bit for the Ministry of Information during the World War. Newspapers he controlled would remain noticeably friendly toward Crowley over the next few years.

Of course, not everyone was happy to see Crowley back in England. *The Patriot*, the organ of the arch-conservative Lord Northumberland (another crony of Makgill, Webster, and the British Fascisti), soon weighed in to defend decency. On 2 May Northumberland's paper had run a piece that raked over Crowley's disreputable past, including his intrigues with the Golden Dawn. Now, countering the *Sketch*'s spin, another *Patriot* article accused the *Sketch* of "doping" the British public by misguided praise of such "subversive persons and doctrines."[32] Crowley still had plenty of enemies in his homeland.

But he also had friends besides Carter and Yorke. The Chelsea hostess Gwen Otter was an old acquaintance of Crowley's and a friend to artists and bohemians of all stripes. Crowley popped up at her gatherings during early summer 1929. Even there British intelligence had eyes and ears. Among his fellow guests at Otter's was Francis

Toye, music editor for the London *Morning Post*. Toye was cousin to the Beast's ex-brother-in-law, Gerald Kelly, and another veteran of Hall's Naval Intelligence during the war. Toye retained spookish connections, and while he passed off his encounter with Crowley as purely casual, there could have been more to it.[33]

On 16 August, Crowley surfaced in Leipzig where he finally exchanged vows with Maria de Miramar, beginning a turbulent and short-lived marriage. The nuptials were necessary for Miramar's British visa. Belgium's laws made it hard for foreigners to contract marriage there, so Germany was a logical choice. Even so, there were German towns much closer than Leipzig. Crowley chose the hometown of his loyal acolyte and likely intelligence contact Karl Germer, who attended the wedding.

Another German attendee, Martha Kuentzel, had become a fanatical admirer of Hitler, in whom she saw a "magickal child" and the embodiment of the New Aeon. In 1925 Crowley had assured her that "the nation which first accepted the *Book of the Law*, officially, would thereby become the leading nation in the world."[34] Apparently on her own initiative, Kuentzel translated the *Book* and sent it to the future Führer. It probably never reached his desk. In fall 1930, however, Crowley tried to contact the Nazi chief through his old friend Col. "Bony" Fuller, now another British admirer of Fascism and later of the Third Reich.[35] There is no sign that the overture elicited a response.

This did not stop Réné Guénon from later asserting that Crowley went to Berlin in the early 1930s specifically to contact Hitler and succeeded in becoming a "secret counselor" of the Nazi leader.[36] A wilder version holds that the Beast actually became Adolf's Svengali or alter ego.[37] Walter Johannes Stein and Trevor Ravenscroft, both followers of Anthroposophist Rudolf Steiner, alleged that Hitler was the initiate of an occult doctrine "similar to, and in part derived from, the horrible sex magic of Aleister Crowley."[38] There is no credible evidence for any of this. However, the claims of Stein and Ravenscroft may somehow relate to Crowley's peculiar relationship with some of Steiner's faithful in the years ahead.

Crowley certainly found Hitler fascinating, but so did many people. Upon reading Herrmann Rauschning's *Hitler Speaks*, the Beast is said to have proclaimed that his and the Führer's intimate thoughts ran on the same rails, but Crowley's fixation on Adolf seems more clinical than personal.[39] In the same vein, the Beast's declaration in a 1933 article for the *Sunday Dispatch* that "before Hitler was, I am," is sometimes cited as proof of an occult bond between the two.[40] Taken in context, however, it is much less provocative, being merely Crowley's claim to a prior, special relationship with the swastika—that he had been born with "four hairs curling from left to right" over his heart. Like so many other things, Crowley's Naziphilia was a pose aimed at gaining attention and influence. It does not seem to have worked on Hitler, but others may have been taken in.

Around the same time Crowley was reaching out to Hitler, he also was courting

Joseph Stalin. In January 1930, he made an overture to the Soviet strongman through Walter Duranty, and he would try again a few years later. Much as before, Crowley offered Stalin "a substitute for the God [the Soviets] had spurned," Thelema, and, of course, himself.[41] The Beast's efforts to curry favor in Moscow meshed with Carter's and friends' concerns about the Red Menace.

On 25 August 1929, Crowley's diary records a very interesting rendezvous, presumably on his way back from Germany, with Col. R.J.R. Brown.[42] The notation indicates that this was at least their second meeting. Most interesting of all, however, is the Colonel's address or site of the get-together: 12 bis du Marechal Joffre, near Versailles, just outside Paris. So, the Beast did return to France after all, despite his later claim that he never set foot there again. Given the circumstances, we must assume that he traveled incognito. The big question, of course, is what was so important that he had to meet with Brown under such circumstances? What relation did Col. Brown have to Carter and British intelligence? The same diary notes a dinner with Carter on 6 September, right after Crowley's return to London. The meeting included a "long talk till midnight at [Carter's] flat."[43] This was undoubtedly a debriefing.

In late October, perhaps after a similar sojourn, the Mage met with both Carter and Yorke.[44] His reports must have confirmed that things in Germany were fast going to Hell. The economic crash that October had sent unemployment soaring. The power of the Nazis and Communists grew with every downward tick in the economy, and the fragile coalition of moderates running the Republic was disintegrating.

Crowley hung around London during winter 1929–1930, unsuccessfully trying to keep Mandrake Press afloat while dealing with his frequently hysterical and inebriated wife. He had not lost his special knack for driving women over the edge. In February, public outcry scuttled his attempt to deliver a lecture on fifteenth-century mass murderer Gilles de Rais to the Oxford University Poetry Society, proof that he had not lost his ugly reputation either.

On 13 April 1930, Crowley headed back to the Reich. The day prior, his diary noted receipt of money, "for Germany", from the aforementioned Robin Thynne.[45] Was this for business purposes, or something else? Thynne's name shows up again in a diary entry for 30 April after the Mage had reached Berlin.[46] In this Crowley suggests that Thynne or MacAllen see a certain "Pax" in Paris who owned a couple of Spanish-language newspapers. Said papers had "copied Paris lies." The main part of the entry, however, concerns a lunch with Arnoldo Krumm-Heller, the German-Mexican occultist and secret agent we last saw headed back to Mexico from the Orkneys. Also referenced is a certain Steiner, though certainly not Rudolf who had been dead since 1925.

The *Berliner Tageblatt* of 3 May ran a short article acknowledging the "gentleman bohemian's" recent arrival and emphasized his past exploits as a mountain climber.[47]

The *Tageblatt* piece did not seem to know quite what to make of this "peculiar personality." Was Herr Crowley a "revolutionary philosopher," or just a "foolish artist"? No thought seems to have been given to the possibility that he was a spy. The article made special note of the fact that the Englishman had offered his advice to the German Himalayan expedition then preparing an assault on Crowley's old enemy, Kangchenjunga. The leader of the expedition was Paul Bauer, a veteran alpinist and friend of Crowley's former climbing partner, Eckenstein. A few years later, Bauer would become chief of the Nazi-sponsored German Alpine Federation and a special adviser to the SS expedition Heinrich Himmler dispatched to Tibet.

Bauer's expedition piqued the interest and suspicions of officials in London and Delhi. The biggest expedition ever sent into the Himalayas, it was rumored to be equipped with all manner of technical innovations. Anything Crowley could have gleaned about those would have been worth his pay. The German attempt failed, but fresh on its heels the British began planning their own expedition, an aerial one, to photograph and map nearby Mt. Everest. One of the planners of the Everest flight was Crowley's supposed contact Col. Percy Etherton.[48]

Réné Guénon invokes Etherton's name in a different context. Around this same time, writes Guénon, Crowley founded a "Saturn-Lodge" in Berlin, and Col. Etherton was involved with it.[49] Guénon may have been on to something, but he seems to be talking about the *Fraternitas Saturni*, the Thelemic offshoot formed in Germany in 1928 by Eugen Grosche (who dubbed himself Frater Gregor Gregorius), not Crowley. According to Germer, Crowley had nothing to do with Grosche or his group. Then again, Germer detested Grosche as a "sex-maniac" and "one of the lowest types of occultists."[50] Still, the Nazis later arrested Grosche, and the Gestapo's suspicion focused in part on his alleged connection to the English Magician Crowley.[51] The Mage and Etherton would have been more than willing to exploit Grosche and his organization for whatever information they could provide. On the other hand, Germer's own mystical name (one of them) was "Frater Saturnus," so the mysterious lodge may have been just a branch of the OTO.

Crowley's latest foray into Germany occurred during a full-blown political crisis. The teetering governing coalition collapsed at the end of March 1930 as the nation sank into a seemingly bottomless depression. The leaders of the foundering Weimar Republic, their grasp weakening, resorted to emergency powers. The secret battle had begun for the soul of the nation.

In Berlin, in summer 1930, Crowley encountered the Viennese psychoanalyst Alfred Adler, mentioned earlier in connection with the Tavistock Institute. It may not have been their first meeting. Adler's name will crop up in a stranger association with Crowley's a few years hence. Their link at present was Karl Germer, who was one of Adler's patients. The Beast later claimed to "know [Adler] personally" and, implausibly, to have "handled" some of the Doctor's Berlin patients and to have "put a lot of my own theory and practice into it."[52] Perhaps Crowley merely referred to Germer, but a larger and more intimate connection between Mage and Psychiatrist cannot be ruled out.

Crowley wasted no time in finding a female diversion, this time a nineteen-year-old German model and aspiring artist, Hanni Larissa Jaeger. He dubbed her "the Monster," which captures the mood of the relationship. Sexual imperative aside, a female traveling companion always made good cover. That summer he and Hanni briefly returned to England, but on 29 August they departed Southampton on a boat for Lisbon, where one of the strangest episodes in Crowley's strange career would occur.

The poet Fernando Pessoa met the couple in Lisbon, and he became the Beast's accomplice in the stunt to come. Pessoa, a friend of Frank Harris, was fascinated by the occult, and an esoteric Freemason and Rosicrucian.[53] Crowley's grand scheme, planned for at least a year, was to fake his own death. As Francis Dickie had understood it in 1929, the basic idea was to get creditors off his back and boost the value of his books, including those recently published by Mandrake Press. He would eventually resurface, reap the rewards, and pay off his and Mandrake's debts. It was a plan hatched in desperation and a telling example of Crowley's capacity for calculated deception.

The Beast later tried to explain the plot as a misguided joke on Frau Jaeger. On 18 September, Hanni, who may or may not have understood her part in the game, stormed off after a noisy brawl and caught a steamer back to Germany. A few days later, a broken-hearted Crowley left a suicide note near the Boca do Inferno, a swirling ocean inlet surrounded by jagged cliffs, and disappeared—sort of. The same day he supposedly took his fatal leap, Crowley, or someone using his passport, crossed the Spanish frontier. Pessoa later admitted that he had seen the Magician alive in Lisbon on 24 September.[54] Over the next few weeks, other reports put Crowley in Portugal, but his existence on Earth remained in doubt. In mid-October, a group of English devotees held a séance in hopes of contacting him on the other side.[55] Stories appeared in the French press claiming that Scotland Yard had sent detectives to investigate the Mage's mysterious disappearance.[56]

As a money-making scheme, the ploy was a bust. There is not even any evidence that it much bothered Hanni Jaeger, although she and the Mage did reunite briefly. Besides money and Hanni, however, there may have been another purpose to the undertaking. Crowley's disappearance created an opportunity to go places and do things in relative obscurity. The Portuguese town where Crowley spent most of his stay, Cascais, was a posh, cosmopolitan resort full of millionaires and exiled royalty, among them the Spanish Bourbons and a whole colony of Germans. In the months following, the Beast maintained a curiously low profile. Stories making the rounds in Paris placed him on a Hollywood movie set, lecturing at Cornell University, or even toasting the Revolution in Moscow.[57]

Crowley did not disappear completely. Two people knew where he was, or at least how to reach him: Yorke and Carter. In October 1930, Carter sent the Beast a letter sternly advising him to stop "knocking around the Continent" and come back to England to take care of his wife. Otherwise, warned the Colonel, Crowley could find himself in "serious trouble."[58] Carter's intervention was not motivated by any sympathy for the former Madame de Miramar. He was concerned that the abandoned, unstable woman's mounting debts would end up landing Crowley in hot water and generate more bad publicity, impairing his usefulness as an agent. Worse still, Scotland Yard might find itself stuck with the bills.

By mid-1931, Crowley was back in Berlin, where political pressure continued to mount. Elections the previous fall saw Nazi seats in the Reichstag jump from 12 to 107, while the Reds' share grew from 54 to 77. In place of Hanni, Crowley picked up a new German Scarlet Woman, Frau Bertha "Billy" Busch, who bore a suggestive nickname, "the Red Angel."[59] If that indicated her political predilections, it would fit the Beast's other affiliations. He and Bertha fought frequently and ferociously, and on one occasion Crowley was pummeled by Nazi Brownshirts who took offense at his slapping around a German woman on the street.

Crowley's diary entry for 6 October 1931 mentions two familiar names, von Alvensleben and Arnoldo Krumm-Heller. He first mentions a call from "Frau v. Alvensleben," who rang him to voice concern about "Germer's insanity." Presumably this had to do with Germer's treatment by Adler, although her interest in it is a puzzle. As noted previously, this Frau von Alvensleben undoubtedly had some relation to Alvo von Alvensleben. Most likely she was Alvo's Canadian wife, Mary, since the couple visited Germany in this period. It again raises the intriguing possibility not only of a past but also an ongoing relationship between Alvo and the Beast.

As for Krumm, the Mage records that he called with a mysterious "anthropophagist" (more probably an *anthroposophist* than a cannibal), "Muller." Krumm could have provided a link to another old associate then in Berlin, Hanns Heinz Ewers. Ewers had become cozy with the Nazis, as had Krumm, affording Crowley even more sources in that camp.

Crowley also consorted with an assortment of British expatriates in Berlin, among them the writer Christopher Isherwood. Most important to us, though, was one of Isherwood's gay friends, an Irish journalist named Gerald Hamilton, whom Crowley let crash at his apartment for a while. This was not altruism; Col. Carter was paying the Beast to keep an eye on the Irishman. Hamilton was a former friend of Roger Casement and had served time in British jails during WWI for his Republican and pro-German sympathies. In Berlin, Hamilton had a reputation for having lots of money and for being a spy, although no one was sure whose. He had ties to the IRA, which was still seeking help from the Soviets in its diehard struggle against London and Dublin. Thus,

Hamilton was *au fait* with Communist activities in the German capital, even while he propitiated German authorities by informing on his Red friends. He also supposedly kept them apprised of the doings of the dubious Englishman Crowley.

Hamilton recalled his first brush with the Mage in fall 1930. Crowley's diary records frequent meetings with the Irishman from October 1931 through the following June, with Hamilton moving in during January. On 1 February 1932, the Beast recorded that "H.[amilton] arrived [from London] with £50 from Yorke." Yorke, it seems, was still playing case officer, but the money came from Carter, in payment for a report Crowley had provided on Hamilton. Hamilton later said that he had had no inkling of this, until Yorke "gave me proof" after Crowley's death.[60]

Hamilton was by no means Crowley's only link to the Reds. By far, his most important Communist contact was still Louis Gibarti. Gibarti struck many as a slightly comical "opera cavalier," but he was a deadly serious and clever conspirator and a kingpin of the Comintern's operations in the West.[61] His main duty was creating and running front organizations such as the League against Imperialism (LAI) and an array of "peace" and disarmament groups. Gibarti also was an active agent of the OGPU and Soviet military intelligence.[62]

MI5 and SIS were aware of the Crowley-Gibarti connection. Buried in Gibarti's MI5 dossier is a 1933 letter from MI5 to SIS stating that "Gibarti has recently been in touch with Alesteir [sic] Crowley in connection with LIA activities."[63] "LIA" must be a typo for "LAI." Officially, Gibarti had severed ties to the LAI in 1928, which raises the questions how and why he and the Beast were still associated with it some six years later. More intriguingly, the LAI's roots led straight back to the League of Small and Subject Nationalities, the radical entity earlier linked to Crowley, Dudley Field Malone, and John De Kay.

In his role as an OGPU (later NKVD) operative, Gibarti played a part in grooming the most infamous British traitor of the twentieth century, the Soviet mole and future SIS officer Kim Philby.[64] Thus Gibarti indirectly connects Crowley to the notorious "Cambridge Five" spy ring. The Ring's recruiter at Cambridge was the Soviet agent Semen Rostovskii (a.k.a. Ernst Henri), a protégé of Moscow's then ambassador in London, Ivan Maiskii—whose name will later be linked to Crowley's by none other than Philby.

Rostovskii's operation got underway in 1933, around the time the Gibarti-Crowley note was written. One of Rostovskii's accomplices was the young Cambridge communist Brian Howard. He, in turn, was a friend of Crowley's erstwhile roommate, Gerald Hamilton.[65] Howard also connects to another of the Mage's left-leaning homosexual associates, Tom Driberg, about whom more in the following chapter.

Gibarti also holds the key to Crowley's link to Albert Einstein. In Berlin in fall 1930, the Beast entertained his old friend John Sullivan and Sullivan's friend, the writer Aldous Huxley. Crowley is usually credited with introducing Huxley to the wonders of mescaline, but he also aided Huxley's plan to interview prominent men of science. On 3 October, the Mage's diary records "wire Einstein for Huxley."[66] The question has been how Aleister and Albert could have known one another. Although it is largely obscured by his scientific achievements, Einstein had a passion for pacifist and left-wing causes, many of them the handiwork of Louis Gibarti. Gibarti knew Einstein well enough to provide all sorts of dirt on the physicist when he later turned FBI informant.[67]

The Beast's appearance in the Gibarti file coincides with an important change in his own main MI5 dossier. In 1916 this file, #2573, bore the prefix "P.F." (Personal File). By 1933, however, the file had added a "P.P." prefix, a subcategory created late in WWI for "Peace Propaganda," i.e. subversive pacifist activity. The P.P. files came under the control of a special section of MI5, G-1, run by Victor Ferguson, an expert on Russian and Communist affairs. Almost every P.P. laureate was a Communist or fellow traveler. The list includes Soviet personalities and pro-Red front groups such as the Women's International to Britons such as George Lansbury, editor of the left-wing *Daily Herald*, and journalists William Ewer, George Slocombe, and Arthur Ransome.

Therefore, as far as MI5 was concerned, the Beast was a Red. Of course, these were the same people who had accepted that Crowley was a German propagandist during WWI. Just as in 1914–1918, MI5's apparent credulity about Crowley's Communist sympathies was a part of maintaining his operative cover, whether they realized it or not. During 1931, a major reorganization of the British secret services consolidated counterintelligence under 5's control, shifting most counter-subversion from Special Branch and SIS to MI5. Once again, Agent Crowley was going to be under new management.

The case of the above Arthur Ransome invites an illuminating comparison with Crowley's. As a reporter in revolutionary Russia, Ransome was an outspoken admirer of the Bolsheviks, especially Trotsky. He even ended up married to Trotsky's secretary. In August 1918, however, the SIS station in Stockholm secretly recruited Ransome as agent S76 and sent him back into Bolo-land.[68] They did not inform MI5 or anyone else of Ransome's true allegiance; all but a select few had to believe him to be a committed Red. Ransome spied on his Soviet hosts, undetected, until 1924. All the time MI5 dutifully included him in a P.P. list of thirteen "dangerous Bolsheviks" who were not to be allowed into Britain.[69] Just like Crowley, he was a suspect to one branch of British intelligence while an asset for the other.

1 "Le mysterieux visage d'Aleister Crowley—mage ou espion?," unidentifiable paper (17 April 1929).

2 Mariel, 64.

3 "La mystere de Sir Crowley: Espionage, magique noire, sadisme," *La Liberte* (18 April 1929).

4 "English Nobleman's Adventures in France," *Eastern Evening News* [Norwich] (16 April 1929).

5 Dherelle & Lazareff, "Sir Aleister Crowley...," *Paris-Midi* (16 April 1929).

6 *Ibid.*

7 USNA, U.S. Army, General Staff, IRR file XE001752, "Final Report in the Case of Walter Schellenberg, " 30 Sept. 1946, Appendix XV, "Jahnke and the Jahnke Büro," 2.

8 The formal basis for this German-Soviet collaboration was the so-called Rapallo Treaty of early 1922, but secret negotiations had started a year earlier. See: Edward Hallett Carr, *The Bolshevik Revolution, 1917–1923,* Vol. 3 (NY: W.W. Norton, 1953), 362–372.

9 Bell worked closely with Ernst Roehm, chief of the SA from 1931 to 1934 and one of Hitler's most dangerous rivals.

10 On Bell's intrigues see: Glyn Roberts, *The Most Powerful Man in the World* (NY: Covici-Friede, 1938), 305–322, *passim.* Deterding was an important money-man behind various anti-Soviet intrigues and an alleged contributor to Hitler's coffers.

11 "Jahnke and the Jahnkebüro."

12 UKNA, KV2/755, 9a, MI5 to Cowgill, SIS, 16 Feb. 1940.

13 Soviet military intelligence was then known as the 4th Department, *Razvedupr* or simply RU. Later it became the GRU. See: Raymond W. Leonard, *Secret Soldiers of the Revolution: Soviet Military Intelligence, 1918–1933* (Westport, CT: Greenwood Press, 1999).

14 Sean McMeekin, *The Red Millionaire: A Political Biography of Willi Muenzenberg, Moscow's Secret Propaganda Tsar in the West* (New Haven: Yale Univ. Press, 2005), 208.

15 *NYT* (8 Dec. 1925), 1, and (14 Nov. 1926), XX9.

16 As of 1925, MI3(b) was a section of British military intelligence concerned with Europe and Russia, excepting Italy and the Balkans.

17 UKNA, KV2/ 1288, and *NYT* (29 Dec. 1926), 4.

18 Francis Dickie, "Aleister 'Black Magic' Crowley," *The American Book Collector,* Vol. II (May 1961), 34–37.

19 Jacques Mousseau, "Un Compagnon de Lucifer: Aleister Crowley, " *Planete,* #19 (Nov.–Dec. 1964), 63.

20 *Ibid.*

21 Paul Newman, *The Tregerthen Horror: Aleister Crowley, D.H. Lawrence*

Ibid., 108.

Lance Sieveking, *The Eye of the Beholder* (London: Hulton, 1957), 254.

Www.bbc.co.uk/radio4/musicfeature/pip/rjmsc.

Francois des Aulnoyes, "Aleister Crowley: Aventurier ou illumine?," *Astrologie* (Oct. 1952), 102.

A. Crowley, "The Worst Man in the World," *Sunday Dispatch* (16 June 1932).

Symonds, 266–267.

Ibid.

Ibid.

Yorke to R. Swinburne Clymer, 28 Feb. 1948, see: *Thelema Lodge Calendar*, Interactive Content (1993 e.v.).

Alfio Bernabei, "The London Plot to Kill Mussolini," *History Today*, Vol. 49, #4 (April 1999), 2–3.

"The Doping of Our People," *The Patriot* (11 July 1929).

[John] Francis Toye, *For What We Have Received* (London: Heineman, 1950), 102–103.

Sutin, 375 and Levenda, 155.

Fuller later was a guest at Hitler's 50th birthday celebration.

Rene Guenon to Marcelo Motta, 1949, as quoted in Giorgio Galli, *Hitler e il nazismo magico* (Milano: Rizzoli, 1989), 129.

E.g., "Before Hitler Was: Looking for a Doppelganger," www.blackraiser.com/nredoubt/ident2.htm.

Trevor Ravenscroft, *The Spear of Destiny* (Boston: Weiser, 1982), 164.

P. Koenig, "Fraternitas Rosicruciana Antiqua: Arnoldo Krumm-Heller, Aleister Crowley Background Information," //user.cyberlink.ch/~koenig/2005/krumm/krumm.htm. Hermann Rauschning, *Hitler Speaks: A Series of Political Conversations with Adolf Hitler on His Real Aims* (London: Butterworth, 1940).

Crowley, "The Worst Man in the World," *Sunday Dispatch* (15 June 1933).

Taylor, 249.

William Breeze to author, 3 Feb. 2008.

Ibid.

"Partie judeo-maconique," RISS (23 March 1930) and *Detective* [Paris] (30 Oct. 1930).

William Breeze to author, *Ibid.*

Ibid.

"Arrived in Berlin: Aleister Crowley," *Berliner Tageblatt* (3 May 1930).

This was also known as the Houston Everest Expedition after one of its sponsors. One of the pilots involved was another intelligence officer long connected to Etherton, Lt. Col. L.V.S. Blacker.

"Martinet," comments re Claudio Mauri, *La Catena Invisibile*, 11 May 2006,

22:31, www.saturniatellus.com, and Galli, 73, n.41, quoting Guenon to Julius Evola, 29 Oct. 1949.

50 Germer to Petersen, 17 Nov. 1950, in P.R. Koenig, "Fraternitas Saturni, History and Protagonists: In Nomine Demiurgi Saturni,", n. 15, //user. cyberkink.ch/~koenig/fs1.htm.

51 "Fraternitas Saturni," //en.wikipedia.org/wiki/Fraternitas-Saturni.

52 Crowley to Max Schneider, 5 Oct. 1944, in Starr, *Hidden God*, 187 n.16.

53 Gary Lachman, "The Magical World of Fernando Pessoa," *Strangeness* (Jan. 2004).

54 "Famous Mystic or His Double ?," *Empire News* (Sept. 1930).

55 *The Oxford Mail* (14 Oct. 1930), quoted in John Symonds, *The King of the Shadow Realm: Aleister Crowley, His Life and Magic* (London: Duckworth, 1989), 456.

56 Aulnoyes, *Astrologie* (Oct. 1932), 104, and *Detective* (30 Oct. 1930).

57 Wambly Bald, *On the Left Bank, 1929–1933* (London: Ohio Univ. Press, 1987), 79.

58 Sutin, 358–359.

59 Gerald Hamilton, *The Way It Was with Me* (London: Leslie Frewin, 1969), 56.

60 Hamilton, 56–57.

61 McMeekin, 208.

62 Stephen Koch, *Double Lives: Spies and Writers in the Soviet Secret War of Ideas Against the West* (NY: The Free Press, 1994), 17, 342–344.

63 UKNA, KV2/ 774 [MI5 file on "Wilhelm Munzenberg"], note to SIS.

64 Koch, 17, 157, 341.

65 Robin Bruce Lockhart, *Reilly: The First Man* (London: Penguin, 1987), 44–45.

66 Diary extract, 3 Oct. 1930, in FAAC "Aldous Leonard Huxley," www. redflame93.com/Huxley.html.

67 Einstein File, FBI FOIA File #61-6629, "Gibarti, Louis."

68 Phil Tomaselli, "Release of MI5's Files on Arthur Ransome to National Archives at Kew [KV2/1904-1904]," (March 2005).

69 UKNA, KV2/1978, P.P. 459/M.I.5.E.1., 11 Jan. 1919.

CHAPTER THIRTEEN

~

A SMALL CIRCLE OF FRIENDS

~

CROWLEY STAYED AROUND BERLIN through early 1932. In addition to his roommate Hamilton, he was in regular contact with Gerald Yorke and Karl Germer. Both would have been useful for keeping tabs on British "renegades" living in Germany.

One such dubious Briton was the convicted German spy and emerging Nazi Vivian Stranders. Another was Norman Baillie-Stewart, who aroused great interest in London. This disgruntled Army officer offered his services to the Germans in 1930. The following year he showed up in the Reich to barter military information for cash and sexual favors. Someone kept London well apprised of these activities, and in 1933 MI5 placed Baillie-Stewart under arrest. He spent five years in the Tower of London for violation of the Official Secrets Act.[1]

During fall and winter 1931–1932, persistent rumors had Crowley materializing in supposedly forbidden Paris. As we know, he had secretly returned to France at least once since his expulsion, so these rumors may well have been based on fact. In November 1931, American journalist Wambly Bald, another fascinated by the Beast, noted recent reports that the infamous *Mage noire* had been spotted in his old haunts in Montparnasse. Bald concluded that the rumors were unfounded, because "the notorious sorcerer has just sent us a letter to prove it."[2] If the tales were just flights of fancy, why did Crowley bother to deny them?

George Langelaan's recollections also speak of Parisian encounters with the Beast after 1929. Moreover, American writer Henry Miller remembered meeting the Mage in Paris (and lending him money), and Miller did not set foot there until spring 1930.[3] A scrap of paper would never stop the Master Therion from doing what he willed. Practiced in slipping invisibly in and out of countries, he needed only a fake ID and a fresh disguise. But what was he doing in France?

In February 1932, *Paris-Mardi* made the sensational assertion that the "chief of German counter-espionage" had come to Paris to deal with Aleister Crowley, who had somehow become "compromised."[4] The German spymaster in question was Ferdinand von Bredow, head of the *Abwehr*. Bredow also was the right-hand man of Gen. Kurt von Schleicher, a rival of Hitler and contender for power in the dying Weimar Republic. True or not, the story is further suggestion of a link between Crowley and German intelligence. If von Bredow was using our man, it was as likely against German political opponents as the French. Politics certainly lay behind Crowley's departure from Germany in June 1932. In this increasingly desperate atmosphere, a new Chancellor took the stage. He was Franz von Papen, the Kaiser's former military attaché in the United States and one of Crowley's "co-conspirators" in the late war. Von Papen surely had not forgotten those days or Crowley's treachery. He also happened to be another deadly rival of Bredow's friend von Schleicher. If Crowley had colluded with either man, putting Berlin behind him was a wise move.

Things begged for Crowley's attention back in England. One was the destitute and deranged Mrs. Crowley, now a patient at Colney Hatch asylum. Soon after his return, he visited there but declined to actually see his wife. Instead, he schemed to get her to agree to a divorce and surrender rights to spousal maintenance. She was not far gone. Another problem awaiting him at home was the departure of Gerald Yorke for the Far East. He was soon headed to China for Reuters, and SIS. This meant the loss of a reliable and familiar intermediary and probably the need for a new case officer.

With or without Yorke, circumstantial evidence suggests that the Mage somehow remained in the intelligence loop. Back in London, he continued cultivating Communists and fellow travelers. For example, in August 1932, he approached the expatriate American singer and actor Paul Robeson. Crowley wanted Robeson to play the Othello-like role in a production of his play *Mortadello*. This may have been just another of Crowley's half-baked schemes, but Robeson was an outspoken Red sympathizer, if not a formal member of the Party. Securing his cooperation would have been further validation of the Beast's own radical credentials. Crowley managed to wangle an interview with Robeson's wife, but neither she nor her husband took the bait.[5]

Crowley's diary for 13 October 1932 mentions a meeting with a Flight Commander Thorton (Thornton?) in London.[6] There is no indication what it concerned, but any time a military officer shows up in the Beast's company it is worth taking notice. Robin Thynne also had a background in the RAF.

In spring 1933, the Mage renewed acquaintance with the shipping heiress Nancy Cunard, whom he had known for some years. She had been one of the first persons he looked up when he first returned to Britain in 1929. Like Robeson, Cunard was never a full-fledged Comrade (so far as can be determined), but she was another passionate advocate of avant-garde and left-wing causes and welcome in Communist circles. That April, Crowley moved into the Astoria Hotel, where Cunard also lived. As ever, how the supposedly broke Magician afforded such ritzy rooms is a mystery. Within two days of his arrival, Crowley had insinuated himself into Cunard's political activities, which centered on the black liberation movement and protesting racism in the United States. He lent his literary talents to a flyer she put together on the Scottsboro Boys case and was at her side at public protests.[7] This also was around the time of his contact with Gibarti and the League against Imperialism. Cunard and her campaign were exactly the sort of things Gibarti sought to draw into his network, if they were not there already.

Soon after sidling up to Cunard, Crowley made or renewed contact with another denizen of the London's avant-garde scene, Evan Morgan. This eccentric Welsh aristocrat later inherited the family title and became Lord Tredegar. The Beast was a regular guest at Morgan's parties, which included the likes of Aldous Huxley. When WWII began, Morgan, like so many of the Beast's associates, found himself in intelligence, in his case a branch called MI8, the Radio Security Service. The new Lord Tredegar maintained his reputation for eccentricity by advocating bizarre, and disastrous, schemes involving carrier pigeons. What landed the Lord in hot water, however, was the impromptu office tour he gave to a friendly young woman. Morgan ended up charged with treason before MI5 intervened to get his release. That suggests that he and "5" had some special relationship. How far back might that have gone? It is said that in the aftermath of his arrest, Tredegar summoned Crowley to put a curse on the officer responsible for the mess. As the story goes, the officer fell deathly ill.[8]

Arguably Crowley's most important contact in the British Left was Tom Driberg. The Beast had known him since the mid-1920s, when Driberg was an Oxford student and aspiring occultist. They re-established contact when Crowley came back to London in summer 1932. In years to come, the talkative Driberg made various wild claims about his relationship with the Beast, including being Crowley's named heir. Driberg also fabricated a tale about the grisly death of the Beast's son "McAleister" during a miscarried occult working in Paris.[9]

Driberg had been a Communist Party member since 1920. He also was a homosexual, like so many others Agent Crowley's path had crossed.[10] Despite (or maybe because of) his politics and sexuality, Driberg had become a gossip columnist at the *Daily Express*. Collecting gossip, after all, is just another way of gathering intelligence. Driberg may have been informing to His Majesty's authorities for years, but about the time he renewed association with Crowley, Maxwell Knight, now employed by MI5, recruited him as an informant.[11] Max used Driberg to keep tabs on "café communists" and fellow-traveler liberals, precisely the crowd Crowley was so busy cultivating.

Driberg introduced Crowley, if an introduction was necessary, to the writer Dennis Wheatley (also linked to intelligence), and Wheatley then introduced the Beast to his friend Maxwell Knight. This occurred sometime in early 1937 or late 1936. However, Knight, former intelligence chief for the British Fascisti, doubtless knew a little something about our man already.

In private life, Knight was a joyful eccentric. In addition to dabbling in the Black Arts, he enjoyed playing jazz and collecting exotic animals.[12] He later confessed to his nephew that he and Wheatley "applied to Crowley as novices and he accepted then as pupils," but he also tried to pass off the interest as "purely academic."[13]

Similarly, Dennis Wheatley, "the prince of thriller writers," explained his involvement with Crowley as a way to collect details on black magic for his stories. Wheatley, however, was much deeper into the occult than he publicly admitted, and convinced that the Beast possessed genuine mystical powers.[14] Among other things, Wheatley was connected with "Rosicrucian" sex rites performed by his aristocratic friends Charles and Joan Beatty. Joan Beatty (better known under her pen name Joan Grant) had an old association with Crowley. As a child, she and her family had sailed for the United States in 1914 aboard the *Lusitania*, on the same voyage as Crowley. In New York, he became an occasional (but not overly welcome) guest at their home. Perhaps her father was involved in more secretive doings with their strange guest.[15]

Wheatley's own ties to intelligence predated the Second World War. In that conflict, he would become a member of the super-secret London Controlling Section (LCS), a body presided over by Winston Churchill. The LCS oversaw military security, code-breaking, and deception.[16] Another associate was Peter Fleming. A curious detail about the LCS is that its "mascot" was a Roman statuette of Pan, a deity Crowley knew well. Could its presence at the gatherings have been more than decorative?

To understand what Knight was up to, we need to go back to that shake-up in British counterintelligence in 1931, which shifted him from SIS to MI5. He became chief of MI5's Section B5(b), also known as "M" Section, which kept track of subversive threats to Britain and the Empire. Under Knight, "M" Section functioned as a practically independent agency. Its staffers did not show up on the regular MI5 roster, and even Vernon Kell seems to have had little idea about what Max was doing and with whom.

While initially focused on the Red Menace, by 1935 Knight and his outfit took on watching fascists and pro-Nazis. Knight's main weapon was the "mole" used to infiltrate suspect organizations. He proved very effective in recruiting such agents, one way or another. Crowley had years of perfectly apt experience and a rich network of contacts ranging from Communists to German occultists. Max Knight could also take special appreciation of Crowley's expertise in the arcane arts.

One tale concerning the two is that Knight's first wife killed herself after an "occult experience with the notorious Aleister Crowley."[17] A past connection between Mrs. Knight and the Mage is not out of the question, but there is no real evidence that she and he ever so much as met on the street. Still, Gwladys Evelyn Amy Poole Knight definitely did die in November 1936, about the time Crowley went to work for her husband, and under questionable circumstances.

An inquest established that Gwladys Knight succumbed to "poisoning by a barbiturate hypnotic prescription," apparently an overdose of the painkillers she took for back trouble.[18] What the inquest left unclear was whether this was suicide, accident, or murder. Maxwell came under suspicion: Gwladys had the money in the marriage, and her substantial bank accounts passed to him. Max admitted not having lived with his wife since 1929, though (he said) they had remained on friendly and even intimate terms. Some suspected that Max had killed his unwanted spouse for her money. Crowley was an expert of sorts on drugs and could have offered some pointers in making a fatal overdose look like a suicide.

Clues to the strange relationship between Crowley and Knight may be hidden in the same Italian dossier that notes the Beast's Sicilian expulsion. At the least its contents offer a glimpse into some the Beast's more enigmatic connections in the 1930s. These are letters from a mysterious Briton, identified only as "M," to a Jesuit priest in Rome, Father Joseph Ledit. The French-born Ledit is an interesting character in his own right. An expert in Russian and Slavic literature and professor at the Vatican's *Pontifico Instituto Orientale*, Ledit associated with the *Collegium Russicum*, a secretive body that trained priests to undertake missions in the Orthodox East, including undercover work in Soviet Russia.[19] Ledit had worked in the USSR incognito and was probably part of the Vatican's clandestine services. Some also associated him with George Monti, the dubious occultist who had proclaimed himself Crowley's French representative in the 1920s. On his own initiative or on orders from Jesuit higher-ups, Ledit compiled a detailed registry of occult and subversive groups. The Father was a die-hard anti-Communist and an active collaborator with Mussolini's OVRA secret police.

The first of the letters, dated 25 September 1935, makes no mention of Crowley. It is a query from "M" to Ledit concerning a "very remarkable English group" called "New Europe" or "New Britain." "M" linked this group to psychoanalyst Alfred Adler, whose name has come up in connection with Crowley, Germer, and the Tavistock Clinic. "M" linked Adler and his International Society for Individual Psychology to the Serbian writer and mystic Dimitrije Mitrinovic. "M" claimed to have been investigating this nexus for "a year or two" and to have unearthed "startling European connections which might be of very grave import politically. . . ." The unstated suspicion seems to be that there was Communist influence on Adler, Mitrinovic, and friends.

Mitrinovic had no evident link to the Beast, but he had lived in England since 1914. He was close to one of Crowley's literary and philosophical acquaintances, A.R. Orage, and was a devotee of both Steiner and Gurdjieff. Mitrinovic also was an ardent follower of Adler and in 1927 set up a branch of the International Society for Individual Psychology in London. Five years later, he expanded this into the New Britain movement.[20] New Britain had its roots in utopian schemes such as Guild Socialism and the Social Credit Movement, long touted in Orage's

New Age magazine. Mitrinovic and his ilk envisioned the reformation of society into a "threefold commonwealth" of autonomous political, economic, and cultural spheres, all run by a hierarchy of voluntary federations. It freely combined elements of anarchism, Marxism, and fascist corporatism with Adler's "Personalism" and more metaphysical notions borrowed from Steiner and Gurdjieff. Its "Do What Thou Wilt" ethic also was consistent with Thelema, as Crowley must have noticed.

The next item is a 16 April 1936 note from the Economic League's John Baker White to "M" commissioning the latter to investigate Mitrinovic and his organization and offering to "pay for the work done on the usual basis." "M" included this to explain the inquiry, and it suggests a long and close relationship between "M" and Baker White. In an attached note to Ledit, dated 20 April, "M" praised White as "a very practical worker" in the common cause. "M" asked Ledit for any information he had on Mitrinovic, "the key man of a very large organization." "M" named another person involved, the journalist and editor Philippe (or Philip) Mairet, a friend of Orage and the husband of the former Ethel Coomaraswamy.[21] She was the first wife of the Anglo-Indian writer and "Black Brother" Crowley had cuckolded and spied on in wartime New York. If nothing else, the Mage's world could be oddly small.

A month later, "M" finally brought Crowley into the picture. "I have been very occupied. . . ," "M" explained, "with the special urgent investigation into the group calling itself XI Hour/ New Britain/ New Europe/ New Order."[22] This array was allied to a group in France, *l'Ordre Nouveau*.[23] Still more tentacles reached out to Vienna and Holland. Most provocatively and cryptically, "M" declared that "I am inclined to link [all these groups] up with 'O.T.O.'—*Ordo Templi Orientis*—which makes it quite dangerous stuff to handle!" He added, "I expect you have the O.T.O.—in its esoteric and exoteric name, C.C. [Celtic Church?] fully documented?" "M" then asked Ledit, "can you tell me anything of the last ten years, and especially the 1935–1936 movements of the world famous Abister [sic] Crowley—*and his many alias names* [emphasis original]? "This is urgent," "M" concluded, ". . . can you give me a description of him recently? Or a drawing? Especially of his *head*?"

Besides enthusiasm for the "Threefold Commonwealth," New Britain/*l'Ordre Nouveau* and associated groups all shared a commitment to European unification. Such groups were of keen interest to Crowley's Commie friend Gibarti, so concerns about Soviet penetration or manipulation may have been warranted. On the other hand, *l'Ordre Nouveau* had more obvious cross-pollination with the French Fascist and esoteric Right, namely the sinister *Mouvement Synarchique d'Empire* and the terrorist *Comite Secrete d'Action Revolutionaire*, or *Cagoule* ("The Hood").[24] Lurking in these same corners one again finds Crowley's "representative" George Monti.[25] The Synarchists or some kindred group may explain Crowley's alleged belief that an ancient and sinister secret society underlay the coming Vichy regime.[26] This strange nexus at once seems to lead everywhere and nowhere. Maybe that is why "M" found it so interesting, and menacing.

"M" never explains how Crowley fit into this picture or why the matter was so urgent. Evidently (s)he lacked recent knowledge of the Beast, including a physical description. "M" could, however, peg him as "Frater Perdurabo" and link him to the A∴A∴, *The Equinox*, and the "temple" at Cefalu, but also repeated the falsehood that Crowley "has been in Sing-Sing." "M"'s odd fascination with Crowley's head suggests a desire to make a physical comparison. Did "M" suspect that the Beast was masquerading as someone else? It would not have been the first time.

Who was "M"? A note in the Italian file states that Ledit identified his contact as female, personally known to him, and a person of "value and courage."[27] This woman was well-disposed towards Fascism and recently had published a book on Mussolini. The problem is that no British or other authoress fits this profile. The closest is Nesta Webster, who certainly admired Il Duce, was close to Baker White, and feared and loathed Crowley. She cannot be excluded as a possibility.

Father Ledit pointedly declined to give his informant's name to OVRA; he or "M" must have thought it vital to conceal. Also, Ledit kept "M's letters and only supplied transcriptions to the secret police as further means of preserving confidentiality. Perhaps Ledit presented "M" as female as misdirection to protect the man behind the letters and copied the letters to hide his telltale masculine handwriting.

"M," of course, is also the nickname used by Max Knight in MI5. Using it in dealings with Ledit would not have been clever unless he could be the Father would obscure his identity in other ways. Knight once had, and perhaps still had, Fascist sympathies, and had worked for Makgill's spy outfit. He also had links to Baker White. The mistaken reference to Crowley's prison time in America and the picture of the OTO as the center of lurid conspiracies fits closely with the view cherished and spread by Makgill & Co. when Knight worked with them. "M"'s evident lack of information about Crowley since the mid-1920s fits with Knight's subsequent shift to SIS. If Knight was discreetly hunting for more recent info on Crowley, Ledit would have been a good source. While the identity of "M" remains a mystery, all things considered, Maxwell Knight is the most likely candidate.

After his return to England, Crowley renewed his campaign to rehabilitate his reputation in the British press, with more unofficial help. During late June and early July 1933, the *Sunday Dispatch* ran three lengthy pieces by Crowley, starting with "'The Worst Man in the World' Tells the Astounding Story of His Life" and continuing with "I Make Myself Invisible" and "Black Magic Is Not a Myth."[28] They painted the Great Beast 666 as an unjustly maligned, colorful eccentric, a benevolent practitioner of white magic who battled the forces of evil. Moreover, he was, and had ever been, a true son of England.

The *Sunday Dispatch* was another of Lord Rothermere's papers, as kind to Crowley as had been the *Daily Sketch* in 1929. By the early '30s, Rothermere had become one more

British cheerleader for Mussolini and Hitler as well as for such home-grown Fascists as Oswald Mosley. Rothermere met Hitler and lauded the budding Third Reich as a "nation of 'he-men'" which Britons should emulate.[29] Another of Rothermere's friends, the familiar Col. J.F.C. Carter, was available to point out the Beast's recent service in the New Germany. Indeed, the first of the *Sunday Dispatch* series contained the infamous "Before Hitler was, I am" statement and took a strong pro-Hitler tone. At the same time, Rothermere wrote columns for his flagship *Daily Mail* heaping praise on the *Führer*.[30]

Crowley next authored five articles in the Manchester *Empire News,* running from September to December 1933, with a sixth piece appearing in May 1934. This series sang much the same song as above but contained more personal and sensational details. One installment, "They Called Me a Renegade," contained the Mage's most candid remarks about his wartime activities in the U.S., including his work for the Admiralty and the Americans. In another, "The Ridiculous Accusation," he sought to set the record straight about his involvement with the occult, placing himself well on the side of the benevolent "White Brotherhood."

The *Empire News* was not a Rothermere publication, but part of a syndicate run by the Berry brothers, Gomer and William (later, respectively, Lords Kemsley and Camrose), who also ran the prestigious *Sunday Times*. The *EN* was a down-market, provincial paper with a yellow reputation. At the time, it was trying to gain a wider readership and respectability, without abandoning its lucrative sensationalism. Mr. Crowley must have seemed an ideal subject.

A few years later, however, Gomer Berry hired young Ian Fleming, the future creator of James Bond, to head a foreign desk. Fleming, as we will see, would later find himself in Naval Intelligence and working with Crowley. His intelligence career almost certainly commenced in 1933, when he went to Moscow as a Reuters correspondent. There he covered the trial of some British engineers (including at least two past or present SIS operatives) accused of espionage and sabotage.[31] At the same time, Crowley's pal Gerald Yorke, also under Reuters cover, was busy spying in China alongside Ian's elder brother, Peter, mentioned above. Crowley may have known the Fleming brothers by the early 1930s. Their mother's paramour during the 1920s was the painter Augustus John, another familiar of the Beast.

Crowley's public relations offensive suffered a major setback in the spring of 1934. Two years earlier, the sculptress Nina Hamnett had published a memoir, *The Laughing Torso*. Hamnett had known Crowley for years, and to spice up her book she repeated some of the more lurid rumors about the Abbey of Thelema, including the tales of a missing infant and of the tragic death of Raoul Loveday. She did not present any of it as verified or with any malice toward the Wickedest Man in the World. Nevertheless, in April 1934 Crowley leapt off a precipice he always had backed away from before: he sued Hamnett and her publisher for libel.[32] Perhaps he hoped that discrediting her stories would complete his rehabilitation. He was also, as usual, broke, and the expected damages would put him on easy street.

He miscalculated gravely. Horrified spectators and an unsympathetic judge heard a parade of evidence, much of it the plaintiff's own words, which made Crowley look less like the incarnation of evil than like a despicable old cad and charlatan. To compound his misfortune, after losing the lawsuit he ended up tried and convicted of "feloniously receiving" letters connected to the case.[33] Even another appeal to Admiral Guy Gaunt to come and defend his honor failed to elicit any open response. Far from restoring his finances, the fiasco pushed Crowley into bankruptcy, where he remained for the rest of his life.[34]

If the Beast had been involved in only of a fraction of the clandestine affairs we have considered, he still would have been privy to many potentially embarrassing or damaging secrets. To leave such a man destitute and twisting in the wind was dangerous. Bankrupt or not, in the aftermath of the trial, Crowley continued to live comfortably. As before, guardian angels seemed to shield him from utter ruin; he was never homeless or hungry, or unable to pay for his weekly packet of heroin from the pharmacist. The common assumption is that Crowley's remaining faithful friends, principally Karl Germer, paid his bills. But they could not do everything; there must have been other helping hands, persons with an interest in the old man's contented silence.

For instance, during the trial and for the decade following, Crowley enjoyed the services of the prominent West End solicitor Isidore Kerman, a noted bon vivant, real estate speculator, and later adviser to the press baron Robert Maxwell.[35] Kerman was best known as a high-profile and expensive divorce attorney. Unless he took on the Beast as a bizarre pro bono case, someone paid Kerman and kept paying him for years. Kerman not only kept Crowley out of the poor house but also helped keep his name—and his chatter—out of the papers.

In the wake of the Hamnett trial a new woman appeared in Crowley's life, the pretty nineteen-year-old Patricia Dierdre Maureen Doherty, whom the Beast dubbed "Pat." According to legend, she ran up to him on the courthouse steps professing her admiration and offering to have his baby. Things did not quite happen that way. At the time, Crowley's Scarlet Woman was a thirty-something Pearl Brooksmith, the widow of a naval (intelligence?) officer.[36] Pat, too, was romantically involved with someone else. She did give the Mage a son, but not for another three years.

Pat Doherty was the granddaughter of the well-known Cornish artist Thomas Cooper Gotch. Here, too, coincidences abound. Her father, Patrick Doherty, perished in South Africa during WWI doing "secret government work."[37] Abandoned by her mother, she was raised by her grandparents until Gotch's death in 1931. An autographed volume in Thomas Gotch's library shows that he and Crowley knew each other, probably from the Beast's visits to Cornwall. They also shared a mutual acquaintance, Augustus John, de facto stepdad of the Fleming boys.

When Pat Doherty met Crowley, she was enmeshed in a passionate affair with the much older and married Robin Thynne, one of Crowley's partners in the failed Mandrake Press. Thynne, also known as Robert Thompson Thynne, has been aptly described as a "mystery man."[38] He claimed to be a descendent of the noted Elizabethan alchemist and Rosicrucian Francis Thynne, a contemporary of Crowley's hero John Dee. Thynne's WWI service record shows his civilian occupation as managing director of timber camps and lumber mills.[39] He listed knowledge of German among his skills. During the war, Thynne became a major in the RAF's Technical Branch attached to the Ministry of Munitions. As such, he may have worked on the development of bombs and rockets. His obituary cryptically notes that he "published several important scientific works anonymously," and that he and his work were "considered vital by certain authorities."[40] Postwar, however, Thynne's most obvious involvement was with questionable business ventures. Besides the Mandrake Press, he ran at least two shady companies, one of which became the focus of a scandal exposed by *John Bull* in 1928. Even Crowley once branded Thynne "a swindler and share-pusher of the worst type."[41]

Another odd thing about Thynne and Pat Doherty is that both were avowed followers of Rudolf Steiner's Anthroposophy. How that meshed with their allegiance to Crowley and Thelema is a puzzle. Perhaps it somehow relates to the odd WWI connection between Crowley and Steiner already discussed. Were they really "followers" of Crowley, or persons sent to watch and manage him? By the early 1930s the Steinerites had become bitter foes of the Nazis, a factor that made them actual or potential allies in certain secret quarters.

In 1932, Thynne, billing himself a "literary agent," showed up in Cornwall and took a house near Newlyn. According to police records, his real job was recruiting for an occult group headed by Aleister Crowley.[42] One of his recruits was a local teenager, Pat Doherty, who soon became Thynne's lover and the "high priestess" of the local band. The Cornwall "coven" connected to a larger group based in London. Other members of the Cornish crew included two local heiresses, Sheila and Marcia Hirst, and Wyn Henderson, a bohemian socialite and friend of Nancy Cunard. In the quaint town of Mousehole Henderson ran a restaurant, the Lobster Pot, which served as meeting place for the group. Another devotee was a lawyer, apparently of German-Jewish origin, Jacob Weinberg. He may have had connection to Isidore Kerman, who also was of Jewish background and a benefactor of German-Jewish refugees. Weinberg became very close to Pat Doherty, and later joined her in the Middle East during WWII. Was he, too, some sort of spy? Finally, there was a "rich man from the Midlands," undoubtedly our old friend Gerald Yorke.

Two others connected to the Crowley and the Cornwall group were James MacAlpine and Greta Sequeira. On the eve of the war, MacAlpine worked for SIS' Section D, a unit specializing in sabotage and assassination. It later became part of the Special Operations

Executive, or SOE. MacAlpine has been described as a "James Bondish sort of character" with the requisite taste for adventure and women.[43] At some point in the late 1930s, the Beast introduced him to Pat, and the two became an item. They married during the war, but MacAlpine perished on a mission in the Balkans. Pat herself then went to work for SOE as a code clerk. How and when did Crowley become so friendly with an SIS man? MacAlpine is one more cryptic thread linking the Beast to the intelligence world.

Glamorous, twenty-nine-year-old Greta Sequeira was a close of friend of Doherty and Thynne, and for a time a rival for Thynne's affections. Like Pat and Thynne, she was also a devotee of Rudolf Steiner.[44] Moreover, she was close to another of Crowley's friends and collaborators, and yet another admirer of Steiner, Lady Frieda Harris. The exotic and rather mysterious Greta was the youngest daughter of Dr. William Sequeira, one of the physicians who worked on the Jack the Ripper case.[45] Like Pat, Greta also aroused the interest of the still concupiscent Beast. Sequeira managed to keep him at bay, however; according to her, he never got her into bed despite all the charms he could muster. Maybe keeping the lustful old goat on the string was part of her job.

Not surprisingly, Sequeira's activities hint at intelligence work. During the late 1930s, she made trips into the Third Reich and helped facilitate the escapes of "a number of Jewish doctors."[46] As mentioned, another benefactor to Jews fleeing Germany was Crowley's attorney, Isidore Kerman. Greta's risk was all the greater because she herself was of Sephardic Jewish ancestry. As it happened, the SIS station chief in Berlin, Frank Foley, was engaged in similar secret rescue efforts.[47] Foley had been stationed in Berlin since the early 1920s, which means that Crowley's name must have come across his desk a few times, each an opportunity for a deeper acquaintance. Foley recruited and ran an intelligence network of Jewish businessmen (like Weinberg). Finally, Sequeira's German escapades coincide with Crowley's own rumored late 1930s forays into Hitler's domain.

Another person who gravitated to Crowley in this period was twenty-something Robert "Robin" Cecil. The Cambridge-educated Cecil joined the Foreign Service in 1936 as a specialist in German affairs. In addition to his interest in Crowley, Cecil studied Gurdjieff and his main expositor, P.D. Ouspensky.[48] Cecil later wrote on the evolution of Nazi ideology and penned a biography of Cambridge Ring spy Donald Maclean.[49] His interest in espionage was not just academic; during WWII, Cecil became personal secretary to Sir Stewart Menzies, then "C" (Chief) of SIS, and was the liaison between SIS and the Foreign Office. Everywhere Crowley turned, it seems, we find a spy.

With that in mind, Robin Thynne, mentioned previously, merits a closer look. Like Gerald Yorke, Thynne's association with Crowley looks like an assignment, a now familiar pattern. Thynne moved into Crowley's inner circle just as Yorke departed the scene, which suggests that he took over the role of the Beast's case officer.

Throughout the early 1930s, Thynne made frequent trips to Switzerland, supposedly to visit the Rudolf Steiner Foundation headquarters at Dornach. Other reports, however, claimed that the Swiss forays included liaison with a "rich group of occultists," presumably German exiles, who were plotting against the Nazis.[50] Some of these must have been Steinerites. Were there others from the OTO or Fraternitas Saturni? That may hold the key to Crowley's relationship with Thynne, Pat, and others.

This is all the stranger because officially Anthroposophy took a dim view of Crowley. As noted, Steiner's successor, Walter Johannes Stein, painted him as a "black magician" and inspiration to Hitler.[51] For his part, Stein also claimed to have been a "confidential adviser" to Churchill.[52] MI5 documents do show that Stein undertook a special mission to Belgium early in WWII.[53] In October 1939, Churchill's close friend Admiral Sir Roger Keyes dispatched Stein to Brussels with a confidential letter for King Albert. The mystically-inclined King was a longtime friend of Stein, who traveled with MI5 man Cecil Liddell, the brother of B Division chief Guy Liddell.

The approach to the Belgian Monarch was a cover for Stein's real mission, to make contact with a group of anti-Nazi "German aristocrats" who thought they could force Hitler to abdicate or bring about his removal. Were they the same group Thynne had cultivated in Switzerland? On his return to London, Stein and Liddell reported to Churchill. The mission did not achieve any tangible success, and Stein's subsequent activities were limited to "economic matters."[54]

Regarding Thynne's mysterious government work, he may have been involved with a shadowy branch of the War Office initially known as "General Staff-Research" (GS-R), and later as MI-R. Its ostensible function was as a think tank for "irregular warfare," including subversive propaganda and psychological operations. Peter Fleming joined the same outfit, as did Col. Etherton's longtime collaborator, L.V.S. Blacker. During WWII, MI-R merged into SOE, alongside MacAlpine's Section D. A problem with the GS-R/MI-R scenario is that Thynne died before it officially formed. It stands to reason, however, that it or something like it existed earlier, perhaps since WWI.[55] Could that be where *The Cactus* ended up?

Another possibility is that Thynne was connected to a "private" intelligence-gathering organization that took shape during 1935–1936, dubbed "The Focus." The man behind this was the disempowered Winston Churchill. The Focus aimed to counter the growing threat of Nazi Germany, something that Winston and others believed the Government did not take seriously enough. Moreover, the man running the information-gathering wing of The Focus was the Beast's old boss, the venerable and ever-scheming Admiral Hall.[56]

Arch-schemer and manipulator Hall, out of an official post since 1919, but never out of the spying game, could have been the hidden hand behind Crowley's intelligence employment between the wars. Through the likes of Feilding, MacBean, Burbury, Yorke, Carter, Thynne, and others, he could have kept the Beast on a leash, setting him loose when they needed him, and while he could still run.

1   Baillie-Stewart returned to Germany after his release and became a Reich citizen in 1940. Even before that he began making propaganda radio broadcasts alongside the notorious William Joyce, a.k.a. "Lord Haw-Haw." The extensive MI5 dossiers on the Baillie-Stewart case can be found in the UKNA, KV2/174-192.

2   Bald, 79.

3   Newman, 43. Miller's lover Anaïs Nin also mentions his association with Crowley.

4   "Hjos—Hist—Tsih," *Paris Mardi* (23 Feb. 1932).

5   Diary, 12 August 1932, in FAAC, "Nancy Cunard," www.redflame93.com/Cunard~ns4.html.

6   William Breeze to author, 3 Feb. 2008.

7   FAAC, *Ibid.*, Diary, 9 April 1933. The Scottsboro Boys were nine African-American youths arrested in 1931 in Alabama on charges of raping two white women. The case dragged on to 1937 when five of the accused were convicted. Eventually, all were acquitted, pardoned or paroled.

8   Diary extracts, 18 and 17 June 1943 in FAAC, "Lord Tredegar," www.redflame93.com/Tredegar.html.

9   Driberg, *Ruling Passions* (NY: Stein and Day, 1979), 82–86.

10   Francis Wheen, *Tom Driberg, His Life and Indiscretions* (London: Chatto & Windus, 1990).

11   Anthony Masters, *The Man Who Was "M": The Life of Maxwell Knight* (NY Blackwell, 1987), 209.

12   Years later, as "Uncle Max," Knight hosted a popular children's show on British television.

13   Masters, 90.

14   On Wheatley's occult ties see: Peter Underwood, *The Ghost Hunters* (London: Robert Hale, 1985), 120–133.

15   Joan Grant/Beatty's maiden name was Marshall. Her father, John Marshall, may have been in the U.S. on an official mission for the British Government, probably related to financial matters. Her recollections of Crowley are in her *Time Out of Mind* (London: Arthur Barker, 1956), 42–44.

16   Wheatley's somewhat selective memoir about this is *The Deception Planners: My Secret War* (London: Hutchinson, 1980). A more recent and broader study is Thaddeus Holt, *The Deceivers: Allied Military Deception in the Second World War* (NY: Scribners, 2004).

17   Bryan Clough, *Tyler Kent and MI5: The Full Story* (London: Hideaway, 2005), 16. Clough credits the origin of this story to Knight's secretary Joan Miller, whom he considers an unreliable source.

18   *The Times* (18 Dec. 1936), 6a.

19   Andrei Soldatov, "Zachem Pape bol'shie ushi?: Vatikanskaia razvedka na

protiazhenii mnogikh let sledit za Rossiei," www.cvni.net/radio/nsnl/nsnl030/
nsnl30soldatov-ru.html. Originally published in *Versiia*, #13 (87) (2000).

20 See: Andrew Rigby, "Training for Cosmopolitan Citizenship in the 1930s: The
Project of Dimitrije Mitrinovic," *Peace and Change*, Vol. 34 (3), 379–399.

21 Philip Mairet was an admirer of Adler and the Social Credit movement. As
editor of the *New English Weekly* he became friends with George Orwell.

22 *XI Hour* was the publication put out by New Britain.

23 One of the leading figures of *L'Order Nouveau* was Alexandre Marc. On
him and the movement, see Christian Roy, *Alexandre Marc et la Juene Europe
(1904–1934): L'Ordre Nouveau aux origines du Personnalisme* (Nice: Presse
d'Europe, 1998).

24 Geoffroy de Charnay, *Synarchie: Panorama de 25 années d'activité occulte*
(Paris: Editions Medicis, 1955), 21–34. The *Cagoulards* twice attempted
armed uprising during the '30s and were responsible for a number of
bombings.

25 Monti died in October 1936, allegedly murdered.

26 Amado Crowley, *Riddles*, 133.

27 Claudio Mauri to author, 2 July 2006.

28 *Sunday Dispatch* (18, 25 June and 2 July 1933).

29 *Daily Mail* (21 March 1934).

30 *Ibid.* (10 July 1933).

31 This was the Metro-Vickers Case.

32 "Crowley vs. Constable & Co…," *The Times* (12 April 1934).

33 "Aleister Crowley set for Trial at Old Bailey," unidentified paper (April 1934),
www.lashtal.com/nuke/module-subjects.viewpage-page.id-59.phtml.

34 UKNA, BT 9/1250, Court of Bankruptcy Records, "Crowley, Edward
Alexander, Commonly Known as Aleister." Crowley faced roughly £ 5,000
in debts.

35 Stephen Aris, "Obituary: Isidore Kerman," *The Independent* (21 Aug. 1998).

36 Newman, 57.

37 *Ibid.*, 48.

38 *Ibid.*, 54.

39 UKNA, AIR 76/506.

40 Newman, 107, quoting obituary in *The Cornishman*, July 1936.

41 *Ibid.*

42 *Ibid.*, 103–107.

43 *Ibid.*, 87.

44 "Greta Valentine…," obituary, *The Telegraph* (28 Nov. 1998).

45 Dr. William Sequeira performed a post-mortem on one of the Ripper victims.

46 Newman, 61.

47 Andrew, 379–380. See also Mike Smith, *Foley: The Spy Who Saved 10,000 Jews*

(London: Hodder & Stoughton, 1999).

48 Martin Starr to author, 11 July 2006.

49 Robert Cecil, *A Divided Life: A Biography of Donald Maclean* (London: Bodley Head, 1988).

50 Newman to author, 5 Dec., 2005.

51 Ravenscroft, 164, 166.

52 Ravenscroft, xiii. On Stein, see also: Johannes Tautz, *W. J. Stein: A Biography* (London: Temple Lodge Press, 1990).

53 UKNA, KV6/47, Cecil Liddell, "Report on Special Mission to Belgium, 5.10.39-11.10-39."

54 *Ibid.*, Liddell report, 22.10.39.

55 In 1918, a special intelligence unit did function under the name MI-R, but in this instance the initials stood for "Military Intelligence-Russia." Officially, this outfit disappeared in the early '20s, but given the peculiar ability of bureaucratic entities to mutate and survive, this may not have been precisely the case.

56 Hughes, Chap. 6.

~
THAT OLD
BLACK MAGICK

~

IN JULY 1936, FIFTY-SEVEN-YEAR-OLD ROBIN THYNNE FELL ILL on his way back to London from Cornwall. His situation deteriorated rapidly. Desperate to save his life, the British government flew in Dr. Ita Wegmann, a Swiss specialist in homeopathic medicine affiliated with Anthroposophy. Her ministrations were of no avail. Like much of his life, Thynne's funeral took place under a veil of secrecy. Another mystery is whether the devastated Doherty's trip to Switzerland afterward was a spiritual pilgrimage, an effort to complete Thynne's unfinished business, or something of both. When she returned that fall, Doherty finally offered to bear Crowley's child.[1] Maxwell Knight also stepped into his life in the wake of Thynne's death. As ever, when one door closed, another opened.

Thynne's legacy lived on in a Cornish mystery involving Crowley, or at least his name, and the usual intimations of clandestine doings. In spring 1938, unnamed persons linked to the Thynne-Crowley coven were dwelling in a remote cottage near the village of Tregrethen, not far from Land's End. Their neighbors and the owners of the cottage were two respected locals, Will and Katherine "Ka" Arnold-Forster (a.k.a. Ka Cox). The story later circulated about the events of 21–22 May went roughly thus: One night a frantic young woman knocked on the Arnold-Forsters' door and blurted out that "something terrible" had happened in the cottage above. Ka accompanied her back to the place, where she discovered a man in a shocked or terrified state, and, supposedly, Crowley. Some sort of violent altercation ensued, possibly involving the Beast, and the result was Ka's sudden death. The actual medical determination was heart failure, but the rumor mill churned out more sinister explanations.

The incident has been fictionalized at least twice, in A.L. Rowse's *A Night at the Carn* and Frank Baker's *Talk of the Devil*, and most recently analyzed in Paul Newman's *The Tregerthen Horror*.[2] As that book makes clear, was Crowley nowhere near Tregerthen or Cornwall at the time; his diary puts him snugly in London. He had frequented that corner of Cornwall, however, and had met Pat and Greta there just a few months later.

But there were at least tangential links between the Beast and the Arnold-Fosters. Both he and the pair affected leftist sympathies. The elfin Will Arnold-Forster ardently promoted the League of Nations, making frequent visits to its headquarters in Switzerland. Both Arnold-Forsters were active in the International Peace Campaign (IPC or *Rassemblement Universel pour la Paix*), a pacifist-disarmament organization headed by Lord Cecil of Chelwood and the French Socialist politician Pierre Cot.[3] Will had recently toured the Low Countries and Scandinavia on behalf of the organization, and IPC representatives attended Ka's funeral.[4] The couple were thus immersed in "peace propaganda," the same affiliation MI5 attributed to Crowley.

The IPC originated at the Brussels World Peace Congress of 1936. Like the Congress, the Campaign was to some degree "Communist-influenced."[5] Crowley's friend Louis Gibarti and his boss Münzenburg helped organize the Congress, and Moscow sought to exploit the IPC as a propaganda vehicle and espionage front. Cot, for instance, turned out to be a Soviet agent who betrayed French military secrets.[6] Someone could reasonably have suspected the Arnold-Forsters of like proclivities.

The picture, though, is complicated. Ka was close to members of the locally prominent Bolitho family, several of whom looked very kindly upon Hitler. In 1938, the Bolithos even played hosts to German Ambassador Joachim von Ribbentrop. Crowley knew some of the Bolitho clan and had performed rites on their Cornish property years earlier.[7] Yet another of Ka's intimates was Lady Violet Bonham-Carter, a key member of Churchill's secretive anti-Nazi group, The Focus.

Paul Newman suggests that a key to what was going on at Tregerthen may lie hidden in Frank Baker's roman à clef, *Talk of the Devil*.[8] Baker, who knew the Arnold-Forsters well, thinly disguised them as the book's central couple, the Actons. Most of the other characters correspond to real persons, including Crowley, who appears as the bloated and sinister occultist Nathaniel Sylvester. The real villain of the tale, however, turns out to be Paul Acton (Will Arnold-Forster), who arranged for his wife to be frightened to death because she had discovered his secret double life as a Nazi spy and mad scientist. Sylvester (Crowley) turns out to be a mere "decoy," while a clever British secret service agent is on hand to monitor the suspect doings.

Just how close did Baker's fiction come to the truth? A man of Will Arnold-Forster's known political bent seems unlikely to have been a Nazi spy. On the other hand, a contemporary, Kim Philby, deliberately cultivated a reputation for Fascist sympathies as a cover for his communist ones. Perhaps Will did the inverse by feigning leftist affinities. Or perhaps Baker fudged the truth by making a fictional Nazi out of a real-life *Red* agent.

Venturing further, writer Steve Jackson speculates that Crowley had been recruited (probably by Max Knight) to run some sort of "occult training school" for selected agents.[9] Using Thynne's Cornwall coven as cover, the aged Mage could offer not only a wealth of arcane wisdom, but also a lifetime's experience of trickery and deceit, not to mention hypnosis and drugs. This scenario would explain the bevy of occult-linked present and future spies—Doherty, Knight, MacAlpine, Sequeira, Wheatley, etc.—who whirled around Crowley in this period.

Another possibility is that the Crowley-Thynne group was a counterintelligence ploy to attract, compromise, and recruit subversive elements. That, too, suggests Knight's guiding hand. Occult rites, especially sexual ones, produced excellent opportunities for blackmail. There are hints of something like this going on in the early part of WWII. They surface in a report Soviet mole Kim Philby sent to his Moscow control in 1942.[10] Philby noted that SIS was investigating a "complicated racket" that linked RAF officers and members of British high society to drug smuggling, sexual orgies (hetero and homo), and black masses. Behind this scheme was the German Embassy in Dublin, which ran drugs into England with the aid of Welsh fishermen and corrupt nightclub owners. The dope, orgies, gambling, and black masses were used to blackmail officers into supplying information. Mingling in this weird milieu, along with a colorful throng of ladies, countesses, wing-commanders, and pornographers, were Soviet Ambassador Ivan Maiskii and "the notorious occultist Aleister Crowley."[11] Unfortunately, the charts mentioned by Philby, which might have clarified these connections, are missing.

Philby and SIS may have stumbled on an MI5 operation (probably Knight's) intended to ferret out security risks and enemy agents. MI5, after all, included the masterminds of the top secret and very successful "Double-Cross" system, which managed to transform most of the Nazi espionage network in Britain into a vehicle for disinformation. The Soviet Ambassador's presumed involvement in the murky doings would make a British agenda more likely than a German one, as would Crowley's.

After the war, self-proclaimed warlock Cecil Williamson alleged that he had been tapped by SIS on the eve of the Second World War to head a "Witchcraft Research Centre."[12] Williamson later became a founding father of modern witchcraft and the curator of the Witchcraft Museum. The goal of his wartime outfit, he claimed, was to discover who in the German High Command and Nazi hierarchy might be influenced by astrology or related superstitions. In this, Williamson claimed to have collaborated with Ian Fleming, Dennis Wheatley, and others definitely linked to Crowley. Another part of Williamson's alleged mission involved investigating "a network spreading from Britain to Germany and Switzerland, with contacts that penetrated the *Abwehr*."[13] That sounds like Thynne's intrigues. On the other hand,

Williamson also gained a reputation as a master fabulator.

Nevertheless, Paul Newman, citing a source with access to classified SOE and Political Warfare Executive (PWE) files, believes that Williamson was telling at least a version of the truth. Similarly, spy writer Donald McCormick (a.k.a. Richard Deacon) once observed that "[the British] might quite easily create a coven as a propaganda weapon against the Germans, but it would be highly impracticable to suggest that the Germans could do the same thing in reverse on our soil."[14] This, he insisted, was because the Germans were far more inclined to take such things as witchcraft and astrology seriously. While that is debatable, and McCormick earned a reputation for sensational and unsubstantiated statements, he did spend WWII in British Naval Intelligence working with the likes of Ian Fleming. He may have learned more about this exotic branch of spycraft than he let on.

Still, why would anyone have picked the relatively callow Williamson over the seasoned Mage to run an occult outfit? At sixty-five, Crowley was not all the way over the hill. In fact, he was a year younger than Churchill. On the other hand, he was a hopeless drug addict in failing health. A bigger problem, though, and one that Williamson did not have to bear, was the Beast's toxic reputation and the fear and revulsion his name aroused inside and outside Government circles. Just as in 1914, Mr. Crowley could have his uses, but never in any *official* capacity.

The use of astrologers by British intelligence is confirmed by wartime MI5 chief Guy Liddell, whose diary entry for 10 April 1941 includes this revealing note:

DNI [Director of Naval Intelligence Admiral John Godfrey] is employing Louis de Wohl to read horoscopes of the most important Admirals in the navy and those of Hitler, Mussolini, Darlan, and Portal. Merritt of NID is his intermediary. It is believed that DNI himself is a strong believer in astrology. On the other hand it may be that since Hitler works on these lines and de WOHL is acquainted with the workings of Hitler's astrologer [illegible] hopes to work out the most propitious [time] for Hitler to act. The whole business seems to me to be highly misleading and dangerous."[15]

This shows that some decision-makers in British intelligence not only embraced astrology as a weapon, but also, contrary to McCormick, took it seriously. McCormick himself also noted that "the links between occultism and astrology on the one hand and intelligence work on the other, though obscure, have nonetheless existed through the Middle Ages to the present day."[16]

As for McCormick's contention that the Germans were more susceptible to such stuff, as noted the Nazi leadership definitely was full of believers, among them

Heinrich Himmler, Rudolf Hess, and to some degree Hitler himself. They certainly were concerned enough about occult organizations to suppress them. Early in 1935, The Nazi regime initiated what author Peter Levenda aptly describes as a "cult war" against "Masonic lodges, other lodges and lodge-like organizations."[17] Besides all forms of Freemasonry, the Nazi crackdown included Steiner's Anthroposophy, the Theosophical Society, and even the venerable *Druiden-orden*. Also on the Nazi hit-list were the Golden Dawn, Grosche's *Fraternitas Saturni*, the OTO, and Crowley's A∴A∴; that is, every esoteric organization the Beast ever had anything to do with.

The Third Reich had room for only one secret society, Himmler's own "Black Order," the SS. Himmler viewed other groups not just as rivals but as security threats. For instance, he believed that Rosicrucianism was a "branch of the British secret service."[18] Donald McCormick argues that Himmler arrived at that conclusion "through knowledge of Crowley's activities," though he does not explain *how* Himmler knew about them.[19] One source could have been the Beast's earlier collaboration with the Weimar era's *Abwehr* under Ferdinand von Bredow. The SS executed Bredow in 1934 but the Nazis inherited his files.

Heinrich Himmler was arguably "a full-fledged man of magic."[20] He conversed with spirits and had his own Rasputin in Karl Maria Wiligut, a former *Schlaraffen* who preached a bizarre amalgam of racist pseudo-history and rune-magic.[21] In 1935, Himmler assumed control of the *Ahnenerbe* (Office of Ancestral Research), sometimes referred to as the SS "Occult Bureau." While only a fraction of the *Ahnenerbe's* more than fifty sections investigated the occult or paranormal, these were serious priorities. Himmler also created a *Hexen-Sonderauftrag* (Witchcraft Special Commission) aimed at recovering the supposed "lost wisdom" of the German *Volk*.[22]

Still, Himmler had nothing on Rudolf Hess, former devotee of the Thule Society and student of Karl Haushofer. Hess was a firm believer in astrology and unlike most of his fellow Nazis retained a certain admiration for Rudolf Steiner, just like many in Crowley's prewar entourage. Even Hitler's cynical propaganda minister Joseph Goebbels formed a special section to exploit "astrology, metapsychology and occultism."[23] He believed that the "Americans and English fall easily to this kind of propaganda."[24] In 1940, Goebbels schemed to use the prophecies of Nostradamus to "prove" the inevitability of German victory.

Like all the organizations to which he belonged, Crowley was officially *verboten* in the Third Reich. Karl Germer tasted this hostility first-hand. He had accompanied Crowley back to England in 1932, but for unstated reasons the Home Office declined to extend his visa in late 1934. Germer ended up back in the Reich just as the Nazi hammer came down on occultists. His deportation may not have been a mere matter of blind bureaucracy and bad timing. If Crowley had used Germer as a British asset, his deportation was a means to get him back into Germany with the advantage of an apparent grudge against England. The Gestapo arrested Germer in Leipzig on 2 February 1935 and charged him with recruiting followers for the "high-grade Freemason Aleister Crowley."[25] Germer spent the better part of the next six months in the SS-run Esterwegen concentration camp.

It seems suicidal for Crowley to have set foot in Germany after 1934, yet there are stories of him doing just that, and given his past behavior in France, it should not be ruled out. He could have resorted to the trusted and simple expedient of a false identity. Germer's case also suggests that the Beast still had some friends in the Reich. Germer got out of internment in August 1935 and in October somehow reached England via Belgium. In Leipzig, his friend Fraulein Kuentzel continued to operate the *Thelema Verlag*, which openly produced and sold Crowley and OTO materials, until 1937. Who or what granted her the special dispensation?

On 30 July 1936, Crowley memorialized an interesting luncheon in his diary. Joining him were the recently arrived Germer, "girl Pat" (Doherty), and an unknown "Rudy" (not Hess, certainly). The guest of honor was another old acquaintance, George Sylvester Viereck, on his way to or from Germany. Viereck had not abandoned his pro-Germanism, and he had become an outspoken admirer of Hitler and National Socialism. Back in America, Viereck became a blatant Nazi propagandist, a role that led to his arrest and imprisonment during the war. Only in Crowley's small, strange world would a pro-Nazi would be breaking bread with an undesirable leftist foreigner he knew to have been connected to British intelligence.

Crowley's recollection of the conversation makes the picture even odder. According to the Mage, Viereck agreed to sign an affidavit attesting that Crowley "had no troubles with authorities in U.S.A."[26] The German-American also admitted that after WWI, "he made friends with our N[aval] I[ntelligence] chiefs who told him that I had been working for them during the war." So, Viereck not only had somehow gained the confidence of NID, but also would vouch for a man who had tricked and betrayed him. Maybe Viereck was just the forgiving type, but more probably he had been, just as we have supposed, a British double agent. Maybe he still was. Viereck, too, could have provided the Beast with some useful channels in Germany.

Another detail suggesting that someone was running interference for Crowley inside the Third Reich is that his name is missing from the *Sonderfahndungsliste-GB*, the "special arrest list" compiled by the Gestapo and SS in 1940 in anticipation of the occupation of Britain.[27] Among its roughly 2,000 names are many real or suspected intelligence operatives (including Sidney Reilly, supposedly dead since 1925) and persons connected to Freemasonry and other esoteric societies. That the Nazi compilers overlooked a world-infamous occultist with long-known connections to Germany and British secret service is strange indeed.

Despite ruthless repression, the Nazis still had plenty of enemies in their midst. One such group was the *Tatkreis* ("Action Circle"), a shadowy cabal of "conservative revolutionaries," which included former Thule Society members and associates of the murdered Ferdinand von Bredow.[28] The *Tatkreis* took credit, rightly or wrongly, for Georg Elser's attempted assassination of Hitler in November 1939.[29] It maintained ties to anti-Hitler elements abroad, and very likely was the group Walter Stein had hoped to contact in Belgium. It may also have included the mysterious persons Thynne schemed with in Switzerland.

A key figure in the anti-Nazi underground was another familiar figure from Crowley's WWI days, Kurt Jahnke. Even though "he hated Hitler and nearly all Nazis" and had past ties to von Bredow and Soviet intelligence, Jahnke somehow secured the confidence and protection of Deputy Führer Rudolf Hess. Moreover, Hess chose Jahnke to run a special intelligence bureau, "Abteilung Pfeffer."[30] The main aim of this outfit was the "strengthening of Anglo-German relations by a mutual, unfettered exchange of views."[31] Jahnke's activities extended to Switzerland, where he traveled frequently. That, too, suggests a connection to Thynne, and thence to Crowley.

In 1935, Jahnke arranged a Berlin meeting between Hess and a "British secret service man," F.C. (or J.C.) Fletcher, who attended with the approval of his superiors.[32] Did Jahnke, using his influence with Hess, also arrange for Crowley's clandestine visits, to meet with his boss or others?

In 1937, Jahnke, still working for Hess, tried and failed to bring about "a comprehensive agreement between Britain and Germany worldwide."[33] In pursuit of Anglo-German comity, Jahnke also employed agents in England who established contact with a pro-Nazi group, the Link. Its adherents included occult expert Arthur Rogers, ex-NID chief Admiral Barry Domvile, and Crowley's old chum J.F.C. Fuller.

One man vitally interested in the Link was Maxwell Knight. His successful infiltration of the organization helped compromise the Nazi "Fifth Column" in Britain and was a masterpiece of counterintelligence. Crowley's personal knowledge of some of the members, his mastery of the occult beliefs that motivated them and others, and his possible access to Jahnke's or other German channels would have made him a valuable asset to Max.

Knight no doubt was interested in the Beast's contact with another German who arrived in Britain in early 1939. Indeed, MI5 would amass a five-volume dossier on him.[34] He was Col. Hans Kahle, a former officer of the Kaiser who became a Communist and Soviet agent in the 1920s. He most recently had served the Party in the Spanish Civil War where he started out commanding a contingent in the International Brigades and ended up leading a whole Republican division. He supplemented his military duties with service to Stalin's NKVD. Kahle knew Jahnke and undoubtedly had ties to Crowley's Comintern contact Louis Gibarti. In London, he assumed the mantle of a "political journalist" while continuing to act on the orders his masters in Moscow. On 19 March 1939, Crowley's diary records a lunch with "Col. Kahle" and three others, Knight's informer Tom Driberg, composer Constant Lambert and writer John Rayner.[35] The Beast's presence at the table may have stemmed from his outspoken support for the Spanish Republic (befitting his leftist affectations), but it seems unlikely that this meeting with an important Communist operative was a purely casual affair.

Driberg's presence at the gathering also is interesting. He and Crowley remained in fairly regular contact right up to the war and beyond, although the Beast seems to have become less and less tolerant of his manners. The frequency of their meetings suggests that Driberg may have been acting as cut-out for Knight.

Knight also must have taken some interest in the Master Therion's ongoing contacts with Gerald Hamilton, the pro-Communist journalist whom Crowley had befriended and spied on in pre-Hitler Berlin. For instance, "Ham" (Hamilton) shows up in the Beast's diary of 23 August 1939, where Crowley notes seeing him "en route for Paris."[36] He is there again on 2 October where Crowley mentions having "conferenced" with him.[37] Not long after, the government interned Hamilton as a potential security risk under Defence Regulation 18B. The order allegedly came straight from Churchill. The official reason was that Hamilton had suspicious communication with the German Embassy in Dublin. Could that have had anything to do with the drug-running plot mentioned by Philby, also based in the Dublin Embassy? As before, there is a sense of looking at scattered pieces of some great jigsaw puzzle. In any case, note that Crowley, who supposedly bore a black mark against his name because of his dalliance with the enemy in the First War, and now associate of the likes of Hamilton, was entirely unmolested. In fact, he resumed relations with Hamilton after the latter's release.

Back in Berlin, some Nazis were convinced that Jahnke was a British double agent, but they could not get enough on the slippery Prussian to prove it. One was the chief of Himmler's *Sicherheitsdienst*, Reinhardt Heydrich, who was sure that Jahnke's real purpose in visiting Switzerland was to exchange information and receive orders from British intelligence.[38] Had Jahnke been one of Thynne's contacts?

Under the circumstances, Heydrich immediately cast suspicious eyes in Jahnke's direction when, on 10 May 1941, Rudolf Hess flew a Messerschmidt-110 to Scotland on his infamous and abortive mission to broker peace between London and Berlin. In the resulting *Aktion Hess*, Jahnke narrowly avoided arrest or worse, but numerous occultists, especially *astrologers*, were not so lucky.

Jahnke surely had some hand in convincing Hess to undertake the gambit, but he did not act alone. Whatever he did to drive Hess toward his fatal decision was linked to a larger plot in London orchestrated by Crowley's "friends" Dennis Wheatley and Ian Fleming and Fleming's boss, NID chief Admiral John Godfrey. Fleming, for instance, practically ran a secret section, 17Z, that worked closely with Wheatley, the abovementioned astrologer Louis de Wohl, and a "black propaganda" outfit run by the Political Warfare Executive's Sefton Delmer.[39] Crowley would have been an ideal adviser to such a group.

Additional inspiration on the Hess front came from Ian's brother Peter Fleming. In 1940, he began writing a novel called *The Flying Visit*, which offered the provocative scenario that Adolf Hitler flew to England and ended up in British hands. The reality was that the war was going very badly for Britain at this point. Hitler had yet to entangle himself in Russia, and American intervention was nowhere on the horizon; Britain stood alone. Many in the establishment, including some in Royal circles, felt that a deal with Germany was the smart move.[40] Others, such as Churchill, looked for a way to confound the Nazis and buy precious time.

A part of this complex scheme involved Albrecht Haushofer, the son of Hess' mystical mentor Karl Haushofer. Albrecht knew Hess, was a secret anti-Nazi, and was a close friend of the Scottish Duke of Hamilton, who was affiliated with the British "peace party." By manipulating correspondence between Haushofer and Hamilton, Fleming and his crew hoped to convince Hess that the peace party was ready to oust Churchill and make a deal.[41] When this effort fizzled, Admiral Godfrey and Fleming hit on another approach: using cooked astrology to persuade that his cause and timing were right. This was the plan Guy Liddell detected and disapproved of. In the end, Hess used astrological readings concocted from various sources to pick 10 May as *der Tag*. Apparently the fact that the 10th had the sun and four planets in Taurus he considered highly significant.

The Beast's name comes up in discussions of a variety of "occult operations" during WWII. He personally claimed to have given Churchill the "V for Victory" sign, which really was, the story goes, the powerful occult symbol of Apophis and Typhon. Weirder tales involve the Mage's name, and sometimes his person, in an alleged effort by British witches to ward off Nazi invasion through forest gatherings and magic rituals.[42] Such tales probably best belong in the large file of Crowley apocrypha, but they may have their origin in the campaign of "occult disinformation" waged by elements in British intelligence.

Among the factors that led Hess to undertake his daring flight was a peculiar dream. He found himself in Buckingham Palace, being received by the King. Hess took this as another auspicious sign. This has led some to speculate that Crowley used his special talents to literally get inside Hess' head and inspire or influence this dream. While obviously beyond objective proof, the notion is not as farfetched as it sounds. The same concept lies behind today's "remote influencing," a psychic technique experimented with by the U.S. Army and the CIA, among others.[43]

Whatever Crowley's role in the Hess affair, there is no doubt that he rekindled his relationship with NID when war came. On 8 September 1939, only days after Britain's declaration of hostilities, the Mage noted that he had "completed form for NID," which sounds like a questionnaire or application. Immediately following, he lists four names: "Sir P.[ercy] Harris. C. Bax. G.[erald] J. Yorke. C.R. Cammel."[44]

Percy Harris was the husband of Lady Frieda Harris, the artist who painted Crowley's Tarot deck. He also was a Liberal M.P. and later a privy counselor and member of Churchill's wartime circle. Only a few weeks earlier, Crowley recorded that he had "educated" Harris about something and the next day Harris arranged the Beast a visit to a meeting of Parliament.[45] Our man still was not without a few friends in high places. The writer Clifford Bax was an old acquaintance who had introduced Crowley to Frieda Harris. His interests included astrology and Theosophy, and he just may have had some connection to intelligence. Gerald Yorke we know, and Cammell, another writer, would pen an early and rather sympathetic biography of the Beast, *The Black Magician*, in 1951. The names look like a list of personal references.

Crowley must have done something right, for on 10 September he received a personal reply from Admiral Godfrey, DNI. The Admiral offered his compliments and summoned the Mage for an "interview," suggesting that Crowley contact Commander C.J.M. Lang of the Naval Intelligence Division to set up a time. He helpfully provided Lang's telephone number: Whitehall 9000, Ext. 484. On the note, Crowley jotted: "Better ring up Mr. Frost—Ext. 46 for an interview?"[46]

Commander Lang's connection to Naval Intelligence went back at least to 1919 and took root in the Far East. The latter recalls Burbury's, Etherton's, and Crowley's earlier interest in "Oriental Evil." During 1932–1934, Lang was NID chief in Hong Kong, coinciding with Yorke's and Peter Fleming's missions in China. His service record shows that he returned to active duty with NID in August 1939. Although the file reveals nothing about his exact assignment, his extension, #484, was used by *"the NID section dealing with the interrogation of POW's."*[47] Remember that Crowley had conducted hundreds of "experiments" with peyote and other drugs and had kept copious notes on the results—further expertise useful to Godfrey and his lieutenants, with or without Hess.

Crowley's "Mr. Frost" is harder to pin down. "Extension #46" existed in NID, but was assigned to a senior civil servant, W.G. Johns. Given the Beast's penchant for nicknames, perhaps "Frost" was his for Johns. In any case, why Crowley thought it best to contact him first remains a mystery.

Two days after his invitation from Godfrey, the Beast recorded a rather cryptic entry that includes "Interview as satisfactory as could be expected," what looks to be a Hebrew code for "NID" and "Job from umbilicals."[48] The latter seems to be his personal code for NID or some related branch of officialdom. Also mentioned is a letter from "V. I.", certainly *Volo Intelligere* (Gerald Yorke). A following entry on 2 October mentions "Col. Ellachie or Commdr. Leeds" and "Executed Harris' mission: better that I had ventured to hope." The same entry also notes the recent conference with Gerald Hamilton and letters from the German-sounding H.L.M. Gertz and Kraemer.

The man who became the NID's point man on the "Crowley business," effectively his case officer, was Godfrey's assistant Ian Fleming. Fleming later recalled how Crowley "put forward some madcap ideas to the intelligence authorities . . . one being dropping occult information [on the enemy] by leaflet."[49] Supposedly, the idea went nowhere, yet Delmer's and other agencies engaged in almost identical activities, whether or not inspired by Crowley.

Fleming later confessed that one of his unfulfilled desires was to have Crowley interview Rudolf Hess.[50] That would make perfect sense if the Beast was already involved in prisoner interrogations. Crowley was willing to oblige, and may have suggested the idea himself. Fleming preserved a letter from him, dated 14 May (four days after Hess' capture), which read: "If it is true that Herr Hess is much influenced by astrology and magick, my services might be of use to the department in case he should not be willing to do what you wish."[51] Interestingly, Crowley noted Tom Driberg as someone who "could testify to my status and reputation in these matters."[52] Had he been doing similar work for Maxwell Knight? Fleming and Godfrey hoped that the old Magician might persuade Hess to divulge intimate details about other top Nazis, such as the degree of their own occult susceptibilities.

Officially, the Beast never got anywhere near Hess. There were, after all, concerns about Rudy's mental stability, and who knew what impact Mr. Crowley might have on that. Fleming attributes the decisive veto to Maxwell Knight.[53] This seems odd, since Knight theoretically had no jurisdiction over NID or Hess (who was MI6's responsibility). But Knight could claim a prior proprietary interest in *Crowley*, and may have objected to Fleming poaching his man. Maybe Knight had his own scheme for getting Hess and Crowley in a room together.

By one account, Crowley did interrogate Hess, not at MI6's Camp Z (Mytchett Place), but at a secret *MI5* facility. This was Camp 020, otherwise known as Latchmere House or Ham Common.[54] According to information received by researcher Peter Koenig, the Beast interviewed Hess there over a three-week period, sometime between Hess' arrival in London in May 1941 and his transfer to a mental hospital in Wales in June 1942.[55] The original source of the tale is a German POW who claimed to have seen the Mage and Hess at the Camp. Ham Common definitely was a top-secret center for interrogation, often rough, of select German prisoners. At least two of them, Kurt Maass and Eduard Semelbauer, were close to Hess, and he had asked to see them after his capture.

The official chronology of Hess' captivity, however, reveals no opportunity for a three-week visit, or any visit to Latchmere House. Perhaps the prisoner did see Crowley there on other business, and falsely assumed that it had to do with Hess. On the other hand, if Max Knight wanted to probe Hess on the sly, a secure location like Ham Common would have been perfect.

A final curious detail: at Camp Z, Hess complained of hallucinations and protested to Red Cross officials that his food was being dosed with "Mexican brain poison," i.e. mescaline.[56] Was Hess just losing his mind, or was someone using Crowley's bag of tricks? As Donald McCormick later observed, "if one examines the remarkable story of Rudolf Hess . . . the triangle of witchcraft, astrology and espionage becomes strangely more predominant."[57] Crowley's connection to all this leaves us a trail of provocative facts and intriguing rumors, but no clear answer.

In early 1942, the Beast put forward what may have been his last proposal regarding clandestine warfare. He called it "Plan 241." Fleming and Godfrey having moved on to other pastures, he used as intermediary his friend and student Robert Cecil. Cecil was in the Foreign Office but had connections in the "spookier" corners of the wartime government. On 14 January, the Beast noted that he had an "excellent talk" with Cecil and that he "agreed to get Plan 241 to Col. Britton personally."[58] The latter was attached to Delmer's Political Warfare Executive. Cecil later described the Plan as "black propaganda" that was "as black as black could be."[59] He is sparse with details, but the gist of it was the deliberate recruitment of persons "whom despair had rendered not only murderous, but suicidal." Such an operative would slay two Germans and then kill himself, leaving "241" somewhere on his corpse. Crowley hoped that this might encourage spontaneous copycat attacks by other desperate men. Cecil noted only that the Plan "did not find favor."

1 The child, Randall Gair (later called Aleister Ataturk), was born in May 1937.

2 Frank Baker, *Talk of the Devil* (London: Angus & Robertson, 1956), and A.L. Rowse, *A Night at the Carn and Other Stories* (London: William Kimber, 1984).

3 Lord Edgar Algernon Robert Gascoyne Cecil (1864–1958).

4 *The Times* (13 Jan. 1938), 9g, and (28 May 1938), 16d.

5 Ursula Langkau-Alex, "The International Socialist Labor Movement and the Elimination of the 'German Problem'," 7–8, www.iisg.nl/publications/respap29.pdf.

6 Gary Kern, *A Death in Washington: Walter G. Krivitsky and the Stalin Terror* (NY: Enigma Books, 2003), 58.

7 Newman, 118.

8 *Ibid.* 140–141.

9 *Ibid.*, 135.

10 Oleg Tsarev and Nigel West, *The Crown Jewels: The British Secrets at the Heart of the KGB Archives* (New Haven: Yale Univ. Press, 1999), 316–318.

11 *Ibid.*, 316.

12 Newman, 128.

13 *Ibid.*

14 Donald McCormick, *Murder by Witchcraft: A Study of the Lower Quinton and Hagley Wood Murders* (London: Arrow Books, 1969), 169–170.

15 UKNA, KV4/186, Liddell Diary. A long-ago destroyed Colonial Office file (CO 875/9/10) bore the interesting title "Use of Astrology in Propaganda." The astrological operation noted by Liddell seems actually to have been under the direct control of Sefton Delmer of the Political Warfare Executive, yet another intelligence spin-off that specialized in "black propaganda."

16 McCormick, *Murder by Witchcraft*, 154.

17 Levenda, 151.

18 Deacon, BSS, 310–311.

19 *Ibid.*

20 Newman, 132.

21 Stephen E. Flowers (Trans.) and Michael Moynihan (ed.), *The Secret King: Karl Maria Wiligut, Himmler's Lord of the Runes* (Waterbury Center, VT: Dominion Press, 2001).

22 Juergen-Michael Schmidt, "*Hexen-Sonderauftrag, Hexenkartothek*," www.lrz-muenchen.de/~u9332br/webserver/webdta/hexenverfolgung/art816.htm.

23 Deacon, BSS, 312.

24 Goebbels Diary, 19 May 1942, //en.wikiquote.org/wiki_Goebbels.

25 Levenda, 156–157, Starr, "Freemason!," and P. Koenig, "Ordo Templi Orientis, Background Information: Karl Germer, Autobiography," //user.cyberlin.ch/~koenig/dplanet/germer1.htm.

26 Diary, 30 July 1936, FAAC, "George Sylvester Viereck," www.redflame93.com/Viereck.html.

27 See: *The Black Book (Sonderfahndungsliste—GB)*, reprint (London: Imperial War Museum, 1989).

28 "Tatkreis," www.btinternet.com/~j.pasteur/Tatkreis.html.

29 William S. Stephenson (ed.), *British Security Coordination: The Secret History of British Intelligence in the Americas, 1940–45* (NY: Fromm International, 1999), 234–235.

30 UKNA, KV 2/755, 8a and 18b. and XV.

31 *Ibid.*, 18b.

32 *Ibid.*, 11b.

33 *Ibid.*

34 KV2/1561-66.

35 William Breeze to author, 3 Feb. 2008. Rayner was the author of *The Shell Guide to Hampshire* (1937).

36 *Ibid.*

37 *Ibid.*

38 Ladislas Farago, *The Game of Foxes: The Untold Story of German Espionage in the United States and Great Britain during World War II* (NY: D, McKay & Co., 1971), 658.

39 Andrew Lycett, *Ian Fleming: The Man Behind James Bond* (London: Turner, 1996), 133–134.

40 On this point, see: Lynn Pickett, Clive Prince and Stephen Prior, *Double Standards: The Rudolf Hess Cover-Up* (NY: Little Brown, 2001), and "Interview: Double Standards: What Really Happened to Rudolf Hess," www.eyespymag/intv.html.

41 Newman, 134.

42 The story is variously credited to Ian Fleming or Crowley himself. See: Gordon Rutter, "Magic Goes to War," *Fortean Times*, #185 (July 2004), www.forteantimes.com/articles/185_magic_war4.shtml, and— Dion Fortune, *The Magical Battle of Britain* (Oceanside, CA: Sun Chalice Books, 2003).

43 Roughly, "remote influencing" is an extension or offshoot of the more commonly referenced "remote viewing." See, e.g., David Morehouse, *Psychic Warrior: The True Story of the CIA's Paranormal Espionage Programme* (London: Clairview Books, 2000) and Turan Rifat, "Remote Viewing: The ESP of Espionage," *Nexus Magazine*, Vol. 3, #6 (Oct.–Nov. 1996), www.nexusmagazine.com/articles/espionage.html.

44 William Breeze to author, 3 Feb. 2008.

45 *Ibid.*, citing diary entries of 23 and 24 August 1939.

46 Martin Booth, *A Magick Life: A Biography of Aleister Crowley* (London: Hodder & Stoughton, 2000), 395. The note from Godfrey later was found among Crowley's personal effects.

47 P. Tomaselli to author, 24 Oct. 2004.

48   William Breeze to author, 3 Feb. 2008, citing entry of 12 Sept. 1939.

49   Deacon, BSS, 311 and Masters, 128.

50   Deacon, BSS, 320.

51   John Pearson, *The Life of Ian Fleming* (London: Companion Books, 1966), 117. A curious detail is that the entire Crowley episode was deleted from the subsequent American edition of Pearson's book. See also, Gerald Suster, *Hitler: The Occult Messiah* (NY: St. Martins, 1981), 166.

52   Undated literary sales catalog describing and quoting Crowley-Fleming letter. Thanks to William Breeze.

53   Pearson, 118.

54   Lt. Col. R.W.G. Stephens, *Camp 020: MI5 and the Nazi Spies* (Kew: PRO, 2000).

55   Peter Koenig, "Crowley Met Rudolf Hess," www.groups.yahoo.com/thelema93-1/message/2733), 31 Aug. 2000, and Koenig to Jackson, 30 Sept. and 1 Nov. 2004.

56   S. Jackson to author, 30 Sept. 2004. The most thorough account of Hess' captivity may be David Irving's *Hess: The Missing Years, 1941–45* (London: Focal Point Press, 2002) [earlier edition, 1989].

57   McCormick, *Murder by Witchcraft*, 154.

58   William Breeze to author, 3 Feb. 2008.

59   *Ibid.* 30 Jan. 2008, quoting excerpts of Robert Cecil's unpublished memoir, *The Will and the Way*.

EPILOGUE

~

†HE DISHOПORABLE GEП†LEMAП

~

WHATEVER HIS INVOLVEMENT IN THE HESS CASE OR OTHER CLANDES-
TINE ACTIVITIES, CROWLEY WAS NOT SHY about showing his patriotism. In
1941, he wrote *Thumbs Up!*, a small volume of verse that included "England, Stand
Fast!" (dedicated to Winston Churchill) and "A Toast," a parody that harked back to
his "German" propaganda in the last war. To some, it was just an aging petty traitor's
cynical effort to rehabilitate himself. On the contrary, these outpourings probably
reflected the genuine sentiments which stirred his Tory heart of hearts.

The Mage's last years saw a final burst of literary work, including the completion
of *Magick without Tears* (published posthumously in 1954) and *The Book of Thoth*
(1944). But the notorious Aleister Crowley was a sick man suffering from bad teeth,
chronic bronchitis, and a failing heart. His lifelong respiratory problems and the
years of abuse, narcotic and otherwise, had taken their toll. Even his vaunted libido
was on the wane, though apparently he still managed to attract a string of willing (if
sometimes ambivalent) partners.[1]

The war buffeted him from one place to another. In 1940, he was bombed out of
the London suburb of Richmond Green and left for the relative security of Torquay
(near Cornwall). Pushy creditors (and perhaps other obligations) drove him back to
London, where by late 1942 he lived in a flat at 93 Jermyn Street, just off Piccadilly.
He left there in early 1944 (Robert Cecil moved in) to find temporary refuge at a
small inn in Aston Clinton, Buckinghamshire. In early 1945, the Beast crept into his
final lair, the bucolic Netherwood boarding house near Hastings.

At Netherwood, on 1 December 1947, the 72-year-old Master Therion shed his
mortal coil. Mystery and controversy clouded even his death. Pat Doherty asserted that
a peal of thunder marked his dying moment, and Frieda Harris later recalled his last
words as the oft-quoted "I am perplexed."[2] Harris, however, left Netherwood the day
before his passing. Crowley's attending nurse remembered the Beast's final utterance
as, "Sometimes I hate myself."[3] Another legend holds that Crowley cursed his doctor
and brought about the physician's death within a day of his own.[4] In fact, Dr. William

Brown Thomson had long suspected that his patient was getting extra, illegal doses of heroin and had threatened to cut him off, much to Crowley's annoyance. Curse or not, Dr. Thomson soon followed his troublesome patient to the grave.

Four days after the Beast's passing, in nearby Brighton, a handful of friends and devotees gathered to pay last respects. Louis Wilkinson read Crowley's "Hymn to Pan," provoking a final spasm of outrage among local bluenoses, who were aghast that a "black mass" had taken place in their midst.

Rumors of espionage and related dark doings clung to Crowley's name in his last years and after his death. His name surfaced, indirectly, in connection with two mysterious wartime murders, the so-called Wych-Elm and Charles Walton (Lower Quinton) cases. The fragile threads connecting Crowley to them deserve brief consideration.

The first case arose from a grisly find near Hagley, west of Birmingham, in 1943. Teenage poachers discovered of the skeleton of a young woman, subsequently dubbed "Luebella" or "Bella," in the hollow trunk of an ancient wych-elm (actually a wych-hazel) tree. Forensic examination indicated that the thirtyish victim had been murdered, probably sometime in 1941. In the opinion of professed witchcraft expert Professor Margaret Murray, the unusual disposal of the body and its severed hand marked a "black-magic" slaying.

The crime naturally generated much rumor and speculation. In the years following, it is alleged, files and evidence from the case, including "Bella's" skeleton, went missing. Recently, one anonymous official who looked into the case offered that "there were clear occult and secret service links," though just how (s)he arrived at that conclusion is unknown.[5] Donald McCormick came to much the same conclusion in his 1968 *Murder by Witchcraft*, which explored the Hagley Wood and Walton killings.

In 1953, Wilfred Byford-Jones, a writer for the *Wolverhampton Express & Star*, found a source who claimed knowledge of the Wych-Elm Murder. According to the source, a woman called "Anna," Bella was killed because of her connection to a German spy ring that had operated in the Midlands and included a "traitorous British officer."[6] McCormick concluded that "Bella" most likely was a Dutch woman whose interests included astrology. She might even have been a witch. He also speculated that a mysterious Hungarian astrologer may have been connected to the case. Other rumors linked the unfortunate woman and the espionage ring to a group of occultists that included associates of Crowley's Cornwall coven.[7] Here we may have another vague glimpse of the weird nexus of Crowley, witchcraft, spies, Black Masses, and blackmail alluded to in Kim Philby's wartime report and other sources.

The Crowley connection is a wee bit stronger in the second case, the Walton Murder of February 1945. The victim, Charles Walton, was a seventy-four-year-old laborer from Lower Quinton, about forty miles from "Bella's" wych-elm. Walton was found pinned to the ground with a hay-fork and slashed to death, his blood soaking the ground. Some took this as evidence of a ritual slaying.[8] The redoubtable Inspector Robert Fabian of Scotland Yard was called in to investigate. His suspicions settled on a man who owed Walton money, but the evidence would not support a charge. The case remained in limbo until 1955 when, once again, an informant came forward to the local press. "Mrs. Jones" claimed to have been initiated into a "witch cult" during WWII. It extended nationwide and was run by "Dr. Gardner," an apparent reference to the father of modern Wicca, Gerald Gardner.[9] Gardner did meet Crowley, but by all accounts not until 1946–1947. Another possibility is that this in some way related to Dion Fortune's Society of the Inner Light which is alleged to have played a key part in the "Magical Battle of Britain."

Mrs. Jones' most sensational accusation was that the killing itself was the work of "Aleister Crowley's widow," Pat Doherty, whom Gardner or whoever called in for just that purpose. This charge prompted a doubtful but intrigued local inspector to inquire of his colleagues in Cornwall. The result was the aforementioned police report, which described the membership and activities of Crowley's devotees around Tregerthen. It is hard to picture the gentle, Earth-motherly Pat as a ritual murderess, but appearances can be deceiving.

One can easily dismiss the supposed Crowley connections to these murders as sensationalist fantasies of the British press, which had lost none of its enthusiasm for laying evils at the feet of the Worst Man in the World. One can also, however, wonder whether Mrs. Jones' story was a distortion of actual events in a wartime campaign of disinformation and counter-espionage that had used occult groups as cover.

Suspicion and intrigue also clung to many of the Beast's associates. Perhaps the most affected was Karl Germer, last encountered having lunch with Crowley and Viereck in London in 1936. When the British Government again refused to grant him residency, he moved to Dublin. In 1937, Germer quit Dublin, reportedly at the insistence of the German Embassy. How he antagonized the Germans is a mystery, but his past, including his association with Crowley, may have convinced them that he was a British operative. Also recall Philby's report that the German Legation in Dublin was the launchpad for occult and drug-linked plots against England.

Germer's next stop was Belgium, where he resumed his trade as a machinery salesman for British firms. Belgium, of course, played host to the murky intrigues of Anthroposophist Walter Stein, among others. Belgium also put Germer relatively close to Greta Sequeira and her secret missions in Germany. Curiously, Pat Doherty also was in the Reich just before the war broke out, escaping just in the nick of time alongside a mysterious "Jewish doctor." Germer remained in Belgium until

May 1940 when, with the German Blitzkrieg thundering along, the Belgians kicked him to France. Staying one step ahead of the Nazis, Germer took refuge in the unoccupied Vichy zone, where he cooled his heels for nearly a year. With the help of his American-based wife, and maybe others, he finally made his way top the Caribbean and wangled a special U.S. immigration permit in spring 1941.

In New York, Germer became the Mage's general factotum in the States. Probably for that reason, he soon attracted the hostile scrutiny of the man who had investigated Crowley back in 1919, J. Edgar Hoover. In December 1941, Hoover pressed the New York Bureau to give "preferred and expeditious attention" to Germer.[10] When FBI agents in Gotham responded that they could not dig up anything negative, J. Edgar simply told them to try harder. Eventually, they found some personal enemy willing to brand Germer a pro-Nazi. It was a baseless charge, but enough to put him and his new wife Sascha under surveillance and justify a search of their apartment. Germer knew that he was being spied upon, and the harried couple resorted to communicating via written notes. Eventually, Germer came to believe that almost everyone was out to get him, and that the FBI was but another manifestation of the nefarious Black Brotherhood. He also believed that Hoover's animus was not against him personally, but part of a larger conspiracy against Crowley. Paranoid or not, in that conclusion Germer was absolutely right.

To understand why, we need to pick up what Ian Fleming and Admiral Godfrey were up to in the wake of the Hess case. In late May 1941, the pair departed on a special mission to the States, which may have been someone's (Max Knight's?) way of getting them out of England and far away from Hess. Their mission was to offer help to the still officially neutral Americans with counterintelligence operations against Axis agents. In discussions with the chief of British intelligence in America, the Canadian Sir William Stephenson, Fleming and the Admiral learned that the biggest obstacle to their plans was the imperious and territorial Mr. Hoover.[11] Hoover may have been an efficient enough policeman, but as far as the British were concerned, he was no spy-hunter.

Fleming found himself working with William "Wild Bill" Donovan, whom President Roosevelt had named Coordinator of Intelligence (COI). Out of that came the Office of Strategic Services (OSS) and out of that the CIA.[12] Officially, domestic counterintelligence remained Hoover's bailiwick, while Donovan's new outfit took responsibility overseas. As usual, the division was never clean or satisfactory to either party. The FBI Director regarded Donovan's operation as a gang of "Ivy League dilettantes" meddling in his territory, some of them outright security risks.[13] Hoover mistrusted the English on principle, and the coziness of Britons such as Fleming with the COI excited his suspicion and hostility all the more.

Hoover also took a dim view of anything unconventional, which naturally included occult groups, though he was a Freemason. He certainly sniffed out Fleming's connection to Crowley. Perhaps J. Edgar worried that the English Magician knew a little too much about the Bureau, and maybe about the Director himself. If, as is today commonly asserted (without being definitively proved), Hoover was a closeted homosexual, someone with Crowley's inclinations and means of ferreting out secrets would have made him nervous.

Hoover's personal attention may have something to do with the dearth of Crowley records in the FBI files.[14] There is nothing in the extant Crowley file dated past 1926, and nothing of any substance after August 1924, soon after Hoover took over the Bureau.[15] Those documents do make numerous mentions of the Beast's connection to George Sylvester Viereck, a fact Hoover used to justify blocking Crowley's admission to the U.S.[16] It was a handy, politically correct objection under the circumstances. The FBI had Viereck dead to rights as a Nazi propagandist and arrested him in 1942.

Imagine then Hoover's reaction when he discovered that Karl Germer, another German, and one of Crowley's principal disciples, had arrived in the U.S. a month or so after Fleming. Hoover must have suspected a connection that led him to set his agents on poor Germer. In their perusal of Germer's papers, Hoover's agents discovered his recent correspondence with the Mage, which further revealed that dutiful Karl was raising money to bring Crowley to the States. Hoover must have smelled a British scheme to bring the old, disreputable, and possibly dangerous agent back to America for some devious purpose. He may not have been imagining things. Unable to employ Crowley's unique talents in England, Fleming and his boss could have hoped to put him at Stephenson's disposal. Another veteran British spy then assisting Stephenson was none other than Sir William Wiseman.

Persons in England were interested in helping Crowley reach the States. Robert Cecil alludes to a scheme to get Crowley to the British West Indies for reasons of health, but he failed to secure the necessary exit permit and passport.[17] Crowley's real intention was to join Germer and other members of the OTO in California. By 1943, Cecil had sufficient clout as a secretary to SIS chief Sir Stewart Menzies, that he could get access to the Beast's MI5 dossier, or one of them at least.[18] Oddly, he mentions no attempt to see SIS' file on the Magician. In the MI5 papers, Cecil claimed to find ample evidence of Crowley's pro-German writing during WWI but nothing to support his claims to have done that on British authority, nor does Cecil mention anything of a more recent nature. Did Cecil see only what someone wanted him to see? However "black" Crowley's record seemed, Cecil admitted that "the case remains open."[19]

Cecil also concluded that the above must have been why the necessary British officials were unwilling to assist Crowley's departure. "He has done nothing for us," they supposedly opined, "[and] we will do nothing for him."[20] Perhaps this was the result of years of disgust and mistrust, and then there was his status as an undischarged bankrupt. But there may have been other good reasons to keep the unpredictable Mr. Crowley on a very short leash. Maybe Max Knight wanted to keep him close to home.

Shortly after the war, there was a final effort to get Crowley to the U.S., led by a young U.S. Army officer, Grady Louis McMurtry.[21] He met the Beast after arriving in Britain in fall 1943. It was no chance encounter. McMurtry was a recent initiate of the Agape Lodge, a thriving branch of the OTO based in Pasadena, California. Leaves from front-line duty allowed Lieutenant McMurtry to deepen his connection with the declining Mage and receive further initiations. In 1946, McMurtry began a "Clear Crowley's Name Campaign" which was to smooth *To Mega Therion's* way back to America. The old man's decline and Hoover's continuing obstructiveness, however, frustrated the plan.

Writers such as Peter Levenda suggest that McMurtry was linked to American military intelligence, and that his cultivation of Crowley somehow served interests in that sphere.[22] While no evidence supports such a link during WWII, when the Korean conflict erupted a few years later, McMurtry did volunteer his services to U.S. Army intelligence (G-2), an unusual offer from a man whose prior experience had been in ordnance.[23]

Had Crowley made it to America, the intention of McMurtry and friends was, as noted, to settle him in California. This brings us back to the Agape Lodge, which had been formed in the early 1930s by Crowley's acolyte, Wilfred T. Smith. By the early 1940s, the dominant figure in the Lodge was the man who had initiated McMurtry, a Cal Tech rocket scientist, explosives expert, and student of the occult, John Whiteside "Jack" Parsons. To no surprise, suspicions of espionage attached to Parsons as well.[24]

Parsons's pioneering work in jet propulsion and rocketry led to his involvement in top-secret government projects. That lay awkwardly against his other role as leader of what FBI reports dubbed the "Church of Thelma" [sic].[25] The same reports pointed out that Parsons and the group "received . . . orders from Sir Allister [sic] Crowley in London." A bigger concern was that Parsons had flirted with Communism and had numerous friends and acquaintances known or suspected to be Reds.[26] The FBI began investigating Parsons in 1943 and continued until his bizarre death nine years later. In the end, Hoover's men found no substantive evidence of espionage, but the investigation raised enough flags to cost Parsons his security clearance.

What really got him into hot water was his removal in 1950 of classified documents from his employer, Hughes Aircraft. Parsons admitted his deed, but explained that he only wanted to copy the documents to include in an application for a new job with the American Technicon Society, an affiliate of the Israel Institute of Technology.[27] The IIT in turn had links to Israeli intelligence, the Mossad.

Several things about Parsons remind one of Robin Thynne, most notably his appeal to women and his association with secret government projects. Another similarity is his mystery-shrouded death. In 1952, Parsons was blown to bits in what investigators deemed an accidental explosion. He kept a variety of explosive materials in his private lab, including extremely unstable fulminate of mercury. Skeptics, however, doubted that Parsons (who was after all a rocket scientist) would have been so careless as to be hoist by his own petard; some hinted at supernatural causes, and others at murderous conspiracies.

Another intrigue that wound through Parson' last years was his unfortunate relationship with a man he identified to Crowley as "Frater H." This was a former U.S. Navy officer, L. Ron Hubbard, the future founder of Scientology. Hubbard did have a brief affiliation with the ONI early in WWII, but his service record indicates nothing of the kind during the time of his acquaintance with Parsons. Soon after the war, Hubbard and Parsons ventured into the Mojave Desert to perform the Babalon Working, a ritual aimed at achieving the Beast's longtime goal of spawning a Thelemic messiah. Hubbard eventually ended up running off with Parsons' money and girlfriend. Years later, Hubbard explained his dealings with Parsons as part of his secret work for Naval Intelligence, or the FBI, or the local police (the story varies) to infiltrate a dangerous black magic cult, the OTO, which was being used by someone to enlist or compromise scientists.[28] It all sounds vaguely like an American version of Philby's tale.

Just before Crowley's death, Karl Germer made a last-ditch effort to visit the Beast. His effort to obtain a visa, however, met with an insurmountable stone wall.[29] Germer assumed authority over the OTO, but the matter of succession was clouded, however, by the machinations of Gerald Yorke. That once and likely continuing intelligence operative stage managed the settlement of Crowley's estate, copying and, perhaps, destroying papers, and withholding a vital charter from Germer. Yorke's may have been the guiding hand behind the excisions made to the Beast's *Confessions*. He likewise may have influenced the dismissive attitude evident in John Symonds' 1951 biography. Did Yorke have an assignment to spin Crowley's legacy in such a way as to discredit or obliterate all evidence of his intelligence activities?

Under Germer's leadership, or lack of it, the Order withered away to almost nothing. The Agape Lodge folded the year after Parsons' death, and by the time

Germer passed away in 1962, the remaining Thelemites were so scattered that it took years for some of them to learn that their master was gone. The situation was compounded by Germer's deepening paranoia, which led him to isolate himself and his wife in the tiny Sierra town of West Point, California. Among the items Germer acquired from Crowley's estate were an archive of OTO materials, a trove of the Beast's correspondence, and various personal and ritual items. Germer jealously guarded these in his mountain hideaway.

Starting around 1965, alumni of the Agape Lodge and others connected to Crowley were victims of mysterious break-ins aimed at the theft of OTO-related materials. Israel Regardie was one. In a terrible realization of her paranoid fantasies, two years later, Sascha Germer was the victim of a brazen assault on her home and person. Her attackers tricked their way into her isolated house, maced and bound her, and stole items from the Crowley collection.

Much suspicion subsequently alighted upon the so-called Solar Lodge. Surfacing in Los Angeles in the late 1960s, it was dominated by Georgina "Jean" Brayton, who apparently aspired to take up where the old Agape Lodge had left off. Besides drugs, it emphasized an apocalyptic and allegedly racist doctrine that had little in common with Crowley's ideas. Though nothing was ever proved in the thefts, the Solar Lodge soon landed in other trouble with the law. This included charges of child abuse and, most notoriously, alleged association with Charles Manson and his homicidal, LSD-addled Family.[30] Such connections, probably coincidental, fed broader speculation that the Solar Lodge, the Mansonites, and groups such as the weird Process Church of the Final Judgment were all parts of a nefarious mind-control experiment run by the CIA or other spooks. If there is any truth behind such theories, perhaps it is more strange fruit of Crowley's long-ago experimentation with mescaline and psychic manipulation.

Germer died without designating a successor, resulting in more schism and secession. Autonomous branches of the OTO soon arose in England and Switzerland. In the Western Hemisphere, Grady McMurtry struggled with the Brazil-based Marcelo Ramos Motta for succession. McMurtry surfaced in 1969 to salvage the remnants of Agape and what remained of Germer's archive. Years of litigation ended with victory in the States for McMurtry, who assumed the title Caliph Hymenaeus Alpha, a name originally given him by Crowley. The unbowed Motta ascribed his defeat to a plot by British and American intelligence "to absorb the OTO into the ideological warfare network of the political right."[31] Abetting this conspiracy, alleged Motta, was "veteran British intelligence agent" Gerald Yorke. Naturally, Motta also alleged that McMurtry was another intelligence asset.[32] Motta's detractors dismissed him as an alcoholic with delusions of grandeur and a persecution complex.

My final nagging doubt is not whether I have overstated Crowley's involvement with intelligence, but whether I have overlooked or misread some critical detail that would make better sense of his activities or cast them in a different light. For instance, how much, if any, reality is there behind Hubbard's alleged conspiracy, Philby's 1940s story of drugs, blackmail, and black magic, Makgill's 1920s "Cult of Evil," or the high weirdness Frances Gregg sensed around Crowley during WWI? Was some of this just misinterpretation of Crowley's involvement in intelligence affairs, or are some glimpses of deeper, more sinister secrets of the Beast?

As noted at the beginning, the available evidence relevant to Crowley's involvement with espionage and attendant activity ultimately raises more questions than it answers. I am forced to conclude that the lack of records about the Mage's role as an agent is intentional. On the British side, a deliberate purge of Crowley materials has decimated the open files. On top of that, misdirection, obfuscation, and stonewalling by MI5, SIS, Scotland Yard, and other agencies reflects a continuing effort to obscure or deny Crowley's role as a British intelligence asset. Much the same may be said of the FBI's implausible denials. Why?

Certainly one factor is the reflexive secrecy of such agencies. The withholding of seemingly innocuous information can be justified simply because someone at some point deemed it a secret. The security of the British Empire can no longer be at stake, but some reputations, personal or institutional, might be. The surmised destruction of Crowley's MI5 files took place in the early 1950s, part of a mass culling of "records no longer worth keeping," which doubtless included many items deemed politically embarrassing. A smattering of these records, thought historically significant by the chief "weeder," Gilbert Wakefield, survive and include references to Walter Stein, the Nazis, and even the *Lusitania*.[33] Of the Beast, however, not a hair remains.

Subsequent releases by MI5 show that dossiers on persons of much less historical significance than Crowley were preserved, which makes the 1950s criteria for destruction hard to infer. Coincidentally or not, the purge began during Churchill's return as prime minister from 1951–1955. Did Churchill take a personal interest in seeing the Beast's records destroyed? As Robert Cecil suggests, Crowley's record may have been too "black" to ever see light of day. The past hides many secrets, many crimes, many uncredited heroes, and many unsuspected villains. Aleister Crowley knew more than his share of each.

1   Sutin, 391.
2   Symonds, *Great Beast*, 296.
3   Symonds, *King of the Shadow Realm*, 578.
4. Warren Hill, "The Beast's Last Curse," *American Weekly* (11 April 1948) and *Daily Express* (4 Dec. 1947).
5   Newman, 129.
6   "Bella in the Wych-Elm– A Midlands Murder Mystery," www.mysteriouspeople.com/Bella_in_the_ wychelm.htm, and Newman, 129.
7   Newman, 129–130.
8   The purported significance did not rest in the fact that Walton's death took place on or about February 14th, modern Valentine's Day, but the correspondence of this day with the pagan festival of Candlemas or Imbolc under the old Julian calendar.
9   Newman, 130. The original stories ran in the *Reynolds News* and *Sunday Pictorial*.
10 FBI file, "Germer, Karl," as quoted in Marcelo Motta, "Intelligence Services Are Not Intelligent, or the O.T.O. since Crowley's Death" [annotated version], member.ozemail.com.au/~realoto/intel1.html [cached].
11 Stephenson, *op.cit.* One of the men assisting Stephenson was Sir William Wiseman. For a more critical view of British clandestine operations in the U.S, see Thomas Mahl, *Desperate Deception: British Covert Operations in the United States, 1939–1944* (Dulles, VA: Brassey's, 1999).
12 Mark Riebling, *Wedge, From Pearl Harbor to 9/11: How the Secret War between the FBI and CIA Has Endangered National Security* (NY: Touchstone, 2002), 3–4.
13 *Ibid.*, 33.
14 FBI, Crowley file, 61-2069.
15 Hoover formally assumed command on 10 May 1924.
16 The Magician, "Jack Parsons and the Curious Origins of the American Space Program," Part 7 [*Laissez Faire City Times* Vol. 2, #7 (16 March 1998)], www.aci.net/KALLISTE/Jpar7.htm.
17 Willam Breeze to author, 30 Jan. 2008, quoting Cecil's *The Will and the Way*.
18 *Ibid.*
19 *Ibid.*
20 Martin Starr to Steve Jackson, 9 July 2002, and Starr to author, 11 July 2006.
21 Jerry Cornelius, *In the Name of the Beast: A Biography of Grady Louis McMurtry, a Disciple of Aleister Edward Crowley*, (2005), Vol. I, Synopsis, *Redflame* #12, www.redflame93.com/RF12.html.
22 Levenda, *Unholy*, 288.
23 Cornelius, *Ibid.* The Army took him back, and made him a captain, but assigned him to an ordnance unit as opposed to MI. That, in any case, is the official story.

24 On Parsons, see two recent biographies: John Carter, *Sex and Rockets: The Occult World of Jack Parsons* (Los Angeles: Feral House, 1999) and George Pendle, *Strange Angel: The Otherworldly Life of Rocket Scientist John Whiteside Parsons* (NY: Harcourt, 2005).

25 FBI file #65-9131. This was available at the Bureau's online reading room, //foia.gov/foiaindex/jparsons.htm.

26 One example was Chinese mathematician Hsue-shen Tsien. Finally deported by the U.S. Government in the early '50s, he returned to China and later helped build Beijing's ICBMs. See Pendle, 301–302.

27 Parsons FBI file, Memo, 27 Sept. 1950.

28 Peter Levenda, *Sinister Forces: A Grimoire of American Political Witchcraft*, Book II, "A Warm Gun" (Walterville, OR: Trine Day, 2006), 92, and Levenda, *Unholy*, 245.

29 William Breeze to author, 6 Feb. 2008.

30 Levenda, *Sinister*, 91–95.

31 Motta, and Alex Constantine, "The OTO and the CIA: Ordo Templis Intelligentis" (1996), www.american-buddha.com/theotoandthecia.htm.

32 Levenda, *Sinister*, 92.

33 UKNA, KV6/47.

İNDEX

A∴A∴ (*Astrum Argentum or Argenteum Astrum*), 35, 37, 38

Abteilung, 1A 99, 206, 245

Abteilung IIIb (Nachrichtenabteilung, Nachrichtendienst), 33

Abteilung Pfeffer, 245

Abwehr, 206, 207, 224, 241, 243

Action Francaise, 181

Adams, Evangeline, 60, 132

Adler, Alfred, 189, 214, 216, 227, 228

Admiralty (British), 18, 20, 32, 36, 42, 45, 81, 82, 84, 85, 133, 140, 153, 159, 170, 230

Agape Lodge (OTO), 260-262

Ahnenerbe, 243

Aiwass, 33,101

Aktion Hess, 246

Alamantrah Working, 149

Albert, Heinrich, 66, 97

Alfonso XIII, King of Spain, 198

Alvensleben, Alvo (Gustav Konstantin) von, 102, 103, 107, 110-114

American Technicon Society, 261

Anarchists and Anarchism, 147, 160, 161, 164, 211, 228

Anational Congress, 141, 149

Anational Grand Lodge, 141, 149

Ancient and Free Gardeners, Order of, 38

Angell, Norman, 84

Anthrax, 129

Anthroposophy and Anthroposophists, 212, 216, 232, 234, 239, 243, 257

APL (American Protective League), 146, 147, 167

Apponyi, Alfred, 164

Ariosophists, 194

Arnold-Forster, Katherine, (Ka Cox), 239, 240

Arnold-Forster, Will, 239, 240

Ascended Masters (Mahatmas), 23, 196

Ashburnham, Lord Bertram, 24-27, 42

Astor, (William) Vincent, 170, 171

Astrologers and Astrology, 241-243, 246-250

Astrum Argentum (or *Argenteum Astrum*, see also A∴A∴), 35, 37, 38

Atlanta Federal Penitentiary, 139, 172

Atlantean Research Society 161

Atlantis, 35

Atonement, Society of, 130, 151

Maugham, William Somerset, 35, 96, 104, 164, 167, 181

Mauri, Claudio, 189

Maxwell, Robert, 231

May, Betty, 188

McCormick, Donald (Richard Deacon), 28, 70, 242, 243, 250, 256

McGarrity, Joseph, 56

McMurtry, Grady Louis (Caliph Hymenaeus Alpha), 260, 262

Medina, Don Jesus de, 31, 116

Melville, William, 21-23, 25, 40, 210

Memphis-Misraim Rite, 70, 184

Mencken, H.L., 128

Menzies, Stewart, 233, 259

Mescaline (*Anhalonium lewinii, see also* Peyote), 31, 39, 73, 108, 132, 153, 189, 218, 250, 262

Mexico City, 116

Meyer, James, 61

Meyer, Kuno, 68

MI1c (see also MI6, Section V, SIS), 42, 121, 146

MI3, 219

MI5 (Security Service), 6-8, 20, 21, 42, 48, 54, 57, 58, 66, 85, 122, 123, 139, 146, 161, 173, 187, 190-192, 206, 207, 210, 217, 218, 223, 225, 226, 229, 234, 235, 240-242, 245, 249, 259, 263

MI6, (*see also* MI1c, Section V, SIS) 6, 8, 20, 42, 48, 249

MI8, 225

MID, (U.S. Military Intelligence) 109, 144, 152

Miguel, Don, (Portuguese pretender) 26

Miller, Anna, 147

Miller, Henry, 223, 235

Minor, Roddie, 147, 149, 152

Minotto, Jacques (James), 125

MI-R, 234, 237

Miramar, Maria de, 198, 209, 212, 216

Mitrinovic, Dimitrije, 227, 228

MK ULTRA, 108

Mohammed, 41

Moltke, Helmut von, 70

Montauk, 169-171

Monti, Georges ("Count Israel"), 181, 227, 228, 236

Moonchild, 17, 27, 28, 142, 197, 209

Moore, James, 191, 192

Morgan, Evan (Lord Tredegar), 225

Morgan, J.P. & Co., 52, 53, 59, 62, 99, 121, 170

Rupprecht, Prince of Bavaria, 25
Russell, Bertrand, 84
Russell, George, 54
Ryan, Thomas, 81, 82
Ryerson, Albert W., 165, 172, 181
SA (*Sturmabteilung*), 206, 207, 219
Sampson, Holden, 69
San Diego, 114, 115
San Francisco, 32, 83, 102, 103, 107, 110, 112-114, 121, 126
Sander, Albert, 139
Sarg, Tony, 152
Sat B'hai, 71
Savinkov, Boris, 38
Schack, Eckhart von, 102
Scheele, Walter, 126
Scherff, George, 171
Schiff, Jacob, 52, 167, 186
Schlaraffia, 71, 73, 74, 78
Schleicher, Kurt von, 224
Schwieger, Walther, 13
Schwimmer, Rozika, 131, 166
Scotland Yard, 8, 21, 97, 117, 123, 144, 179, 185-187, 190, 210, 215, 216, 257, 263
Scottish Rite, 31, 32
Seabrook, Kate, 172
Seabrook, William, 151, 152, 195
Secret Chiefs, 17, 24, 39, 193, 194
Secret Church, 22
Secret Service (U.S.), 85, 89, 97, 113, 121, 122, 133, 150, 162, 167, 168
Section 17Z, 247
Section D (SIS), 190, 232, 234
Section V (*see* MI1c, MI6, SIS), 121, 124, 144, 146, 160, 166
Seidlitz, Ida Leonie von, 131, 148-150, 152, 167
Sektion Politik (*Sabotage-Abteilung*), 65, 70
Semelbauer, Eduard, 250
Semenovskii, Apollonarii, 147, 148, 150
Sequeira, Greta, 232, 233, 241, 257
Sequiera, William, 233, 236
Service de Renseignements, 184
Services des Affaires Indigenes, 37
Shambhallah (Aghartha), 195-197
Shumatov, Lev Arkadievich, 147